Guide to
Baby
Products
Fifth Edition

Guide to
Baby
Products

Fifth Edition

**SANDY JONES WITH WERNER FREITAG
AND THE EDITORS OF CONSUMER REPORTS BOOKS**

CONSUMER REPORTS BOOKS
A DIVISION OF CONSUMERS UNION
YONKERS • NEW YORK

Copyright © 1996 by Sandy Jones and Consumers Union of United States, Inc., Yonkers, New York 10703.

Published by Consumers Union of United States, Inc., Yonkers, New York 10703.

Library of Congress Catalog Card No.: 94-32295

ISBN: 0-89043-854-4 pb

ISSN: 1091-0557

Design by Joseph DePinho

Page composition by Maggie Brenner

First printing, November 1996

This book is printed on recycled paper ♲

Manufactured in the United States of America

Guide to Baby Products, Fifth Edition is a Consumer Reports Book published by Consumers Union, the nonprofit organization that publishes CONSUMER REPORTS, the monthly magazine of test reports, product Ratings, and buying guidance. Established in 1936, Consumers Union is chartered under the Not-for-Profit Corporation Law of the State of New York.

The purposes of Consumers Union, as stated in its charter, are to provide consumers with information and counsel on consumer goods and services, to give information on all matters relating to the expenditure of the family income, and to initiate and to cooperate with individual and group efforts seeking to create and maintain decent living standards.

Consumers Union derives its income solely from the sale of CONSUMER REPORTS and other publications. In addition, expenses of occasional public service efforts may be met, in part, by nonrestrictive, noncommercial contributions, grants, and fees. Consumers Union accepts no advertising or product samples and is not beholden in any way to any commercial interest. Its Ratings and reports are solely for the use of the readers of its publications. Neither the Ratings, nor the reports, nor any Consumers Union publications, including this book, may be used in advertising or for any commercial purpose. Consumers Union will take all steps open to it to prevent such uses of its material, its name, or the name of CONSUMER REPORTS.

Contents

Introduction Guidelines and safety tips 1

1   Backpacks and soft carriers..13

2   Bassinets, carrycots, and cradles 23

3   Bathtubs and bathing accessories.................................29

4   Bottle-feeding equipment and pacifiers........................35

5   Breast-feeding and nursing accessories 53

6   Changing tables..65

7   Child safety seats 69

8   Clothing and footwear 95

9   Cribs and crib mattresses 105

10 Diapers and accessories..121

11 Foods for babies 131

12 Gates...153

13 Hazard reduction and childproofing products 165

14 High chairs and booster seats.......................................205

15   Infant seats 215

16   Monitors 219

17   Nursery decor and accessories 225

18   Playpens 233

19   Portable cribs 241

20   Portable hook-on chairs 245

21   Strollers 249

22   Swings 261

23   Toilet-learning aids 265

24   Toys 269

25   Walkers 293

Appendix A Babies and accidents: A national overview 299

Appendix B List of manufacturers 313

Index 319

Acknowledgments

We are proud to offer new readers the same team and methodology that have made *Guide to Baby Products* an indispensable tool for selecting baby gifts and products.

Guide to Baby Products, Fifth Edition, involved a unique collaboration within Consumers Union that began in 1975 with the first edition of *Guide to Buying for Babies*. Werner Freitag, a Consumers Union engineer who has done most of the baby-product testing for CONSUMER REPORTS magazine for 35 years and has helped formulate national safety standards for baby products, has tested products specifically for this book under the direction of Consumers Union's Technical Division. Sandy Jones, author of six parenting books, created the concept of this book and proposed it to Consumers Union. She continues to research and evaluate products not tested by Consumers Union, and provides practical information regarding product selection and use.

The editors of Consumer Reports Books would like to express their appreciation to Michael Mitariten, manager in Consumers Union's Recreation and Home Improvement Department, for his review of this book; to Maurice Wynn, senior project leader in Consumers Union's Recreation and Home Improvement Department, for his work on the chapter on childproofing products; to Linda Greene, senior project leader in Consumers Union's Foods Department, for her work on the chapter on baby foods; and to Donald Mays, testing director of Consumers Union's Recreation and Home Improvement Department, for his contributions to the fifth edition of *Guide to Baby Products*. They would also like to thank Thomas Mutchler, a technician in the Recreation and Home Improvement Department, and John Walsh for the photography in the fifth edition.

Sandy Jones would like to express her appreciation to Donna Waterman for her invaluable assistance in updating the fifth edition.

Sandy Jones and the editors of Consumer Reports Books are grateful for the cooperation and dedication shown by everyone associated with this project.

Guide to
Baby
Products
Fifth Edition

Introduction

Guidelines and safety tips

Given the vast number of cribs, child safety seats, strollers, and other costly pieces of baby equipment available, buying for a baby can be a challenge for parents and grandparents. The average cost for feeding supplies and food, clothes, diapers, safety devices, and child-care services for the first year of a baby's life is estimated to be between $3,000 and $26,000.

Nationally, new parents and grandparents spend over $10 billion on baby products. And every year, manufacturers and retailers spend millions of dollars to convince parents and grandparents to buy their wares.

The three most important factors to consider when shopping for baby products are safety, durability, and convenience. Saving money is an important issue, too. Using this book can help you plan your purchases, enabling you to save hundreds of dollars.

Baby product safety standards

Simply because a product has been designed for a baby is no guarantee that it's going to be safe. Thousands of babies are injured each year in accidents related to baby products because parents overestimate the protective qualities imparted by manufacturers to their products.

As a result of advances in record keeping by the government, and specifically by the U.S. Consumer Product Safety Commission (CPSC), we now know that an alarmingly high number of injuries are associated with the use of baby products each year. Nationally, the U.S. government addresses product safety for child safety seats through the National Highway Traffic Safety Administration (NHTSA). All baby food (except meats, which are the domain of the Department of Agriculture) and skin care products are regulated by the Food and Drug Administration (FDA). In the opinion of Consumers Union, the products administered by these two agencies are well regulated and relatively safe. Cribs and toys, though, are regulated nationally by the CPSC, and applicable standards are not as complete for these products as we think they should be. In fact, cribs and toys are covered by few requirements, although voluntary standards have been created to give children added protection not covered by the mandatory federal regulations. To be legally sold in the United States, cribs and toys must comply with the CPSC's limited standards. Products that are not in compliance are sometimes recalled by the manufacturer as part of the remedial action asked for by the government, and sometimes manufacturers recall products voluntarily.

Some consumer protection also results from voluntary standards set by industry associations, but those standards are only as stringent as the association decides. The Juvenile Products Manufacturers Association (JPMA), for example, sponsors and administers a voluntary certification program for certain juvenile products. Voluntary certification programs are currently in effect for full-size cribs, high chairs, portable hook-on chairs, playpens, strollers, gates, and walkers. The JPMA retains an independent testing laboratory (Detroit Testing Laboratory, Inc.) to perform the tests or witness tests of sample units on a periodic basis. Products are certified if they meet the minimum safety performance standards developed by the American Society for Testing and Materials (ASTM). Although *voluntary* industry safety standards exist for many baby products, *mandatory* federal standards, as noted above, cover only child safety seats, pacifiers, rattles, cribs, and toys (to a certain extent). Federal regulations also apply to most products in respect to lead in paint.

Certification stickers

When you shop for baby products, you will find some with stickers that say "CERTIFIED: This model tested by an independent laboratory for compliance with ASTM safety standard." Products with these stickers are supposed to have passed certain tests, based on industry "safety" standards. (The JPMA oversees the sticker program, whereas the standards are controlled by ASTM.)

Stickers, however, are no guarantee of safety. Here's why: Some safety standards require only minimum levels of safe performance and may not address all hazards; they vary in strictness from one product category to another; and the tests specified in the safety standards generally are conducted on products in their new, unused condition. Except for full-size cribs, the standards for most products do not adequately take into account the normal stresses that could make a product deteriorate with use. And even with full-size cribs, the sticker program is not 100 percent reliable. For example, some crib manufacturers have had to recall full-size cribs that had rail-to-slat separations, even though a standard exists to prevent such defects.

Some product categories, such as full-size cribs, are tested according to relatively stringent government (16 CFR Part 1508) and ASTM standards (ASTM F1169 and ASTM 5966). The two ASTM standards have been used to certify the companies that make or market cribs, rather than to certify the cribs themselves.

We believe that a full-size crib with a current certification sticker is preferable to a crib that lacks the sticker. Cribs without stickers from companies that are currently certified may be less safe because they were produced before standards were set, but cribs from noncertified companies are not necessarily less safe.

Other product categories are certified by the JPMA (individual products are certified, not companies). But, based on our tests, these products, such as walkers and gates, need to be subject to stricter standards. Unfortunately, the consumer does not really know at the point of sale which hazards are addressed by the safety standards and which are not.

The absence of a certification sticker does not necessarily mean that the product is unsafe, since manufacturers can choose not to subject their products to certification tests. Hence, a product without a sticker might have passed the industry test or it might have failed—or the product might never have been tested at all. It should be emphasized that the voluntary ASTM standards address only major hazards, and that only minimum requirements are contained in the standards.

On balance, we think the industry's standard setting and its certification program are a big step in the right direction, but consumers would be better served if there were industry-wide participation and a recognition of normal use and abuse incorporated into all standards. To call the CPSC, use their hotline number, 800-638-2772, through which you can either receive prerecorded updates on product recalls and related information or report an injury. For complaints regarding baby food or skin-care products, call the FDA at 301-443-1240. For concerns about child safety seats, call the NHTSA at 800-424-9393.

Money-saving tips

Shopping at yard and garage sales is sometimes a good way to stock up on items like baby clothes that simply need a thorough laundering to be usable or baby toys that are still in good condition. The same goes for shopping at thrift and consignment stores.

But beware of used child safety seats and cribs. If a restraint has been in a crash, it may have small cracks or stressed components that aren't visible to the untrained eye. These cracks could affect the seat's crash protection. Older cribs and cradles can be hazardous, too, if they have broken slats or malfunctioning hardware, or have been painted with lead-based paint. Cribs built before 1991 may not have all the important protective features that have been federally mandated or are now routinely incorporated into new cribs. (For more information on how to buy a crib, consult chapter 9.)

Baby products sold in small specialty stores may carry a higher price tag than items sold in the larger retail chains. The price difference among big-ticket items, such as cribs, child safety seats, and strollers, may be substantial.

The advantage of shopping in smaller shops is the personal attention customers receive from salespeople who usually have an intimate knowledge of every product in their store. In most instances, these salespeople, often store owners and managers, will go out of their way to please you and will be willing to assemble cribs and other do-it-yourself items for you, saving you both time and labor.

Larger discount operations, such as Burlington Coat Factory's Baby Depot, Toys 'R' Us, Baby Superstore, LiL' Things, Target, Wal-Mart, and Kmart, while offering better prices, usually offer minimal help or information that will enable parents to make a sound buying decision. Some of these stores carry only certain domestic brands. For example, you are not likely to find expensive imported strollers or high chairs in these stores. In addition, floor samples may be fastened down, products may be in sealed cartons, or items may be displayed up high and out of reach, making consumer evaluation difficult. If you live in a location with limited baby offerings, JC Penney offers a wide selection of cribs in its mail-order catalog (toll free: 800-222-6161). Sears and other catalog retailers of baby merchandise can also be a good source. Here are some practical strategies for saving money on various products:

Baby bath seats. Use the kitchen sink, lined with a towel, or use a tub that fits the sink.

Baby food. Prepare your own baby food using a baby-food grinder, an electric blender, or a food processor.

Bibs. Rather than purchasing a number of terry-cloth bibs, buy one or two flexible, molded-plastic bibs and wipe them clean after every meal.

Changing table. Install a sturdy wall-to-wall shelf at a comfortable height in baby's closet, or change the baby on a waterproof pad placed on your bed or on the floor. (Always keep one hand on your baby during changing.)

Child safety seat. Investigate loaner or rental programs sponsored by hospitals and childbirth education associations or the state police in some states. Typically, you'll be able to rent a seat for a refundable deposit and a minimal monthly or flat fee. Some states administer loaner programs through the state highway safety department.

Clothing storage. Use brightly colored plastic bins or laundry baskets to hold clean diapers and shirts, or buy used shelves for clothes storage and paint them with nontoxic, lead-free paint.

Diapers. Use and recycle cloth diapers. Unfolded diapers allow you to devise the best-fitting shapes for your own baby. They can also be cleaned better.

High chair. Feed the baby in your lap, or use a child safety seat that converts for indoor use.

Infant formula and bottles. Breast-feed your baby. Breast milk is sterile and warm, and requires no preparation.

Infant seat. Use a child safety seat that converts for indoor use.

Stroller. Buy a safe used stroller at a yard sale.

T-shirts and nightgowns. Buy used garments from other parents or from a secondhand clothing store. For maximum whiteness, soak them in very hot water with dishwashing detergent to get them clean and then wash them with regular detergent and a cup of vinegar or bleach, with an additional hot rinse. Just avoid clothing with strings, like hooded sweatshirts.

Creating your buying plan

Before you enter the baby-product retail realm, it helps to know in advance what you're seeking. That's especially true for costly investments like child safety seats, strollers, and high chairs. Over the years,

Consumers Union's tests have clearly shown that price is not always an indicator of quality and durability. Less expensive models from reputable manufacturers of strollers, child safety seats, and cribs have often tested well compared with more expensive versions and offer the same quality materials and craftsmanship as costlier, "designer" versions from the same companies. The higher price tags on "super-deluxe" models are often due to the use of fancier fabrics, plusher seat stuffing, and unneeded extras, such as canopies or toy trays.

If you're economizing, consider buying a stripped-down, streamlined stroller, child safety seat, or high chair from a reputable company and then add on the extra accessories you want. Save money by buying a crib with only one side that lowers, a crib with a less fancy wood finish, etc. Add better casters if the crib doesn't roll easily, and buy a top-of-the-line mattress with the money saved. A child safety seat with a simple five-point harness is not only as safe as a fancier model with a shield, it's just as easy to use.

Expensive strollers come with a "boot"—a casing that covers baby's feet. A cozy blanket or a blanket sleeper will serve the same purpose for a lot less money. Large baby outlets such as Toys 'R' Us, Burlington Coat Factory's Baby Depot, and Baby Superstore carry well-padded stroller seat cushions, umbrellas that clamp onto strollers or fasten on play trays, and other handy extras.

Here are some questions you should ask yourself as you create your baby-product buying plan:

◆ **How soon will you need this product?** All hospitals require that you have a child safety seat before they allow you to take your baby home. You'll probably want a crib and a mattress on hand before baby comes home, too. And you'll want to have a basic supply of baby clothes, diapers, and a few bottles on hand. (For a basic clothing list, see p. 95.)

It makes sense to postpone buying products you won't need right away. For example, you can decide later about purchasing a high chair, a changing table, a front carrier, baby toys, or a bath seat. In fact, once your baby comes home, you may discover you don't really need some of these products at all.

◆ **How is the product going to be used?** Which stroller you choose depends on whether you plan to take baby on long walks in the country or just for quick shopping jaunts. If you want your baby's child safety seat to double as an infant seat, you'll want to choose a small, portable model with a carry handle designed for babies under 20 pounds; otherwise, plan to purchase a heavier, more cumbersome convertible model with a longer period of usefulness—to be used from birth to 40 pounds.

❖ **How long before this product is outgrown by baby?** All baby products you buy now will be obsolete in two to three years or won't find use until you have another child. Take that fact into account as you eye costly baby suites with matching bureaus and changing tables, expensive wall hangings, or $100 or more quilt-and-bedding sets that usually end up folded in the closet. Baby swings are useful for four to five months at most. Baby mobiles, walkers, and jumpers are useful only for a few months.

❖ **Does baby really need this product?** People buying shower gifts for baby may need coaching when buying products that fall into the nonessential (and sometimes unsafe) category: scratchy or constricting baby clothes, clothes and toys that can't be washed repeatedly; uncomfortable, elasticized baby headbands; bottles shaped like animals or footballs, with nooks and crannies that harbor bacteria; stuffed quilts, pillows, and large stuffed toys that can suffocate a baby; battery-operated baby toys; walkers; baby bath seats; hook-on high chairs; playpens; automatic swings; most baby toys; door-mounted jumpers; and fabric diaper stackers. Other optional items include baby monitors and playpens.

Gathering information

Use this book to create a master list of products you wish to buy. Write down the manufacturer's name, the product description, and current model number for your selections. Sometimes the same or a very similar model will be assigned a different model number by the manufacturer, depending on the year. If you're unable to locate a specific model, you may want to check with the manufacturer directly. Most have toll-free consumer numbers. (See Appendix B.)

Next, check on current recalls of child safety seats by dialing the NHTSA's automated, toll-free Auto Safety Hotline telephone number: 800-424-9393. To check on recalls of other baby products, call the CPSC's Product Safety Hotline, 800-638-2772. For information on breast pumps and other breast-feeding equipment or techniques, contact La Leche League, International, toll-free: 800-525-3243. For information on baby formula, baby food, and skin-care product recalls, call the Consumer Inquiries Hotline of the FDA: 800-FDA-4010. Certain baby-product categories have voluntary safety standards set by the JPMA. To find out which products are certified, call for a free list or send a stamped self-addressed envelope to JPMA, P.O. Box 955, Marlton, NJ 08053; telephone 609-231-8500.

Now you're ready to start your search for the best prices on the products you've chosen. You can save time by telephoning stores to compare prices. Stores carrying baby products are usually found in the Yellow Pages under "Furniture—Children's" and "Children's & Infants' Wear—Retail."

If you're anticipating receiving gifts at baby showers or from friends and relatives, you may want to register your choices with baby registries available in superstores such as Toys 'R' Us, Babies 'R' Us, Baby Superstore, and Burlington Coat Factory's Baby Depot.

Beware of sales tactics

Knowing in advance what you're looking for can help keep you from being distracted by the allure of plush, designer patterns and extra padding on strollers, or cribs decorated with fancy wood or brass that will have no effect on product performance. Armed with knowledge, you can fend off the advances of salespeople who may try to manipulate you into considering costlier options.

Does this sound like car shopping? Well, in some ways shopping for baby products can be very similar. If you walk into a store looking for an advertised bargain, you may encounter salespeople trained to "bait and switch"—a tactic used to get you to purchase models that are more expensive than the low-profit, advertised "loss leader."

Manipulative sales tactics also emerge when it's time to purchase a crib and a crib mattress. Most parents don't realize that cribs and mattresses—although they're displayed together on the showroom floor—are sold as separate items. But a low advertised price for a crib that includes a mattress most likely means that an inexpensive crib has been combined with a really cheap and poor mattress. Our advice is to forgo fancy woods and finishes in a crib and opt for a single dropside crib of painted wood. With the money saved, you could buy a good, firm mattress (the firmest you can find).

Beware, too, of some one-product-does-everything designs—high chairs that double as play tables, gigantic crib units that convert into toddler bed/chest/couches—they all are usually more expensive and more cumbersome, and their use is usually limited to one child. There are also design deficiencies that are absent in single-use products. Crib/chest combinations, in particular, may have pull-out drawers that offer a dangerous leghold to a climbing tot.

When it comes to nursery furniture other than cribs—chests or rockers, for example—consider piecing together your child's nursery from quality used or unfinished furniture that you put together yourself. Conversion kits allow you to turn the top of any waist-high chest into a changing table by screwing a support frame into the rear of the chest. (*Note:* These units don't have guardrails. They're only safe if they are sturdy and you always put the safety belt around baby.)

Dangers to babies

Injury statistics reported to the CPSC and private injury-prevention organizations send a strong message about the dangers of baby products because of the high number of deaths and injuries. And, as you will discover throughout this book, there are no across-the-board safety standards that apply uniformly to all baby products.

The CPSC estimates that baby products injure over 70,000 babies a year. Understanding how babies get hurt can help you in choosing safe products and becoming aware of ways to use products correctly. Once you've brought products home, you still have the responsibility of guarding your baby from accidents. Here's a listing of the most prominent injuries and what you can do to protect your baby from hazards:

◆ **Falls.** Babies are active, squirming, dynamic beings, and they've got enough torque to roll out, squeeze out, or pull themselves free from any product. All baby products designed to raise a baby off the floor, such as cribs, changing tables, backpacks, and high chairs, have the potential for causing injuries when babies tumble out of them. Babies routinely plummet out of child safety seats, strollers, and infant seats when their seatbelts aren't fastened properly or not fastened at all, or crash into sharp-edged objects—including coffee tables, fireplaces, doors, or objects with corners—that are not padded.

  Protective action: Look for sturdy seatbelts that fasten around both the waist and crotch. Check latching mechanisms on folding products to ensure they're easy for you to use but hard for a toddler to release. Select baby products with no sharp or protruding edges, and don't allow your unsteady tot to carry objects, including a baby bottle, in his or her mouth, or to push the stroller as if it were a toy, or to run with objects in his or her mouth. Shield sharp-edged furniture with soft safety protectors.

◆ **Choking.** Babies are capable of biting off small parts of toys, the tips of bottle and pacifier nipples, and pieces of vinyl covering or the foam under the covering on playpens and other products. They can swallow chunks of foam from toys and bath cushions, and pull off buttons, pom-poms, and other add-ons to toys and clothes. They may also choke on chunks of food, such as hot dog pieces, and on nonfood items like coins, bolt heads, and ballpoint pen tops. Sometimes these objects get stuck in their throats, cutting off their air supply.

Protective action: Heed manufacturers' safety warnings for toys, and examine all products periodically for small parts that could be swallowed. Dispose of toys or other products with small broken parts. Keep chunky or hard foods with choking potential away from your baby. Lock the door to an older sibling's room that might contain unsafe toys and small objects like marbles and small balls.

◆ **Strangulation.** Young babies have soft, vulnerable throats that can easily be compressed when pressure is applied to the outside of their necks, cutting off their air supply. They can strangle when strings, necklines on shirts and hooded sleepers, and pacifier ribbons snag on crib posts or other protrusions. Or they can strangle on loose ribbons, strings, or cords from crib bumpers, wall hangings, and window blinds. Death can result when their necks become compressed by rigid playpen floorboards, when they get wedged between the edges of adult bed frames and bedside tables or between the wall and an adult bed, or when they get hung up by their necks after their bodies slip through the leg holes of strollers, out the bottom of high chairs, or between the wide-spaced bars of old cribs and cradles. They can also strangle when they fall on crib mobiles and other items strung across cribs and playpens.

Protective action: Remove all strings from hoods and sleepers. Clip strings and ribbons on crib bumpers so that each individual string does not exceed nine inches in length. Clip off strings or ribbons from wall decorations, and keep the child well away from them. Always keep the sides of playpens up. Position the crib away from windows, and tie up blind cords so they can't be reached by your child. Keep hard toys out of the crib, and remove crib mobiles after the first few months.

◆ **Suffocation.** Babies can asphyxiate when small pieces of latex balloons get caught in their throats. Some suffocations occur because babies have a limited ability to lift their heads. If they're placed facedown, their faces get buried in the "suffocation pocket" created by cushioned surfaces, such as soft-padded mattresses, beanbag cushions and chairs, animal skins, plastic dry cleaning and garbage bags, and single-bladder waterbeds. They die from rebreathing their own exhaled carbon dioxide.

Protective action: Never let your baby have a balloon to play with, or tie a balloon on the side of the crib. Avoid placing your baby on soft-padded surfaces, and always lay your baby faceup for sleep unless otherwise directed by a pediatrician.

◆ **Finger entrapment.** Babies' fingers can be crushed between hinged parts of toys, strollers, high chairs, playpens, and gates, sometimes causing amputation. Fingers can also get cut on sharp-edged tubing and metal hardware on strollers, high-chair trays, and wherever open-end tubing is present.

Protective action: Check products to be sure safety locks actually prevent accidental collapse of the hinges or the entire product. Be sure that all tubes have caps that can't be removed by a baby. Don't open or fold products with your baby in them or when your baby is nearby.

◆ **Burns.** A baby's skin is far more sensitive to burns than an adult's skin. Babies can get scalded by hot water from faucets and tub spouts, or when they touch the steam from some vaporizers. They can get burned when they touch overheated bottles, or when hot coffee or the water used to sterilize bottles is spilled. They can suffer shocks and electrical burns from biting extension cords, lamp wires, and electric plugs. Their mouths and throats can also be burned from ingesting chemicals such as dishwasher detergent.

Protective action: Turn the hot water thermostat down to 120° F, or purchase an antiscald device for the tub spout. Purchase a cold-water humidifier. Buy protective safety devices for appliances and electrical outlets. Use a hardware-mounted baby gate or playpen to keep baby out of the kitchen. Use a covered coffee mug, and place it far from baby's reach. Don't use a microwave oven to heat a baby bottle (although the outside of the bottle may feel cool, the milk inside may be hot enough to cause burns). Hide or wrap up cords, and replace old ones with newer, safer designs. Store household chemicals out of reach, and don't put detergent in the dishwasher when baby's around.

How we tested products for this book

Child safety was an important criterion in testing and judging the products covered in this book. Consumers Union's rationale is that a baby product has to be "baby safe" first, "parent convenient" second, and, where these criteria apply, durable enough to last at least until the child has outgrown its use.

Not every product category covered in this book was actually tested in Consumers Union's laboratories. Such products were, however, evaluated by the authors and are appropriately identified by the statement "These products were not tested by Consumers Union."

Selection of the models for testing within each product category was based on information obtained from manufacturers. Only nationally distributed models were selected.

The testing itself exposed the products to a battery of trials intended to check such performance parameters as safety, convenience, durability, comfort, and serviceability. Safety tests for some products were performed according to the applicable government standards or voluntary industry standards. Where necessary, we modified the tests and the requirements, and where no tests existed, we devised our own.

Tests and judgments for convenience were made by panels of staffers, most of whom were also new parents. Durability was checked by performing such routine procedures as drop tests and cycling of the products, or running them repeatedly through all intended functions. Comfort was assessed by judging the effectiveness of padding, the absence of protrusions, and general user-friendliness.

Backpacks and soft carriers

A baby carrier allows you to tote your baby on your body, and offers a convenient alternative to a stroller. A carrier won't make your baby any lighter, but a well-designed carrier can help distribute your baby's weight more evenly for less strain than carrying your baby in your arms—and it will leave your arms free.

All babies love and need to be carried, but it's hard to get much else done while cradling a baby in your arms. From ancient times onward, parents have tied babies onto themselves with animal skins, or knotted long strips of fabric to station baby in front or back. There are basically two types of carriers used today: pouchlike fabric models that you wear either in front or on the back, and framed carriers designed to be worn only on the back. Pouch carriers are for young babies who need head support, whereas framed carriers are for babies and toddlers who can already sit up independently.

Soft and framed carriers offer some advantages over other devices for transporting baby. For example, they offer more mobility than, say, a stroller while boarding a bus, hiking, or getting through a crowd. Having your baby strapped to you offers a feeling of greater security than carrying the baby in a baby seat or carrycot, which may tip over when your baby's position shifts. In addition, babies are usually soothed by the close contact and rhythmic movements of a parent's body, making a carrier very useful for periods of fussiness. Carriers can provide physical closeness for both you and your baby.

There are use differences between soft and framed carriers. Soft fabric carriers are, for the most part, designed to give head support to a very young baby. With the exception of the *Baby Wrap* (see p.18), the weight of the baby is carried almost completely on your shoulders.

Framed carriers are designed to be used after a baby can sit up independently, an ability that babies usually develop between six and seven months of age. These models offer some structural support by redistributing the baby's weight on your upper body instead of placing all of it on your shoulders.

Some disadvantages of carriers

Most manufacturers claim that their packs are constructed to carry children until they weigh about 30 to 35 pounds, which is around three years of age, but you're sure to find that your child is too heavy for comfort long before that. Your baby's weight in comparison to your own size is an issue that should be considered before purchasing this product. A tall, strong parent will probably manage carrying a baby or toddler quite comfortably, whereas a short, slender parent may struggle with the discomfort of the carrier's straps cutting into the shoulders and the imbalance caused by baby's increased weight. Also, keep in mind that your child will probably have lost interest in being confined to a carrier long before three years of age—in fact, around the time he or she starts to walk.

All carriers tend to be quite awkward and difficult to mount on your body until you get the knack of it. Bending over with your baby in the carrier can be quite difficult, and dangerous for the baby. Some soft carriers are relatively easy to buckle or tie on, but some models require practice and skill to use, and frame carriers are difficult to put on without the help of another person. Hefting your baby or toddler around to the back in a frame carrier or pulling the baby around from back to front for dismounting is unwieldy at best.

Some framed packs have built-in stands that help make back-mounting easier. Use these packs with caution. The stands have caused numerous injuries when parents tried to use the packs with open stands as baby seats, rather than as temporary aids to help mount the carrier. The baby's movements may cause the stand to topple over with the baby inside the pack. Fingers may also get pinched in the hinge mechanism of the stand.

In an informal survey, we found that parents were most likely to complain about aching backs, shoulders, and calves when their baby exceeded approximately one-fourth of their own body weight. Frame carriers usually felt most comfortable when parents were able to use long walking strides, as during hiking. On the other hand, these carriers felt least comfortable when parents did a lot of stop-and-go walking, as in shopping. Most parents found that their comfort level could be built up with time and practice. But since the baby's weight increases quickly, comfort can change to discomfort quickly. When carrying a baby in a pack, bend at the knees when you stoop down rather than leaning forward from the waist. Never use a baby carrier or sling while in a car, on a bicycle, or while jogging or skiing. And don't use the carrier while cooking, or in situations that could injure the baby.

As with all devices that restrict a baby's movements, use of a carrier should not be a substitute for allowing your youngster natural freedom to crawl, walk, and explore under your supervision. Once your baby is over seven months of age, you should limit use of the carrier to less than an hour at a time.

Buying advice

As with all baby products, safety should be your number-one shopping consideration. Examine the pack closely to be sure that it will fit your baby comfortably (it should not bind or scratch around the baby's legs). Packs for younger babies should offer firm, padded head support that adjusts to the size of your baby. There should be a way to safely secure your baby into the pack, such as with a seatbelt, to diminish the danger of your baby falling or climbing out. Check all buckles and other securing hardware to be sure seams won't tear and straps won't slip. If a framed pack has a kickstand, it should lock firmly into the open position and be hard to tip over. In fact, most manufacturers recommend that babies not be left in backpacks that are not being worn. Be sure the metal frame is padded around the baby's face to prevent bruises.

When shopping for a carrier, consider your own comfort. Try it on. Check to see that the shoulder straps are amply padded, and that they stay in place without slipping. Leg holes for the baby should be wide but not so wide as to let the baby slip through, and soft so that they don't bind the legs. The straps' hardware should be easy to operate and should hold securely without slipping. Clasps, especially those that fasten in the back, should be easy to open and close with one hand, since you're likely to have your baby in the other arm when you're putting on or taking off the carrier. Fabrics should be easy to wipe clean.

The only way to find out how your baby will respond to a carrier is to try one out with your baby in it, preferably before you purchase it. You may discover, for example, that your baby protests loudly at being zipped into a carrier, perhaps because of oversensitivity to confinement, especially to pressure on the back of the head.

Soft carriers

Soft carriers are especially serviceable during the early weeks and months after birth, when most babies are easily comforted by physical closeness. Fussy babies can often be calmed by being strapped in a carrier and rocked or walked.

There are three major varieties of soft carriers: those that resemble zippered pouches with an inner fabric seat for the baby; those that are simple, soft seats that hold the baby like a small pair of pants; and hammocklike slings that hold the baby in a reclining position, to be carried by a single shoulder strap.

Slings usually come in brightly patterned fabrics. Older tots can be supported on the side while straddling your hip. A young baby can be carried on your back or in a semireclining position in front. The sling allows a baby to be laid in a natural sideways position for nursing.

An advantage of a baby sling over other soft carriers is how easy it is to put on and take off. A disadvantage is that you have to carry your baby's full weight on one shoulder instead of distributing it more evenly on your body, which can cause fatigue.

Slings also have two big safety problems: There's no safety strap to hold baby in, and there's no backup for the dual rings that most slings use for cinching the fabric straps, which can cause accidental slippage.

Most soft carriers are designed so that the baby faces you, but there are a few models that also give the option of facing the baby outward toward the world. If the pouch comes with a headrest, check it for comfort with your baby inside. Such a carrier will adapt better to older babies if the headrest is removable. If elastic is used in the leg area, test to be sure it's stretchy and won't constrict your baby's legs. The carrier should be completely washable.

Less expensive strap-on carriers

These carriers are usually designed only for young, relatively small babies. Most of them come with headrests that are either permanently attached to the carrier or designed to be removed when your baby outgrows the need for such support. They have minimally padded shoulders and are usually tied or fastened on with adjustable latches. The advantage of the strap-ons is that they are less cumbersome and usually less expensive than bulkier pouch counterparts. The disadvantages are that strap-ons are difficult to put on without the help of another person and that they offer little or no support for the infant, who may topple out when an adult leans over. We recommend that you try the carrier out before buying it, and use caution when wearing it.

Listings: Soft carriers

Note: These products were not tested by Consumers Union. This alphabetical listing does not include all models available but rather is a selection of some widely distributed models. Descriptions and Special Features are derived from authors' observations and manufacturers' claims.

MODEL	DESCRIPTION, SPECIAL FEATURES
Babies' Alley Denim Backpack *La Rue International* Model 13415, $35	Denim backpack with suede accents. Elasticized side pockets and front zipper organizer pocket. Vinyl, waterproof lining. Padded, adjustable shoulder straps. Removable padded changer. Drawstring closure. Detachable bag for soiled diapers. **Special features:** Handy pockets are useful for storage of bottles, toys, and other small items.
Babies' Alley Soft Baby Carrier *La Rue International* Model 13118, $20	Soft, cotton pastel gingham carrier with padded headrest, leg holes, and shoulder straps. Removable, washable bib. Carrier can be worn on chest or back, with baby facing you. Adjustable padded shoulders and waist belt. Shoulder straps cross in back. Zipper in front for nursing. Available in mint, pink, and blue. **Special features:** Accommodates breast-feeding. Can be adjusted for maximum comfort.
Baby Bjorn New Baby Carrier *Regal & Lager* Model BB–120, $80	Carrier straps adjust in front rather than in back for easy removal. Two rings in crotch area allow baby's seat to be lengthened for growth. Wide, well-padded shoulder straps. Adjustable snaps convert the carrier for use with newborn to larger sizes. Baby can also face outward. **Special features:** Keeps baby's body directly against parent's. Front tabs allow private nursing. Navy blue, sailor motif.
Baby Bundler Soft Carrier $40 plus unspecified S&H	Long, stretchable cotton/poly knit wrapper that ties baby to parent for maximum flexibility. Allows multiple positions: upright, reclining, inward or outward facing, baby in front or back. Machine washable. **Special features:** Although tying techniques seem complex, step-by-step photographs and directions are provided. Available in a variety of colors.

Listings: **Soft carriers** *continued*

MODEL	DESCRIPTION, SPECIAL FEATURES
Baby Wrap Products Baby Wrap, $45	Strapless baby carrier wraps baby around parent's chest, distributing the child's weight to the back without straining shoulders or neck. Baby's seat has foam-padded head/backrest. Zipper-back seat pocket. **Special features:** Adjusts to the parent's chest width, using long Velcro strip at rear of upper portion and a long tie-sash at base. Model available for large chests.
Basic Comfort Pack-N-Ride Model 30050, $32	A hip-carrier with a firm side platform for baby with a built-in Velcro-closed storage area. Baby's weight is carried on back and hips, not on neck. Attaches quickly with two buckles. Carries toddlers up to 35 pounds. Washable. **Special features:** Carries a child with little reduction in mobility of the parent to stand, sit, or climb stairs. Weight on hip minimizes neck and upper back strain.
Evenflo Grand Tour Baby Carrier Model 515901, $25	A soft carrier for babies 0–18 months. Quilted, padded interior and seat for baby, terry-cloth lining, heavily padded straps, headrest, leg openings, pockets, front nursing zipper, detachable bib, and handy pocket. **Special features:** Front zipper allows for easy breast-feeding. Headrest reduces strain on baby's developing neck muscles.
Evenflo SportCarrier Baby Carrier Model 517101, $20	Padded straps and leg openings, front nursing zipper, removable bib. Washable. Babies 0–9 months. **Special features:** Well padded for baby's comfort. Zipper accommodates nursing needs.
First Years Clip & Go 2-Way Carrier Model 4080, $25	Inward- or outward-facing carrier with separate parent harness that makes putting it on and taking it off simpler. Mesh seat for comfortable, all-season use. Pacifier tether. Snap-on burp cloth. Machine washable. Fits into standard infant car seat. For children up to 20 pounds. **Special features:** Lets parent carry baby facing in when newborn, or facing out when older. Separate harness makes picking up and putting down baby easier.
First Years Clip & Go Warm & Cozy Carrier Model 4082, $30	Soft, water-resistant carrier resembles a front-zipping baby sleeping bag or bunting. The carrying sack can be clipped on and off parent's separate body harness to lay baby down for sleep or to put in child safety seat. Roll-down hood for wind protection. Seat adjusts inside to hold child at the right level. Machine washable. For children up to 20 pounds. **Special features:** Separate parent's harness makes it easy to pick up or put down baby. Bunting is warm for traveling and napping in cool weather.
Fisher-Price Deluxe Perfect Support Carrier Model 9249, $39	Can be used as a sling, an upright front carrier, or an outward-facing front carrier. Removable outer shell can be used as a baby sling or a weather shield. Adjusts for nursing privacy. Padded head support for baby. Harness distributes baby's weight; waist and back straps are adjustable for increased comfort. One-handed buckle operation. Padded head support. Removable bib. Machine washable, dryer safe. For children up to 26 pounds. **Special features:** Three ways of carrying make this a very versatile carrier. Can be quickly attached to separate parent harness.
Fisher-Price Perfect Support Carrier Model 9248, $29	A machine-washable carrier that allows baby to face toward or away from parent. Wide, padded waist belt for parent. Parent's belts cross in back. Firm spine on baby shell makes mounting easier. Buckles readily onto the parent's harness at waist and chest. Machine washable with removable burper bib. For children up to 26 pounds. **Special features:** Weight distribution reduces strain on parent's shoulders and neck. Easily attaches to parent's shell.

MODEL	DESCRIPTION, SPECIAL FEATURES
Gerry Snugli Cuddle Up Soft Baby Carrier Model 055, $25	This pack features fully padded back, seat leg, and arm openings, including padded head support that cradles young infant's head. Also includes adjustable seat size, strap for pacifier or toy, removable bib, nursing zipper, padded shoulder straps, and a pocket for storage. **Special features:** This pack is loaded with padding for the comfort of both parent and child.
Gerry Snugli Double Take Soft Baby Carrier Model 045, $20	Younger babies can be carried facing in or, when older, changed to face forward. Chest padding cushions baby when in face-in position. Other features include fully padded leg openings and head/neck support, removable bib, and strap to hold pacifier or toy. For ages 0–12 months. **Special features:** Offers good support and flexible use in a small pack.
Gerry Snugli Front & Back Pack Soft Baby Carrier Model 075, $45	Pack offers three carrying positions: face in, face out, and backpack. Backrest flips front to back to change position. Padded belt strap carries one-third of baby's weight, relieving shoulders for increased comfort. Other features include fully padded head pillows, adjustable seat height and size, pacifier holder, and drool bib. For ages 0–20 months. **Special features:** Weight distribution reduces stress on parent's shoulders.
Gerry Snugli Legacy Soft Baby Carrier Model 018, $35	Can be used as a sling carrier or for carrying young infants facing in. The outer cover keeps baby warm, the inner seat can be zipped off to remove a sleeping baby without disturbance. Other features: padded head and neck support, bib, pacifier holder, and adjustable seat size. **Special features:** Yoke design helps distribute baby's weight and lessens strain on parent's back.
Indisposables Indi Sling Small or large, $40	A pleated, over-the-shoulder sling with 3-inch padding on sides for baby comfort and containment. Large shoulder pad for parent. Double-loop adjustable rings. Can be used as a reclining sling and later as a hip holder or front-facing carrier. Cotton print fabric. Hand wash. Accommodates babies and tots up to 30 pounds. **Special features:** Large shoulder pad increases comfort for parent. May be worn on either shoulder.
Infantino All-Weather Convertible Carrier Model 150-041, $40	Outer shell zips off for warm weather comfort. Padded shoulder straps. Locking clip in back. Smaller seat inside with firm head support. Adjustable drawstring. Burp bib. Zipper front for nursing. Two rear and one inside storage pack. Machine washable. **Special features:** Accommodates breast-feeding. Roomy pockets.
Infantino Heart-to-Heart Carrier Model 150-025, $20	Especially suitable for small babies, this fabric carrier provides firm back and neck support. Sides fasten around baby with buttons and Velcro. Softly cushioned seat for baby and thick padded straps for parent. Removable terry-cloth bib. Available in navy blue with white polka dot pattern or aqua. Washable. **Special features:** Easy-care fabric. Adjustable straps.
Infantino Lil' Traveler Color Block Carrier Model 150-011, $20	Inward facing front carrier made of fabric in bright primary colors. Nursing zipper. Padded headrest and leg holes. Satchel in rear of baby seat for storage. Crisscross, padded shoulder straps. Adjustable waist strap. Rear head support. Removable burper bib. For infants up to 21 pounds. **Special features:** Accommodates breast-feeding. High back headrest offers neck support.
Infantino Side Traveler Model 150-052, $18	A hip carrier for toting a toddler. Parent's heavily padded shoulder strap and waist strap are adjustable. A full seat with crotch is provided for the tot. Sturdy fabric and webbing in bright red and blue. **Special features:** Adjustable straps allow for changes as tots grow. Weight is carried by both shoulders and hips.

MODEL	DESCRIPTION, SPECIAL FEATURES
Infantino Tot Tender 6-in-1 Model 150-013, $38	Baby can ride in front, facing inward or outward, or in back. Can also be used in grocery carts, as a chair restraint, and in child safety seats. Back collar rolls down to offer extra head support for preemies or when baby faces outward. Toy or pacifier snap. Adjuster snaps on side and crotch. Padded shoulder straps for parent. Rear storage pocket. Padded leg holes. Padded bib. Demonstration video included. **Special features:** Highly versatile carrier meets the many different needs for holding babies.
Medela Little Navigator Baby Carrier Model 37065, $40	Fully adjustable, easy-to-use baby carrier. Distributes baby's weight over parent's hips, back, and shoulders through a unique shoulder yoke and waist strap. Baby can be carried facing in or out or on back. Loops for toys and clip-on bib. Cotton chin support. Reversible headrest. Sleeved leg openings. For babies up to 25 pounds. **Special features:** Versatility in use can provide for the changing needs of growing babies. Weight distribution reduces strain on parent.
NoJo Cuddle Me Carrier NMN, $20	A soft front carrier with padded head support, shoulder straps, and a soft cotton drool bib. Baby faces you. Shoulder straps cross in back, and hip strap helps distribute baby's weight. Machine washable. Available in assorted fashion prints. For babies up to 18 pounds. **Special features:** Padded head support helps reduce risk of neck injury.
NoJo "Discovery Two" Soft Baby Carrier NMN, $24	Baby can face inward or outward in this front carrier. Extra padding and support around legs, back support, shoulder, and waist belt. Adjustable back support accommodates baby's growth. For babies up to 22 pounds. **Special features:** Well-placed padding and support provide comfort for both baby and parent.
NoJo Original BabySling NMN, $29	Flannel side sling for baby that fastens over one shoulder using a double-ring fastener. Baby can be carried in sling position or sitting upright, facing parent. Available in a variety of prints; coordinating diaper bags and other accessories available. For babies up to 35 pounds. **Special features:** Simple, yet versatile, the sling allows bonding between parent and baby.
Parenting Concepts Sling-Ezee Models 101 and 117, $40 plus S&H	A fabric shoulder-sling that carries baby in front like a hammock. Baby can be laid down for nursing or sat semiupright or across the hip. Fastened with plastic double rings. **Special features:** Thickly padded side edges and shoulder strap.
Sara's Ride Side Hip Carrier $30	Hip carrier sling with patented waist belt to carry baby's weight. Single padded shoulder strap. Two plastic squeeze-release buckles. Baby must be able to hold head up (approximately 4 months). **Special features:** Baby can ride facing frontward or outward, or on adult's back.

Metal-framed backpacks

Metal-framed packs are designed for babies six months of age and older who can sit up on their own to ride on your back. Modeled after backpacks for hikers, these carriers have comfort features such as padded shoulder straps for parents, roomy adjustable seats inside with safety belts for passengers, and pockets underneath or in back for storing extra baby gear.

Frames are usually made of lightweight aluminum, and seats and straps are sewn from moisture-resistant fabric. Some models come with U-shaped rear support stands that lock in an open position to allow the pack to stand on its own on the floor.

Costlier baby carriers for serious adult hikers, available in sporting goods stores and through direct mail, have frames that adjust to fit adults who are five feet three inches to over six feet tall. These models have both shoulder straps and hip belts (to shift some of baby's weight to the adult's pelvic area). Padding on straps and belts is usually much denser on costlier carriers than that found on less expensive models.

The advantage of metal-framed packs over fabric packs is that their frames help provide additional support for baby's weight, distributing it more evenly along the back and hips, instead of concentrating it all on the shoulders. And hip belts are great for providing extra carrying comfort.

Listings: Metal-framed packs for toddlers

Note: These products were not tested by Consumers Union. This alphabetical listing does not include all models available but rather is a selection of some widely distributed models. Descriptions and Special Features are derived from authors' observations and manufacturers' claims.

MODEL	DESCRIPTION, SPECIAL FEATURES
Baby Trend Home & Roam Convertible Baby Carrier Model 2210, $58	A framed backpack that unzips to become a soft carrier. Nylon, moisture-resistant fabric that is machine-washable. Absorbent cotton interior. Wide-stance support stand. Safety buckles and locking zipper. Padded waist and shoulder belts for parents. Rear headrest and inner seat belt with dual inner seat that adjusts to baby's size. Built-in storage pocket. For children up to age three. **Special features:** Adjustable to baby's size and shape for maximum comfort. Frame folds flat for travel. Versatile; accommodates changing needs as baby grows.
Gerry Explorer Backpack Model 740/750, $70	A new frame design offers comfort and durability. A wide-stance fold-up loading frame. Child's seat is adjustable and is padded firmly in the front. Firm foam hip belt adjusts to five positions for different parent sizes. Has many features of soft packs, including adjustable seat height, baby shoulder restraint, padded back support, bottle pockets, change pocket on hip belt, adjustable sternum strap, and a storage pouch. Fits children up to 40 pounds. **Special features:** Very adjustable; lots of storage. At 3½ pounds, pack is lightweight but sturdy.
Remond Dandy Handy Chair Carrier Model 9118, $70	For serious hiking. Rear-facing carrier with washable seat made of coated nylon. Safety harness. Side pockets. Collapses flat for storage. **Special features:** Sun/rain shade. Retractable rear support converts carrier into an on-the-ground seat. Optional kit converts to a regular two-compartment hiking backpack.

Listings: **Metal-framed packs for toddlers** *continued*

MODEL	DESCRIPTION, SPECIAL FEATURES
Safety 1st Light 'N' Rugged Back Pack Carrier Model 91720, $45	Lightweight backpack designed to carry toddler with headrest. Cushioned shoulder harness and adjustable cushioned belt. Roomy storage compartment for snacks, toys, and bottles. Durable nylon fabric helps repel water. Mickey Mouse design. Easy-to-use locking tabs on straps. **Special features:** Lightweight design makes it easy to carry child and take along toys and snacks. More compact and maneuverable than a stroller.
Tough Traveler Kid Carriers Prices range from $70 for the Pony Ride to $170 for the Stallion	Infants can start riding in the Pony Ride carrier, a soft, front carrier. When baby can sit up unsupported, between four and five months, baby can move up to the tubular-framed back carriers, starting with the Colt and going up to the Stallion. Framed packs have loading stands, which can be folded flat when not in use. All framed models have safety harnesses, ample legroom, comfortable seats, and cargo pockets. Designed for hikers, these packs are also useful when shopping, riding on the bus, or doing housework. Deluxe models have higher backs, greater range of adjustment, and other features. Accessories are available to increase the potential use of these packs. **Special features:** Framed styles can stand alone for use as a seat. Adjustable straps provide high level of comfort and mobility for even strenuous hiking.

2

Bassinets, carrycots, and cradles

Bassinets, carrycots, and cradles are specialized devices for holding recumbent babies. Bassinets and cradles are smaller than cribs. They are usually placed in parents' bedrooms so that parents can monitor baby in the early weeks and months following birth. Although it might be more economical to simply invest in a crib from the start, both bassinets and cradles have an old-fashioned charm and take up less floor space than full-size or even portable cribs.

Choose a bassinet or cradle with a sturdy bottom and a wide base. Follow the manufacturer's weight guidelines.

For a bassinet, check to see that its folding legs have locks so that the unit won't fold during use. Periodically check screws and bolts, especially on the base, to be sure they're tight.

Both bassinets and cradles offer an alternative to putting your newborn into a large crib, but they are meant to be used only in the first few months of a baby's life. Bassinets and cradles are unstable and can, therefore, be unsafe once your baby is able to pull up. As with other bedding, we suggest that you not use a pillow in a bassinet, carrycot, or cradle; and if you use side cushioning, be sure that it is firm so that baby's face won't smother against it.

Neither bassinets, nor carrycots, nor cradles are covered by the federal safety standards that cover cribs and portable cribs. However, some requirements contained in other federal standards, such as the ban on lead paint, apply to these products.

Bassinets

Bassinets are small, wheeled baby beds with hoods, usually woven of basket material. Their advantages are that they take up little space and can be rolled easily from one room to another. Their disadvantages are that the large hood may get in the way when you pick up or lay down your baby, and some models have relatively rough, sharp edges on the inside that could cut a baby.

Between January 1994 and June 1995, over 30 babies in the United States died while lying facedown in bassinets. The cause of these deaths is not clear, but one possibility is that the softness of the mattresses supplied with the bassinets may have smothered the babies' faces and caused asphyxiation. The bassinet mattress pad you use should be firm and fit snugly against the edges of all sides of the bassinet.

Some bassinets are designed to fold. Their legs have hinges that lock into an open position. There have been incidents involving hinges that have accidentally folded, collapsing the bassinet to the floor and entrapping babies in a position that caused them to suffocate. Other babies have suffocated when their heads became trapped between the soft mattress and the hard sides of the bassinet, even when the bassinet was in an upright position. Nonfatal bassinet accidents usually happen when siblings try to lift babies from bassinets and accidentally drop them or cause the bassinet to topple over.

If there are older siblings in the house, you may want to consider a safer bed for your baby, such as a crib. Should you decide to purchase a bassinet, we recommend that you always place baby faceup (unless your pediatrician advises otherwise) for sleeping. Resist the temptation to add more mattress padding, to cover the mattress with plastic bags, or to use pillows of any size. Your baby may get his or her face trapped against those items.

Carrycots

Carrycots, which are small baby beds with carrying handles, are designed for toting very young babies from place to place. They are not widely used in the United States but are very popular in Europe. Although carrycots can be useful, especially for daytime naps while away from home, a stroller, an infant child safety seat, or a fabric front-carrier could serve the same purpose.

Carrycots come in two basic styles: those made of fabric that fold down for storage and those made like woven baskets.

Safety is a critical issue with carrycots. Be sure that the attachment points for each handle are widely spaced so that when your baby shifts position, the carrier won't tilt from head to toe. Handles that are not adequately reinforced may eventually pull loose and break, causing the baby to fall. Models that rely on cardboard sewn inside the fabric for backing may warp or deteriorate if the material gets wet.

Woven basket carrycots have handles that are scratchy and uncomfortable to carry for any length of time. These handles also tend to fray and break, and may allow a baby to fall. If you do opt for a woven carrycot, be sure to look under the fancy lace and fabric for sturdy construction, especially with respect to the handle attachments. Also check that the basket is well balanced while the baby is in it.

In spite of their limitations, carrycots can offer an easy way to tote a young baby around when visiting, and they are especially cozy for daytime naps. Collapsible models could conceivably be handy on camping trips. But remember, a carrycot must never be used as a substitute for a safe, sturdy child safety seat while riding in an automobile. In fact, to do so is illegal.

Cradles

Cradles have a romantic, old-fashioned look about them, but we suggest that you resist buying one. Their side-to-side motion can roll a tiny baby until the child is helplessly pressed against the side (the baby's weight can cause the cradle bed to shift to one side).

It's true that babies love rhythmic motion, but the kind of rocking motion that is most effective for them is a head-to-toe motion, similar to what they experience when they're rocked on a parent's shoulder in a rocking chair. Many parents who buy cradles, especially those with floor rockers, are disappointed with the results. The side-to-side motion simply rolls a tiny baby back and forth. Cradle frames that are suspended on hooks may have less radical side-to-side action, but again, the motion will only cause a newborn's body to shift back and forth.

In addition, cradles may not be as safe for babies as they appear. One recent Australian study found that many cradles had locking pins that were not secure. Researchers showed that when cradles were tilted 10 degrees or more, babies were pushed into the side of the cradle with their faces pressed against the bars. Some babies got their arms trapped through the bars and were unable to breathe, with the exception of those babies that had pacifiers in their mouths.

The study recommends that babies should never be left unattended in freely rocking cradles, and that locking pins should be bolted into place so cradles cannot tilt to an angle greater than 5 degrees.[1] In other studies, infant deaths were attributed to the marked tilt angle of the cradle. All of the cradles in question had inadequate or nonchildproof locking devices.[2]

Instead of spending several hundred dollars for a cradle, consider investing in a comfortable padded rocker/recliner for use during those late-night times when your baby seems to want to be held and have rhythmic movement, or look for a rocking infant seat. Another alternative is a baby carriage with a good, springy suspension system that allows you to provide a head-to-toe motion while wheeling it about the house or outdoors.

Listings: Bassinets, carrycots, and cradles

Note: These products were not tested by Consumers Union. This alphabetical listing does not include all models available, but rather is a selection of some widely distributed models. Descriptions are derived from authors' observations and manufacturers' claims.

MODEL	DESCRIPTION
BASSINETS	
Badger Basket Handwoven Bassinet *Winnie-the-Pooh liner* Model P-411, $279; Model 4095, $225 *White liner*	European-style basket bassinet with hood, wooden legs, and 9-inch wooden wheels. Pad included. Available with white or Winnie-the-Pooh print lining. For infants up to 4 months, or when baby starts to turn.
Badger Basket Swinging Bassinet Model 306-7, $109	A white, suspended cradle with bars. Comes with pad. Locks into stationary position. For infants up to 4 months, or when baby starts to turn.

[1] Beal, S.M., et al., "The Danger of Freely Rocking Cradles," *Journal of Paediatric Child Health,* no. 1 (February 3, 1995), 38–40.

[2] Byard, R. W., Beal, S., and Bourne, A. J., "Potentially Dangerous Sleeping Environments and Accidental Asphyxia in Infancy and Early Childhood," *Archives of Disease in Childhood,* 71 no. 6 (December 1996), 497–500.

MODEL	DESCRIPTION
Badger Hand Carry Bassinet Model 850, $109	Bassinet with fold-down, detachable hood, bottom pad and sheet, quilted liner, and comforter. Carrying handles with hand grip. Comes with sturdy stand that has 2-inch casters. Stand folds for easy transport and has antifold locking ring. Mattress pad available in standard and jumbo size. For infants up to 4 months, or when baby starts to turn.
Century Bedside Bassinet Model 10-450, $90	Bassinet fold-down hood. Two fabric handles and nonskid rubber feet for use out-of-stand. Stand has stage compartment and casters for easy moving. Four locks snap bassinet into stand. Thick, vinyl-covered mattress. Available in white or print fabric.
Delta Travel Sleeper Bassinet Model 4430, $50	Vinyl and mesh sides. Top zipper can totally enclose bassinet for protection from insects and pests. Metal-tube frame has wheels and safety-lock side hinges and folds flat for storage. Includes mattress.

CARRYCOTS

Baby Bjorn Carrycot Model BB-200, $150	Well-padded, 100 percent cotton carrycot with two straps. Two long zippers allow front to open completely. Fits inside all pram-type strollers. Can be used as a changing area. Particleboard base removable so that the fabric carrier can be washed. Can be hooked onto a stroller to form a warm bunting; belt loops hold it in place. Interior is soft, quilted flannel. For infants up to 5 months.

CRADLES

Cosco Brass Cradle Model 10-T48, $89	A gentle rocking angle. Fashion design, white metal tubing with brass-tone accents. Locks in stationary position.
Delta Rocking Cradle Model 4440-1, $130	Resembles a crib with bars on the side. Has teething rails. Can be locked into a stationary position. Comes with mattress. White finish.
Gerry Contemporary Cradle Model 6141, $135	This sturdy hardwood suspended cradle has rounded suspension hardware that attaches toward the outside of the support frame for quiet swinging. Slats spaced for safety. Comes with vinyl-covered foam pad. Locks to prevent rocking. Available in white, natural, or misty white.
Longwood Forest Classic Rocking Cradle Model 4095, $119	A white, one-piece rocking cradle made of solid hardwood with a non-toxic finish. Bars on all sides. Reversible waterproof pad. Braced floorboard. Brake pins allow freezing into stationary position.
Million Dollar Baby Futura Cradle Model 403-W, $120	White finished cradle with flat head and end bars. Suspends by hooks from a frame. Comes with 2-inch foam mattress with vinyl covering.
Simmons Contemporary Cradle Model 0260, $320	A hardwood rocking cradle with bars on all sides. Has a rock-lock feature to hold the cradle still while baby sleeps. Available in natural and Aspen white finishes. Company also makes more traditional cradle models in darker woods.

Bathtubs and bathing accessories

Bathing a baby can be an anxiety-provoking activity for parents, especially with a first baby. We recommend "damp-mopping" a baby during the first few weeks. Eventually, though, the baby has to be bathed. Baby bathtubs are helpful because they provide a comfortable, secure environment for bathing. We recommend a tub that offers a semi-reclined seat, slip-resistant backing, and a drain hole with an attached plug. Certain products are unsafe to use as bath aids: bath rings; baby flotation devices that can flip over; suctioned seats without restraining belts, which can lead to drowning; and foam cushions that can be torn into pieces and swallowed, causing the baby to choke. Resist the temptation to answer the phone while bathing your baby. Never leave your baby alone in a bathing device. Always have one hand on your baby during bathing.

Baby washcloths and hooded baby towels are both optional purchases. Any soft washcloth will do, as will any soft towel, as long as it is large enough to enfold your baby. Special baby soaps can be expensive; whatever soap you choose, to prevent skin reactions make sure that it is relatively free of perfumes, deodorants, antibacterial agents, and other additives. Soap can be used to wash baby's hair as well, but if you plan to use shampoo, choose a baby shampoo because it will probably be gentler to eyes and skin.

Very young babies often heartily protest being bathed, not because their parents aren't doing it right but probably because a baby's primitive warming system is stressed by rapid changes in temperature. Babies don't need as many baths as we think they do, especially in the early months. Babies don't really get *dirty*, except for spitting up milk or soiling the diaper area. Damp-mopping with a moderately warm, soft baby washcloth will often suffice to keep your baby's skin in good shape.

CAUTION
Never leave a baby unattended in water. If you need to interrupt a bath, wrap your baby in a towel and take him or her with you. During bathing, always keep one hand on your baby.

The compulsive routines that some parenting instructors teach about rolling up cotton balls and carefully swabbing each eye, each nostril, and each ear really aren't necessary. Don't use *Q-Tips* or other cotton swabs; they only tempt you to poke into orifices, which could result in harm. A cotton swab used to clean the ear canals could rupture an eardrum. A boy's uncircumcised penis should not be paid any special attention beyond washing, rinsing, and gentle drying. The foreskin will not be retractable for years, and any attempts to retract it may cause tearing.

Baby bathing basics

Damp-mopping. First, don't give your baby a regular bath until the navel heals and the umbilical cord falls off. Even then, a very young baby will feel much more comfortable with damp-mopping while being covered by a warm towel or blanket. You can damp-mop your baby on your lap, on the diaper-changing table, or even on a bed, if you have the protection of a waterproof pad. If your baby seems frightened or overly upset, postpone bathing until another time. The places that most need attention are the face, neck creases, hands, and diaper area. Warm water without soap is adequate for cleansing unless there are signs of a diaper rash.

Bathing supplies. Before you begin, have all the supplies you need handy so that you can reach them while you're bathing your baby: towel, soft washcloth, soap, a plastic rinsing cup, diapers, and clothing. (Soaps without heavy perfumes or deodorant additives are less likely to cause skin reactions.)

Bathing tips. An important rule to follow from the first bath onward is *never to leave your baby unattended*, even for a moment. Babies can drown in an inch of water. Your baby will be slippery when wet. Gradually lower the baby into the tub, cradling the head with your arm. The room should be comfortably warm and draft free. To prevent slipping, line the tub or sink with a bath towel and use only about three inches of warm water. Test the water temperature with your elbow or wrist—it should be comfortable but not too hot (no more than 100°F).

Suggested bathing routine. Start by gently wiping your baby's face with a damp washcloth and no soap. If you decide to shampoo the head, you can use either soap or a baby shampoo. Cup the head in your hand so that it's angled backward, and mop the soap toward the back with a damp, wrung-out washcloth. Clean within the creases and folds of the body, especially in the diaper area. You can get to this area conveniently by holding on to both of your baby's ankles and raising the legs. Rinse with a damp washcloth or by pouring water over soapy parts. It's easiest to dry your baby in your lap while you're sitting down. Towel-dry the hair and pat down the rest of the body, again paying attention to creases and folds.

Fingernails are best clipped when your baby is asleep. To make the clipping less awkward (some parents have accidentally cut off more than nails), hold the hand so that it faces the same direction as your own.

Bathroom safety

Every year, many babies die or are involved in near-drowning incidents. Some are severely scalded by hot water in bathrooms. Often parents have been careless in watching their babies—perhaps because they have gone to answer the doorbell or the telephone, or they entrusted the task of watching baby to baby's brother or sister.

 WARNING! DROWNING HAZARDS
▲ **Keep small children away from buckets, toilets, and other containers of water.**
▲ **Supervise young children at all times in the bathtub to reduce drowning hazards.**

Exercise special caution when baby is around water sources. Children have drowned in bathtubs, basins, showers, and jetted bathtubs. Children have even drowned in toilet bowls, usually when they fell in headfirst. Install a toilet lid locking device to prevent the lid from being raised by a child, but don't rely on the device to protect your baby from all harm. Allow your toddler in the bathroom only if you keep a close watch.

Be aware of scalding hot water. Scalds from steaming hot bath or sink water happen with alarming frequency to babies and toddlers under five. Most scald injuries happen when children fall into a tub filling up with hot water. In other instances, the hot water is turned on by the child or the child's older brother or sister. Some children burn their hands simply by putting them under running water, and, in other cases, parents have burned children when they failed to sense the temperature of hot bathwater.

The single best answer for protecting your baby from being accidentally scalded is to turn down the thermostat on the water heater. According to the American Academy of Pediatrics, thermostats on water heaters should be set no higher than 120°F. Studies show that a temperature only five degrees hotter can result in a full-thickness skin burn in only 30 seconds.

Avoid suctioned bath seats for babies. A suctioned bath seat usually consists of a seat with three or four support posts and a ring at the top. Suction cups under the seat attach to the tub. These cups may suddenly release, allowing the seat and the baby to tip over. Modern bathtubs have slip-resistant surfaces to which suction cups do not readily attach (if at all). A baby may also slip between the legs of the seat and become entrapped. According to reports, 18 babies since

Avoid suctioned bath seats for babies.

1983 have died when they either climbed out of or slipped under bath seats, or when the seats tipped over. In most cases, the babies, ages 6 to 11 months, weren't being watched by their parents. Seats without safety belts are especially dangerous.

Use diaper pails with care. Children have drowned in diaper pail accidents. Purchase a pail with a locking lid, and keep the pail locked.

Be cautious with large buckets. Approximately 228 children, most about 8 to 14 months old, drowned in five-gallon utility buckets from

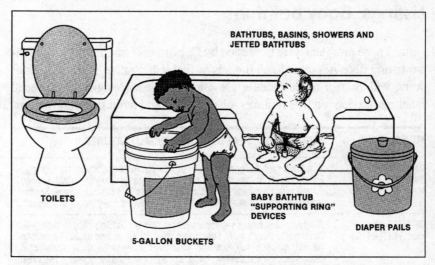

Exercise special caution when your baby is around water sources.

January 1984 to March 1994, according to reports from the U.S. Consumer Product Safety Commission. In the typical bucket-drowning incident, a parent brings a bucket home that originally held paint or other substances. The bucket is then used to mop floors, or to wash a pet. An unattended toddler crawls to the bucket and begins to play with the water. The tot falls into the bucket, can't get upright again, and drowns. It's important to empty all buckets completely when not in use, and always supervise your baby when you are using a bucket containing liquid.

Avoid foam bath sponges. Bathing sponges and sponge bathtub cushions for babies can be picked apart and ingested, causing choking. Avoid spongelike bath products when bathing baby.

Baby bathtubs and bathing accessories

Baby bathtubs are useful because they provide a comfortable, secure environment for bathing a baby. You'll need a sturdy baby tub with a smooth, rounded lip that makes carrying easier. Look for a model made of thick plastic that won't fold in the center from the weight of the water. The seat should be slip resistant and positioned at a comfortable angle for a small baby. A plug at the base of the tub makes it easy to drain.

Listings: Baby bathtubs

Note: These products were not tested by Consumers Union. This alphabetical listing does not include all models available but rather is a selection of some widely distributed models. Descriptions, Seat Designs, and Special Features are derived from authors' observations and manufacturers' claims.

MODEL	DESCRIPTION, SEAT DESIGN, SPECIAL FEATURES
Delta Luv Ergo BathSeat Model 9420, $13	A molded seat designed to hold baby safely and comfortably for bathing. European design has smooth contoured sides that hug the infant, leaving parent with both hands free. **Seat design:** Molded contour shape. **Special features:** Contour shape holds baby in place, reducing risk of accidents.
DEX EZ Bather Model EZB-01, $6	A vinyl-coated frame supports a fabric sling for bathing baby in sink or tub. Contours to baby's body, supporting head, shoulder, and back. Slip-resistant fabric is quick-drying, reducing germ and mildew build-up. Washable cover dries quickly. **Seat design:** Fabric sling on metal frame. **Special features:** Light and compact for travel. Support holds head safely above water.
First Years 2-Stage Baby Bather Model 3101, $14	Rigid, molded plastic with drain spout and plug on base. Can be used on single or double sink, or on any flat surface. **Seat design:** Foam-backed reclining seat on one end is for babies; upright seat at the other end is for older babies and toddlers. **Special features:** Small indented section at one end is for storing soap, washcloths, or shampoo.
Fisher-Price Deluxe Bath Center Model 9326, $16	Deep tub keeps baby warmer while bathing. Convenient container sections hold soap, shampoo, and other bathing products. Rinse pitcher has removable lid with spouts for pouring or sprinkling. Tub has carry handles on each end. Closed-cell foam cushion. Drain plug on base. Fits in one- or two-cavity sinks, or for use in bathtub or on countertop. **Seat design:** Contoured. **Special features:** Closed-cell foam cushion resists mildew. Drain plug allows emptying without lifting.
Gerry Infant to Toddler Tub Model 466, $18	A firm plastic insert fits in the larger tub, adjusting to two positions for bathing smaller babies. Remove the insert, and the tub provides support for children who can sit up. Fits in adult bath or on countertop. Sensi-temp plug indicates by turning pink if water is too hot. For children up to 24 months. **Seat design:** Contoured insert. **Special features:** Sensor to indicate high temperatures could help prevent scalding.
Gerry Teddy Tub Model 431, $20	Tub interior is lined with closed-cell foam for comfort and slip resistance. The bear-shaped foam and terry pad can be used to support baby while washing, or used as a drying pad. Plug at base turns pink if the water is too hot for the baby. **Seat design:** Contoured. **Special features:** Sensor to indicate high temperatures could prevent scalding.
Gerry Warm Bath Cushion Model 432, $7	Water-filled cushion with nonslip surface makes baby's bath warm, cozy, and safe. Fill inner cushion with water from faucet; inflate outer cushion with air for safety and support. Cushion folds for easy storage or travel. **Seat design:** Not applicable. **Special features:** Two separate cushion sections allow for the cushioning of water in the center and the buoyancy of air around the edge for maximum comfort and safety.
Safety 1st 2-in-1 Two Stage Tub Model 41641, $14	An oval-shaped white tub with a firm carrying rim. Snap-closed drain at foot of tub for easy emptying. Has slip-resistant foam pad. Accommodates babies age 0–2 years. **Seat design:** Closed-cell foam (infant shell); plastic contour (toddler tub). **Special features:** Converts to accommodate a range of ages safely. Foam support shell is mildew resistant.

Bottle-feeding equipment and pacifiers

Babies should not drink only whole cow's milk because it does not contain sufficient nutrients. In addition, babies' immature kidneys can't handle the by-products of foods such as whole cow's milk or high proteins. Cow's milk can also cause microscopic bleeding and blood loss in the baby's digestive tract, and cause allergic reactions. Skim milk is not good for babies, either. Babies need fat in their diets to supply them with energy and enable them to grow properly, and for proper development of their nervous systems. Not getting enough fat may cause a baby to drink more liquid to compensate for the shortage.

The use of formula (without any solids) can meet a baby's nutritional needs during the first six months of life. Although evaporated cow's milk formed the basis of formulas in the 1950s and earlier, newer formulas are based on an artificial milk in which homogenized vegetable and animal fats and oils are added to skimmed cow's milk to simulate the fatty-acid content of human breast milk. Various thickening and stabilizing agents are added to stabilize liquid formulas and provide uniform consistency.

In some instances, physicians recommend that soy-based formulas be substituted for cow's milk-based formulas when babies have an allergic reaction. Diarrhea, constipation, runny nose (with clear mucus), crankiness, frequent inner-ear infections, unusual sluggishness, or rashes may indicate such an allergy. The American Academy of Pediatrics recommends that babies who truly show signs of allergies to cow's milk not be given soy milk as a substitute, since soy has similar allergenic properties to cow's milk. The other alternative is pre-digested formulas, which are the least allergenic. Their biggest drawbacks are expense and taste.

How to prepare formula

In the early weeks after birth, your baby will probably feed six to eight times in 24 hours. Studies show that babies are more apt to be awake at night than in the daytime, so nighttime feedings are normal and should be expected. While a newborn will consume only about two to four ounces of formula during a feeding, your baby will increase the amount of formula needed up to about seven to eight ounces from four to six months of age. A simple rule of thumb is that a baby will take about two to two and a half ounces of formula per day for every pound of weight.

 Your baby's physician is the best source of advice on choosing an appropriate formula for your baby. We suggest that you stay with major formula brands and resist the urge to experiment with off-brand formulas from health-food stores or other sources.

Your baby should be fed whenever the baby seems hungry. Don't try to enforce an arbitrary schedule. In the early months, crying is the number-one signal of hunger, and if hunger cries aren't answered, they quickly turn to pain cries. The amount of formula that your baby needs can be expected to vary from one day to the next. Growth spurts, activity, and illness can all affect how much and how often your baby wants to be fed.

Basically, there are three types of formula: concentrated liquid that needs added water, powder that must be reconstituted with water, and ready-to-feed formula that comes in bottles or quart cans. All formula products should be carefully measured and diluted according to the container directions. If the formula is too concentrated, it can cause a serious overload to the baby's kidneys. Adding too much water to formula can result in malnutrition or serious overdilution of the baby's body fluids.

Be sure to read the can or bottle carefully and use it before the expiration date printed on the container. Formula should be prepared for no longer than a 24-hour period, refrigerated, and then discarded if it's not used within that time. Leftover formula in the baby bottle should be thrown away after feeding, since milk is an ideal breeding ground for bacteria. Opened cans of powdered formula should be covered; they can be safely stored for up to four weeks in the refrigerator. Opened liquid formula should be covered and refrigerated, but should be discarded after 48 hours. Freezing infant formula is not recommended.

Rules about sterilizing baby bottles and formulas and about heating formula before feeding have become much more lax in the last decade. Most physicians now recommend that all baby-bottle equipment be sterilized before being used the first time. After that, bottles and nipples no longer need to be sterilized if your home uses tap water rather than well water. If you use well water and septic systems, then you should boil the water used for formula to kill any harmful bacteria. Bottles, nipples, caps, and rings should be washed thoroughly in warm, soapy water after every use, or washed in the dishwasher. Very young or vulnerable babies, such as premature babies, may need to have their formulas sterilized initially. Your baby's physician is the best source for advice on what to do. Formula manufacturers' pamphlets give clear directions on sterilization procedures.

Most parents prefer to give their newborns warmed formula in the early weeks, but in time they shift to formula that is room temperature and then to refrigerated formula. Some babies show clear preferences for warmed or cold liquids. But all formula should be refrigerated immediately rather than "left out until baby wants the rest of it." Formula should not be prepared with hot water from the tap, since lead is much more soluble in hot water and in hot-water pipes and water heaters. The faucet should be run for several minutes if pipes have not been used for six hours or longer, since standing water may pick up contaminants from the plumbing.

Although automatic bottle-heating units can be handy in the night, the easiest way to warm formula is to run warm water over the lower portion of the bottle for a few minutes, or to place it in a pan of warm water and then shake the bottle to distribute the warm contents evenly. To prevent scalding, microwaving is not recommended for warming baby bottles.

Selecting bottles, sterilizers, and heating units

There are two basic kinds of feeding systems: bottles, which can be plastic or glass, and disposable bottle systems. Disposable systems consist of a hard plastic holder, called a *nurser*, that holds a plastic bag in the center, called a *bottle*. They use a special nipple design, and most have screw-on collars to hold the nipple and secure the bottle in place. The bottle is folded lengthwise and inserted into the nurser, and the top rim is stretched over the nurser edge. Formula is then poured into the bottle. The system must be thoroughly cleaned after each use, just as with regular bottle nipples.

The advantage of disposables is that bottles are ready to use and don't have to be cleaned. An advantage touted by manufacturers of these systems is that they can be squeezed to prevent the baby from sucking air, but positioning a standard bottle correctly has the same effect. Disposables are expensive and, as with disposable diapers, there is always the problem of running out of them at times when it's not convenient to go to the store. If overheated, the disposable pouch can rupture, spewing scalding liquid on parent or baby. Occasionally, disposable pouches can have flaws, causing tears and ruptures that leak milk. And there have been reported incidents of babies choking on plastic tabs from the sides of the bottle. From an environmental perspective, disposable bottles add more poorly decomposing plastic to the nation's landfills, and there may be a remote but potential danger of formula becoming contaminated from plastic particles and residues.

Standard baby bottles offer numerous advantages over disposables. They can be used over and over, and therefore they offer a considerable

QUICK TIPS
FOR SUCCESSFUL BOTTLE-FEEDING

◆ Follow the baby's signals for feeding times.
◆ Feed promptly when baby is hungry, before baby becomes aroused from heavy crying.
◆ Nestle the baby in the crook of your arm, in a half-sitting position, to prevent choking.
◆ Hold the bottle so that the neck and nipple are always filled.
◆ Don't jiggle the bottle or the baby.
◆ Be sure the bottle doesn't block the baby's nose, which forces harder breathing and makes feeding uncomfortable.
◆ Never prop the bottle in a baby's mouth, or leave the baby unattended while feeding. (The baby might choke.)
◆ Never try to change your baby's feeding schedule by withholding the bottle. Crying will only burn up calories and make baby hungrier.
◆ Notify your physician if your baby has diarrhea, spits up frequently, is constipated, or shows the following signs of allergies: skin rashes; clear, running mucus from the nose; frequent crying spells; or frequent colds.

saving over the long run. Setting them up for filling is easier, and you can gauge formula amounts more accurately. They're easier to hold on to, and they offer many more nipple options, including more durable silicone versions. Most breast pumps and all baby-bottle warmers are designed solely for use with standard bottles. Standard bottles can pose a cleaning challenge, however, especially models that don't have straight necks and bodies. Soft, opaque bottles tend to hold stains from juices, and those made of glass break if they're dropped.

Nursing bottles generally come in four-ounce and eight-ounce sizes. The four-ounce size is useful with small babies, for storage (freezing) of expressed breast milk, and later on for juice or water. Eight-ounce bottles are more versatile. We suggest you buy four of each of the following: four-ounce plastic bottles if you're breast-feeding or four-ounce and eight-ounce plastic bottles if you're using formula, with several extra nipples and caps. Clear plastic bottles are a good purchase because you can see inside when you're cleaning, you can observe how the milk is flowing when your baby is drinking, and you don't have to worry about breakage, as you would with glass bottles.

Nursing bottles now come in a number of designs. Bottles with angled necks are designed to help keep the nipple filled with liquid and the baby's head in a semiupright position. When shopping for baby bottles you should:

◈ Purchase clear, straight-sided, unbreakable bottles with no decorative patterns printed on the sides.
◈ Avoid bottles molded into shapes that are difficult to clean, or opaque bottles that absorb juice stains.
◈ Boil new bottles and nipples for five minutes before using them.

As discussed earlier, you may not need to contend with sterilization procedures unless your doctor instructs you to. The two basic styles of units for bottle sterilization are stove-top models, which have rings or racks for holding bottles, and self-standing electric units, which have to be plugged in. The stove-top models are more economical. But most electric units offer the advantage of automatic shutoff mechanisms that prevent meltdowns if the water boils away. An ordinary pot of boiling water can be just as effective as the stove-top models, although it won't have rings or racks for holding bottles.

If you want a bottle heater for, say, an upstairs bedroom, for maximum safety choose a model that has an automatic shutoff device to prevent overheating accidents. Remember to monitor the temperature of heated formula carefully by testing it on your wrist before serving it to your baby.

Injuries from bottles

Between January 1994 and March 1996, there were 262 baby bottle-related injuries reported to the U.S. Consumer Product Safety Commission (CPSC). Most accidents occurred when toddlers fell down while walking around with bottles in their mouths. Severe mouth and tongue injuries were the result. Other incidents included serious cuts caused by broken or exploding glass bottles, burns from hot liquid when bottles were being sterilized on the stove, and babies biting the tips off of nipples and choking on them. One serious accident that occurs with alarming frequency results when plastic bottles left to boil in a pot catch on fire. Babies exposed to the fumes from the melting bottles can be overcome by severe, life-threatening smoke. Parents have also reported that the decorative patterns on the interior of some plastic bottles have melted into clumps found floating in heated formula. Our suggestion is to purchase clear plastic bottles and to exercise extreme caution when sterilizing them or heating them on the stove.

The politics of formula

A decade ago, the U.S. surgeon general established the goal of increasing the nation's breast-feeding rate to 75 percent of all babies by 1990. But the U.S. breast-feeding rate remains below 60 percent, despite overwhelming medical evidence that breast milk reduces infant susceptibility to illness, especially gastrointestinal illnesses and ear infections. The reason for the lack of progress in breast-feeding may be the influence of the $3 billion-a-year formula industry.

It is generally agreed by nutritionists that baby formula brands are all basically the same. At current prices, U.S. babies consume $75 worth or more of formula a month, a significant burden for many families. And it has been calculated that out of every dollar that formula manufacturers charge wholesale for formula, approximately 16 cents represents the cost of production and delivery of the product.

In 1993 alone, spending for baby food and formula promotion more than doubled, increasing to $61 million, with the formula market growing an unprecedented 7.8 percent in the first quarter of 1995. The largest purchasers of baby formula aren't America's parents but state governments, which buy about 35 percent of all formula through their Women, Infants, and Children (WIC) programs for low-income mothers.

Infant formula was once marketed solely as a pharmaceutical product. Formula salespeople would call on pediatricians personally in an attempt to influence their recommendations to their patients. This interpersonal system was shaken in 1988, when the federal government directed the states to purchase all of their infant formula from one manufacturer to lower costs. That caused formula makers to compete directly with one another for lucrative WIC contracts.

In 1990, the Federal Trade Commission charged Abbott Laboratories, Bristol-Myers Squibb, and American Home Products with price fixing of infant formula in government nutrition programs. Bristol-Myers was accused of anticompetitive practices in marketing its *Enfamil* brand, as was American Home, whose Wyeth-Ayerst laboratories manufacture *SMA* formula.

From 1980 through 1993, Abbott (Ross Laboratories) raised the price of its *Similac* formula 18 times for a total of 207 percent—six times the increase in the consumer price of milk, its basic ingredient. Company and industry records show that Abbott played a central role in persuading rivals to agree to an industry sales code that erected a barrier to new competitors by discouraging consumer advertising of formula.

In 1994, the State of Wisconsin's Department of Justice filed civil antitrust charges against Abbott Laboratories and Bristol-Myers Squibb Company and its subsidiary Mead Johnson & Company. The companies sell milk-based infant formula under brand names such as *Similac* (Abbott/Ross Laboratories) and *Enfamil* (Mead Johnson & Company), which are responsible for more than 85 percent of industry sales. The state of Wisconsin alleged that the companies used cash grants, free formula, and other baby products to persuade hospitals and physicians to endorse a particular formula to their patients rather than marketing the products to consumers. The antitrust action also alleged that the companies raised the price of infant formula in a lockstep fashion, producing nearly identical prices. In 1993, Abbott agreed to pay $8 million to the state of Florida, $79 million to wholesale purchasers of formula, and $53 million to three major supermarket chains. Two other companies, Bristol-Myers and American Home Products, settled charges in the state of Florida separately from Abbott.

In May 1996, Abbott agreed to settle lawsuits from 17 states for a total of $32.5 million for having fixed the price of baby formula. The company also agreed to provide $7.5 million worth of formula. The states involved were Alabama, Colorado, Florida, Illinois, Kansas, Kentucky, Louisiana, Michigan, Minnesota, Mississippi, Nevada, North Carolina, North Dakota, South Dakota, Tennessee, West Virginia, and Wisconsin. At the time of this writing, Mead Johnson faces price-fixing suits in 15 states.

The result of the federal and state antitrust actions has been a free-for-all among manufacturers to convince new mothers, through direct mail, new-baby clubs, and TV and print advertising, to buy formula. Ninety percent of all breast-feeding materials being distributed to new mothers in hospitals today are being produced by formula companies. Studies have shown that women given hospital discharge packs that include infant formula samples and/or coupons are much less likely to breast-feed their babies. The packs are successful because they imply that the hospital and medical professionals endorse formula feeding.

In 1993, the American Academy of Pediatrics, which represents 45,000 pediatricians nationwide, admitted it had received grants of about $1 million annually from the nation's top three formula makers, and, according to the *Wall Street Journal*, a $3 million grant from formula manufacturers to build the academy's $10 million headquarters in Illinois in 1983.[1] Other medical groups funded by the formula industry include the American Medical Association, the American Dietetic Association, and the Association of Women's Health, Obstetrics and Neonatal Nurses.

After returning home from giving birth, new mothers are being bombarded with promotional literature touting the wonders of infant formula. Even though the brochures insist that "breast milk is best," this disclaimer does little to dampen the dominant message that breast-feeding is inconvenient, embarrassing in social situations, and possibly unnecessary. Many new mothers are receiving more than $50 in redeemable checks for various brands of formula. Without asking for it, mothers are being mailed seemingly impartial parenting guides designed to promote bottle feeding. Ross Laboratories, the makers of *Similac*, mails out cases of ready-to-serve formula designed to target women during the periods of maximum anxiety about their ability to nourish their babies with human milk.

Indigent mothers are the most vulnerable to these freebies, the least able to afford to buy formula, and the most likely to give up breast-feeding prematurely. Some companies are distributing handouts in clinics that falsely imply that a few bottles of formula each day will help a breast-feeding mother keep a good milk supply. In truth, supplementing with formula, especially in the early months, effectively begins the weaning process.

Unfortunately, breast-feeding proponents do not receive the immense

---

[1] Burton, T. M., "Spilt Milk: Methods of Marketing Infant Formula Land Abbott in Hot Water; It Pushed Baby-Food Rivals to Bar Ads, Limiting a New Player's Chances, A Big Antitrust Settlement," *Wall Street Journal* (25 May 1993), A-1.

financial backing that the formula-feeding industry does, even though scientific studies document the superiority of human milk in protecting and promoting the health of babies. The formula industry bestows major contributions on many hospitals to snare the privilege of giving away products there. Hospitals are provided with unlimited free formula along with cash if they're willing to promote one brand of formula. A typical case is Northwestern University's Memorial Hospital in Chicago, which accepted $210,000 from Bristol-Myers Squibb Company's Mead Johnson Nutritional Group over a three-year period in return for using only their formulas.

In spite of incentives, there is a growing movement among hospitals to pull away from participating in formula marketing in the belief that distributing free formula and hospital discharge packs actively undermines breast-feeding and makes hospitals beholden to large formula manufacturers. Dozens of U.S. hospitals have stopped distributing maternity discharge packs laden with formula samples and coupons, and more than 200 U.S. hospitals state they plan to join a voluntary pro-

TO PARENTS: BEWARE OF BOGUS FORMULA WARNING LABELS

In February 1995, more than 50 babies became ill when mislabeled formula cans coded with fictitious expiration dates were sold in California grocery stores.

A month later, the criminal investigative unit of the FDA announced that counterfeit-labeled cans of *Similac*, a milk-based baby formula manufactured by Abbott Laboratories, had been sold in 15 states. Some of the cans sold in California that were labeled *Similac* contained *Isomil* instead, a soy-based formula. California's Lucky Stores removed more than 17,000 cans of the mislabeled formula.

FDA investigators announced that some of the counterfeit labeling was the result of a widespread underground selling of brand-name formulas. Traders, known as "diverters," had bought bargain-priced formula from retailers who were selling the formula at a discount to attract customers. The diverters then resold the formula at a profit to other stores or to formula distributors. The counterfeit labels became necessary when the formula passed expiration dates.

It's suggested that parents examine labels carefully and throw away formula that has an unusual odor or texture.

gram sponsored by the World Health Organization and UNICEF that offers "Baby Friendly" certification to hospital nurseries that discourage hospital formula marketing.

Formula precautions

The Infant Formula Act of 1980, administered by the Food and Drug Administration (FDA), was designed to ensure quality infant formula that meets all the needs and requirements of infant nutrition. All formula manufacturers test their products to ensure they meet nutritional requirements and are free from such contaminants as bacteria. Here are some precautions you can take to be sure that your baby is being fed the freshest, safest product:

◆ Check the expiration date on the can before you buy it. Some small grocers may sell formula that has gone beyond safe storage dates.

◆ Store liquid and powdered formula in a cool, dry place, and out of direct sunlight.

◆ Follow the written instructions on the can carefully. Formula makers change directions periodically.

◆ Before opening a formula can, shake it to be sure it's well mixed, and wipe off the top of the can with a clean cloth.

◆ Add exactly the right amount of water to powdered mixes, and don't dilute formula to make it last longer. Doing so can cause water intoxication and deprive your baby of needed nutrients.

◆ Don't use formula that doesn't smell or look right (e.g., lumpy, grainy liquid, or clumped powder).

◆ Don't store open, prepared formula or reconstituted formula in the refrigerator for longer than 24 hours. Unrefrigerated formula should be used within 4 hours.

◆ Discard partially used bottles of formula—don't save them up to be "finished" later.

Juices and sweetened beverages

Adults seldom consume more than one apple or orange at a time, yet drinking fruit juices represents the consumption of the liquid from as many as four or five apples or other fruits at one time. According to the U.S. Department of Agriculture's Food and Nutrition Service, some fruit juices, such as apple, pear, cherry, peach, and prune juice, contain significant amounts of sorbitol, a type of carbohydrate called a "sugar alcohol."

When children consume these juices in excessive amounts, they may experience diarrhea, abdominal pain, and bloating. Sugar alcohols create a laxative effect due to their slow and incomplete absorption in the gastrointestinal tract. For that reason, these juices should be given to a baby only in moderation, especially when babies are under six months of age. Citrus juices, such as orange, tangerine, grapefruit, pineapple, and tomato, should not be consumed by babies until they are six months or older because citric juices may cause allergic reactions.

When babies drink too much water, juice, or liquids other than breast milk or formula from a bottle or cup, it may slow down their intake of breast milk or formula, which contains all the nutrients they need to thrive. In addition, juices are acidic in nature and may contribute to baby tooth decay, sometimes called baby bottle mouth. Feed your baby juices in moderation and from a cup, rather than a bottle with a nipple (even if the juice comes in a four- or eight-ounce bottle designed for a nipple). And don't feed your baby sweetened powdered drinks, or caffeine-containing beverages such as tea or soda. They can be harmful, depriving your baby of needed nutrition and causing baby tooth decay.

Honey has been found to carry bacteria that are harmless to children but can cause botulism poisoning in babies. The symptoms of botulism are listlessness, irritability, diarrhea, droopy eyelids, and difficulty swallowing and breathing 24 hours after exposure. Severe cases can lead to seizures, brain damage, or, more rarely, death.

Most canned juices made in the United States are packed in cans coated with a lining designed to reduce the rate at which the can corrodes. Once a can is opened, the exposure to air may increase corrosion. For that reason, juices should be poured out of the can and stored in a clean glass or plastic container. Fruit juices should never be stored in lead crystal containers or pottery containers—both of which may leach lead into the juice. Canned juices from ethnic stores or imported from other countries may have lead soldering in the seams and should be avoided.

Bottled water

Even though baby food manufacturers are now marketing bottled water for babies, babies shouldn't be given boiled or bottled water to drink as a substitute for breast milk or formula. The U.S. Centers for Disease

Control warns that bottled water can cause seizures in babies under six months old who are not yet eating solid foods. Bottled water contains little or no sodium, which babies need, and it can dilute the sodium they get from human milk or formula. Since breast milk and formula contain enough water for babies, they should not be given bottled or tap water or juice without a physician's advice. Breast-fed babies seldom have diarrhea, and should continue to nurse if they do. If your bottle-fed baby has diarrhea or vomiting, he or she should be given a special oral rehydration solution, rather than water.

Although the FDA requires that bottled water products be clean and safe for human consumption, the FDA's overseeing of bottled water doesn't ensure water safety. Bottled water may contain potentially high levels of harmful contaminants that are not allowed in public drinking water. One study of 37 brands of bottled mineral water found that 24 of them contained one or more substances that did not comply with federal drinking-water standards. Fluoride levels also vary among different brands. It makes sense to consider contacting the water bottlers for information on the quality of their products.

If you have reason to believe that your water system is contaminated with lead, copper, nitrates, or agricultural by-product runoffs, or excessive amounts of naturally occurring fluoride, then you may want to stick to premixed formula for your baby, or buy bottled water to mix instant formula. Distilled water contains fewer contaminants than bottled, spring, or mineral water. Consult your physician before buying any water product or before using well water for your baby.

Choosing nipples

Both bottle and pacifier nipples are available in rubber and silicone. Rubber nipples tend to deteriorate, swell, and crack after two or three months of normal use. Rubber nipples whiten when they're wet for a long time, and saliva, heat, and sunlight can cause them to become sticky and clogged.

Silicone is a clear, odorless, taste-free material that is heat resistant enough to be washed in a dishwasher. It is less porous than rubber, making it less apt to harbor bacteria. Although silicone nipples do not rot and become sticky as rubber nipples do, they have a tendency to split and tear. According to the CPSC, there have been numerous reports of both silicone and rubber nipples and pacifiers being bitten through by babies.

Nipples come in two basic shapes: the traditional bell-shaped nipple (available with hole sizes ranging from standard to smaller for newborns and larger for toddlers or for use with pulpy juices) and the irregularly shaped "orthodontic" nipple, which is elongated on one edge of the top and indented in the center.

Standard vs. orthodontic nipple

According to manufacturers, orthodontic nipples resemble a mother's nipple when it is elongated in the baby's mouth. Supposedly, such a shape evokes a tonguing action similar to the one used by breast-feeding babies, so that tongue-thrusting and bite problems believed to be caused by standard nipples are reduced. Such claims have not been scientifically substantiated, and there is little difference between the performance of orthodontic and traditional nipple shapes. There have been problems with rubber orthodontic nipples quickly deteriorating and becoming sticky, perhaps because the indented center of the nipple makes thorough cleaning more difficult. When an orthodontic nipple ages and becomes sticky, the narrow center often collapses.

Bottle nipples vary among brands, and even nipples from the same manufacturer with the same model numbers can differ in the size of the tiny flow hole that allows milk to be sucked from the bottle. One way to find the best nipple flow is to test different brands yourself by sucking liquid through them. You will discover that the nipples offer different resistance to flow. While your baby is nursing, nipple flow can be increased and decreased by tightening or loosening the neck of the bottle. You may find that so-called dripless nipples produce such a strong resistance that they block milk flow, making them more of a disadvantage than an advantage.

The standard nipple is bell-shaped; the orthodontic nipple dents in the middle.

A nipple should offer some resistance so that milk won't pour into your baby's throat, causing choking. Too much milk flow during feedings can cause babies to adopt an abnormal tongue thrust from trying to stop the milk. It is thought that this habit may later affect speech patterns. On the other hand, overly resistant nipples may cause your baby to struggle to get milk and make the nipple collapse. Of the four major brands of silicone nipples—Gerber, Evenflo, PlaySkool, and Pur—only Gerber's nipple has a reinforced neck that gives it a tighter spring-back action, resisting collapse during feeding.

Although latex nipples can be boiled with a toothpick through the center to enlarge their holes for better flow, the holes in silicone nipples can't be enlarged because they are easily ruptured by tears or scratches. If you're using silicone, throw out any malfunctioning nipples.

WHICH NIPPLES SHOULD YOU BUY?

Experiment. Let your baby try out both an orthodontic and a regularly shaped nipple, and see which one is accepted better.

Use silicone nipples, but with caution. Silicone offers fewer deterioration problems than rubber. Hold silicone nipples up to the light and inspect them carefully prior to each use to detect punctures or tears. Discard those that show signs of problems, and file a report with the U.S. Consumer Product Safety Commission.

Pacifiers

A pacifier is a nipple mounted on a plastic shield for the purpose of allowing a baby to suck and mouth while not actually drinking milk. Some pacifiers have rings on the back, and others have small knobs. Sometimes babies who are restless and fussy can be calmed by being given a pacifier to suck on, and some experts theorize that babies have a built-in need for "nonnutritive" sucking—that is, sucking that offers no breast milk or formula. Parents sometimes offer pacifiers in an effort to prevent their babies from establishing a thumb-sucking habit, with some success. It is thought that pacifiers are less likely than habitual thumb sucking to interfere with tooth alignment.

Sometimes babies become so addicted to using a pacifier that they

WARNING!
Strings around the
neck can strangle
a child. Never tie
pacifiers or other
items around your
child's neck.

cry in the night when it falls out of the mouth, and parents may find themselves pinning it onto sleeves or nightgowns. Never use the pacifier's ring to hang it from a string around the baby's neck or to tie it to crib bars because of the risk of strangulation. Discard a pacifier when the nipple becomes old, sticky, and crumbly, or when your baby begins to chew off pieces of it.

A federal standard now in effect requires that all pacifiers be constructed with two ventilation holes in the shields to admit air in case a baby accidentally gets the shield caught in the mouth or throat. Pacifiers must pass a "pull test" after boiling and cooling to ensure that they will not come apart. The size of the shield is regulated to prevent accidental choking, and a warning label must appear on all pacifier packages advising against use of a string to hang a pacifier around a child's neck because of the strangulation hazard.

Pacifier dangers

Recent research suggests pacifiers aren't completely harmless. For example, pacifier use has been associated with early weaning from breast-feeding. In addition, a 1995 Finnish study of 845 day-care centers found that children who used pacifiers had significantly more middle ear infections than children who did not use pacifiers. In fact, the researchers concluded that pacifiers were responsible for one out of four middle ear infections in children under three.

Here are the ways to inspect a pacifier for safety:

◆ Handle can crack. Pull to see that it is securely attached to the nipple and shield bracket.

◆ Shield may crack, allowing the nipple section to come off, causing choking. Shield should be firm and large enough so babies can't take it into their mouths.

◆ Ventilation holes are designed to keep babies from suffocating if the pacifier becomes entrapped in their mouths.

◆ Nipple can tear or pull off from shield. Make sure it is securely fastened on, has no tears or holes, and hasn't become sticky with age.

Listings: Bottles and accessories

Note: These products were not tested by Consumers Union. This alphabetical listing by category includes new or unusual accessories. Descriptions are derived from authors' observations and manufacturers' claims.

MODEL	DESCRIPTION
BOTTLES	
Evenflo Clear Angled Nurser *8- and 4-ounce* Models 12200, 12240; $2.65	Reusable clear plastic nursers with silicone nipples and nipple covers in assorted colors. Comfort grip design makes holding the bottle easier for adult. Also available in 4-ounce size.
First Years Tumble Mates Nurser Model 1054, $2.15	Bottle section is shaped like a tumbler with measurement markings on the side. Base is textured for easy grip. Unit is dishwasher safe on the top rack and stackable for efficient storage. Nurser lid snaps on and off. Comes with standard latex nipple and nipple cover. Accepts all other standard nipples. Entire unit may be sterilized by immersing it in boiling water for two to five minutes.
Gerber Glass Nurser Model 76100, $1.35	Standard glass bottle with easy-grip sides. Dishwasher and sterilizer safe. Comes with rubber nipple that can be replaced with a silicone nipple, which tends to resist cracking. Available also in 4-ounce size. Similar models available with rubber Nuk nipple.
Sassy Man 3-Step Nurser System Model 517, $4	Short, wide nurser bottle with a removable plastic neck ring that forms small handles on either side. Comes with orthodontic-shaped silicone nipple. Nipple cap of bottle turns over to become a small drinking cup. Dishwasher safe.
BOTTLE ACCESSORIES	
Evenflo Snap & Fill Formula Funnel for Angled Nursers Model 11260, $1.10	Plastic funnel especially designed for angled nursers to prevent spills when mixing formula or filling with prepared formula. Fits most brands of angled or conventional nursers.
First Years/Cool Tote Model 1026, $11	Insulated zippered bag with reusable cold pack for storing up to three 8-ounce bottles and three 8-ounce baby food jars. Side pocket for utensils.
First Years Drink Link Model 1112, $2.45	Elasticized band goes around a bottle's neck and is fastened to a plastic snap-on strap for fastening bottle to stroller, high chair, or grocery cart.
Mommy's Helper Better Baby Bottle Brushes Model 01352, $6	Comes with two brushes—a large one for bottles and a small one for nipples. Suction-based brush holder adheres to bottom of kitchen sink, making bottle and nipple washing a one-handed operation. Place bottles neck down on brushes for easy scrubbing.
Pearcy Wooden Bottle Dryer Model CRI, $12	Solid maple rack that holds up to six bottles, nipples, and retainer rings for air drying. Designed to sit on kitchen counter or drain board.
Prince Lionheart Bottle Booties Model 1201, $4	Soft, textured, padded sleeves for 8-ounce bottles for maintaining temperature and providing gentle tactile stimulation.

MODEL	DESCRIPTION
Prince Lionheart Sani-Stor Baby Bottle Sanitizing and Storage System Model 1010, $8	Heat-resistant rack holds bottles securely by the neck for dishwashing. Rack then slides into a tray mounted onto a kitchen cabinet shelf for storage until time for use.
Safety First 1st Stage Smart Feeder Model 24023, $2.20	Angled, contoured cap screws onto all standard-size bottles to keep nipple filled with liquid to reduce baby's air intake. Clear hooded cap helps keep nipple clean when not in use. Silicone nipple resists cracking and increases feeding comfort. Unique grip shape is easy for parents and for baby to use when old enough to grasp bottle alone. The 1st Stage Smart Feeder is suitable for infants up to 3 months; a 2nd Stage Smart Feeder is also available for babies 4 months and older.

BOTTLE CARRIER AND HEATING DEVICES

First Years Day & Night Bottle Warmer System Model 1058, $32	Keeps two bottles cool for up to 8 hours using cold packs. Central section warms a chilled bottle in approximately 5 minutes. Built-in night-light. Automatic shutoff.
Prince Lionheart Hip Hiker Model 4501, $15	Insulated fanny pack for parents designed to keep warm things warm and cool things cool. Ideal for nursing and feeding supplies. Thermally reflective lining with foam insulation combines to minimize loss of heat or cold from foods or liquids. Waist strap adjusts for comfortable fit. Outside mesh pocket holds car keys or sunglasses.

STERILIZERS

Gerber Electric Bottle Sterilizer Set Model 76044, $46	Complete 34-piece set includes sterilizer, four 9-ounce and two 5-ounce plastic nursers, complete with ribbed rubber nipples, collars, and snap-off hoods. Tongs, bottle, and nipple brushes also included. Automatic shutoff.
Evenflo Automatic Electric Sterilizer Model 41150, $33	Unit converts water to steam. Comes with base and cord, lift-out rack, and cover. Empty bottles, nipples, caps, and other small items are sterilized in 30–45 minutes, formula-filled bottles in 60–90 minutes (two-hour cooling time). Automatic shut off at end of process or if water boils away.
Prince Lionheart NAP Sanitizing Device Model 1001, $6	Plastic basket holds teething and bottle-feeding necessities for washing in an automatic dishwasher. Patented design features a compartment for small, hard-to-clean items like nipples. The compartment, which has a flip-top lid, holds nipple upright, directly above the water source, for thorough washing and rinsing. Rust-proof material withstands the high temperatures of automatic dishwashers.

Recalls

EUGENE TRADING CO. Deary Baby Rattle/Pacifier
Nipple can separate from base. Also, shield lacks ventilation holes, and it can penetrate too far into mouth.
Products: 194,000 pacifiers sold between 8/92 and 11/93 in Arizona, California, Illinois, Maryland, Montana, New York, and Texas. Pacifier has pink, yellow, or

blue shield and ring with rubber nipple. Packaging consists of plastic bubble attached to perforated display panel that reads: "Deary Baby Rattle Baby Soother Spain Style." Package also shows blond baby with pacifier in mouth.

What to do: Destroy pacifier or mail it to Eugene Trading Co., 3841 Broadway Pl., Los Angeles, CA 90037, for refund.

GERBER PRODUCTS CO. NUK Pacifiers

Could come apart and choke child.

Products: 10 million pacifiers sold singly or in multipacks for $1.29 to $4.99. "NUK" is on mouth shield. Date code on back of package ranges from 070193 (7/1/93) to 063094 (6/30/94). Package reads, in part: "Nipple made in Germany. Plastic parts molded and unit assembled in USA. Printed in USA. Distributed by Gerber Products company." Pacifiers with "NEW" on front of packaging are not being recalled. Nor are pacifiers distributed by hospitals.

What to do: Call 800-443-7237 for replacement pacifier. Gerber will also replace any NUK pacifier that lacks packaging.

M.J. HARRIS AND ASSOCIATES Dubby Pacifier-Thermometer

Nipple could come off and choke child.

Products: 340 pacifier-thermometers sold at pharmacies and through mail-order catalogs between 4/93 and 8/93 for up to $12.50. Device is pink or blue with clear silicone rubber nipple. Built-in electronic LCD thermometer displays temperature when baby sucks on nipple. Product was sold in blue box with "Dubby" on top panel; sticker reads, "Made in Taiwan."

What to do: Return product to store or mail-order house.

PACI-FACES INC. Pacifiers

Nipple could come off and choke child.

Products: 35,000 pacifiers sold between 1/94 and 6/94 for $3. Pacifier comes in 3 styles: Mustache pacifier, model 00001, resembles black handlebar mustache with red lip below; Lip pacifier, model 00002, and Smile pacifier, model 00003, have two large lips and two rows of teeth. Pacifiers are 2½ inches wide, 1½ inches long, and have small air hole on either side of beige rubber nipple. Label on back of shield reads, in part: "MADE IN CHINA 1986 Paci-Face, Inc. Patent pending." Pacifiers whose packaging bears date code of 5/1/95 or later are not being recalled.

What to do: Return pacifier to store for refund.

Breast-feeding and nursing accessories

Every year, something new is discovered about the value of human milk to the growth and health of babies. Scientific studies have shown, for example, that, unlike cow's milk, human milk is more like living tissue that is transferred to a baby from its mother. Mother's milk offers food for brain growth and protection from disease as no other liquid can do.

Breast milk delivers not only antibodies to protect babies but also a battery of other infection-fighting agents. Substances in a mother's milk ingest and kill harmful bacteria and virus cells, while promoting the growth of helpful bacteria. Other disease fighters disarm certain bacteria and viruses so they can't succeed in attacking the baby. Hormones are delivered to the baby to speed up the maturation of the digestive tract and immune system. And research is showing that the effects of breast-feeding can endow children and adults with a better chance for a healthy life.

Breast-feeding your baby can help to reduce your own risk of getting breast cancer. The younger you are when you start breast-feeding, and the longer you breast-feed, the lower your risk of breast cancer. If you're under 20 and breast-feed for at least six months, you can reduce your chances of getting breast cancer before menopause by as much as 46 percent. Women who feed their babies solely breast milk will probably not menstruate during those months when they are breast-feeding, which is an aid to birth control.

Here are some of the health benefits of breast-feeding your baby (for information on feeding your baby formula or cow's milk, see chapter 4):

◈ **Fewer allergies.** Your baby will be less likely to have lifelong allergies to dairy products and other foods. He or she will also be less likely to suffer from allergic skin reactions such as eczema.

◈ **Protection from viruses and bacterial infections.** Babies receiving human milk have fewer colds and stomach upsets than babies fed formula. Factors in human milk fight against polio, mumps, measles, chicken pox, tetanus, strep, staph, pneumonia, meningitis, and *Giardia* infections. It doesn't mean your breast-fed baby won't come down with these illnesses, but your milk may strengthen the fight against them.

◈ **Protection from urinary tract infections and life-threatening forms of diarrhea.** Substances in your milk will help to strengthen your baby's urinary tract and will offer protection from the most life-threatening forms of diarrhea.

◈ **Better teeth.** Human milk has components that help to form strong, cavity-resistant teeth, and the process of suckling leads to better jaw formation than sucking on a baby bottle. Both of these benefits mean fewer dental problems down the road.

◈ **Reduced chance of having anemia.** Even though breast milk appears to contain less iron than artificial milk, iron deficiency anemia is rare in young breast-fed babies. That's because breast milk's iron is easy to absorb. Iron absorbtion is reduced once baby food is introduced.

◈ **Fewer middle-ear infections.** One study of 1,000 babies found that babies who were breast-fed during their first four months had 50 percent fewer ear infections than bottle-fed babies, whereas babies who were formula-fed or breast-fed with formula supplements were more likely to have middle-ear trouble. The antibodies in breast milk appear to prevent these infections.

◈ **Fewer chances of becoming an overweight adult.** Breast-fed babies tend to be leaner than formula-fed babies and have less trouble later as adults with being overweight. One factor contributing to fat bottle-fed babies is the tendency to coax them to "finish the bottle."

◈ **Protection against juvenile diabetes.** Breast-fed babies who haven't been exposed to formula have a reduced risk of developing insulin-dependent diabetes later on in childhood. Chances of having appendicitis or developing arthritis in childhood or multiple sclerosis in later life are also reduced.

◆ **Intelligence benefits.** Children who have been breast-fed as infants show a small but statistically significant increase in intelligence over babies who have received no mother's milk. Breast milk is thought to contain "brain food"—substances that enhance human brain development.

Prepare to succeed

Consumers Union's medical consultants advise any woman who is undecided about whether to breast-feed or bottle-feed her baby to try breast-feeding initially. It's always possible to wean your baby gradually if breast-feeding doesn't work out, but if nursing isn't started immediately after birth, it is difficult to initiate later.

If you want to succeed in nursing, a few words of advice are in order: Resist the urge to impose a schedule on your baby's nursing, since milk production is dependent upon how often and how long a baby is allowed to nurse. Don't offer your baby both the breast and formula, because additional fluids will reduce a baby's demand for the breast, which affects milk production and starts the process of weaning. In addition, some newborns will refuse the breast once they've been exposed to commercial nipples, a situation called nipple confusion.

The best way to satisfy yourself that your infant is getting enough milk is to count wet diapers. Six wet cloth diapers or five disposables in a 24-hour period means your baby is getting enough fluids. Contact a physician right away if your baby shows signs of dehydration.

It may be a good idea to familiarize yourself with breast-feeding techniques before your baby is born rather than trying to wing it on instinct. Your pediatrician may be able to provide you with a videotape, or you can read up on breast-feeding. Two excellent books on this topic are *The Womanly Art of Breast-feeding*, written by La Leche League, International, a worldwide support organization for breast-feeding mothers, and *Nursing Your Baby*, by Karen Pryor. Both books are available in moderately priced paperback editions and in libraries. La Leche League also has well-informed leaders who offer telephone counseling and monthly support groups for nursing mothers in nearly every city. For information about your nearest group, look in the white pages of your telephone directory, or contact La Leche League, International, P.O. Box 4079, Schaumburg, IL 60168-4079; phone 847-519-7730, or toll-free 800-LALECHE (523-3243).

....

Choosing a nursing bra

Here are some suggestions on shopping for a nursing bra:

Comfortable fit. The best time to shop for a nursing bra is between your 28th and 36th week of pregnancy, before your rib cage expands. That way you'll be sure to get a comfortable fit for after pregnancy. Your breast size and chest dimensions will change over time, so look for a stretchable bra with fasteners that allow you to adjust chest and cup sizes. You'll need room for pads and shields to prevent leaks.

Nursing features. The latches that allow the cup to lower for nursing should be easy to operate with one hand. Some mothers prefer opening a front-latched bra in the center rather than dealing with each cup-opening device at the top. A roomy, stretchable regular bra can also be used for nursing.

Washability. Since you will be using the bras over a span of time, they should be completely machine washable, with no special launder-ing or care requirements. Elasticized garments like bras hold up better when dried at low clothes-dryer heat.

Supply. Three to eight bras should be sufficient, depending on whether you use bra pads. Milk leakage can be a problem during the early months of nursing, so if you don't use pads, you may be changing bras several times a day. One way to economize is to use your nursing bras during the last months of your pregnancy as well.

Nursing pads. Pads are available in washable fabric and foam combi-nations, and in disposable paper versions. The advantages of washable pads are that they are less likely to chafe and are more absorbent. Disposable pads are convenient to use, but they often contain a layer of vinyl that keeps air from the moist nipple area, making nipple infec-tions more likely. If you use disposables, change them frequently so that the breast stays dry.

Use only cotton pads without plastic or waterproof liners for best cir-culation. Other alternatives to nursing pads: cotton handkerchiefs, squares cut from terry cloth, cotton diapers, and folded cotton T-shirt fabric. Toilet paper and facial tissues shouldn't be allowed to stay on the nipple for long because they hold moisture in. Motherwear, Inc., has an excellent catalog of nursing fashions offering bras, nursing shields, discreet nursing shirts and dresses, mother/baby coordinates, nightgowns, bras, shields, portable pumps, diapers, baby hats, and many other items. To order, contact Motherwear, Inc., P.O. Box 927, Northampton, MA 01061, or call toll-free 800-950-2500 (9 A.M. to 10 P.M., Saturday 9 A.M. to 5 P.M.).

Breast pumps

Do you really need a breast pump? Your baby, in fact, is the best breast pump. If you plan to work away from the home and need to express your milk regularly, or if you want to go out without baby occasionally, you may want to consider investing in a pump to keep your breast stimulated for milk production and for storing your milk for later use. (Freezing is the best storage method.)

All breast pumps operate on a vacuum principle that, unfortunately, does not duplicate actual nursing. Mothers often find themselves dissatisfied with a breast pump because they mistakenly employ a constant vacuum on their nipple area, which can cause discomfort and even actual bruising. Some pumps, such as those produced by Medela, have an autocycling pull-and-release action.

A baby doesn't nurse by a simple suction process in the same way that vacuum pumps operate. Rather, a moist seal formed by the baby's mouth helps to keep a mother's nipple and areola (the colored portion of the breast) in the mouth. When a baby is first put on the breast, it tongues and mouths until, in a few moments, the breast "lets down" milk—that is, the milk arrives in the larger ducts just behind the nipple. Then the baby rhythmically pulls and tongues in a way that stretches the mother's nipple toward the back of the mouth, in a suction and draining process.[1] So don't be disappointed if the unrelenting suction of a pump doesn't seem to be effective.

Most manufacturers now supply informational brochures with their pumps to help mothers in using them. The two critical factors in the successful use of a breast pump are making sure that the nipple adapter fits the mother's breast contours well and operating the suction action correctly.

The most important element of pumping success is the letdown reflex, an anatomical response that signals the body that it's time to release milk into the ducts behind the nipples. Warm, wet compresses applied to the breasts and light, circular massage of the breast, looking at a picture of your baby, or imagining your baby nursing can all help the letdown to occur prior to pumping.

Once the milk lets down, a rhythmical, gentle tugging action that imitates a baby's nursing (i.e., pull . . . pull . . . pull . . . pause) is usually the most successful. For the best results, pump one breast for about five

[1] Smith, W. L. et al., "Imaging Evaluation of the Human Nipple During Breastfeeding," *American Journal of Diseases of Children* 142 (1988), 76–78.

minutes, then shift to the second, going back and forth until the breasts are drained. Usually a pumping session will last about 20 minutes.

Your body produces milk more readily if you pump during the times of the day your baby is most likely to nurse. Your milk supply will probably be the most plentiful in the morning. Get comfortably seated and relaxed. The color, consistency, and odor of your breast milk may change depending on your diet. Moms who exercise vigorously may raise lactic acid levels in their breast milk, giving it a sour taste that some babies dislike. And dieting while breast-feeding can affect your milk quality by lowering needed protein.

Storing breast milk

Human milk is a perishable food that must be stored properly to be safe for baby to drink. If you wash your hands well before pumping, your breast milk will be safe for a few hours at room temperature (68°F), but immediate refrigeration is recommended. Also, put leftover breast milk in the refrigerator or freezer immediately after feeding. Defrosted milk may be kept for up to 24 hours in the refrigerator.

Breast milk, like most liquids, expands as it freezes, so leave space at the top of the container. Freeze milk in two- to four-ounce portions. These smaller amounts will thaw quicker and will waste less milk.

CAUTION
Freezing breast milk can be convenient for mothers, but recent research has found that freezing milk for more than a month may affect the milk's folate, a vitamin essential for baby's growth. Short-term freezing for periods up to one month does not affect this vitamin.

Milk should be gathered in a clean glass or a rigid plastic bottle and tightly capped after filling. Label the bottle with the date. Sterilize the bottles if your baby is less than three months old. Use refrigerated bottles of breast milk within 48 hours after gathering. Store milk in the back section of the refrigerator, which is colder than the front or the shelves on the door. If you're away from home, milk can be kept for a short time in a cooler packed with ice or with a frozen ice pack.

Breast milk can be stored for up to one month in a freezer (0°F and below). Use the oldest milk first. It should be used quicker if it's kept in the freezer section of a refrigerator. If the freezer isn't cold enough, or there's a power failure, the frozen milk may thaw and spoil. The best indicator of spoilage is a sour smell.

Thawing frozen breast milk

Breast milk and formula should never be mixed in the same bottle. This may affect the potency and protective qualities of the human milk. Breast milk doesn't resemble bovine milk. It is watery, bluish white, and appears thin in comparison. Its color may take on a light tint if the mother has eaten certain vegetables. Just as cow's milk does before homogenization, human milk will separate with standing, the milk's fatty portion floating to the top.

To thaw breast milk, place it in the refrigerator overnight or hold the bottle containing the breast milk under cool running water and then shake it to mix the parts. If your baby prefers warm milk, then briefly hold the bottle under warm running water. Thaw only as much milk as your baby will drink, and use previously frozen milk immediately after warming, or the milk will start to spoil.

Heat and light can alter some of the milk's protective qualities. Don't thaw at room temperature or on a stove or in a microwave oven. Such thawing methods change the milk's composition, and microwaving may burn the baby. Even though the outside of a microwaved bottle may remain cool, the liquid inside may have dangerous hot spots that could burn your baby's mouth.

Thawed breast milk should never be refrozen. Once you've thawed it, use it immediately. Fresh human milk contains living cells that destroy bacteria and viruses in the milk. Freezing the milk kills these protective cells, which causes the milk to be more vulnerable to spoilage. Once the baby has drunk from a previously frozen bottle of milk, the contaminated milk should be discarded.

Choosing a breast pump

Breast pumps come in a variety of models, ranging from manually operated suction devices to small, handheld units that are operated by electric motors that use batteries or can be run both on batteries and with electric plug adapters. Some can be used for both manual and electric pumping. Manual, nonelectric pumps create suction through a syringelike piston action that is produced by moving an interior cylinder in an in-and-out motion, or through a spring-action pumping movement. The advantages of manual pumps over electric ones are that they are generally less expensive, offer more sensitive control of pressure, and require no electrical source. The advantages of small electric pumps over manual pumps are their ability to be used with one hand and the strength of the suction they produce. (Whether this is really an advantage depends on the sensitivity of their vacuum control knobs.) Most newer small pumps offer several sizes of collection funnels to better fit breast sizes, and some use flexible silicone funnels with rotating heads for comfortable positioning.

Simple, bicycle horn-style pumps sold in drugstores should be avoided. They are not only ineffective but may also cause tissue damage.

Hand-operated pumps should be easy to clean, and milk should not make contact with the gasket that separates the pump from the collection unit. If there is contact, the gasket should be easy to reach and clean. Small, battery-operated pumps probably aren't worth the money—they simply don't have the power to do the job, and their cycles are so slow that they can't do the job well.

If you're breast-feeding a hospitalized baby, and don't have much time to do it, you'll probably want to buy or rent a piston-operated pump that can empty both breasts in only 10 or 12 minutes. The most effective pumps are full-service, heavy-duty electric units designed for use in hospitals. These piston-driven models are designed to imitate the rhythmic sucking action and pressure of actual nursing, and have sensitive controls for regulating suction rhythm, intensity, and pressure. They also offer accessories that allow pumping of both breasts at once. But these units are heavy (as much as 11 pounds) and cumbersome. If you're at work and don't have a private office or a company medical suite to use, a large pump may be impractical.

Smaller, lightweight pumps that are similar to the larger models, but less efficient, are a good alternative for milk expression while you're on the job or away from baby. Their drawback is that they take as much as 20 minutes to empty both breasts, and you may have to manually operate the vacuum to re-create a sucking rhythm. The parts of the pump that come in contact with your breast and the milk containers should be washed in the dishwasher or with hot, soapy water and drained dry before each use.

Listings: Hand-operated breast pumps

Note: These products were not tested by Consumers Union. This alphabetical listing does not include all models available but rather is a selection of some widely distributed models. Descriptions and Attachments are derived from authors' observations and manufacturers' claims.

MODEL	DESCRIPTION, ATTACHMENTS
Ameda Egnell One-Hand Breast Pump Model R3660, $30	Spring-action manual pump that screws on top of a standard baby bottle. Can also be used with plastic freezer bag. Operated by one hand with a single-squeeze release action. **Attachments:** Pumping unit, flexible breast funnel, polycarbonate bottle, neck ring, latex nipple, and bottle cap.
Gerber Manual Breast Pump Model 78076, $17	One-handed breast pump uses a pistol-grip pumping handle for comfort and convenience. Funnel swivels to prevent muscle fatigue. Suction is controlled by user's pumping action. Dishwasher-safe. **Attachments:** None.
Omron Comfort Plus Breast Pump/ Infant Nurser Model 900CP, $20	Suction is applied by a back-and-forth movement of the outer cylinder in a pistonlike motion. Adapter cap and nipple attach to outer cylinder for feeding. Can also be used as a storage container. Dishwasher safe on top rack. **Attachments:** Two cylinders, two nipple adapters, feeding nipple (silicone) adapter cap, storage disc, cleaning brush, two extra gaskets, and dust cover.
Sassy Infa Breast Pump and Milk Storage System Model 718, $17	Piston-action syringe cylinders with two different-size nipple adapters designed with a natural tilt for easy, two-handed use. Comes with presterilized plastic bags for freezer storage. **Attachments:** Two sealing discs, two nipple covers, two nipple collars, orthodontic and standard nipple, two nipple adapters, piston cylinder, two collection cylinders, labels, presterilized freezer bags, labels, and twist ties for bags.

Listings: Battery-operated and electric breast pumps

Note: These products were not tested by Consumers Union. This alphabetical listing does not include all models available but rather is a selection of some widely distributed models. Descriptions and Attachments are derived from authors' observations and manufacturers' claims.

MODEL	DESCRIPTION, ATTACHMENTS
Evenflo Deluxe Breast Pump Kit Model 52132, $66	Electric pump with swivel horn that can be adjusted for maximum comfort. Uses either a 3-volt AC adapter (included) or two C alkaline batteries (not included). **Attachments:** Pump kit includes bottles, nipples, and pump shield adapters, and a two-compartment tote bag for storing breast pump and keeping milk chilled with ice pack.

Listings: Battery-operated and electric breast pumps *continued*

MODEL	DESCRIPTION, ATTACHMENTS
First Years Simplicity Electric/Battery Breast Pump Kit Model 1068, $50	A portable unit that can pump either a single breast or both breasts at once. Adjusts with soft shields for comfortable fit. Uses two C batteries (not included). **Attachments:** Includes carrying case, multiple nipple adapters, reusable cold pack for refrigeration.
Gerber Battery or Electric Breast Pump Kit Model 76198, $46	Expresses breast milk easily and comfortably into nurser for immediate feeding or storage. Fingertip vacuum control. Soft silicone funnel conforms to mother's shape and size. Funnel and funnel adapter are dishwasher safe. Uses two AA Renewal Reusable batteries (not included). **Attachments:** Includes 120-volt AC adapter.
Medela Mini-Electric Breastpump Model 71001, $87	Battery-operated unit mounts on a standard baby bottle. AC/DC transformer for plugging into an electric outlet. Unlike other small pumps, provides an auto-cycle action to resemble infant suck-and-release patterns. Adjustable vacuum. **Attachments:** Motor unit, AC/DC transformer, breast shield and insert, valve, membrane, collection bottle, bottle stand, lid, carrying bag, piston, seals, cylinder, vacuum regulator ring, instruction booklet.
Medela Pump In Style Breastpump Model 57000, $198	Professional-grade pump in a discreet size and style. The 7-pound electric breast pump comes with an insulated bag that carries the fully automated pump, the double-pumping kit, collection bottles, and cooling elements to store breast milk. The pump is designed to operate on both breasts simultaneously for maximum efficiency and speed in milk gathering. Fully automatic cycling simulates baby's suck-and-release nursing action. Vacuum can be adjusted for individual comfort. Quiet operation. **Attachments:** Bag, bottles, and cooling elements. (Optional PowerPak powers the pump by recharging the battery when electricity is not available.)
Medela Manualectric Breastpump Model 50001, $32	For manual and electric pumping. Contains everything needed for manual pumping, with ExpressSpring and comfort cushion for ease in pumping. **Attachments:** Contains parts necessary for single pumping using either the Lactina or Classic electric breast pumps.
Omron MagMag Advanced Breast Pump Model D893, $60	Lightweight motor operates from the base of the collection unit. Milk funnel screws on at the top of the nonstandard collection bottle. Suction-control and pressure-release valves work together to simulate nursing baby. Operates either on batteries or using an AC adapter unit. (Motor may jam from milk backflow, requiring a flushing action.) **Attachments:** Pump base and AC adapter, two hard nipple adapters, silicone nipple, collar and cap, collection funnel, bottle seal.
White River Concepts Portable Electric Breast Pump System Model 9050, $1,050 Rental approx. $2.25/day	Rental-grade pump, recommended for mothers who need to express 50 percent or more of their milk. Patented 15-pound electric pump with soft cup system that emulates human suckling. Provides 10 levels of suction, and variable control. Easy clean. Double pumping kit available. **Attachments:** Includes bottle, carrying case, hospital-grade power cord, and manual breast pump.

Listings: Nursing accessories

Note: These products were not tested by Consumers Union. This alphabetical listing by category does not include all models available but rather is a selection of some widely distributed models. Descriptions are derived from authors' observations and manufacturers' claims.

MODEL	DESCRIPTION
NURSING ACCESSORIES	
Medela Hand Expression Funnel Model 80001, $8	Large, easy-to-use, rounded funnel fastens onto a standard baby bottle for collection of milk during hand expression. Fits any standard baby bottle; bottle not included.
Parenting Concepts Pretty Private Cover Model PPNC, $20	Attractive, lightweight knitted shawl to drape over you and your nursing baby for a touch of privacy when nursing in public. Hand-knitted, with weighted shoulder piece to hold it in place. Hand wash, hang dry.
NURSING PILLOWS	
Noel-Joanna NoJo Nursing Pillow Model BNP, $26	Soft, wedge-shaped foam pillow covered in quilted terry cloth to support baby's weight and reduce nursing back strain. Curved shape reverses for nursing on either side.

6

Changing tables

Of the three kinds of changing tables—wheeled, folding ones; railed, wooden versions; and hinged chest adapters—the first two are the most acceptable purchases. The higher the protective guardrail around the table, the better. Some tables offer only several inches of protection and are not adequate to prevent a falling accident. Use the safety belt, and never rely on the guardrail. Open shelves that run the entire length of the changing table are far more convenient for storing items than are small, high-sided basket containers. Changing tables are available with padded baby cushions and come in a variety of finishes. Some can convert to other pieces of furniture for use after your baby is out of diapers.

Like other products, including cribs and high chairs, which put babies high up for the parent's convenience, changing tables present the danger of a baby falling. Usually this happens when a parent turns for a moment and doesn't anticipate that the baby is capable of unexpected gymnastics. Sometimes, too, parents have too much confidence in their baby's ability to follow a parent's command not to move.

We suggest that you gather up whatever you need for the changing job, whether it's a damp washcloth or a fresh change of clothing, on the way to the table, and use its storage shelves to keep basic necessities, such as clean diapers and clothing, right at hand. Always keep one hand on the baby while he or she is on the table, and never walk away and leave the baby lying on the table for any reason. If you have to answer the phone or get something, take the baby with you.

Buying advice

Sturdiness and resistance to tipping are important. If the table is light-weight, make sure it has a wide stance. Rattle it with your hand to see how steady it is. In general, all-wood tables are less likely to sway or fall over with pulling, which babies will try to do from the floor.

Of the three commercial table choices, the least desirable is the fold-down wooden adapter for the top of a nursery chest. Such adapters have been known to cause the entire chest to topple when a baby's weight is placed on the outer edge.

Both folding tables and permanently standing wooden tables are equally acceptable, although a few features are worth looking for with-in each type. A wooden changing table could conceivably be adapted to a bathroom storage shelf or other use once your baby has outgrown the need for diapers.

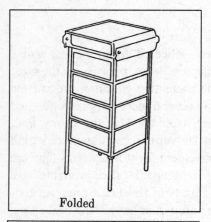

Folded

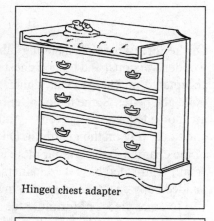

Hinged chest adapter

Furniture style

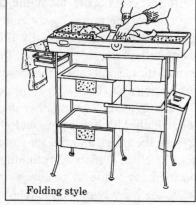

Folding style

Types of changing tables

An alternative to purchasing a changing table is to build a waist-high plywood platform that runs the length of the inside of a closet. Again, always keep one hand on your baby during changing.

Of the three table choices, the least desirable is the fold-down wooden adapter for the top of a nursery chest. Such adapters have been known to cause the entire chest to topple when a baby's weight is placed on the outer edge.

Listings: Changing tables and accessories

Note: These products were not tested by Consumers Union. This alphabetical listing does not include all models available but rather is a selection of some widely distributed models. Descriptions and Special Features are derived from authors' observations and manufacturers' claims.

MODEL	DESCRIPTION, SPECIAL FEATURES
Bassett Sugarplum Dressing Table Model 5068-590, $229	A pine dressing table with two shelves and decorative safety railings on all sides. Tabletop has a padded baby cushion and safety belt. Available in a variety of woods. **Special features:** Useful for storage as well as changing table.
Child Craft Encore Dressing Table Model 1376, $250	Dressing table has two open flat shelves beneath the dressing surface. Dressing area is enclosed on all four sides to prevent baby from rolling off the table. Equipped with pad and security strap to ensure baby's safety and comfort. Hardwood tables are available in a variety of finishes. **Special features:** Raised sides and security strap help to reduce accidents.
Gerry Changing Table Model 3610, $75	Full-size hardwood changing table has two large shelves for storage. Safety railings on all sides. Comes with vinyl changing pad and safety belt. Optional drawer kit available. **Special features:** Safety railings and security strap help to reduce accidents.
Kinderkraft Changer-N-Desk Model 540, $179	A wooden changing table with a high guardrail on four sides, shelf, and an extra-large storage drawer. Converts into an inclined art board or can be made into a desk/play table combination. White surface wipes clean. Comes with changing pad. Available in natural, aspen, and cherry finishes. **Special features:** Convertible to desk, after need for changing table has passed, for many years of continued use.
Million Dollar Baby Futura Changer Model 402-W, $138	White dressing table with arched, railed ends, guardrails on both sides, 1-inch-thick pad, safety belt, and one lower shelf. **Special features:** Can be converted to a desk with a laminated writing surface.

Listings: Changing tables *continued*

Simmons Dresser/Desk Model 6816, $1,100	Shaker-style dresser/desk has fold-down work area that rests on pull-out wooden supports. The diaper-changing conversion kit, which includes a thick pad and waist belt for baby, transforms the desk into a safe and comfortable dressing area. Cabinet and drawers underneath and small drawers above offer storage space for diapers and other products. When baby is grown, simply remove the diaper-changing kit to convert the dresser back to a writing desk. **Special features:** Versatile design means that this piece of furniture will offer many years of useful service.
Simmons Genova Dressing Table Model 0130, $190	Rail-sided diaper-changing table with two shelves, vinyl-covered foam pad, and safety belt. **Special features:** Two storage shelves, high side railings, and a variety of finishes to match Simmons cribs and chests.
Tracers Contemporary Beechwood Dressing Table Model 2320, $120	Sturdy beechwood dressing table with three shelves for convenient storage. Comes with standard 1-inch pad and nylon safety straps with squeeze-release buckles. Upper shelf is a changing area with solid rails on all four sides to protect baby from rolling off while being changed. Available in white, natural, or cherry finishes. **Special features:** Safety rails and straps protect from accidents.
Tracers Deluxe Dressing Table Model 3220, $150	Sturdy European beechwood dressing table with three shelves and a pull-out drawer. Includes deluxe plastic-lined nesting pad. Upper shelf is a changing area with solid rails on all four sides and a safety belt to protect baby from rolling off while being changed. Optional rail-side plastic organizer is available. **Special features:** Safety rails and straps protect from accidents. Drawer offers additional storage.

7

Child safety seats

Using child safety seats has saved the lives of many babies and children and prevented numerous injuries, but motor vehicle-related accidents are still the leading cause of death among U.S. children. Car crashes are estimated to kill some 600 youngsters under five and injure another 60,000 to 70,000 every year. In 1994, approximately 673 children younger than five years of age were killed while riding in motor vehicles. Of those who died, 362 were either unrestrained in a child safety seat or weren't restrained properly. If restraints had been used, over 200 lives might have been saved. For babies under a year old, child safety seats can potentially reduce fatal injury by 69 percent; they can reduce deaths of toddlers one to four years of age by 47 percent.

The laws of physics have particularly cruel consequences for children. A crash at 30 miles per hour will propel an unrestrained 15-pound baby with some 300 pounds of force—the equivalent of a fall from a third-story window. The same 30-mile-per-hour crash can be just as lethal if an adult cradles a baby. An adult wearing a safety belt won't have the strength to hold on to a child in a crash, and an unbelted adult will crush a baby being held with one to two tons of force.

Just as with adult safety belts, child safety seats can provide protection in all but the most violent crashes. Every state requires infants and small children to travel in an approved child safety seat, and all manufacturers of child safety seats must certify that their seats meet government standards. The seats must pass crash tests that include a simulated 30-mile-per-hour head-on collision into a fixed barrier.

Safety seat options

There are basically three types of seats for protecting babies from vehicle crashes: infant-only seats, convertible seats, and booster seats.

Some infant-only seats are designed to protect babies from birth to 22 pounds. They are to be positioned only with the baby facing the rear of the car, in order to protect the baby's vulnerable neck and spine from injury. (Infant-only seats manufactured prior to September 1996 are safe only for babies up to 20 pounds.)

Convertible seats are designed to face both rearward for newborns to babies 22 pounds, and forward for children from about 22 to 40 pounds. Convertibles come with several securing options (see photos below): with a set of straps for shoulders, legs, and crotch (called a

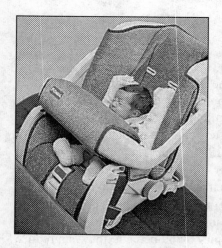

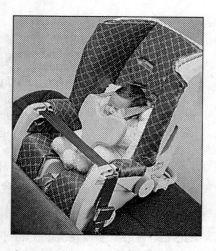

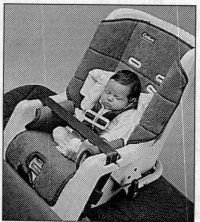

A convertible seat with an overhead shield (above, left) or T-shield (above) will not fit an infant properly. The shield should be chest-high; it should not obscure the child's face. A convertible seat with a five-point harness (left) fits babies better, but an infant seat is really the best choice for a baby up to about 20 pounds.

five-point harness system); with a T-shaped shield that pulls over a baby's head and latches at the crotch; and with a front shield/harness combination that can be raised for installing the child and then latched with a buckle at the crotch.

Booster seats, designed for kids weighing 30 to 60 pounds, are usually a combination of a riser seat and a removable front shield for use with younger children. Most boosters adapt to use with lap belts for children in the larger weight range. Below is a more detailed discussion of each option.

Infant seats

These seats are the best choice for newborns or small babies weighing less than 22 pounds because they combine protection, convenience, and comfort features. They're designed for babies to ride facing the back of the car in a semireclined position. The back of the shell, in combination with a simple V-shaped harness and car lap belts, acts as a restraining system to spread the forces of a head-on crash across a baby's back.

These lightweight seats, with their U-shaped carry handles, can double as infant carriers, feeding chairs, or rockers when used out of the car. Some can be detached from the base, which is designed to remain installed in the car. Some models have flaws, however (see crash test results on p. 73). A few infant-only seats come with an accompanying stroller frame, and at least one model comes with recessed wheels and handles that pull out to convert the unit into a stroller.

Once your baby is placed in an infant safety seat, all harness straps should fit snugly across the "strong" parts of your baby's body (shoulders and thighs) and lie flat when buckled. If there's a plastic or metal clip holding the shoulder straps together, adjust the clip so that it's at the level of your baby's armpits.

If your baby is riding in a convertible seat, shoulder straps should be threaded through the lowest slots for use in the rear-facing position. Some models require the shoulder and crotch straps to be adjusted by a metal buckle found behind the seat. For the buckle to hold securely, you must thread the end of the strap back through a second time. If you don't, a crash could cause the strap to come loose, allowing your baby to be thrown from the seat. (Refer to the manufacturer's instructions.)

If your baby slumps down in the seat, you can wedge a rolled cloth diaper between the crotch and the seat buckle—but *never* place padding under your baby, or buckle a blanket or other padding under the seat straps, as this may affect the restraining function of the straps.

Using separately purchased cushioned head and neck supports is not recommended. At least two babies have died as the result of being ejected from their safety seats when padded neck supports widened the space between shoulder straps, negating the holding power of the straps.

In May 1996, the American Academy of Pediatrics issued a statement warning parents that babies who weighed over 20 pounds but who were still under one year of age should continue to ride in the rear-facing position to avoid the risk of neck and spine injuries in a crash. As mentioned earlier, new regulations require that infant-only seats manufactured after September 1996 may be labeled as safe for babies weighing up to 22 pounds. If you've got a baby who weighs over this limit but who isn't yet a year old, you may need to purchase a rear-facing seat designed for a larger baby. The only current safety seat on the market that has passed crash tests in the rear-facing position for babies up to 32 pounds, or about three years of age, is the *Safeline Sit'n'Stroll*, a molded seat/stroller combination with retracting wheels and handle. Consumers Union's tests showed that the seat was not without problems, however. The straps were particularly stubborn, and the pathway through which the vehicle safety belt is fed is positioned so that it can restrict the child's movement. (Worse, the child can dislodge the belt if it isn't tightly secured.) Even with these flaws, the *Sit'n'Stroll* may be the only seat available for big babies under a year old. (See bottom left photo on p. 251.)

Convertible seats

Convertible seats are designed for use by children from birth up to about 40 pounds. Most convertibles have shoulder harnesses that can be adjusted to different heights as a child grows larger. Until the child is a year old, a convertible seat should be installed in a vehicle in a rear-facing position, with shoulder straps threaded through the lowest slot; later it can be reinstalled in the forward-facing position for use by young children (with straps threaded through higher slots).

Since convertible seats follow the growth of your child during the first few years, they're more economical than purchasing two separate seats. But one major drawback of convertibles is that the safety of tiny babies can be compromised by these "one-size-fits-all" models—particularly the larger versions with shields. These overhead and T-shields, which might comfortably fit a larger baby, will engulf most newborns and have the potential to cause face and head injuries in a crash.

Of the three most common convertible restraint options—five-point harness systems, T-shields, and overhead front shields—we found the five-point design provided the best protection against head injury for all sizes of babies and children, including infants. Five-point systems are relatively easy to buckle and unbuckle, but manipulating the harness straps takes a bit more doing than with other convertible designs. When seating the child, you have to move all the straps out of the way and then gather and insert two separate latch plates from the shoulder and thigh belts into a single buckle. That may take some fumbling around, particularly if you're leaning over in the backseat of a small car. Nonetheless, we found this design provided better protection than seats that did not provide enough room for a baby's head to clear the front shield.

We judged the *Century 1000 STE Classic*, with a five-point harness and an average price of $53, A CR Best Buy. Its performance in our crash tests was very good. In addition, it is easy to use and clean. (If you can't find that Century model, look first at the higher-rated models in the Ratings that use a five-point harness.)

In Consumers Union's judgment, models with T-shields or overhead shields are appropriate for larger infants and toddlers who weigh up to 40 pounds—children who are tall enough so that their necks clear the top of the shield.

Crash test results

In past reports on child safety seats, CONSUMER REPORTS took manufacturers' statements of compliance with the federal standard as assurance of a seat's safety. When 25 widely sold safety seats were tested for a report published in the September 1995 CONSUMER REPORTS, we crash tested the seats ourselves to find out how well they performed in trials that were similar to, but slightly tougher than, those the government specified at that time. We tested widely sold child safety seats priced from $30 to $140.

While that report was in progress, the National Highway Traffic Safety Administration (NHTSA) announced that it would institute new, tougher certification criteria for safety seats in 1996. The new tests are similar in many ways to the ones we used.

For safety seats made before September 1996, one aspect of the government's certification tests required the use of a 17½-pound crash-test dummy (the size of a typical six-month-old) for infant seats used facing the rear of the car. The infant seats that passed could be labeled for use with infants weighing up to 20 pounds, about the weight of a typical nine-month-old.

Since the infant seats could be labeled for use with a 20-pound baby, we used a 20-pound dummy for our crash tests. The government's

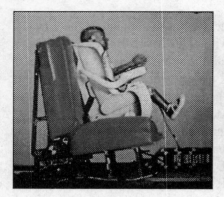

Not acceptable performance. Film footage of our crash demonstrates what can happen when a safety seat fails. On impact, the safety seat's buckle failed, releasing the harness and the crash-test dummy. When the dummy

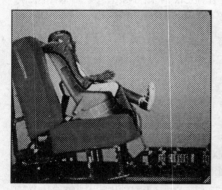
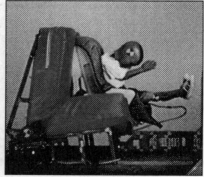

Safe restraint. This test of the Century 1000 STE Classic illustrates how an

(September 1996) criteria requires using a 20-pound dummy, too. Seats that meet the new standard can be labeled for use with infants weighing up to 22 pounds, the weight of a typical one-year-old. The new standard was set to encourage the practice of having infants ride in the rear-facing position until they reached their first birthday.

In government tests, convertible seats used for children over age one are tested in the front-facing position using a 33-pound test dummy, comparable to the weight of a typical three-year-old. Most are labeled for use with children up to 40 pounds. For our tests in the forward-facing position, we used the same size dummy as required by the government, since a 40-pound dummy did not exist.

We checked the performance of convertible seats for infants in the rear-facing position (the recommended installation position until a child is one year old) by testing representative designs from each

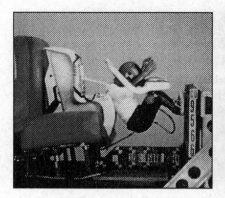

struck the shield, the shield broke away, completely ejecting the dummy from the safety seat.

effective safety seat should perform in a crash.

manufacturer using the "nine-month-old" dummy. Similarly designed models (see Ratings) should perform the same.

Testing procedures

Our tests included infant-only seats, convertible seats, and booster seats. As the government does, we used "sled tests" that simulated a 30-mph head-on crash into a fixed barrier to assess the safety of the seats. The tests were done under our direction by a contract laboratory that also does safety testing for many manufacturers.

Following the manufacturers' instructions, each safety seat was installed securely on an automobile seat that was mounted on the test sled. Then a crash-test dummy was snugly harnessed into the seat. High-speed cameras tracked the movement of the dummy and the safety seat. After the crash, the seats' structural integrity was examined.

Twenty-two of the 25 safety seats tested passed the crash tests. Three did not: the *Century 590* and the *Evenflo On My Way 206*, rear-facing seats for infants, and the *Kolcraft Traveler 700,* a convertible seat for infants and small children. These three seats were found to be more likely to fail than other seats when used in certain ways. Consumers Union judged them Not Acceptable.

The *Century 590* and the *Evenflo On My Way 206* consist of a base that's installed in a vehicle (held in place by the car's safety belt) and a carrier that snaps into and out of the base. Or, the carrier can be strapped into the car alone, using the vehicle's belts. Tests were conducted both ways. Although the *Century* and *Evenflo* have similar designs, they failed the crash tests for different reasons.

The *Century 590* failed to provide appropriate protection when installed *with* its base. Under the force of the impact, the carrier, while holding the 20-pound (or nine-month-old) test dummy, separated from the base. The same failure occurred in two of three repeat tests with new samples of the *590*. In the third test, the seat rotated backward enough to compromise an infant's safety. In a final test, with a 17½-pound (or six-month-old) test dummy, the seat's performance was acceptable, but just marginally.

Consumers Union paid just $35 for the *Century 565*, an infant-only seat identical to the *Century 590* but without a base. Based on price and performance, it was judged A CR Best Buy. The *Century 590* also performed well when used *without* its base. If you own the *Century 590* infant seat, we recommend that you throw away the base and install just the carrier in the vehicle. The seat is safe when used that way. At the time of this writing, the *Century 590* with its base remains on the market, although an investigation is being conducted by the NHTSA.

The *Evenflo On My Way 206* failed the crash test when installed *without* its base. The carrier broke at one of the hookups for the vehicle belt. That left one side of the carrier, with the 20-pound (or nine-month-old) dummy strapped inside, unsecured from the vehicle seat. The same failure occurred in a second test. In testing a third sample with the "nine-month-old" dummy and a fourth sample with a smaller "six-month-old" dummy, the belt hookup cracked but did not break. *With* the base, however, the *Evenflo On My Way 206* performed well.

Based on independent testing conducted by the manufacturer, some 200,000 models of the *Evenflo On My Way 206* made between May 7, 1994, and May 31, 1995, were recalled voluntarily by the company. Owners of the problem seats were instructed to call Evenflo's special toll-free recall number (800-225-3056) to obtain a retrofit kit designed to solve the safety defect. So Consumers Union decided to test the *Evenflo On May Way 206* fitted with the retrofit kit.The retrofit is supposed to reinforce the area where the safety belt threads through the carrier. In the follow-up crash test, the safety belt continued to hold the carrier; however, the reinforcements dislodged, and the carrier cracked in the same general area as in the first test. Therefore, our original recommendation still stands: For *Evenflo On My Way 206* infant seats made between May 7, 1994, and May 31, 1995, install the base in the car and leave it there. With this model, crash protection is inadequate when the carrier is installed *without* the base. The *Evenflo On My Way 206* has since been discontinued and replaced by the *Evenflo On My Way 207*. The *Evenflo On My Way 207* performed well in the safety tests and is considered a safe seat.

The *Kolcraft Traveler 700* proved safe when installed in the rear-facing position for infants under a year old. It failed crash tests when installed in the forward-facing position using a 33-pound ("three-year-old") dummy. The harness buckle let go, releasing the crash-test dummy. When the shield was struck by the dummy, the shield broke away. In one test, the dummy was ejected from the safety seat; in another, it was left hanging from the safety seat's harness straps. Such a failure could eject a child from the seat. It's safe to use the *Kolcraft Traveler 700* as an infant seat in the rear-facing position.

About 100,000 models of the *Kolcraft Traveler 700* manufactured between November 1994 and August 1995 were recalled by the company following our report. Free replacement buckle assemblies were made available through the toll-free number: 800-453-7673.

The replacement buckle assembly, provided via the recall, held tight in the follow-up crash test. But the harness straps slipped on impact, so the test dummy's upper body wasn't restrained quite as well as Consumers Union's testers recommend. Nonetheless, parents who have installed the replacement buckle can feel confident that the buckle and shield will stay intact in the forward-facing position. The *Kolcraft Traveler 700* has recently been discontinued.

As part of the ongoing testing of child safety seats, Consumers Union evaluated three more infant seats (not included in Ratings) in 1996 that share the same basic, convenient design as the *Century 590* and the *Evenflo on My Way 206* and *207* models. The *Century Smart Fit* ($65), the *Cosco Turnabout* ($60), and the *Evenflo Travel Tandem* ($50) all have a detachable base that can remain strapped in the car, allowing you to snap the infant carrier in and out; you can also use them without the base, strapping the carrier in like any other infant seat. The *Century*

Smart Fit and the *Cosco Turnabout* were new for 1996, while the *Evenflo Travel Tandem* is an older seat we hadn't tested before.

As with other infant seats, these three models were tested by simulating a head-on crash into a fixed barrier at 30 mph. A 20-pound dummy was used to evaluate the *Century* and *Evenflo*, since these models are labeled as suitable for that weight. The *Cosco* was tested with a 22-pound dummy, its labeled weight limit.

Both the *Century Smart Fit* and the *Cosco Turnabout* performed well in crash tests. The *Evenflo Travel Tandem*, when tested *with* its base, failed catastrophically. In two of three runs, the shell broke around the buckle assembly and the buckle released, leaving the dummy unrestrained. The *Evenflo Travel Tandem* was judged Not Acceptable when used with its base. It's safe when used *without* the base, however. Following our report, the manufacturer offered all owners of *Travel Tandems* made before April 1996 a reinforcement kit designed to help this seat pass our crash test. As of this writing, we are still investigating the efficacy of this retrofit kit.

Comfort—yours and baby's

Among convertible models, seats with a T-shield and shoulder straps take the least amount of effort to use: Simply pull out a length of webbing, slip the strap and shield over the child's head, and latch the T-shield to the seat in a single motion.

Models with a T-shield harness use a plastic yoke to draw the shoulder straps over the child. The yoke then buckles into the seat at the crotch. The design is easy to position on the child and buckle up.

Other models have a padded, traylike front shield that swings down over the child's head, pulling the shoulder straps over the shoulders. A short third strap buckles the shield to the seat at the crotch. Consumers Union's testers found that the overhead shield models did not protect against injury as well as other designs. However, these models were generally easy to use, and some versions (for example, the *Century 5500 STE Prestige*, the *Cosco Touriva 02045*, and the *Evenflo Ultara I 235*) offered the advantage of being adjustable so the shield could be tightened to fit a smaller child or loosened to accommodate bulky winter clothing. Their drawback was that they required more overhead clearance than the other seat types, and some blocked the view of the buckle, making buckling more difficult.

Neither T-shield nor overhead shield versions are appropriate for an infant if the infant's head does not clear the shield. The shields should be no more than chest high, but, as the photos on p. 70 show, they may be only head high on some infants. Take a measuring tape with you when shopping for a convertible seat. To prevent your newborn from slumping forward, the distance between the crotch strap and the baby's seat back should be less than 5½ inches. Measure the distance between the lowest shoulder strap slot to the seat bottom. It should be less than 10 inches long, to prevent the straps from pressing into your baby's ears. The seat's harnesses should be easy to position, the straps simple to adjust, and the latch easy to fasten.

WARNING!

Leaving a child in an unattended car can be lethal. In hot weather, temperatures inside a car can soar to over 140°F—a danger to babies, who are extremely vulnerable to heatstroke. Never leave a baby or child alone in a car, even in your own driveway. Consider hiding an extra key in a magnetic holder under the car's frame as a safety measure should you accidentally lock your child and keys inside the car.

The straps on most child safety seats are usually easy to adjust, but there are some exceptions. The *Gerry Guard With Glide 627* and the *Safeline Sit'n'Stroll* (mentioned earlier) have straps that are particularly stubborn. In contrast, the *Gerry Guard Secure Lock 691* (also called the *Gerry Guard One Click*) has automatically adjusting harness straps. That can be a major advantage in changeable weather, when a child requires warm clothing one day and lightweight clothing the next.

The *Gerry Double Guard* has a bulky shield that is hard to manage. Fingers and other body parts can easily get pinched if the shield inadvertently closes before it is supposed to. Also, removal of the shield requires tools, and even with tools it is difficult to do.

A child may be less likely to balk at the mere sight of a child safety seat if it's well padded and has plenty of head and back support. A two-position crotch buckle, featured in several Century models, is a particularly nice feature; it makes the harness less constricting as the child grows or when the child wears several layers of clothing.

The *Century Smart Move* and *Gerry Guard Secure Lock 691* offer a more reclined rear-facing position for better support for a baby's head and neck. (Unfortunately, the reclining mechanisms are hard to use.) A few seats come with pillows, cushions, and harness pads. With some, extra-cost inserts for extra support for an infant's head are available; rolled-up towels or diapers do the trick at no added cost.

The tested *Kolcraft Rock'n'Ride* infant seat has vinyl upholstery, which when exposed to summer sun would likely get hot in a vehicle before other fabrics. Burn potential is a problem with three Century convertible seats: When exposed to sun, metal near the latch on the *2000 STE,* the *5500 STE Prestige,* and the *3000 STE* could get very hot.

Installation

Whichever convertible model you use, it is always safer to place the seat in the most upright position when your child graduates to the front-facing position. For models offering slots to adjust shoulder harness heights, shoulder straps should be threaded through in the highest slots for the forward-facing position. When moving the straps, be sure to thread them completely through the back of the seat's hard shell, not simply behind the pad.

Some seatbelts on child safety seats have to be threaded over or around a metal bar on the frame. If the seat has an adjustable crotch strap, keep it as short as possible so that the harness or shield is in its lowest position.

Always test the temperature of metal and plastic parts before placing your child into a seat. During hot weather, when it's not in use you can place a blanket over the seat to protect it from getting too hot.

Babies can also be injured in child safety seat accidents that occur outside of a car. In the home, seats can tip over, drop off counters or other household furniture, or fall from grocery carts. When the seat is in use, it's safest to keep it on the floor while monitoring your baby at all times.

In the early weeks of life, certain babies experience low oxygen levels when they ride upright for long periods of time in child safety seats. Premature or low-birthweight infants, babies with certain genetic disorders (such as Down's syndrome), and those with breathing problems (such as apnea) are most susceptible. If your baby has apnea, he or she may stop breathing periodically and appear to turn blue. If you suspect that sleep positioning may be affecting your newborn's breathing or color, consult with your physician about the type of child safety seat your baby should use—for example, an upright seat or a horizontal car bed.

According to guidelines issued by the American Academy of Pediatrics, babies born at less than 37 weeks gestational age should be monitored while sitting in their seats before being discharged from the hospital to identify those at risk for apnea associated with child safety seat use. Those babies may need to use a seat that reclines into a horizontal car bed.

Of the infant seats Consumers Union tested, only the *Cosco Dream Ride Ultra (02-719)* can be reclined to serve as a bed. But be cautious about purchasing a used model. Cosco recalled about 15,000 seats manufactured between April 8, 1994, and June 15, 1995. Crash tests revealed that these seats rotated farther from the upright position than required by the federal standard when in the rear-facing position. Other *Dream Ride* models manufactured on other dates were not affected by the recall. Reinforcement kits are available from the manufacturer by calling 800-314-9327.

Installation problems

There's a big difference between fiddling with car seat straps, buckles, and buttons in a store and trying to do it in a car. To install a child safety seat, parents often have to work in cramped quarters, at uncomfortable angles, with an uncooperative child. Because of these problems, we advise you to try a child safety seat out in your car to be sure it fits properly before you purchase it.

The most critical factor in selecting a child safety seat is to choose one that you will use, and use correctly, every time you are traveling with your child in the car. If one design seems more convenient to you than others, choose that seat—because you're more likely to use the seat right each time you put your baby in the car.

Ease of installation is not only a convenience factor but also an important safety issue, too. A seat that's hard to install may not be installed properly, and a seat that isn't installed properly may not be safe. Installation problems may be related to the design of the vehicle and its safety belts, or to the design of the child safety seat.

Studies show that many parents fail to install and use child safety seats correctly. Recent random traffic safety surveys have found that between 70 and 90 percent of all child restraints are used improperly. With 27 different car seatbelt systems available, and about 50 different child safety seats on the market, it's no wonder that parents often fail to follow instructions and install seats correctly. In any given vehicle, there are a myriad of possible restraining-belt and safety-seat combinations, and there can be as many as three to four completely separate methods for installing restraints, depending on where you position the seat in the car.

In the face of these complexities, it's critical that you take the time to carefully read the instructions that come with your child safety seat, and that you refer to the car owner's manual when you install a child safety seat. If you're in doubt about safe installation, the best source for technical advice is the automaker.

Installation tips

Use the full weight of your knee to press the seat portion of the child safety seat down into the car's upholstery while tightening the car's seatbelt through the designated slots on the child safety seat. (The child safety seat should be held firmly against the car's seatback.) Then remove your knee and test how tightly you have installed the seat by pulling on the back of the seat with both hands. You shouldn't be able to tip the seat very much, either from side to side or forward and backward. Perform this check every time you put your child into the seat.

If the seat moves more than one or two inches even when belted tightly, then you may want to consider returning it to the store for another model. Another alternative is to contact the automaker for instructions to install the seat. Most state highway safety offices also have child-occupant-protection programs, with experts on board who can offer advice about how to correctly install a child safety seat.

Your vehicle's seat may be the problem. You'll have problems installing a child safety seat if your car has bucket or deeply contoured seats, such as those found in smaller cars. These types of seats often fail to firmly support a child safety seat and allow tipping to occur. Some small cars may not have a center rear seat, or the center rear seat may be elevated enough to cause the child safety seat to wobble (it will shake during normal braking and turning). If that occurs, placing the seat in the outer positions in the backseat is still a safer alternative than letting your child ride in the front seat.

If the vehicle seat slopes down so that your baby's head flops forward, you may need to wedge a rolled towel under the front edge of the child safety seat. The goal is to secure the back of the child safety seat firmly against the car's seatback. The child safety seat should recline back at approximately a 45-degree angle.

Using a car's seatbelts to secure a child safety seat can present major problems. Manual lap belts are the best for securing a child safety seat. They're usually located in the center of the backseat, which is also the safest position for your child's seat. Belts in newer cars are often anchored 4 to 10 inches farther forward than they were a decade ago. That means they fit adults well—resting across the bony pelvic area rather than on soft abdomens—but those few inches of slack may affect a child safety seat's protective abilities in a crash.

A child safety seat cannot be secured by a car's shoulder belt. Therefore, never use a child safety seat in the front seat of a car that doesn't have an independent lap belt. Avoid placing the child safety seat in a seat equipped with a motorized shoulder harness that automatically shifts into position when the door is closed. This type of system requires a special supplemental belt or other modification device (provided by the automaker) for use with a child safety seat. You can also have your car dealer install a stationary lap belt to secure your child safety seat.

Some cars have seatbelts positioned too closely together to accommodate a child safety seat, and some newer car models come with seatbelts mounted on a stiff stalk or stitched onto a latch plate. Both designs interfere with the firm, tight fit necessary for maximum safe use of a child safety seat.

If the car's seatbelt has a free-sliding latchplate that doesn't stay in one place, you may need to use the locking clip that comes with the child safety seat. Heavy-duty locking clips are available from Ford, Toyota, and Nissan dealerships. These big locking clips are designed to enable you to shorten a car's lap-shoulder belt combination so the child safety seat will not slip or slide. Vehicles manufactured as of September 1995 no longer require locking clips. Instead, they use automatic locking mechanisms on their seatbelts. The seatbelts must first be pulled out all the way and then retracted to lock them in place.

Since it's not clear how compatible your child safety seat and your car seat will be when you purchase a seat—you may discover you need to purchase a special device, such as a tether strap, a locking clip, an attaching belt, or an auxiliary belt—we recommend that you install your child safety seat well in advance of using it. That way you won't encounter any unexpected surprises.

A 1995 panel formed at the request of the NHTSA found that the best solution to child-restraint and vehicle-compatibility problems may be to require all automobiles to provide a separate anchoring system for installing child safety seats. The International Standards Organization is currently developing and evaluating a system called ISOFIX, which would put four attachment points in every car so parents can secure child safety seats directly into a vehicle's seat. But it will take years to make this system a standard auto feature. In the meantime, parents will simply have to cope with the confusion that installation brings.

Air bag dangers

Federal safety standards require that all new passenger cars and light trucks be equipped with both driver-side and passenger-side air bags by the year 2009 (most new cars and light trucks already have them as standard equipment). When used as a supplement to safety belts, air bags can effectively prevent deaths and serious injuries to older children and adults involved in frontal motor-vehicle crashes. In fact, since the late 1990s, air bags have saved over 900 lives.

But air bags do not provide the same protection for infants. At least 26 children, ranging from a few days old to nine years of age, are known to have died as the result of injuries suffered from passenger air bags. Most of the deaths occurred in crashes so minor that other passengers were barely injured, if at all.

WARNING!
Never strap an infant seat or a rear-facing convertible seat in the front seat if your car is equipped with a passenger-side air bag. For maximum safety, place your child's rear-facing infant seat, forward-facing convertible seat, or booster seat in the center of the backseat of the car. A secondary, but less safe, choice is the passenger side of the rear seat. If the safety seat must be placed on a front-passenger seat equipped with an air bag, push the front seat as far back as possible.

Part of the problem can be traced to the design of air bags. By federal standard, air bags are designed to protect the average male not restrained by a seatbelt in a 30-mph head-on crash. To achieve this, air bags inflate at a speed of up to 200 mph. While that provides enough force to protect a 165-pound man, it can exert deadly force on the neck and head of a young child—even one properly belted—seated in the front seat.

Air bags pose a unique safety risk for babies restrained in rear-facing infant seats positioned on the passenger side of vehicles with dual air bags. Typically, the upper edge of the back of the rear-facing safety seat extends forward to a point near the dashboard where the air bag is stored. When an air bag deploys, it can slam the baby head-first into the seatback, resulting in severe head and neck injuries.

If you own a dual air bag vehicle, position your baby's safety seat facing rearward in the center of the backseat of the car. (That's also the best position for front-facing seats.) If you have no choice but to position your baby or child in a front seat equipped with an air bag, then push the vehicle's seat as far back from the dashboard as possible.

Under a rule issued by the NHTSA on May 23, 1995, manufacturers of sports cars and light trucks may now install manual cutoff switches for passenger-side air bags so that they can be disabled when a safety seat is in use. The cutoff switch is intended for vehicles that cannot accommodate a child safety seat in the rear seat, such as pickup trucks, sports cars, certain other passenger cars with no rear seats, or those that are too small to accommodate typical rear-facing infant seats or convertible child safety seats in their rear-facing mode. The vehicle's ignition key is used to deactivate the passenger-side air bag.

Maintenance

Most safety seats are upholstered with a polyester/cotton or velour upholstery. Some seats offer terry-cloth upholstery. We recommend avoiding vinyl. At best, it's sticky in hot weather; at worst, it can be uncomfortably hot. For easy maintenance, look for seats with removable pad covers that can be tossed into the washing machine. We found the pad covers on the *Evenflo Ultara I* and *Gerry Guard Secure Lock 691* quite difficult to remove. Instructions for the *Gerry Guard Secure Lock 691* also stated that the pads should not be machine washed.

Dealing with a recall

Just as with automobiles and other consumer products, child safety seats are frequently recalled because of defects that could cause injury. In fact, child safety seats are among the most commonly recalled of all consumer products.

Safety-seat recalls rarely make headlines. Few publications other than CONSUMER REPORTS routinely publicize them. Since March 1993, the NHTSA has required manufacturers to include registration cards with all child safety seats. To ensure you're in the "recall loop," fill out the card immediately and return it to the manufacturer. If a recall occurs, you will be notified by the manufacturer, who is required to repair the problem at no charge.

In the event of a recall, keep all receipts and installation instructions for your child safety seat in a secure place. Try taping an envelope or zippered plastic bag directly onto the back of the seat.

If you're not certain whether your child safety seat has been recalled, you can contact the manufacturer directly (see Appendix B), or call the Auto Safety Hotline of the U.S. Department of Transportation (DOT):

800-424-9393. This number also allows you to report problems, which is important when you consider how many recalls have resulted from parents' complaints.

When you call the manufacturer about a recall, bring the seat to the telephone with you. You will need to provide the seat name, the model number, and the seat's date of manufacture. That information is usually printed on a label attached underneath or on the side or back of the seat. In some instances, this information may appear as number codes.

Although many defects announced by recalls are minor, some can signal serious defects in a seat, such as faulty buckles, broken shields, or unsecured harness straps. In most instances the seat won't have to be replaced. Instead, the manufacturer will supply (upon request) free substitute parts and replacement instructions. Remember to ask the manufacturer if it is safe to continue using the recalled model until repair parts arrive.

Recommendations

CONSUMER REPORTS Ratings list models by types, primarily in order of performance in safety tests. Using any child safety seat is better than using no seat at all, but some seats perform better than others.

BUCKLE PROBLEM: CENTURY SAFETY SEATS, STROLLERS

Century Products Co. is trying to contact the owners of certain infant safety seats and safety seat/strollers because some have defective buckles that may release upon impact.

The problem affects *Century 560, 565, 590,* and *Smart Fit* safety seats and *Century 4-in-1* safety seat/strollers made between September 12, 1995, and May 13, 1996. The safety seats carry the following suffixes after the model number: 4525, 4535, 4560, 4575, and 4590. The safety seat/strollers carry these suffixes: 11-570, 11-597, 11-600, and 11-650. In addition, the affected buckles have date codes 255-95 through 365-95 and 001-96 through 131-96 stamped across the top. The company says no injuries related to buckle failure have been reported. If you have one of the affected products, the manufacturer will send you a free replacement buckle kit and installation instructions. Call Century Products Co. at 800-762-7463.

If you're on a tight budget, or if your baby infrequently travels by car, you may want to investigate loaner or rental programs sponsored by hospitals and childbirth-education associations. Typically, you'll be able to rent a seat for a refundable deposit and a minimal monthly or flat fee. Some states administer loaner programs through the state highway safety department. You can also check to see if your insurance company offers child safety seats at a discount.

Since 1993, Midas Muffler & Brake Shops has distributed more than 115,000 child safety seats nationwide as part of its Project Safe Baby program, which makes the seats available to consumers at cost from any franchised Midas shop. When they're no longer needed, the seats can be returned to Midas with the original price credited toward automotive services. Thanks to the project, at least five children are known to have survived serious automobile crashes.

If you buy a used seat (which we do not recommend) or receive one that has been handed down, check the seat's make, model, and date of manufacture against the recall files maintained by the DOT. Government regulations require that the make, model, and date of manufacture be affixed to the seat. Also, be sure you have the seat's instructions. The seat should have been manufactured after January 1, 1981, when modern safety standards took effect. Inspect the seat for cracks or any other sign of damage.

A seat that's been in a crash should never be used again. A seat that is unsafe—either because it cannot be repaired or because it's been in an accident—should be completely destroyed, not simply put in a trash dump

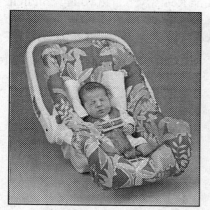

For infants. *The Century 565, like most infant seats, doubles as a carrier. It's easy to use and clean. And, at $35, we judged it A CR Best Buy.*

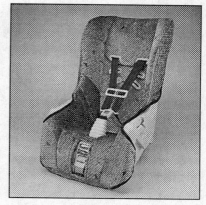

For small children. *We recommend a convertible seat with a five-point harness for optimum protection against head injury. The Century 1000 STE Classic, at an average price of $55, was judged A CR Best Buy.*

where someone else may see it and be tempted to use it. With an indelible-ink marker, write "UNSAFE" in large letters on the body of the seat.

Built-in seats

Some GM, Ford, Chrysler, and Volvo models offer optional child safety seats built into the rear seats. They can be used as front-facing seats for toddlers. Some adapt into booster seats for larger children. Built-ins solve the problems associated with safety-seat installation and provide added security because they won't dislodge in a crash. In addition, they place the child farther away from the front seat, reducing the risk of head injury. But you will need to purchase a separate, rear-facing infant seat if your baby weighs less than 22 pounds.

Shields and boosters for older children

Children who have outgrown child safety seats are safer using a car's seatbelts than not using any restraints at all. But poorly fitting seatbelts—lap belts that cross the abdomen or shoulder belts that cross the face or throat area—increase the risk of a child being injured in a crash. (According to the National Pediatric Trauma Registry, belted young children are more likely to suffer injuries to the abdomen than to suffer severe or life-threatening injuries to the head, neck, chest, or other body part.)

A properly fitted shoulder belt should fall across the shoulder and

Built-in safety seats. Some automakers offer built-in safety seats as an option in some vehicles. Built-ins can be used like a forward-facing convertible seat for small children. They convert to a booster for larger children.

the breastbone. Lap belts should cross the pelvic area, not the abdomen.

Booster seats are recommended for those children who weigh approximately between 30 and 60 pounds who have outgrown a convertible seat but are too small to make use of a car's seatbelts. The old certification criteria for booster seats required testing with the "three-year-old" dummy only. The new criteria require testing with the "three-year-old" and a larger, 47-pound dummy representing a typical six-year-old.

Some boosters come with a removable shield. Boosters used with their harness and shield are best for younger children, who may not remain seated unless confined. To minimize the risk of neck injuries, make sure your child's ear isn't higher than the car's seatback.

Older children, who understand the importance of buckling up, are safest when boosted by a high or no-back model, without the shield, so that the vehicle's seatbelts fit the body directly. When used this way, a booster simply elevates the child while the vehicle's own lap and shoulder belts do the job of restraining. When used without the shield or harness, booster seats are relatively easy to use. But if your car does not have shoulder belts, you cannot use a booster without its shield or harness. For younger children who may not stay put unless restrained, we recommend the *Century Breverra Premiere 4885* or *4880 Booster Seat* (used with the shield or harness).

A number of devices now available are designed to make a car's shoulder belts fit bigger children and small adults better. When we tested the *Child-Safer* and the *SafeFit,* we found they were inconvenient, but they worked. Unfortunately, these products are not subject to federal testing procedures, so parents have no real standards for judging their performance during crash conditions. If your child weighs less than 60 pounds, we recommend a booster seat rather than one of these devices.

For bigger kids. Booster seats like the Century Breverra, used with the shield and harness, are best suited for younger children who may not stay seated and buckled up unless they are confined. Most safety experts—and the manufacturer—advise against using the shield with larger children.

Additional do's and don'ts

Using a child safety seat properly takes a bit of doing. Here are some simple procedures to make the going smoother:

◆ **Wear a seatbelt if you're pregnant**. There's no indication that seatbelts harm infants in utero when pregnant mothers are involved in crashes. And seatbelts reduce injuries to mothers as well.

◆ **Store objects away from baby.** Keep heavy or pointed objects (for example, groceries) out of your child's reach. Place them somewhere in the car where they cannot strike the child in case of a sudden stop or crash.

◆ **Stop the car.** Don't try to tend to your child while driving; pull to the side of the road to do that. And never take your child out of the child safety seat while the car is in motion.

◆ **Remove trays or hard toys**. Toy trays that fasten onto child safety seats or other hard objects should not be used while your baby is riding in the car. They could cause injury in the event of a crash.

◆ **Prevent tip-overs**. Hundreds of babies have been hurt (some have even died) while strapped into child safety seats that fell or were pushed (for example, by siblings) off kitchen counters, couches, or other elevated surfaces in the home. For safety's sake, keep the seat on the floor, and don't leave baby unattended.

Using child safety seats in airplanes

The practice of permitting airline passengers to carry children under two years of age in their laps has been challenged by the National Transportation Safety Board. The board, which investigates airline accidents, favors mandatory use of child safety seats on airplanes, claiming that children who were recently injured or killed in crashes would have avoided injury or survived had they been in child safety seats.

Currently, there is no law requiring that children traveling by airplane use child safety seats, unlike the laws that govern ground vehicles. That's probably because so few infant deaths can be attributed to the absence of child safety seats on airplanes. Nonetheless, in the event of an air crash, an unrestrained baby can be sent flying like a projectile into other passengers, seatbacks, or luggage compartments.

Since 1985, the Federal Aviation Administration (FAA) has agreed to allow child safety seats approved by the NHTSA on commercial aircraft. All child safety seats manufactured after January 1, 1981, bearing a label stating they conform with federal safety standards, qualify for use on an airplane.

But, although the FAA recommends the use of child safety seats on air flights, the organization opposes legislation requiring them. One argument against mandating child safety seats on airplanes is that it would increase the cost of air travel for many families. To avoid paying for an additional ticket, more families might forsake traveling by airplane in favor of a riskier means of transportation—traveling by automobile.

Most of the child safety seats tested for the September 1995 issue of CONSUMER REPORTS (see Ratings) are certified for use on airplanes. But crash tests the FAA conducted suggest that certification doesn't ensure safety. Of eight randomly selected convertible seats, six failed to provide adequate head protection. Two couldn't be secured properly with an airplane's seatbelt. (*A number of models couldn't be tested simply because they were too large to fit an airplane's seat.*) Nevertheless, the FAA recommends using convertible seats for children between 20 and 40 pounds because they are safer for small children to use than the airplane's seatbelts.

Rear-facing infant seats proved safe in the FAA tests. Children under 20 pounds should be restrained this way. Once a child reaches 40 pounds, the FAA recommends against using child safety seats. In fact, the FAA has banned the use of booster seats, harnesses, and child-restraint vests aboard all U.S. carriers.

The FAA's findings suggest that child safety seats used for airplanes require a design different from the convertible seats used for vehicles. Seats need to be designed specifically for the narrow spaces of an airplane.

Unless the FAA changes its position on child safety seats, it's up to you to decide how to protect your children when traveling by airplane. You may continue to carry a child under two years old on your lap. But if the child is a baby, using an infant seat would be much safer. You can pay full fare for the additional seat or try to book a flight that isn't full and hope an empty seat will be available. If your child is over two, you'll have to pay for your child's seat anyway, so it makes sense to bring the convertible car seat with you.

Airline personnel will show you where a child safety seat can be placed. The child safety seat cannot be placed in a row next to an emergency exit, in an aisle seat, or where it would limit access to emergency equipment.

In summary, when traveling with your child by airplane, observe the following guidelines:

◆ For infants up to 20 pounds, use a rear-facing seat. (It's best to use a rear-facing seat until your baby is at least 12 months old.)

◆ For toddlers weighing 20 to 40 pounds, use a forward-facing seat.

◆ For kids over 40 pounds, use the airplane's seatbelt.

Ratings: Child safety seats

As published in the *Consumer Reports 1997 Buying Guide*.

Listed by types; within types, listed primarily in order of performance in safety tests.

The tests behind the Ratings. Safety scores are based on the seats' performance in our tests simulating a 30-mph head-on crash. Column headings list the "age" of the dummies we used, the seats' orientation (front- or rear-facing), and (for boosters) whether we used the seats' harness or shield or lap-and-shoulder belts like those found in real vehicles. Price is approximate retail. Model availability: Ⓓ means model is discontinued.

Standard features for these models. Adequate protection in a 30-mph head-on crash. • Fully assembled product, with adequate instructions. • Locking clip for use with vehicle safety belts, if needed. • Mail-in registration card in case of a recall. • Rear-facing convertibles require more space between safety belts than front-facing ones.

				E VG G F P ⊖ ⊖ ○ ◐ ●	
Brand and model	**Price**	**Safety**		**Ease of use**	**Instal-lation**	**Comments**
INFANT SEATS		**9-MO.**				
Century 565, A CR BEST BUY	$35	⊖		⊖	○	V-shaped harness. Requires installation with each use.
Evenflo On My Way 207 Ⓓ	65	⊖		⊖	○	V-shaped harness. Detachable auto base.
Kolcraft Rock'n Ride 13100	30	⊖		⊖	⊖	V-shaped harness. Requires installation with each use.
Gerry Guard With Glide 627	56	⊖		⊖	○	V-shaped harness. Requires installation with each use. May not fit with short safety belts. Vehicle belts can be difficult to weave through the safety seat. Hard-to-adjust harness straps.
■ NOT ACCEPTABLE WHEN USED WITH THE BASE						
Century 590	55	②		⊖	○	V-shaped harness. Carrier released from base in our safety tests. Without base, requires installation with each use.

CONVERTIBLE SEATS		**3-YR. FRONT FACING**	**9-MO. REAR-FACING**	**Ease of use**	**Instal-lation**	**Comments**
■ The following models are judged suitable for small infants as well as larger infants and small children.						
Century 1000 STE Classic, A CR BEST BUY	55	⊖	③	⊖	○	5-point harness. Rear-facing, requires installation with each use and may not fit with short safety belts.
Century SmartMove 4710	115	⊖	⊖	○	○	5-point harness. Wide base may not fit some vehicles. Hard-to-operate reclining mechanism.
Cosco Touriva 02514	68	⊖	⑤	⊖	⊖	5-point harness.
Kolcraft Auto-Mate 13225	60	○	⊖	⊖	○	5-point harness. Harness-adjustment dials let straps slip somewhat. Rear-facing, requires installation with each use and may not fit with short safety belts.

Brand and model	Price	Safety		Ease of use	Instal-lation	Comments
Safeline Sit'n'Stroll 3240X	$140	○	⊖	○	●	5-point harness. Requires installation with each use. Wide base may not fit some vehicles. When rear-facing, may not fit with short safety belts. Safety-belt pathway may restrict child's movement. Belts could be dislodged by child if not tight. Hard-to-adjust harness straps.

■ *The following are judged less suitable for small infants, but suitable for large infants and small children.*

Brand and model	Price	Safety		Ease of use	Instal-lation	Comments
Century 2000 STE	65	⊖	[3]	⊖	○	T-shield. Rear-facing, requires installation with each use and may not fit vehicles short safety belts.
Evenflo Scout 225	63	⊖	[4]	⊖	○	T-shield. Vehicle safety belt may interfere with buckle on safety seat in rear-facing position.
Evenflo Champion 224	64	⊖	⊖	⊖	○	Overhead shield. Vehicle safety belt may interfere with buckle on safety seat in rear-facing position.
Century 5500 STE Prestige	85	○	⊖	⊖	○	Overhead shield. Rear-facing, requires installation with each use and may not fit vehicles with short safety belts.
Gerry Guard SecureLock 691	80	○	⊖	⊖	⊖	Overhead shield. Hard-to-operate reclining mechanism. Automatic harness straps.
Century 3000 STE	65	○	⊖	⊖	○	Overhead shield. Rear-facing, requires installation with each use and may not fit with short safety belts.
Cosco Touriva 02045	90*	○	[5]	⊖	⊖	Overhead shield.
Kolcraft Traveler 700 13405 D 6	60	○	⊖[7]	○	○	Overhead shield. Buckle failure released harness and dummy. Instructions error may lead to incorrect harness usage for infants. Retrofit judged effective. Rear-facing, requires installation with each use and may not fit with short safety belts.
Cosco Touriva 02014	60	○	○	⊖	⊖	Overhead shield.
Evenflo Ultara I 235	85	○	⊖	⊖	◒	Overhead shield. Wide base may not fit some vehicles. Vehicle belt may interfere with buckle on safety seat in rear-facing position. Overhead shield may not adjust tightly for small child.

BOOSTER SEATS		3-YR. +SHIELD	3-YR. +BELTS	6-YR. +SHIELD	6-YR. +BELTS	Ease of use	Instal-lation	Comments
Century Breverra Premiere 4885	65	⊖	⊖	[8]	⊖	○	◒	5-point harness. Vehicles belts may be hard to weave through safety seat. High-back.
Gerry Double Guard 675	60	○	⊖	●	⊖	○	◒	Swing-out shield. Shield could pinch child or installer when being lowered. No back.

[1] Evenflo has discontinued *206*, which we rated Not Acceptable when used without the base. We found the retrofit kit offered by the mfr. ineffective and advise use of the *206* only with the base.
[2] Without base, score is ⊖.
[3] Not tested rear-facing. Should perform similarly to *Century 3000 STE*.
[4] Not tested rear-facing. Should perform similarly to *Evenflo Champion 224*.
[5] Not tested rear-facing. Should perform similarly to *Cosco Touriva 02014*.
[6] Kolcraft is offering a replacement buckle for owners of seats made between November 1994 and August 1995. That allows the seat to safely be used in the forward-facing position.
[7] Rear-facing score is ⊖.
[8] Mfr. advises against using shield with children over 45 lb.

Recalls

ALL OUR KIDS JUVENILE PRODUCTS All Our Kids Child Safety Seats
Padding is too flammable, a violation of federal safety standards.
Products: 25,482 safety seats, model 600, made between 4/93 and 3/94, and model 602, made between 3/94 and 9/94. Date of manufacture appears on label on seat. Seats, designed for use in vehicles or airplanes by children weighing 25 to 40 pounds, include: model 600 BK (black fabric, black webbing); 600 HP (green and purple fabric, pink webbing); 600 PR (blue/red); 600 SI (silver/silver); 602 BK (black/black); 602 CW (black and white cow-print fabric, black webbing); 602 PF (purple/pink); and 602 PR (blue/red).
What to do: Mail seat to All Our Kids, 1540 Beach St., Montebello, CA 90640. Company will treat fabric with flame-retardant agents.

CENTURY PRODUCTS CO. Century 4750 SmartMove Child Safety Seat
In forward-facing mode, seat may not provide adequate protection in crash.
Products: 11,000 seats, model 4750, made between 12/5/95 and 2/13/96. Model number (first four numbers) and date of manufacture (last six numbers) appear on label on side of base seat. Affected seats also have white label attached to black Y-shaped adjuster strap on back of seat that bears one of the following codes: WO#-136716; WO#-136716-02; WO#-136716-03; and WO#-138442-01.
What to do: Phone 800-583-4093 for replacement latch assembly.

COSCO INC. Cosco Convertible T-Shield and Soft-Shield Child Safety Seat
Might not provide adequate protection in crash.
Products: 1,397 seats, models 02-084 and 02-404, made between 5/6/94 and 8/10/94. Model number and date of manufacture appear on label on seat shell.
What to do: Call 800-221-6736 for replacement buckle housing and installation instructions.

COSCO INC. Cosco Dream Ride Ultra Child Safety Seat
May not provide adequate protection in crash.
Products: 15,370 seats, model 02-719, made between 4/8/94 and 6/15/95. Model number and date of manufacture appear on label on seat shell. Unit can be used as conventional infant seat or as traveling bed. In rear-facing position, device could tip too far backward in crash, increasing risk of injury.
What to do: Phone 800-314-9327 for free repair kit.

EVENFLO JUVENILE FURNITURE CO. Evenflo Trooper Child Safety Seat
With child weighing less than 20 pounds, seat must be used only in rear-facing position. Instruction pamphlet wrongly implies seat can be used facing forward by such a child.
Products: 10,423 seats, models 219140, 219164, 219180, 219186, and 219188, made between 11/95 and 1/96. Label bearing model number and manufacture date appears on seat.
What to do: Phone 800-837-4002 for new instruction pamphlet.

Clothing and footwear

You'll probably discover that baby shower clothes, although cute or clever, sometimes aren't practical for everyday use. For example, many parents are given fancy sweater/bootie/hat sets with weaves wide enough to trap a baby's tiny fingers. It's smart to take back duplicate or impractical items that you receive as gifts and exchange them for useful items such as white cotton T-shirts with snap fronts or tie sides, waterproof pants (if you're using cloth diapers), or sleepwear.

How many clothing items should you buy for your newborn? With spit-ups and drooling, infants can run through three or four shirts a day. If you have a washing machine, you may be able to make do with a smaller number of shirts by washing them frequently. Your baby will need fewer items of sleepwear and other pieces of clothing during warm months. Realistically, however, you and your baby can get along with just a few shirts, gowns, and sleepers in the beginning. Later, when you have a clearer picture of what is needed and what will fit best, you can always shop for more.

Getting ready

Here's a list of some basic baby clothes you can have on hand before your baby arrives:
◆ Six to eight snap- or tie-front T-shirts (six-month size)

◈ Three or four sleepwear items (six-month size)
◈ Three or four dozen diapers
◈ Three pairs of booties or bootielike socks
◈ Three or four pairs of waterproof pants
◈ Two small knit sweaters
◈ Knitted tie-on cap (winter) or small tie-on brimmed hat (summer)
◈ Bunting or hooded jacket (winter)

It makes sense to shop at yard sales or to buy handed-down clothing from other mothers. For the price of one or two new shirts, you can supply your baby with a dozen bright outfits. And having a wide variety of shirts, sleepers, and other clothing can cut down on how often you have to do the laundry.

Premiewear makes clothing and caps for tiny premature babies, size three to eight pounds. For information or a catalog, the company's address is 3258 E. Ridge Place, Twin Falls, ID 83301, or call toll free: 800-992-8469.

Selecting baby clothes

Baby sizes are often difficult to decipher. Since manufacturers vary in their interpretation of the size of a six-month-old baby, you can't rely on your baby's age as an accurate way to choose the size of a shirt or sleeper. Many manufacturers' sizes are much smaller than real-age sizes.

The best way to select a right-size garment is to read the pound/length chart on the back of most baby garment packages, or to take the garment out of the packaging to judge the size for yourself. Keep in mind that cotton garments are often sized large because they naturally shrink and become more dense with washing. Since babies grow so rapidly, many parents buy shirts and other clothing one or two sizes larger than needed.

Footed stretch suits are popular daytime and nighttime wear for babies. Although stretch suits do offer advantages, such as close fit and the ability to expand as the baby grows, they also have their drawbacks. Poor-quality suits tend to shrink in the dryer and quickly become too tight. Stop using suits when they get tight on your baby, especially in the foot area. Baby knee pads are available to help prevent chafing during crawling. You can find these suits in shops that sell baby products. Access to the crotch area is important, so look for suits with snap-open flaps.

When it comes to shopping for tots' clothes, fashion-conscious parents may wish to decide ahead of time which will have patterns: the pants or shirts. Usually it's easier to purchase solid-colored pants and patterned T-shirts. Some major manufacturers color coordinate their whole children's line so that shirts and pants will automatically go with one another. The most economical thing to do is to buy used clothing from other parents or from consignment shops. Fortunately, no one gives fashion ratings for this age group, so it's all right to be casual about how shirts and pants go together, and your tot couldn't care less.

Although parents and grandparents occasionally like to "showcase" babies in fancy frills, babies themselves are most comfortable in simple, comfortable clothes for everyday wear. Dresses, for example, can get caught under a crawling baby's knees, frustrating the urge for forward movement. Instead of thinking pink and blue, think red and yellow; at least that's what psychologists say. Babies seem to prefer bright, primary colors over the blander pastels.

Since babies aren't respecters of fine fabrics and manage to spit up and wet on even the most expensive clothing, all baby clothes you buy should be able to withstand repeated machine washing and drying. Buy clothing that can be machine washed at regular temperatures without having to be separated by colors, since sorting clothes and having to wash them separately is time-consuming. Inspect the inside seams of garments to see that they are even and that they will not fray with repeated washings. Quality garments have thread bindings along the edges of the fabric so that fraying is virtually impossible.

Examine the weave of the fabric in T-shirts and gowns. Choose thick, well-finished shirts rather than thin, semitransparent garments or those that show signs of poor finishing, such as unclipped strings. Most babies hate having shirts pulled over their heads, so front-opening shirts are less likely to cause wails of protest when being put on. If you purchase pullover T-shirts, look for overlapped shoulders and extra-wide neck openings. T-shirts that snap closed at the crotch are invaluable because they don't ride up, they keep baby warmer, and the snaps help keep diapers in place and provide added protection against leakage.

Look for clothes that are easy to put on and take off. Until your toddler is toilet trained, you will want to have pants that offer quick and easy access for diapering. Snap-open legs are indispensable. Velcro closures, although they offer the advantage of quick release and expansion room, lose their holding power unless they are laundered in the closed position. The tiny hooks that make the closures work weaken with repeated washings and become filled with loose strings and lint. Tiny buttons, bows, and other decorative fasteners only make dressing baby more time-consuming and difficult. (They're also a choking hazard.)

As with adult apparel, according to law, a label has to state the fiber content of the item. Most baby clothing sold today is made of cotton blended with polyester fibers. Poly/cotton blends are less expensive than pure cotton clothing, more wrinkle resistant, and less likely to shrink. Pure cotton garments, on the other hand, are more absorbent. Although some parents are purists about wanting their baby's clothing to be 100 percent cotton, we feel that resistance to shrinking and wrinkling are worthwhile qualities to look for when shopping for garments.

WARNING!
Overdressing your baby on very hot, humid days can cause overheating and possible heatstroke —especially if your baby already has a fever. Heatstroke can cause high fever and convulsions. In extremely hot weather, dress your baby in just a diaper and avoid being out during hot spells or being in or near traffic—automobile exhaust can increase outdoor temperatures. Ask your physician about giving your baby water in addition to formula on hot days.

Look for clothing that has a high comfort potential. Inspect the inside finishing of garments. Seams should be soft rather than scratchy, and lie flat rather than stick out. Elastic bands on the arms or ankles may be irritating or restrict circulation. Stop using garments that leave red rings around your baby's wrists, arms, or legs. Look at the finishing on the opposite side of appliqués, since manufacturers often back them with scratchy, stiff materials. If the appliqué is made of heat-welded plastic, be sure there are no small tags of plastic on the back that could be uncomfortable.

Dressing tips

Your newborn baby has little body support for the head. The baby normally rests with arms and legs in a contracted position. When you dress the baby, keep arms and legs in their flexed position rather than forcing them straight.

If you are putting a slipover T-shirt on your baby, first stretch the neck of the shirt so that it will not rub or upset the baby as it goes down over the face. Next, roll up the front part of the shirt, slip it first over the back of the head, and with a quick movement pull it over the face so that it doesn't result in distress as the face is covered. Grasp each hand and arm through the shirtsleeve and then gently pull it through.

Nightgowns and pajamas

Keeping a baby warm during the night presents a perpetual challenge. Many babies get thoroughly wet before morning, even with waterproof pants on. You'll probably discover after the first few weeks that it's better to "let a sleeping baby lie" rather than wake him or her; a baby will usually signal distress. Some parents have found that zippered sacks that enclose a baby's legs like a pillowcase are the best way to provide enough warmth during the night in winter, since regular quilts or blankets usually slip off.

Newborns in the first weeks of life do seem to need extra warmth from outside of themselves because of their primitive self-warming system. After that, most babies can manage at the same temperature that is comfortable for adults.

Toddler clothing

Toddlers' high energy level and curiosity keep them climbing, touching, and exploring with little regard for what they are wearing. Clothing for this age needs to be durable and stain repellent. Durability in toddler clothing means sturdy fabrics, well-sewn seams with overcast stitching to prevent unraveling, and reinforcement, such as additional backstitching at points of stress—for example, at the top and bottom of zippers or around buttonholes. Some manufacturers make children's pants with additional knee reinforcement.

Many parents today opt for a unisex dress code for their tots from crawling age through the early childhood years. The most practical shirts are colorful T-shirts with snap openings on one shoulder or down the front to make taking them off and putting them on a painless activity.

Crawling babies fare well in overalls or dungarees with shoulder straps and snap-open crotches for diaper changes. Pants with elastic waistbands are often too restricting and can ride down as the baby crawls. Overalls are also handy for hiding the shirt gaps that cause a tot's belly to stick out when rapid growth outdistances wardrobe. The best fabrics for overalls are soft knits or cotton/polyester blends for relatively wrinkle-free appearance without ironing.

Several easy-to-make patterns for baby overalls with adjustable shoulder straps are available in fabric shops. If you have the time to make them, a few pairs sewn with a cushioned, quilted fabric or with padded knee patches will be a welcome addition to your baby's wardrobe, since they offer protection to tender knees.

When your baby begins to near the two-year mark, you will naturally want to shift to elastic-waisted paints for potty training. Your child will need to be able to pull the pants up and down alone. Upon purchase, examine the waistband. It should not be overly tight, nor should it have scratchy seams that could cause discomfort on bare skin.

Underwear

Although manufacturers make thick, absorbent underwear called training pants, some parents find that regular underpants may give babies brought up on cloth diapers a better signal to use the toilet than bulky undergarments that feel much like what they've been wearing.

Examples of training pants include *Dappi Early Training Pants* from TL Care ($5 per pair), *Gerber First Trainers* ($2 per pair), and *Gerber Reversible Terry/Vinyl Training Pants* ($2.26 per pair). The problem is that most training pants shrink considerably during washing, and they tend to bunch and lose stretch quickly. Comfortable fit and ease of pulling off and putting on are more important considerations.

Disposable training pants are also being sold by major manufacturers of nonreusable diapers. Their main drawback is that their absorbency makes them feel little different from diapers when it comes to your child's ability to perceive wetness and its discomfort, thus delaying toilet learning.

Underwear should absorb moisture in order to prevent crotch irritations. Therefore, nylon knits—even though they may be imprinted with colorful patterns of animals or super heroes—are not the best choice. The most comfortable underwear is made of cotton or of cotton/polyester blends with an absorbent cotton panel sewn into the crotch. (*Note:* For information on diapers, see chapter 10, and for training pants, see chapter 23.)

Winter wear

Coats whose cleaning instructions specify "dry clean only," such as those constructed of thick wool with insulated linings, are not practical for babies and young children. It's children's nature to get dirty—to be climbing, falling down, and making mud pies—and a garment that can't be washed is going to spend most of its time at the cleaners.

For the young baby, a thick blanket with a knitted tie-on hat is sufficient for most winter weather. A zip-up bunting or sack that encloses baby's body below the arms and has sleeves and a hood at the top is an excellent purchase until the baby can crawl. These cold-weather products are useful for keeping baby warm outdoors in strollers, child safety seats, or backpacks. They should not be used indoors without supervision, nor should babies sleep in them, since they may pose a hazard of overheating, suffocation, or strangulation, particularly for small infants.

Ideally, snowsuits or other winter outerwear for a child should be water resistant, since there is a real danger of deep chilling from getting wet from the outside, especially if there are damp diapers inside as well. Purchase a winter garment with a built-in hood, and use it in conjunction with a knitted hat for maximum warmth. (Snip off any strings from the built-in hood to avoid the potential for strangulation or asphyxiation.)

Mittens offer more efficient cold protection than fingered gloves; they are also much easier to put on and take off. Ideally, mittens should have a nonslip surface sewn onto the palm and thumb area to make it much easier for your tot to pick up objects or to turn doorknobs.

Most toddlers enjoy wearing low-cut rubber or plastic boots on slushy winter days, particularly those boots they can slip on and off themselves. It's wise to purchase boots a size larger than your tot's shoes, since they can otherwise be difficult to put on and take off.

Coats with hood strings or dangling waist strings, or mittens with strings that fasten one glove to the other, should not be used. Children have been injured or suffocated when these strings became entangled on outdoor play equipment, especially sliding boards.

Summer clothing

Babies' skin sunburns much faster than the skin of children or adults, but babies under six months of age should not use sunscreens or insect repellents. The chemicals in these products have not been safety tested for infants. The best strategy is to stay inside during the time of day when sunburn is more likely to occur—between 10:00 A.M. and 3:00 P.M. If you do go out, make sure your baby is covered with a lightweight, absorbent receiving blanket. A brimmed hat, a pair of baby-size sunglasses, and a stroller parasol can all help to protect baby's sensitive skin.

Clothing hazards

For more than 20 years, federal law required that children's sleepwear be flame-resistant. To comply with this law, manufacturers had to produce clothes made of 100 percent polyester and some acrylic fabrics. (In tests using a ⅝-inch flame, these and other flame-resistant fabrics can extinguish themselves within a few seconds after the flame is removed.) Manufacturers who wanted to sell cotton garments that continued to burn after the same flame tests were applied had to treat their fabrics with flame-retardant chemicals. Recently, however, the U.S. Consumer Product Safety Commission (CPSC) relaxed its children's sleepwear standards to allow manufacturers to make sleepwear for children under six months of age using fabrics without added flame retardants, including 100 percent cotton, as long as the sleepwear is tight-fitting. The regulations are not expected to be implemented until early 1998.

The CPSC's decision was based on the fact that tight-fitting sleepwear does not trap the amount of air needed for a fabric to burn. Tight-fitting sleepwear also reduces the chances of contact with a flame and shortens the amount of time it takes for the wearer to be aware of what is happening.

In 1995, the CPSC also issued guidelines to help prevent strangulation deaths of children from strings that tie hoods, waists, mittens, or other clothing and become entangled on crib posts, playground equipment, doors, and other protrusions. Most major clothing manufacturers have now agreed to remove or sew down and shorten the strings for hooded clothing, including baby clothes. We recommended that parents cut strings on children's clothing or buy clothing without strings.

Babies can choke on small ribbons, pom-poms, or laminated decals that peel off of their clothing. Their fingers and toes can also get pinched when they become entangled in strings from clothing or blankets. In rare instances, baby boys have had their penises strangled by tight strings. Our recommendation is to inspect baby's clothing for loose strings or threads after each washing, then clip them. Also inspect your baby's appendages closely if your baby seems to be in pain.

Booties and socks

Your newborn's hands are usually tightly closed and seem to be warm, but the feet will often seem cold to the touch. It's hard to know whether cold feet worry babies as much as they worry the babies' grandparents, but many parents like to keep feet warm with booties or socks.

A baby should have enough space in the booties or sleepers to freely move the toes. Avoid socks that are too tight, or sleepers that cause the feet to be "crimped." When the baby begins to crawl, you may notice that both the toes and the knees get cherry red from chafing against carpets or rough surfaces. Some babies feel so uncomfortable with the rubbing that they develop a crablike stance, with their back ends hiked up in the air. Socks that cover the knee, or pants with socks or booties, can help the crawling baby to be more comfortable.

Choosing shoes

A baby learns to stand and balance by adjusting the pressure of the feet and toes on the floor or ground. The main reason for putting shoes on your newly walking baby is to protect the feet from splinters, cuts, and other foot injuries, and to keep them warm. So-called orthopedic shoes with stiff soles and artificial arches are of no benefit to a normal baby's feet, and may even impede balancing skills.

Choose shoes that have soft sides and soles, such as *Soft Steps* ($24), which are flexible leather shoes designed especially for new walkers. Sneakers are perfectly suitable, although crepe soles may catch on carpeting, causing falls. To fit your baby's shoes, choose a pair that has about half an inch of room beyond the big toe to allow for growth. You should be able to get a pinch of the leather or fabric across the widest part of the foot.

As your baby grows, the main qualities to look for in shoes will be soles with a good grip, flexibility, and fasteners that make it easy to put them on and take them off, such as a single buckle or a Velcro strap.

Recalls

ANGEL-ETTS OF CALIFORNIA Infant and toddler sandals
Buckle could come off strap and choke child.
Products: 170,000 pairs of sandals, made by Angel-etts of California, licensed

under Gerber name and sold in 1995 in Kmart. Infant sandals are white (model 55101) or brown (model 55103) and sold for $5. Toddler sandals are white (model 59006), brown (model 59401), or blue denim (model 59682), and sold for $9. "Gerber" appears on insole, and model number is on inside of strap.
What to do: Return sandals to Kmart for refund.

KMART Three-Piece Clothing Outfits for Newborns
Snap fasteners could come off and choke child.
Products: 6,000 outfits sold between 1/94 and 2/94 for $13. Outfit consists of cotton/polyester cardigan sweater, short-sleeved top, and checkered pants. Outfits came in two shades of blue and white and have airplane appliqués on sweater and top.
What to do: Return outfit to Kmart for refund.

LEVI STRAUSS Jeans, Shortalls, Rompers, and Koveralls
Snap fasteners could come off and choke child.
Products: 40,000 boys' garments sold between 7/93 and early 1994 and girls' garments sold since 5/92. Recalled boys' clothes include Rib Bottom Jeans (product code 29370-7011); Koverall, pants-length version of traditional adult overall (code 19379- 7011); Shortall, short pants version of adult overall (code 19375-7011); and Romper, loose-fitting denim playsuit (code 19377-7011). Garments are in dark blue or indigo blue stonewash with gray trim. Recalled girls' garment is Koverall with pink elastic suspenders; item is in indigo blue stonewash (code 38966-0491), bleached blue (code 38966-0435), pink stonewash (code 38966-1088), or pink (code 38966-1287). Product code is on underside of care label.
What to do: Return garment to store for refund.

SCHWAB CO. Little Me Baseball uniform for infants
Wooden buttons can come off and choke child.
Products: 5,000 one-piece, white-cotton jersey garments with thin blue stripes, sold during the spring of 1992 for $27. Red "24" is stitched onto left front of garment with blue thread. Outfit, which came with matching blue-and-white baseball cap, has three round wooden buttons, each measuring ¾ inch. Label on garment reads, in part: "Little Me . . . 100% Cotton . . . Made in USA . . ."
What to do: Send garment to Schwab Co., P.O. Box 1742, Upper Potomac Industrial Park, Cumberland, MD 21501, for refund, including shipping costs.

Cribs and crib mattresses

Today's cribs are safer than those of past generations. Most newborns, however, will start life in an old and potentially unsafe crib. Hand-me-downs can be risky. Even cribs made as recently as 1991 can have unsafe design features.

Crib mattresses are normally a separate purchase. Buy the firmest one you can find. Save money on the purchase of a crib, and apply the savings to the purchase of a high-quality mattress. Twenty-five years ago, crib accidents accounted for 150 to 200 child deaths and 50,000 injuries every year. Often, the worst injuries occurred when an infant's head was restrained by the crib slats after the legs, torso, and arms had slipped through, when decorative cutouts on end panels trapped a child's neck or arm, or when dropsides were not high enough to keep an active baby from falling to the floor.

Mandatory safety standards, issued by the federal government in 1973, addressed many of the hazards. Those standard requirements are as follows:

❖ The distance between the crib's slats must be no more than $2\frac{3}{8}$ inches —too narrow for a baby's body to slip through.

❖ To keep an infant from falling out, a lowered dropside's top must be at least 9 inches above the mattress support at its highest setting. To keep an older baby safe, the top of the raised dropside must be at least 26 inches above the support at its lowest position.

❖ A dropside must be next to impossible for an older baby to activate. Releasing the dropside must take either a strong force (at least 10 pounds) or two distinct actions at each locking device.

◆ The crib interior must snugly accommodate a standard-size mattress (at least $51\frac{5}{8}$ inches long by $27\frac{1}{4}$ inches wide), so there's no gap between mattress and crib to trap a baby's body or head.

If your child has older siblings around, place casters in caster cups. This will help prevent a nursery version of the Indy 500 powered by the siblings.

Recent voluntary safety standards, followed by all leading manufacturers, have made cribs safer still. Those standards make the following specifications:

◆ The top of corner posts must be practically flush with the top of the end panels, or the corner posts must be very tall (over 16 inches), like those on a four-poster bed.

◆ Mattress-support hangers must be firmly secured to brackets at each end of the crib so that the mattress won't teeter and trap a baby between mattress and side.

Although nearly all new cribs on the market today are safe, cribs are still associated with more children's deaths than any other nursery product—50 or so annually. Cribs are also associated with some 13,000 injuries a year. Older cribs that predate the federal standards are largely to blame. (See the section beginning on p. 110 for guidelines on how to judge the safety of a hand-me-down crib.)

Safe and sound. Most new cribs on the market comply with both mandatory and voluntary safety standards. Frequent inspection of all parts of the crib is still the best way to ensure your child will be safe and sound in the crib.

Beyond safety

Cribs come in two basic types: single and double dropside. The latter is usually more costly, but it's also more versatile, allowing easy access to the child from both sides.

Most modern cribs have slats or spindles on all four sides. The days when cribs had solid head and foot end panels with fancy cutouts, or with trimmings like spinning balls, are pretty much gone. Cutouts are still allowed, but they must be small enough to keep out a child's neck or limbs. End panels usually have rounded top edges. Most cribs are wood, either stained or painted—usually white. Most models have casters. Some have drawers underneath. Others are convertible for toddler use.

 During the time your baby uses a crib, you should monitor the crib's condition. Inspect all the nuts, bolts, washers, and screws now and then, and tighten loose joints. Certain parts may have worked loose so that a child could complete an unexpected disassembly and, worse, swallow some metal parts in the process. Don't let your baby sleep in a crib that has broken hardware, loose spindles or slats, or other malfunctioning parts that could endanger him or her.

There are design factors that make some cribs easier to live with than others. Here are some factors that make a crib convenient.

Assembly. Cribs usually come unassembled. The easiest to put together take about 10 minutes and don't require tools. Most others take about a half hour and can be fastened with a screwdriver or hammer. If you want to avoid the chore, many retailers will do it for a small fee at your home. When you reassemble a previously used crib, you must not reuse the original wood screws, since they may not hold. Use screws that are one size larger, or opt for a crib that does not use wood screws in the first place.

Dropsides. Lowering the dropside makes it easier to reach into the crib to lift the baby, change the sheets, or flip the mattress. To lower the dropside on most models, you pull it up with one hand, then release the locking device by using a foot-operated treadle or U-shaped rod (see photos on p. 108). Considering that you may be cradling a baby in one arm, that's a good design—more convenient to use than designs that require two hands to release locks at either end of the dropside.

We particularly like one simple release: Just lift the dropside a fraction and push it inward. Another takes only one hand to carry out the necessary steps to lower the side: Simply place your index finger on a lift tab in the lock, lift the side a bit, then squeeze a release with your thumb. Unfortunately, some parents may not be able to muster the force necessary to depress the release with only one hand. Most cribs have the conventional release in which you lift the dropside a little, then release it with one foot on the treadle.

Rolling. Broad or rounded casters make a crib easy to move on a hard or carpeted surface. Narrow, disk-shaped wheels roll poorly. Some cribs have lockable casters that help keep the crib stationary if you lean lightly against it.

Mattress adjustment. Most cribs let you position the mattress at three or four height levels. A high mattress position is safe enough for a

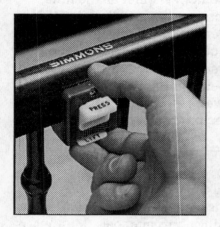

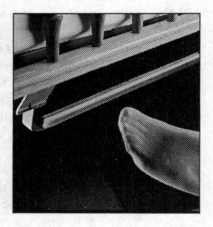

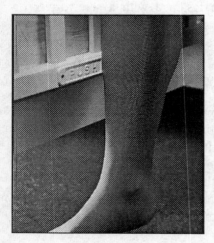

Three ways to lower a dropside. This release (above left) takes just one hand. You lift the dropside a little and press. Try it in the store, though. Some parents may lack the strength to do it with one hand. Most have a conventional release (above), in which you lift the dropside a little with one hand, then release it with one foot on the treadle. Here (left) you lift the dropside a little with one hand, then push it inward with your leg.

docile infant, but as the child grows and becomes more mobile, lowering the mattress will provide safer confinement. Some models let you adjust the height easily by snapping the mattress-support hangers in and out of the brackets without using tools.

Crib recommendations

Federal and voluntary standards have eliminated most of the worries, so you can safely base your choice on convenience, price, and appearance.

The largest manufacturer of cribs is Child Craft. Other common brands are Simmons, Bassett, Cosco, Okla Homer Smith, and Evenflo. Prices for cribs start at less than $100. Fancy designs can set you back $1,000.

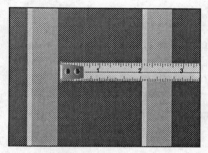

Measure up. If slats are wider apart than 2⅜ inches, a child's body may slip through but the head may not, resulting in strangulation.

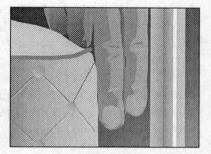

Snug fit. If two fingers fit between mattress and side, the mattress is too small. A baby can get trapped in the gap and suffocate.

No cute stuff. Fancy decorations can come off and break apart, and a child can choke on pieces. Cutouts can trap a baby's arm or neck.

No tall stuff. Corner posts or finials that stick up above the top of the end panels can snag garments and strangle a baby.

Models with a single dropside are usually cheaper than those with double dropsides. The end panels look the same, and therefore it does not matter which way you turn the crib. So, if you plan to locate the crib against a wall, you may want to save your money and buy a single dropside. Choose a double dropside if you want access from either side. A double dropside also gives you a backup, should one dropside mechanism break. A Jenny Lind-style crib carried by major retailers is a low-priced alternative to more upscale cribs.

Any crib, new or old, should be inspected periodically for wear and tear. Look for broken or missing parts, make sure all slats and hardware remain secured, and check for peeling paint. As soon as the child can stand, remove bumper pads and any toys on which the child can stand to climb out.

Cribs in compliance with voluntary standards usually bear a certification label. All new crib models from the following manufacturers are certified to meet the requirements of the American Society for Testing and Materials Standards F1169 and F966 for full-size cribs. The manufacturers are Child Craft; Cosco, Inc.; Evenflo Juvenile Furniture Company; Nelson Juvenile Products, Inc.; Okla Homer Smith; Simmons Juvenile Products Company, Inc.; and Stork Craft Ltd.

One final note: Even with a new crib, you must still follow certain rules (see Basic Rules for Safe Crib Use, p. 111) to help prevent your baby from becoming part of the injury or death statistics we mentioned at the beginning of this chapter.

Risky hand-me-downs

Many parents keep their babies in secondhand cribs—bought at tag sales or handed down from one generation to another. Cribs made before 1973, when government safety regulations took effect, are likely to pose hazards that have been removed from later models. But even cribs made just a few years ago can be risky. It's best to buy a new crib, one made after 1992. But if it's an older crib you're considering, look it over carefully. Here's what to look for:

◆ Avoid a crib with loose, broken, or missing slats, or slats spaced more than 2⅜ inches apart.

◆ Make sure the end panels extend below the mattress support in its lowest position, so a child can't get caught in a gap between panel and mattress.

◆ A lowered dropside should be at least 9 inches above the mattress support at its highest setting, so an infant can't fall out. The top of the raised side should be at least 26 inches above the support at its lowest setting.

❖ Avoid a crib with a dropside that can be released too easily or that can be opened with only a single motion for each lock.

❖ The mattress should fit snugly into the crib. If you can fit two fingers between mattress and sides, the mattress is too small (or the crib is too large). If you're buying a new mattress, a crib interior that measures about $52\frac{3}{8}$ by 28 inches should give you a snug fit.

❖ Mattress-support hooks should stay firmly in their brackets when the mattress is jostled about, as when you're changing sheets.

❖ Push, pull, and shake the crib by its end panels and sides to gauge the integrity of hardware and components.

❖ Cribs made before 1978, and especially those made before 1970, may be coated with a finish that contains lead—a toxic hazard to children, who will chew on anything.

❖ Avoid a crib that has vertical protrusions at the corner posts. (Measure a distance of at least 3 inches from the outer edge of the post. That section must not have a vertical protrusion of more than one-sixteenth of an inch; in other words, the top edges of the four posts should be flush with the top edges of the crib's end panels.) Many strangulations have occurred when children hung themselves on those protrusions. Such tragedies occur when a child wears a necklace or something with strings around the neck or when loose-fitting clothing such as a "football jersey" gets entangled on a corner post. (Posts

Entrapment area. *The "early American" design of the cutout headboard leaves a gap in which a child's neck and head could be trapped. Although these models are no longer made and the manufacturer, Bassett, tried in 1984 to recall them, people are apparently obtaining them secondhand.*

that are more than 16 inches tall are considered safe, provided you do not hang diaper bags or other things around them.)

❖ Pass up a crib with cutouts that can entrap a child's head, neck, or limbs.

Basic rules for safe crib use

Whether you buy a used crib or a new one, here are some important rules to help ensure that your baby isn't seriously injured or killed in a crib-related accident:

Instructions. Before assembling the crib, read all the instructions and keep them for future use.

 To prevent strangulation, measure the length of the tie tapes on bumper pads (also called bumper guards). Ties must not be longer than 9 inches. Snip off the ends of the ties.

Broken hardware. Inspect the crib for broken or bent hardware, loose joints, missing parts, and sharp edges. *Do not* use the crib if any parts are missing or broken. Ask your dealer, or write to the manufacturer, for replacement parts and instruction sheets.

Plastic bags. Never use shipping bags, garment bags, or other plastic bags as mattress covers, since these can cause suffocation.

Teething rails. Replace any cracked or loose rails.

Nontoxic finishes. Refinish a crib with a nontoxic finish labeled as suitable for children's products. Avoid using a vaporizer near the crib. Vapor can cause the wood to swell and the finish to peel, enabling your baby to ingest the finish.

Mattress hangers. Check that the mattress-support hangers are fully engaged before putting your baby in the crib. Hangers can become disengaged when you change the crib sheets, or they can accidentally

Strangulation hazard. Remove all crib toys that are strung across crib or playpen area when your child is beginning to push up on hands and knees or is about 5 months of age, whichever occurs earliest.

Other dangers. Keep wall decorations with ribbons or streamers away from cribs and well out of reach where children play to prevent entanglement and strangulation.

unhook when an older sibling or a dog pushes up the mattress support from underneath the crib.

Dropsides. Do not leave your baby in the crib with the side lowered. Be sure the side is in its raised and locked position whenever your baby is inside.

Strangulation hazards. Babies can get clothing caught on the protrusions of corner posts and end panels or on the cutouts on end panels. Avoid cribs with these hazards. Never put strings or necklaces around your baby's neck or dress your baby in hooded sweatshirts with drawstrings, in loose-fitting T-shirts, or in jerseys with necks that could get caught on the crib.

 Plastic bags, such as garbage bags or thin garment bags from dry cleaners, can suffocate babies. Never use them as crib-mattress protectors. Knot the ends of filmy plastic bags and discard them safely.

Objects on crib. Don't hang anything on the crib ends or sides. Babies have been seriously injured or killed when they became entangled in diaper bag straps and purse straps hung on crib ends. Hooks on diaper stackers can also cause entanglement.

Hazards in or near the crib. Keep the crib well away from window blinds or wall hangings. Keep canopy covers or canopy tiebacks out of the child's reach. Strings on bumper pads must not be longer than nine inches, whereas all other strings or ties must not exceed seven inches in length. The bumper pads should be tied at the four crib corners and in the center of the crib sides, at both the top and the bottom edge of the pad.

Dangling toys. To prevent accidental hanging, remove all crib toys that are strung from one side of the crib to the other as soon as your baby is able to push up on hands and knees. Don't simply untie one end and let items like toys, crib gyms, mobiles, exercisers, and kickers dangle freely. The loose strap may entangle your baby.

Overloading crib. Don't let siblings or heavy pets get into the crib with baby. This could cause the hardware to break or cause other accidents.

Mattress safety. Check and replace the mattress immediately if it gets torn.

Rules for toddlers. Set the mattress at the lowest position when your baby can pull up to a stand. Remove bumper pads and large toys that could be used for climbing out. Once your toddler reaches 33 inches in height, it's time to change to a safe youth-size or regular bed.

Warnings about beds and babies

Adult or youth beds can pose serious risks to babies up to one year of age. A baby on such a bed may suffocate after becoming trapped between the mattress and the wall, or between the mattress and the bed frame, footboard, or headboard. A water bed, too, is a danger to small babies if they become wedged between the bed frame and the water mattress, or if they lie on their stomachs in depressions in the bed. The single-bladder adult water bed has been associated with several child deaths. The U.S. Consumer Product Safety Commission (CPSC) recommends that infants not be left on youth beds or water beds, but that a safe crib be used instead.

WARNING!
Infants 12 months or younger can suffocate while sleeping when they:
▲ **become trapped between mattress and frame or wall**
▲ **become wedged against adult and mattress**
▲ **sink into waterbed mattress while on stomach**
Never let infants sleep on adult beds. Use a crib that meets federal safety standards and industry voluntary standards for cribs and has a tight-fitting mattress.

Sleeping position and Sudden Infant Death Syndrome

When an apparently healthy baby dies suddenly with no clear explanation, the cause of death is often attributed to Sudden Infant Death Syndrome (SIDS). There appears to be a connection between a baby's sleeping position and some cases of SIDS. Although the connection between a baby's sleeping position and SIDS is not completely understood, it is believed that the pressure of the baby's face on the surface of the mattress creates a pocket, allowing stagnant, rebreathed air to be captured. Babies then suffocate from breathing in their own carbon monoxide.

Current U.S. estimates are that SIDS can be reduced 20 to 67 percent simply by putting babies to sleep on their backs. Sleeping position is not the only factor that has been connected with SIDS prevention. Researchers at Loyola University Medical Center in Chicago found that the use of a soft mattress resulted in a fourfold increase in a baby's

SIDS DROPS 30 PERCENT

A major decrease in the number of babies dying from sudden infant death syndrome (SIDS)—the mysterious syndrome that strikes infants less than a year old—is being linked to a national campaign launched by the National Institute of Child Health and Human Development in 1994 that urged parents to put infants to sleep on their sides or backs.

Today, scientists at the National Institute of Child Health and Human Development credit a 30 percent decline in deaths from SIDS to their aggressive outreach program that urges pediatricians, nurses, and new mothers to avoid putting young babies to sleep on their stomachs, despite long-held beliefs that this was the safest sleeping position. In addition, parents should never put their babies to sleep on soft bedding like pillows, comforters, or sheepskins. Researchers believe soft bedding can cover the mouths and noses of babies, causing death from carbon monoxide poisoning as a result of breathing in the trapped exhaled air.

SIDS is the leading cause of death in infants. Prior to the campaign initiated by the National Institute of Child Health and Human Development, SIDS claimed the lives of 5,000 to 6,000 babies a year in the United States. But deaths linked to SIDS declined by 1,500 between October 1993 and October 1995, federal officials report. Even more dramatic results have occurred in Europe, Australia, and New Zealand, where more parents now place their babies to sleep on their backs while overdressing them less. In the past six years, since parent-education efforts began in New Zealand, SIDS has been reduced by 600 percent.

Danger. *To help prevent a suffocation death, place infant on back or side to sleep (unless otherwise instructed by a pediatrician) on a firm, flat crib mattress. Remove pillows, sheepskins, and toys from crib.*

risk of dying from SIDS. Giving a baby a pillow increased the risk of dying by more than two and a half times. A similar study by the CPSC found there was also a relationship between SIDS and putting babies to sleep on quilts, beanbag chairs, and water beds.

Babies most susceptible to SIDS include babies whose mothers smoked during pregnancy, babies whose parents exposed them to passive cigarette smoke after birth, babies who were bottle-fed instead of breast-fed, and babies who had respiratory infections within two weeks of death. SIDS occurs more frequently in the wintertime, when wrapping babies in heavy sleep clothing and blankets in overheated rooms raises the SIDS risk.

How to buy a crib mattress

Most adults, we suspect, wouldn't think of purchasing a bed without giving equal heed to the mattress. But the choice of which mattress to mate with a crib often comes as an afterthought. A mattress is more important to a baby's comfort than the fancy woods or finishes of a crib, and a good-quality mattress is more apt to please parents as well, for it offers superior resistance to punctures and tears and protection in keeping out wetness.

What to look for

The basic choice in crib mattresses is between foam and innerspring models. Prices range from about $30 to more than $100. Innerspring models usually keep their shape better, although high-density foam can be just as good. An innerspring usually has a metal spring unit, layers of light padding, and insulators to keep the padding from migrating into the springs. The layers are covered in liquid-resistant ticking material. Foam mattresses are generally cheaper than innersprings and may weigh half as much, making lifting easier when you change the sheets.

On cheaper mattresses, whether foam or innerspring, the ticking is a single layer of vinyl. More expensive mattresses have quilted vinyl or multiple layers of vinyl laminated together and reinforced with nylon. That makes the mattress more waterproof and sturdier—not only more resistant to tears and holes, but also able to prevent such damage, if it occurs, from worsening.

The binding that joins the top, sides, and bottom pieces of ticking around the edges of the mattress is either vinyl or fabric. Fabric is better because it allows air to escape as the child's movements compress the mattress. Otherwise, the pressure may cause the seams to strain and split over time.

Vent holes on the ticking alleviate air pressure against the seams as well. The holes also help to keep a mattress fresher by allowing odors to escape. All but the cheapest mattresses have vents—the more vents, the better.

Although crib mattress manufacturers are not required by law to make mattresses that comply with the interior dimensions specified in the federal mandatory standard for full-size cribs, they adhere to those dimensions voluntarily. Among those manufacturers are Colgate, Cosco, Kolcraft, Evenflo, and Simmons.

Foam mattresses are available in different firmness levels, depending on the density of the foam. A high-density foam mattress is likely to keep its shape as well as an innerspring mattress, but flimsier foam may soften with use. The trouble is, there's no way to compare the firmness of foam mattresses by reading labels. For that, you'll have to conduct your own squeeze test.

The same holds true for innersprings. Although manufacturers frequently equate higher coil count with firmness, the equation doesn't always hold up. For instance, a model with 150 coils can be firmer than another with 600 coils.

To prevent sagging along the edges, innerspring units are bordered by wire rods. Generally, the thicker the rod, the better the edge will hold its shape. The material used as an insulator also can affect how well a mat-

CHOOSING A MATTRESS

Select the firmest mattress you can find, foam or innerspring. To compare firmness of crib mattresses, squeeze the mattress at the edges and at the center. Look for double- or triple-laminated ticking, fabric binding along the seams, and plenty of vents. Select a safe but lower-price crib with less fancy finishes or woods. The money you save can help pay for a high-quality crib mattress. A high-quality crib mattress has all the features mentioned above. Prices are usually around $100. You can also save money by selecting less-fancy accessories (such as sheets or blankets). Never use the mattress's plastic shipping bag, a garbage bag, or a dry-cleaning bag as a mattress cover. Plastic bags can suffocate your baby.

tress holds up. Look for coir fiber—the hairy material on the outside of a coconut—it generally provides superior strength. Some retailers may have actual "cutaway" samples of crib mattresses that allow you to assess the hidden mattress components.

Mattress recommendations

Select the firmest mattress you can find, foam or innerspring. Check by squeezing the center and edges. Look for double- or triple-laminated ticking, fabric binding along the seams, and plenty of vent holes.

Most mattresses are 6 inches thick. If you opt for a 4- or 5-inch-thick mattress, the sheets you buy may not fit tautly. A high-density foam mattress (better than cheaper low-density foam) typically weighs 7 or 8 pounds. That makes it easier to handle than innerspring mattresses that can weigh a hefty 20 to 25 pounds.

Carefully measure the crib, especially an older crib, before you shop for a mattress. New crib mattresses must be approximately $51\frac{5}{8}$ inches long by $27\frac{1}{4}$ inches wide. The mattress should fit snugly in the crib. If you can fit two fingers between the mattress and any side of the crib, the mattress is too small or the crib too big, and a child's body or head can get trapped in the gap between mattress and crib.

Crib bumpers

If you buy bumper pads (bumper guards) for the crib, make sure they (1) fit around the entire crib, (2) tie or snap into place, and (3) have straps or ties for at least six locations on the top edge and an equal number at the bottom edge. To prevent your baby from chewing on the straps or becoming entangled in them, trim off any excess length. A good rule of thumb is to keep the ties or straps as short as possible, not to exceed nine inches per individual tie or strap. Use bumpers only until baby can pull up to a standing position, then remove them so that baby will not use them to climb out of the crib. Use bumpers with care, since a safety standard for this product is not yet in effect (as of this writing). But industry voluntary efforts are under way to set such standards as length of tie tapes and type of stitching.

CPSC bans infant cushions

The CPSC has voted unanimously to issue a final rule to ban infant cushions, which have been involved in numerous infant suffocations. (According to the CPSC, the use of soft bedding like pillows, comforters, and sheepskins may contribute to the death of as many as 1,800 American infants a year.) The CPSC's action stems from the concern that manufacturers might begin production of products the same as, or similar to, ones previously removed from the marketplace. "A ban of infant cushions can assure that this product does not reappear into the marketplace," said the CPSC.

Here are the essential features that define the banned products:
◆ They have soft fabric coverings.
◆ They are loosely filled with a granular material, for example, plastic foam beads or pellets.
◆ They are easily flattened so that the infant lies prone on them.
◆ They are capable of conforming to the face or body of an infant.
◆ They are promoted for use by children under one year of age.

Of these features, the one that probably contributes most to deaths is the ability of the cushions to conform to an infant's face or body. In addition to publishing a final rule to ban future production of infant cushions, the CPSC urges consumers who may still have infant cushions to call the CPSC's toll-free hotline at 800-638-2772 for recall information and instructions. If the manufacturer of the infant cushion cannot be identified, the CPSC urges that the cushion be destroyed immediately.

Should you decide to bring a baby into bed with you, it would be wise

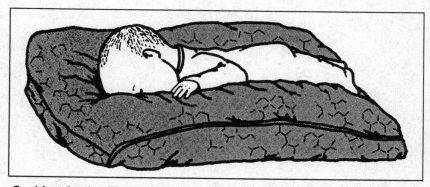

Cushion deaths. *The key characteristic that probably contributes most to deaths is the ability of the cushions to conform to an infant's face or body.*

to take the bed's mattress off the frame and springs and place it directly on the floor, well away from the wall on all sides to reduce the danger of entrapment or wedging. Better yet, refrain from sleeping in the same bed with your baby. In some incidents, an adult has rolled onto an infant during the night. The drawing on p. 114 illustrates how infants become trapped as they wedge themselves between the bed and the wall.

Diapers and accessories

Like feeding, diapering is a regular part of baby care. All told, your baby will undergo about 6,000 diaper changes in the first two and a half years. There are three basic diapering options today: buying and laundering reusable cloth diapers, paying for a diaper service, or using disposable diapers. While disposables are most convenient, they are also the most expensive choice. Which choice you ultimately make will depend on where you live: Do you have a diaper service nearby for handling cloth diapers? Can using water for laundering be a problem in your area? Is the landfill problem so acute in your area as to make use of disposable diapers environmentally irresponsible? You may even decide to select a mix of the three methods.

Whether you plan to buy reusable cloth diapers, pay for a diaper service, or stock up on disposable diapers, you can count on your newborn using as many as 100 diapers a week in the first four months.

Diaper changing and laundering are two of the most time-consuming tasks that parents have to face. Newborns need changing about 12 times a day. That means you can expect to change 350 diapers in the first month after your baby gets home. The frequency lessens as your baby grows older.

Whereas some parents use only disposables, or all-in-one fabric and cover systems, many find that they manage best by using a combination of diapering alternatives. For example, you may want to use a diaper service in the first months after your baby is born, since it saves the labor of laundering or toting home cases of disposables. Later, you may want reusable cloth-and-cover combinations for home and disposables for travel, outings, and at the baby-sitter's or a child-care facility.

Reusable cloth diapers

Reusable cloth diapers are more economical than disposables. But many parents who have decided to use these do so because they feel that they are softer and more comfortable than disposables. Or, parents concerned about the environment may opt for cloth diapers because of the poor biodegradability of disposables, which contributes to the over-burdening of the nation's landfill areas and the depletion of forests and wood resources.

Traditional cloth diapers come in gauze and bird's-eye fabrics, in flat and prefolded styles. Prefolded models of the conventional rectangular style can be purchased in larger (toddler) sizes, and some brands come with an additional center fold to absorb wetness. Gauze is more comfortable than bird's-eye fabric, and its porousness means that air can circulate, which helps prevent diaper rash.

Newer cloth diapers are cut and styled to resemble disposable diapers. They come in several sizes and styles, and close without diaper pins. The latest types of cloth diapers are fast drying and absorbent, some made of heavy flannel and thick woven fabrics that soak up moisture. By 1996, about a dozen companies were marketing these new cloth diapers.

To begin with, you will need approximately four dozen diapers (sold in boxes of 12). The price generally ranges from $11 to $17 per dozen. You will also need diaper pins, preferably with locking heads to prevent accidental release, and at least four pairs of waterproof pants (the snap-on styles are easier to use than pull-on varieties, and allow some air circulation) or diaper wraps, which use snaps and Velcro closures to make the use of diaper pins obsolete. Diaper wraps come in many colors and print designs.

The proper laundering of cloth diapers is critical, since, if they're not rinsed well, soap residue can remain embedded causing ammonia buildup and a possible diaper-area inflammation, popularly called diaper rash. Using hot water, a low-sudsing detergent, a water softener (not a fabric softener), and a vinegar rinse all can help to prevent ammonia buildup in diapers. (See Diaper Rash, p. 126.)

Commercial diaper services

With relatively few new parents using commercial diaper services that pick up soiled diapers and deliver freshly laundered ones each week, many services have found their business squeezed out by the $3.63 billion disposable-diaper industry. Lately, however, they have been making something of a comeback.

Diaper services offer a convenient and economical alternative to disposables, and they provide the softness and comfort of fabric diapers without the accompanying laundering hassles. The front door delivery means that you won't have to lug home bulky packages of diapers as you would with disposables.

Many services now offer a variety of diaper designs, from fitted diapers to special diaper/diaper-cover combinations that require no pins, in a range of sizes to fit your baby's needs. Some offer twice-a-week delivery and the option of using new, rather than used, diapers. Most services are listed in the Yellow Pages. Not everyone has a diaper service nearby, however.

Disposable diapers

All disposable diapers are constructed in more or less the same way: They have a waterproof plastic outer layer, a center layer of absorbent padding, and an inner liner that keeps wet padding from touching the baby.

In the three decades since Procter & Gamble introduced *Pampers*, manufacturers have regularly improved on that basic design. Adhesive-tape fasteners replaced diaper pins. A form-fitting hourglass shape and elastic around the legs made for a more leakproof fit. Elastic at the waist and extra strips of plastic help prevent leakage when the baby is lying down. Extra plastic waist shields keep the diaper shell from tearing if you have to refasten. Some brands are lightly scented. Because of the absorbency gels used nowadays, most disposables are so absorbent they can hold 80 to 100 times their weight in liquid, which amounts to an improbable two quarts.

Three national brands dominate the disposable-diaper market: Procter & Gamble's *Pampers* and *Luvs* and Kimberly-Clark's *Huggies*. There are also some 100 regional and store brands. The latest products incorporate different designs for boys and girls, although Procter & Gamble decided to switch back to unisex diapers in 1996.

What works well for one baby may not work well for another. Babies come in all shapes and sizes, and there's a wide variety in the way parents put diapers on, how often they change diapers, and how active babies are.

All those variables contribute to the inconsistency of diaper performance. Some parents may encounter leakage with one brand but not with another. Disposables are far more absorbent than cloth, and cloth is generally significantly stronger than disposable.

Other things being equal, there is one overriding factor that should guide your choice of a diaper brand: price. Buy the least expensive brand that performs satisfactorily for you.

If you decide to use cloth diapers, you can supplement their absorbency by double-diapering (using two at a time) or by using diaper doublers, strips of absorbent material you put inside the diaper. Diaper doublers can, of course, be used with disposables too, and are especially helpful for overnight use or trips (particularly air travel).

Advantages/disadvantages of diapering methods

Using disposable diapers is definitely more convenient and less time-consuming than laundering your own cloth diapers. On the negative side, disposables are more expensive to use than either laundering cloth diapers or using a diaper service.

Reusable cloth diapers

Advantages. The least expensive option because they can be reused. Thought by some parents to be softer and more comfortable against tender skin. The cloth diapering systems come in several sizes to fit growing babies.

Disadvantages. Soaking, laundering, and drying require time and labor. Additional diaper wraps, diaper covers, or diaper doublers may be required to prevent wetness on clothing or furniture. If not laundered correctly, may cause diaper rash. If pins are carelessly used, a puncture wound may result or the child could even swallow the pin. Inconvenient for travel.

Diaper service

Advantages. Fresh diapers are delivered to your door once or twice a week. Soiled diapers are carried away. Most services supply a diaper pail at no additional charge. Less expensive than disposables (but on average more expensive than laundering cloth diapers).

Disadvantages. Not available in all locations. You have to call for extra diapers if you run low. Inconvenient for travel.

Disposable diapers

Advantages. No soaking, wringing out, or laundering required. These come in a range of sizes to fit growing babies. Superior absorbency. Waterproof outer shield keeps wetness from clothing and furniture. No pins are needed, so there's no danger of baby getting stuck. Convenient for travel.

Disadvantages. More costly than other alternatives. Transporting and storage of packages can be inconvenient. Some babies have choked on tab papers and on linings that have been pulled apart and ingested. Because of these diapers' effectiveness, there may be a tendency to change them less frequently than cloth diapers, possibly resulting in an increased incidence of diaper rash. They are also not readily biodegradable, which becomes important when you consider that each baby uses approximately one ton of disposable diapers before graduating to underpants.

The great disposable-diaper dilemma

Throwing away a disposable diaper doesn't get rid of it. The diaper may no longer be in your home, but it will still be around on the planet for a long time. Disposable diapers are a significant part of the nation's waste-management problem.

Environmental issues are rarely painted in black and white but only in shades of gray. Disposable diapers create garbage, so using cloth diapers is better for the environment in that respect. But using cloth diapers exacts its own environmental price. The diapers have to be washed; that takes a lot of water, a resource in scarce supply in some places. The water has to be heated; that takes fuel and contributes to air pollution. Drying also takes fuel, unless you let the sun do it.

Recommendations

Your first decision should be which diapering method you're going to use. Although cloth diapers are kinder to the environment, the convenience offered by disposables will keep those diapers popular for the foreseeable future.

The best answer may be a combination of disposables and cloth diapers. You might, for example, start with a diaper service for the first three to six months of your baby's life (provided you live in an area that still has a service). That's the time when you'll go through the most diapers each day, so it's nice to have someone else take care of the laundering. You'll still save quite a bit of money by not using disposables.

You might then switch to your own cloth diapers, with disposables plus extra liners for times when you won't be able to change baby frequently.

If you use cloth, choose standard gauze fabric over bird's-eye; it's more comfortable and more porous, reducing the chances of diaper rash. Diapers with an extra center layer are more absorbent. Look for fast-drying designs, those with flaps or layers attached only in the center or at the ends, permitting greater air flow. Also for cloth users, all-in-one diaper and diaper-cover combinations use Velcro or snaps instead of pins. Their outer covers dry quickly and can be used more than once. Look for covers made of lightweight polyester that is porous enough to allow air circulation (important for preventing diaper rash). Interior diapers are made of highly absorbent soft flannel, terry-cloth and terry/flannel combinations, and heavyweight, multilayer cotton weaves. As for disposable diapers, choose the lowest-cost brand you can find. If one brand leaks or doesn't fit right, try the next cheapest.

Diaper rash

Diaper rash, medically called diaper dermatitis, is one of the most common problems parents encounter with a baby's skin. The rash usually begins with a few red bumps and spreads around a baby's diaper area in a matter of days. The rash occurs most often on babies between 9 and 12 months of age, when approximately one out of three babies develops it.

Skin wetness is the major cause of diaper rash. Moist skin is more easily damaged, particularly by the friction of a diaper rubbing against the skin. When a baby's urine and feces mix together, chemicals are activated that also irritate a baby's skin.

Other causes of diaper rash are diarrhea and illnesses. Babies have very sensitive digestive tracts, and that sensitivity is reflected in their bowels. The faster the stool material moves through the baby, the more apt the baby's stools are to be carrying irritating enzymes. Illness also lowers a baby's resistance to infections, setting the stage for diaper rash. A rough washcloth or soap can irritate the diaper area even further.

Babies don't need daily baths. They don't sweat very much, and they're not working in coal mines. Except for their bottoms or when they spit up on themselves, they don't need bathing at all.

Baby-skin specialists suggest the following strategies for combating an outbreak of diaper rash: Change diapers frequently, 8 to 10 times a day. If the baby is soiled with urine and stool, rinse with plain tap water or sit the baby in the tub or sink with water in it. Use diapers that keep the baby as dry as possible. Keep urine away from stool, either by double- or triple-diapering with cloth diapers or by using disposable superabsorbent diapers that bind moisture away and won't release it back onto the skin. Allow the child to go without diapers for a while each day until the rash subsides.

If the diaper area becomes damaged, with skin broken or blistered, or if the rash lasts more than four or five days, you should contact your physician. There are a number of diaper-area infections that may start out as a common diaper rash and develop into something more serious. For example, a fiery, red, bumpy rash, sometimes with scaly edges, may signal a yeast infection. A brilliant red, swollen ring around a baby's rectum with little tears, or fissures, that lasts for weeks and results in painful bowel movements may be caused by a strep infection. In either case, prompt medical treatment should be sought.

One solution for diaper rash might be to relieve the tightness of the disposable diapers' elastic bands around the leg a little to permit some air circulation. Snip the elastic once on one leg in the front part of the diaper and once on the opposite leg at the back part of the diaper. You might get occasional leakage, however.

The dangers of talcum-based baby powder

Inhaling baby powder has been reported to cause pneumonia and even death. Accidental inhalation of talcum powder accounts for about 1 percent of all calls to poison-control centers for babies under three years of age.

About 7 out of 10 parents use baby powder regularly—to keep the baby's diaper area dry, to make the baby smell good, and (mistakenly) to kill germs that cause diaper rash.

The shape of baby-powder containers, which resemble nursing bottles, may contribute to accidental inhalation, along with the fact that containers have no safety caps and no warnings to parents about powder dangers.

A study in Massachusetts found that 47 percent of the calls about babies to a statewide poison-control number were about baby powder,

27 percent about ointments and creams, and 16 percent about baby wipes. The babies' symptoms included coughing, wheezing, choking, shortness of breath, and vomiting. Sometimes the babies had grabbed the powder container from their parents, but in other cases parents had given them the can or jar to play with during diapering.

Your baby's skin will probably do just as well without baby powder and other toiletries; they may even increase skin irritation. If you must use baby powder, use a cornstarch-based powder rather than one containing talc. Powder your hands, rather than directly powdering your baby, to decrease dust storms. Don't use product containers as toys, and be careful to keep lids in the closed position. Always store all baby-product containers well out of your baby's reach.

Diaper pails

Diaper pails are responsible for numerous injuries and even deaths to young children. The U.S. Consumer Product Safety Commission (CPSC) has received many reports of children who got hold of diaper-pail cake deodorizers and ate them. The CPSC also has received reports of children who fell headfirst into diaper pails and drowned.

Always keep a diaper pail (and all other pails, for that matter) tightly closed and out of the reach of young children. When shopping for a pail, choose one with a foot-operated pedal to keep your hands free for baby. Whether you plan to use disposables or cloth diapers, this feature will be a plus. For cloth diapers, look for easy-to-use handles and pouring spouts to make emptying simpler.

Newer diaper pails now employ plastic garbage bags in a system to shut off odors. These pails are specifically designed for use with disposable diapers.

Diaper pins

The plastic heads of some diaper pins can become brittle over time and break, exposing the sharp pin rod that could puncture a baby's skin. Dispose of pins that become dull with use, since applying extra pressure to the pin can lead to accidental puncture wounds. Sticking the pointed end of the pin in a bar of soap before diapering helps to make it slide through the cloth easier.

Listings: Diaper bags and diaper pails

Note: These products were not tested by Consumers Union. This alphabetical listing by category does not include all models available but rather is a selection of some widely distributed models. Descriptions are derived from authors' observations and manufacturers' claims.

MODEL	DESCRIPTION
DIAPER BAGS	
Babies' Alley Denim Backpack *La Rue International* Model 13415, $35	Denim backpack with suede accents. Elasticized side pockets and front zipper organizer pocket. Vinyl, waterproof lining. Padded, adjustable shoulder straps. Removable padded changer. Drawstring closure. Detachable bag for soiled diapers.
Baby Boom/Carter's "Plaid About You" Diaper Bag Model MC4708, $35	Gray- and khaki-colored fabrics that can be carried by sporty dads. Large side pocket. Shoulder straps. Holds bottles and accessories.
Children on the Go Joanna Changing Bag Model 40200, $30	This bags holds a lot yet stays organized, with two outside bottle pouches, a large, zippered "envelope" pocket with clear plastic front, and elasticized holders for baby needs. Main compartment has double-zippered opening for easy access to the three inside storage compartments. Interior is waterproof vinyl. Includes a separate changing station, featuring a large pad and separate compartment for soiled diapers. Adjustable shoulder strap.
Children on the Go Diaper Attaché Model 40700, $50	Two large compartments, a mesh organizer, an outside bottle holder, a large changing pad, a waterproof bag for dirty duds, and a key ring. Has both snap-together purse handles and an adjustable shoulder strap.
First Years Full Day Diaper Bag Model 4090, $25	Machine-washable tote has six labeled compartments, mesh pockets, and two zippered sides. Outside pocket with Velcro closure for parent's things. Removable vinyl changing pad inside. Large enough to carry toys, blanket, or other accessories. Has both carrying handle and adjustable shoulder strap with support.
Lands' End Backpack Diaper Bag Model 28872, $30	A nylon pack with waterproof vinyl lining. Padded shoulder straps, detachable bag for wet items. Two insulated bottle pockets. Burgundy or royal navy.
Lands' End Do-It-All Diaper Bag Model 35070, $30	Sturdy, lightweight zippered bag made of water-resistant nylon-backed vinyl. Zippered section for change of clothes. Two side bottle pockets. Exterior, wallet-size pocket. Clear plastic storage pouch and attached key clip inside. Carry handles plus adjustable shoulder strap. Removable changing pad. Comes in navy, green, red, or plum. Monogram available.
Lands' End Deluxe Diaper Bag Model 22413, $45	Larger than most diaper bags. Four pockets for baby food jars and two insulated bottle pockets. One outside compartment zips open wide with two waterproof pockets, one in clear vinyl for wet items. Soft nylon changing pad. Nylon-backed vinyl. Bound seams for strength. Navy, burgundy, or hunter green.

Listings: Diaper bags and diaper pails *continued*

MODEL	DESCRIPTION
McKenzie Kids "Better than a Diaper Bag" Diaper Bag Model 8001, $45	A sturdy bag made of durable polyester duck with a front organizer pocket to hold parent's stuff, two insulated, covered bottle pockets on the side, a changing pad in its own pocket, a key leash, mesh pockets inside for baby things, and dual zipper front opening. Can be worn as shoulder or waist pack. Comes in blue, teal, and black.
McKenzie Kids Baby Gear Briefcase Model 8002, $56	An alternative to cutesy diaper bags, this sturdy bag has two front pockets with quick-release buckles, a key hook inside front pocket, a shoulder strap that converts to a backpack, removable changing pad, and mesh bottle holders in main compartment. Zippered compartment opens completely, with mesh organizer pockets. Comes in blue, teal, and black.
Omron Way to Grow Packs a Lot Model B1200, $20	A zippered, fully insulated tote for bottles and baby food with a sturdy, mesh carryall duffel bag section on top. Single shoulder strap can be unzipped to form two straps for wearing the tote as a backpack. Water resistant; wipes clean with a damp cloth. Available in assorted colors.
Omron Way to Grow Fanny Pack Plus Model B1700, $14	Two totes in one: one is an insulated, zippered fanny pack, the other a detachable, zippered bottle tote with self-adhering strap for belt or stroller. Bottle tote accommodates 4-ounce and 8-ounce baby bottles or soda can. Waist belt adjusts to fit most waist sizes. Key strap on side.

DIAPER PAILS

First Years Diaper Dispoz-all Diaper Pail Model 3027, $20	Traps up to 25 disposable diapers inside with an airlock system. Uses standard 13-gallon trash liners. Lid opens with a foot pedal. A lever opens the top, locking the diaper, and odor, inside the bag. Liner removes easily for disposal. Double barrier keeps odors in check, even when pail is open.
Fisher-Price Odor-Free Diaper System Model 9229, $19	Uses kitchen-size garbage bags to seal away diaper odors. Lever on front of pail seals soiled diapers off to control odors. Holds up to 20 diapers before having to be emptied. Foot pedal opens lid. Lid has child-resistant compartment for odor filter or deodorizer.
Gerry Odor-Free Diaper Pail Model 478, $16	Double lids with charcoal filters in each section trap odors. Foot pedal opens locking flip-top lid. Inner ring holds standard plastic trash bags. Charcoal filters reduce odors but are an ongoing expense.
Safety 1st Odor-Less Diaper System Model 41681, $18	Turn 'N Seal design allows you to twist the bag closed before you open the lid, locking odors in the bag. Spring-loaded top automatically flips open to let you drop diaper in. Top locks into place, and deodorizer compartment has locking tabs, to prevent children from opening.

Foods for babies

When we looked at more than 500 baby foods from five baby-food makers, including an organic and a frozen baby-food manufacturer, we concluded that you can properly feed your baby nutritious commercially prepared food, but it is important to read the product labels thoroughly. The labels were read for nutrients, ingredient lines, and label claims.

Nutrition: What babies need

For their first six months of life, most babies get all the nutrients they need from breast milk or formula. The digestive system of young infants isn't mature enough to handle foods other than breast milk or formula. Babies may even push food out with their tongues, a reflex designed to protect them from substances they can't properly swallow or digest. Some studies suggest that introducing solids to infants younger than six months just adds needless calories, since the baby will still be drinking the same amount of milk.

Somewhere around four to six months, babies develop the neuro-muscular mechanisms needed to recognize a spoon and to swallow solids and digest foods. They begin to grow too hungry to be satisfied by milk alone. Watching others eat, they may open their mouths and lean forward. But every baby is different, so starting on solids should be determined by a baby's readiness, not by weight or age.

It's best to introduce the various solid foods one at a time, at intervals of a week or so. That makes it much easier to identify any food intolerances, which might show up as loose bowel movements or rashes or other allergic reactions. Pediatricians usually recommend starting with infant cereals, which are fortified with vitamins and minerals—particularly iron—that complement baby's diet of breast milk or formula.

Keep in mind that each new food presents a new taste and texture. Try to make feeding time relaxed. Offer food in small amounts, and don't worry if you're getting more on the baby than in the baby.

Don't feed the baby straight from the jar; spoon what you need into a bowl, then cover the remainder in the jar and store it in the refrigerator for no more than a few days. If you spoon the food into the baby's mouth right from the container, bacteria from the baby's mouth can be transferred from the spoon to the jar, where they will continue to grow.

By the time babies are around a year old, their digestive processes should be functioning at nearly adult proficiency, so most foods can then come from the family table.

The players

The dominant player in the baby-food industry is Gerber Products Company, the only national brand, with about 70 percent of the market. Beech-Nut Nutrition Corporation and Heinz U.S.A. each have approximately 15 percent of the market. Internationally, however, Heinz claims to have the largest market share. All others (including Earth's Best, Inc., and Growing Healthy, Inc.) total up to about 3 percent of the market.

Gerber, which has been making baby food since 1928, now sells approximately 200 different food products. With some exceptions, the brand is conventionally processed (heat treated) and packaged (in jars). Sugars and starches are added ingredients in some of their products, although Gerber announced that it would stop adding sugars and starches to its fruit and vegetable products because of "changing customer preferences."

Over the past few years, Gerber has placed a heavy emphasis on consumer acceptance (both for baby and adult) via a technique called Response Surface Methodology (RSM). RSM incorporates sensory evaluation with computerized mathematical models to develop what Gerber claims are the best-tasting products on the market. They claim to be the only baby-food manufacturer using RSM.

Beech-Nut has been producing baby foods since 1931 and is currently strong in the New York, California, Illinois, Ohio, and Florida markets. Their line includes about 100 products. Like Gerber, most of their products are conventionally processed and packaged. As highlighted in their advertising campaigns, Beech-Nut differentiates itself from Gerber as offering a higher proportion of the total line of products that contain no added sugars and no products with modified food starches. (While this is true, there are a considerable number of Beech-Nut products that do contain regular/unmodified starches.) Beech-Nut once offered an organic line, Special Harvest, but owing to ingredient quality problems and poor profitability, it was dropped in 1993.

Heinz, available primarily in the Central and Southeastern states, is not as much a key player in the United States as it is abroad. According to Heinz, its market share is greater than 50 percent in eight countries, including a 97 percent share in New Zealand, a 90 percent share in Australia, and an 89 percent share in Canada.

In the business since the 1930s, Heinz conventionally produces and packages about 110 baby foods. Its product line is closer to Gerber's than to Beech-Nut's, as sugars and modified food starches are added to some of the products. Like Gerber, Heinz has also stated that it is reformulating some baby foods to eliminate added starches and sugars. Since Heinz does less advertising, this brand is cheaper (actual savings depend on the region of the country) than Beech-Nut or Gerber, which are comparably priced.

Earth's Best was incorporated in 1988 by two brothers looking for healthier, safer food for their own infants, a better world for their children to grow up in, and a means to support the development and viability of organic agriculture. Currently, it is the only organic line of baby food on the market, offering approximately 40 products.

All of their products are certified organically grown and processed according to the Oregon Tilth standards and the California Organic Foods Act of 1990, which, according to Earth's Best, is scheduled to be federally implemented in 1997. Organic farming, as practiced by Earth's Best, avoids the use of synthetic pesticides or fertilizers, but rather uses botanically derived compounds and techniques, such as integrated pest management, pheromone traps, and niche growing.

Earth's Best's organic claim also includes the animals used in their meat-containing products. These animals are:

◆ fed organically grown feed
◆ allowed to roam freely
◆ raised without synthetic growth hormones or antibiotic feed additives (Those cattle requiring antibiotics to treat an infection are removed from the organic herd.)

All of Earth's Best's foods are free of added sugars and starches. Unlike those of their competitors, many of the products incorporate whole grains (offering the benefits of naturally occurring micronutrients) into their formulations. Earth's Best's foods cost more than Gerber, Beech-Nut, or Heinz.

Earth's Best was acquired by H. J. Heinz Company in the spring of 1996. According to Earth's Best, Heinz is committed to preserving the product line and the philosophy of the company. Depending on Heinz's marketing strategy, distribution could increase.

Growing Healthy, founded in 1989, is the only frozen line of baby food currently on the market. Promoted as all-natural, the 30 products contain no sugars or starches. They undergo minimal heat treatment (e.g., blanching of fruits or vegetables) and are then frozen so that, according to Growing Healthy, the "natural fresh taste and nutrition are locked in." Unlike the rest of the baby-food industry, the foods are not packed in jars, but rather are all packed in microwaveable and recyclable high-density polyethylene trays. Currently available in 15 percent of the United States, Growing Healthy is the most expensive brand.

The products and stages

The manufacturers organize their foods into product-specific (juices, cereals, fruits, etc.) and, via label information, age-specific categories. Earth's Best offers age-specific suggestions via a promotional brochure only. Within these categories, the manufacturers take into account the

	FOR BEGINNERS AND OLDER	FROM ABOUT 6 MONTHS	FROM ABOUT 9 MONTHS	FOR THE OLDER BABY
Gerber	1st Foods	2nd Foods	3rd Foods	Graduates
Beech-Nut	Stage 1	Stage 2	Stage 3	Table Time
Heinz	Building Blocks 1	Building Blocks 2*	Building Blocks 3**	N/A
Earth's Best	Basic Beginnings	Building Blocks	Table Trainers	N/A
Growing Healthy	1st Bites	2nd Bites	3rd Bites, 3rd Bites Chunky	N/A

* Labels for some foods are for babies from about 4 months.
** Labels for these foods are for babies from about 7 or 8 months.
N/A Brand does not offer foods for the older baby.

baby's nutritional needs, the ingredients (including possible allergens), the baby's ability to handle different textures, and portion size. The age-specific category names for the manufacturers appear below.

For the most part, the categories are defined as:

MANUFACTURER	TOLL-FREE NUMBER
Gerber	800-4GERBER
Beech-Nut	800-523-6633
Heinz	800-872-2229
Earth's Best	800-442-4221
Growing Healthy	800-755-4999

Toll-free numbers. Each manufacturer offers a toll-free number so that consumers can obtain product information. In some cases, additional material on a variety of topics (such as nursing, pregnancy, discipline) is provided.

❖ **For beginners and older:** These are usually single-ingredient foods (this way allergic reactions can be easily identified) that are pureed for easy swallowing. In all five brands, all are free of added sugars and starches.

❖ **From about 6 months:** This category introduces multi-ingredient foods, such as dinners and desserts, which offer added variety and flavors into the baby's diet. Depending on the manufacturer, starches and sugars are introduced at this stage in some of these foods. The texture is smooth, but not as fine as those for beginners.

❖ **From about 9 months:** These are larger-size portions formulated to keep up with baby's appetite. The chunky texture of these foods encourages chewing.

❖ **For the older baby:** At present, only Gerber and, to a limited extent, Beech-Nut offer baby foods for the older baby. These foods include microwaveable dinners, fruit and vegetable dices, meat sticks, and snacks, and are intended to extend the brands' lines and market share by extending the time a baby/toddler will use baby foods.

Trends in the market

Marketing baby food, as with pet food, presents a challenge, since the actual consumer doesn't make the purchasing decision. Baby-food makers have tried to attract buyers in various ways over the years. They've put every imaginable food and combination of foods into jars. They've added sugar and salt to make the products more palatable. Later, the baby-food makers took out the salt, and now they are taking the sugar and starches out of some of their products.

Some notable industry trends since the last edition of *Guide to Baby Products* include:

✦ **The downsizing of products.** As of the last edition, Gerber was the only company that had reduced the jar size and amount of food in their jars (from 4.5/4.25 ounces to 4 ounces, and from about 6.25 ounces to 6 ounces). Beech-Nut, Heinz, and Earth's Best have now followed in Gerber's footsteps, a move probably dictated by the competitive pressure.

✦ **Line extensions.** As with any processed food, manufacturers are continually developing line extensions on many of their product lines. For example, items like mashed potatoes, lasagna, and yogurt-containing juices are now included with the original line of products.

✦ **Products for the older baby.** Gerber and Beech-Nut are still trying to get parents to purchase their products for the older baby, thereby extending the dollars spent on baby food. Gerber has expanded its *Graduates* line (originally introduced in 1992) to include more snacks and diced fruits and vegetables. Both Gerber and Beech-Nut offer an extensive line of microwaveable dinners that are intended to compete with boxed macaroni and cheese, *SpaghettiOs*, and the like.

✦ **Products for the Hispanic population.** Tropical juices and desserts for the Hispanic population are still being offered by Gerber and Beech-Nut, although cereals and dinners have been discontinued. Because of the different cultural and eating habits of this population, Gerber intentionally does not assign stages to these foods.

✦ **Nonmeat dinners/pasta sauces.** To keep in line with the eating habits of some of the U.S. population, many vegetarian/nonmeat dinners are being offered. In addition, since increased consumption of complex carbohydrates has been recommended for adults, Gerber offers a selection of sauces for babies, so they too can join the family in a pasta meal.

✦ **Simple dinners.** These products typically combine either a fruit or vegetable with a meat as the sole ingredients (other than water). Unlike other dinners, these products do not contain any added starches, sugar, or salt. Originally offered only by Gerber (*Simple Recipe*), they are now available from Beech-Nut (*Delicious Duos*) and Heinz (*Simple & Delicious*). These products were developed to eliminate the need to open two jars of baby food (a fruit or vegetable and a meat) by combining the dinner into one jar.

Changes brought about by the NLEA

Before the Nutrition Labeling and Education Act (NLEA) was enacted, only those packaged foods that had added nutrients or those making nutritional claims were required to be nutritionally labeled. Now almost all packaged foods, including baby foods, are required to carry complete nutritional labels.

While dietary guidelines recommend that adults restrict fat intake to no more than 30 percent of their total calorie intake, these guidelines don't apply to young children. Fat plays a crucial role in the growth and development of the young child; therefore, consumption of fat-containing foods should not be restricted. Consequently, nutritional labeling for young children (under four years) is unlike that for adults, primarily because of the role of fat.

For foods intended for children under two, the regulations forbid fatty-acid profile and cholesterol labeling. According to the Food and Drug Administration (FDA), the presence of such information may lead parents to wrongly assume that certain nutrients should be restricted in a young child's diet, when in fact they should not.

In addition, labels of baby foods for children under two cannot carry the FDA-approved health claims about the relationship between a nutrient or food and a health problem (e.g., folic acid and neural tube birth defects) nor claims about the foods being "low-fat" or "low-cholesterol." Only a few claims are allowed:
◆ the percent Daily Value (DV) that a vitamin or mineral in the food provides
◆ the terms "unsweetened" and "unsalted"

The nutritional labels on foods for children under four show saturated fat and cholesterol content. However, they, along with the labels on foods for children under two, cannot show how fat, cholesterol, sodium, and dietary fiber correspond to DVs. This is because DVs for these nutrients have not been established for children under four. (The FDA has set DVs for young children only for protein and certain vitamins and minerals.)

Basic nutrition for a careful parent

We looked at more than 500 baby foods from five baby-food makers: Gerber, Beech-Nut, Heinz, Earth's Best, and Growing Healthy. We approached this project much as a careful parent would, reading labels and checking ingredient lines and nutritional content. Where it made sense to do so, we compared homemade baby food with commercial equivalents—but without tasting the products, since adults are not the consumers of these products. (Besides, babies don't have the highly developed sense of taste that adults do.) We did not test these products for nutritional components.

Ingredients

The entire product lines from the five manufacturers were compared for the following added ingredients. *Note:* After we completed our report, Gerber announced plans to reformulate 42 of its products to remove starches and sugars.

Added sugars

Adding sugars to certain foods makes them easier to process and perhaps makes them more appealing to babies (and adults) who like sweet things. If the baby is eating a varied diet, he or she will do fine with a baby food that contains some added sugar. Although parents should try to avoid feeding baby large amounts of added sugars, if baby is a finicky eater, choosing a food with some added sugar is better than dealing with a child who will not eat at all.

However, it should be noted that added sugars lower the nutrient density of the other nutrients provided by the food. Additionally, sugars may mask flavor and textural differences among some foods. As one role of baby food is to acclimate the child to table food, a baby should experience a wide variety of tastes and textures early on.

Feeding babies foods with or without added sugars is a matter of choice. If the decision is to avoid added sugars, it's important to read ingredient lines and to compare brands. Sugars can be found in many forms—for example, sucrose, high-fructose corn syrup, or dextrose. Neither Earth's Best nor Growing Healthy add sugars to any of their products.

One will not find added sugars in foods for beginners. They are almost always found in desserts, are spotted in many fruits and cereals (primarily jarred cereals), and occasionally in a few juices (Gerber only), vegetables, and dinners. Actual amounts of added sugar can't be determined from the label.

Added starches

As with sugars, added starches and flours make baby food easier to process. They aid in providing a final product of consistent texture, and when chemically modified, they make acidic foods, like fruits and desserts, more stable so they are less likely to weep (or separate out in a watery layer). It has been suggested that adding modified food starches (MFS) may make the final product more palatable as well.

There is no doubt that foods containing starches are less nutrient dense for most nutrients. However, the average baby will thrive on foods containing added starches. Nevertheless, a great deal of publicized controversy over diluting "real" food with fillers has surfaced.

In 1995, the Center for Science in the Public Interest (CSPI) released a report entitled "Cheating Babies," accusing Gerber and Heinz of "adulterating" some baby foods with water, starches, and sugars, safe ingredients commonly found in adult foods and generally not considered "adulterants" by the food industry. The paper claimed that these manufacturers were offering nutritionally inferior products, and by deceptive labeling, not providing what buyers thought they were paying for. CSPI also petitioned the FDA to require all baby-food labels to list the actual percentage of the product's main ingredients. That petition was still pending at the time of this writing.

In mid-February of 1996, CSPI filed a petition with the Federal Trade Commission (FTC) to halt what they called a pervasive campaign of false and misleading advertising by Gerber. CSPI once again accused Gerber of watering down their products with cheap fillers while maintaining that their products are nutritionally equal or even superior to competing brands. CSPI is asking that the FTC halt Gerber's campaign, fine the company, and require Gerber to run corrective advertising. CSPI did not target Heinz, as Heinz makes no advertising claims about nutritional superiority.

Since then, both Gerber and Heinz have announced that added sugars and starches will be removed from some products. Both claim that product changes are a result of parents' interests, not the criticism of consumer groups.

As with sugars, if you want to avoid added starches, it's important to compare brands and read ingredient lines. Earth's Best and Growing Healthy do not add starches to any of their products. Starches appear most often in dinners and desserts, and in some fruits, creamed vegetables, and meats.

Added salt

Added salt has long since come out of most baby foods. While absent from Earth's Best and Growing Healthy products, it can still be found in some Gerber, Beech-Nut, and Heinz dinners and other products intended for the older baby. However, the sodium level is generally much lower than what might be added to adult processed foods. For example, six-ounce servings of *Beech-Nut Table Time Macaroni and Cheese* and *Gerber Graduates Pasta Shells & Cheese* respectively contain 230 milligrams and 390 milligrams of sodium, while *Franco-American SpaghettiOs* contains about 1,000 milligrams.

Added vitamin C

Vitamin C fortification is found in juices, fruits, jarred cereals, and desserts. In many cases, fortification is at 45 percent of the DV. (Some manufacturers stated that this level was chosen years back and continued for historical reasons.) Juices are typically fortified to 100 percent of the DV.

In a couple of Growing Healthy's fruits, fortification approaches 400 percent of the DV. When asked why, Growing Healthy responded that the company needs to be competitive with the rest of the market, and that, in their opinion, babies need this level of fortification. A more likely reason for the heavy dose of vitamin C is to prevent discoloration of the fruits. While babies do not require excess amounts of vitamin C in their baby foods (breast milk and formula have adequate amounts, although cow's milk is low), the amount found in baby foods is not considered toxic. However, excessive amounts are not recommended either.

Food categories

For this report, we looked primarily at eight food categories—cereals, juices, fruits, vegetables, meats, dinners, desserts, and other foods—comparing the brands on the basis of the key nutrients each product had to offer and the ingredients the products contain.

Cereals

Commercial infant cereals are precooked and fortified to supplement the nutrients in breast milk or formula. (We did not look at any commercial adult cereals or homemade versions, since they were not appropriate alternatives.)

Infant cereals are usually a baby's first solid food, since they are good sources of energy and supply many vitamins and minerals. Pediatricians generally recommend single-grain cereals, such as rice, for infants so food intolerances can be easily identified. Wheat and mixed-grain cereals, which are more likely to cause allergic reactions, are introduced later.

There are many types of grains used in baby cereals (e.g., rice, wheat, oat, barley, corn, rye, millet, mixed), and the selection is further increased by the addition of fruits, and for some, three available forms: dry, jarred, or frozen.

Dry cereals require the addition of breast milk, formula, juice, or water. The nutrition panels do not include the nutrients provided by these added liquids. All (except Growing Healthy) are enriched with iron, since some infants and young children are vulnerable to iron-deficiency anemia. Other than Earth's Best, which incorporates whole grains into their formulations and therefore does not enrich, they all contain added B vitamins. Cereals from Gerber, Beech-Nut, and Heinz claim added calcium. In addition, Gerber, Beech-Nut, and Heinz add vitamin E to selected cereals. Other than cereals for beginners, most of Gerber's cereals contain added sugars.

Perhaps because of the convenience, jarred cereals to be served as is (warmed if desired) have increased in number. As with the dry cereals, all but Earth's Best contain added B vitamins and iron, and most contain added vitamin C. Both Gerber and Heinz add sugar, whereas Beech-Nut does not.

Growing Healthy's frozen cereals contain added B vitamins and vitamin C. Both Growing Healthy and some of the Earth's Best's cereals for beginners are multi-ingredient cereals (e.g., *Earth's Best Plums, Bananas & Rice*), which are not recommended as a first food for infants just starting solid foods. Rather, they should be offered once baby is known to tolerate all the individual ingredients (in this case, the rice, bananas, and plums) in the product.

Juices

Infant juices are one of the most popular baby foods. Other than the standards (apple, pear, grape), many combinations of juices, including Gerber's tropical, yogurt-containing, and fruit/vegetable varieties, are being offered.

Both Gerber and Beech-Nut offer juices with added calcium. These and the yogurt-containing juices are marketed toward those babies who don't drink enough milk/formula. However, it's important to stress that juice should not be a substitute for milk/formula, since juice does not contribute much of anything nutritionally to a baby's diet, other than vitamin C.

Fortification of all juices with vitamin C is typically to 100 percent of the DV. One can replace baby juice with adult juices (diluted with water if desired), although many adult juices are not vitamin-C fortified to the same extent. Regardless, baby will probably get enough vitamin C from other foods.

 Avoid putting baby to bed with a bottle of juice or milk. As baby dozes, the natural sugars and acids from the liquid linger in the mouth and can cause tooth decay.

Baby orange juice, which is somewhat acidic and can produce allergenic reactions, is usually introduced once baby is older. The combination fruit/vegetable juices typically have ample amounts of vitamin A.

Fruits

Fruits are usually introduced after cereals; hence, there are several baby foods that incorporate fruits with cereals. Most of the manufacturers claim that bananas are the most popular fruit (and most popular product overall), even though the number of different fruit combinations offered is close to 30.

Fruits are popular among infants because they are sweet. While there is less fruit in products containing added sugars (and/or starches), their overall nutritional profile, when compared with the others, is similar.

All manufacturers fortify most products to 45 percent of the DV for vitamin C, although certain fruits (e.g., prunes and plums) are not fortified. The orange-colored fruits (e.g., apricots and peaches) and prunes are often high sources of vitamin A.

As with its cereals, Earth's Best offers multi-ingredient fruits for beginners. Gerber's *Graduates* line offers diced fruit for the older baby, which is similar to unsweetened canned fruit, although these products contain smaller-size pieces.

Vegetables

Most vegetables are good sources of vitamin A, and peas and legumes contain more protein and B vitamins than most other vegetables. None are important sources of vitamin C, and few are fortified. Only a few vegetables contain added sugars, starches, or salt.

Whereas some canned vegetables (e.g., sweet potatoes and carrots) can be easily mashed for babies, vegetables such as peas and corn for young babies must be pulverized in a blender or run through a baby-food grinder to separate out the skins or hulls.

Additionally, certain vegetables are not suitable for babies. The higher fiber vegetables, such as broccoli and brussels sprouts, may give a baby gas.

Earth's Best offers multi-ingredient vegetable products for beginners. Gerber offers slightly salted diced vegetables, which look similar to some canned vegetables, for the older baby.

Vegetables, especially the creamed type, sometimes contain dairy products like milk and butter. Parents of babies sensitive to dairy products (those who are lactose intolerant or allergic to the proteins found in milk) should read all the labels to avoid these foods.

Wheat is listed as an ingredient in some of the mixed vegetables we checked. Since some babies may be sensitive to wheat, these vegetables should be avoided or introduced later, when the baby is older.

Meats

Meats are better sources of protein, iron, zinc, and the B vitamins than most other baby foods. Six types are offered: beef, chicken, ham, lamb, turkey, and veal.

Starches (modified) are added only to Gerber's meats, which mandates that the products be labeled "with gravy," as opposed to "with broth." Growing Healthy's meats are generally substantially higher in protein and fat than the other meats.

 It is always important to check the expiration dates on the packages of baby food (and all dated products). All but Growing Healthy have open-date coding. According to the manufacturers, the shelf life of the unopened products is from one to three years. Opened jars of food should be used within two to three days.

The salted meat sticks from Gerber are considerably higher in sodium than other baby meats, and they also contain added sugar. Meat sticks and, for that matter, hot dogs are dangerous even for older babies to eat, since their shape and pliability can form a plug, blocking off a baby's air passage. A parent must closely supervise a child eating these (and, in fact, all) foods, or wait before serving them until the child can properly chew such foods.

Parents may choose to prepare home-cooked meats instead of buying their baby-food counterparts. However, they must be pureed or minced to a consistency suitable for a baby.

Home-cooked meats are usually cheaper. A serving of beef or chicken, the meats Americans most commonly eat, should cost less than the commercial baby-food servings. On the other hand, prices of less-common meats, such as lamb and veal, may be cheaper in the baby-food version.

Dinners

There is a tremendous selection of products in this category, since about one-fourth of the baby foods on the market are dinners. Following the eating trends of the adult population, there has been an increase in the number of pasta dinners, as well as the introduction of nonmeat/vegetarian dinners.

These products typically combine meat, vegetables, noodles, and, occasionally, fruits. Many contain added starches or flours (Gerber, Beech-Nut, and a few Heinz dinners also contain added sugars and salt), so a baby may get less (but still adequate) nutritive value from some of these dinners than if a jar of straight meat and a jar of straight vegetables were served. Manufacturers have obviously responded to this concern, because Gerber, followed by Beech-Nut and Heinz, now offers dinners where, for some, the only ingredients, other than water for processing, are a meat and a vegetable or fruit. (Gerber's line is called *Simple Recipe*, Beech-Nut's is *Delicious Duos*, and Heinz's is *Simple & Delicious*.)

Some dinners that contain cheese are slightly higher in sodium than those dinners that do not contain cheese. While Gerber's and Beech-Nut's microwaveable dinners for older babies contain even more sodium, it is substantially less than some of the canned Chef Boyardee products.

Desserts

As with desserts for adults, desserts for babies offer little nutritionally. However, some, such as the Earth's Best's yogurts and some puddings, are good sources of calcium. (Earth's Best's breakfast yogurts also do not contain added sugars or starches.) All, except the puddings, are fortified with vitamin C.

Other foods

Most of the foods in this category are Gerber products: sauces for pasta and rice, and snacks, such as zwieback toast, cookies, and pretzels, for the older baby.

Both Gerber and Beech-Nut offer fluoridated water, designed to prepare formula, to be mixed with juices, or to serve as a drink. It's possible to get too much fluoride, so consult your pediatrician before adding this element to baby's diet.

Beech-Nut offers chicken soup, although apparently the consistency of the soup is more like that of a jarred dinner than a soup. (Feeding soup to a baby would be difficult.)

Choking on food

Babies and young children can choke to death on a variety of foods. Sometimes the food gets stuck in their throats, sometimes the food goes down the wrong pipe and blocks their air passages, and sometimes the choking happens when they vomit food.

Statistics reported in the *Journal of the American Medical Association* pointed to hot dogs as the most dangerous food for babies. Of the 100 choking deaths of children under four that were studied, 17 were caused by hot dogs. Nuts were next most dangerous, causing eight deaths. Seven deaths were caused by candy and grapes, seven by cookies and biscuits, six by carrots, five by apples, and four each by beans, bread, popcorn, and meat. Other foods on the list included macaroni and noodles, peanut butter, cheese, chewing gum, and shrimp.

The message is clear: Babies can choke on almost anything, so feeding time should be closely supervised. Many baby-food labels don't warn parents about this. Parents should use common sense about which foods to give their baby, and stay close by while baby is eating. Hot dogs, a particular problem, should be sliced lengthwise into thin strips before serving.

Allergens

The estimated incidence of food allergies is less than 1 percent for the general population but from 2 to 4 percent for babies and young children. Some babies are more prone to food allergies than others, but for all babies it is best to introduce new foods one at a time, at intervals of a week or so. That makes it much easier to identify the specific food for which allergies might exist.

Some symptoms of food allergies are diarrhea, wheezing, vomiting, skin rashes, and watery eyes. An adverse reaction is most likely to occur within 24 to 48 hours of exposure to the food, although an immediate response is also possible.

Although all foods can cause allergic reactions, those foods that are more likely to cause them, and that are also found in baby foods, are dairy products, egg whites, grains such as wheat, legumes such as soy and peanuts, tomato products, and citrus fruits.

Beginner foods will generally not contain these potential allergens. They are more likely to show up in wheat-containing cereals, dinners, and desserts. However, especially if a child is prone to food allergies, the ingredient lists of all labels should be checked. If a baby is suspected of having an allergic response to a food, a pediatrician should be contacted. The doctor will probably take the child off the offending food for a period of time, and reintroduce it once the baby is older.

Pesticides

In July 1995, the Environmental Working Group and the National Campaign for Pesticide Policy Reform released results of tests conducted on baby foods from Gerber, Beech-Nut, and Heinz. Half the products they tested contained pesticides, although the levels detected were well below (ten to one hundred times less) the federal limits, which are generally based on toxicity data for adults, not children.

The objective of this report was to urge the government to set limits for babies and children. Indeed, these organizations were hoping to put pressure on Congress, which is considering changing pesticide laws to make them less stringent.

One important piece of information not included in the report was the levels of pesticides found in raw fruits and vegetables (unwashed and unpeeled) that might be used to make homemade baby food—of special interest to parents worried about pesticides in commercial products. In fact, more types and greater levels of pesticide residues are generally found in nonorganic fruits and vegetables from supermarkets than in commercially processed baby foods.

According to the pesticide policy statements issued by the five baby-food manufacturers, concerted efforts are being made to maintain the lowest achievable levels of pesticides in their finished products. (We did not test these products for pesticides.) Beech-Nut, for example, sets its own standards at 10 percent of the government tolerances. Even Earth's Best—the organic brand—did not claim to contain lower levels of pesticides in their products compared with their competitors.

A sensible approach to making your own

Commercial baby food makes sense when the family has sent out for pizza, but it seems silly to sit baby down with a jar of mixed dinner while everyone else enjoys fresh-baked chicken and steamed vegetables. We recommend feeding baby the family's food when practical, when baby is of the appropriate age, and when it's convenient to prepare.

Homemade baby food can be cheaper than the kind you buy, and it may be quite convenient. Although we've found that commercial baby foods usually compare favorably to fresh foods if you simply count up the quantity of appropriate vitamins and minerals, high temperatures involved in processing can destroy some trace nutrients that remain in carefully prepared home-cooked foods. Further, when you do your own mashing and chopping, you have control over variety and texture.

CHECKING FOR SAFE BABY-FOOD JARS

To help ensure that products you feed your baby are free of glass or any other foreign particles, the FDA offers the following advice:

◆ Don't buy a sticky or stained jar of baby food. A jar in that condition is either cracked or has been in a case with broken jars.

◆ All baby-food jars have a depressed area, or "button," in the center of the lid. Reject any jars with the button popped out.

◆ Listen carefully when you open a glass jar. You should hear a characteristic "whoosh" or "pop" when you break the vacuum seal. A grating sound may indicate glass particles stuck under the lid.

◆ If the jar is hard to open, don't tap it with a utensil or bang it against a hard surface. Instead, run it under warm water for a few minutes to loosen the lid's seal.

◆ Always examine the food when you transfer it to a feeding dish.

◆ If you suspect something is wrong with a jar of baby food, call it to the attention of the manager at the store where you bought the food, or contact the manufacturer.

Making food for baby doesn't require a big production, but you should be sure to keep all your tools and work spaces as clean as possible. Wash dishes, pots, and silverware with hot, soapy water, and rinse with water as hot as possible. Plastic dishes and utensils should get an extra cleaning, since tiny cuts or other damaged surfaces can trap foods and bacteria. Wash your hands with soap and warm water as well.

When you're cooking food, make sure you don't put your tasting spoon back into the food or into the baby's mouth. Feed the baby from a serving dish, not from a storage container. And don't store the cooked food for more than a few days. (Extra food can easily be frozen and stored in ice cube trays.)

All fruits and vegetables should be washed and peeled; seeds, if any, should be removed. Take the skin and excess fat off meat, and debone it *before* you cook it. Otherwise, especially with chicken, it's hard to find all the small bones. Taking the bones out before cooking also assures you that bacteria from dirty hands will be destroyed by the heat of cooking.

Meats and vegetables should be baked, broiled, or steamed. Steaming (even with a microwave) retains the most nutrients. If you do boil fruits or vegetables, use as little water as possible. If you're feeding baby what you feed the rest of your family, separate out the baby's portion before you add sugar or seasonings. And if you buy frozen or canned fruits and vegetables (frozen is recommended over canned), use those with no added salt or sugar.

A blender or food processor is obviously a boon for mashing and chopping, but you really don't need special equipment. Many cooked foods can be mashed finely enough by hand. Add formula, juice, or even the cooking water to thin the food. If you do use a processor or blender, note that vegetables puree best in large quantities and meats in small ones. Use the "puree" setting when the baby is little; as baby grows, switch to "chop" or "grind" for a coarser consistency.

You may be able to buy a special food mill in the infant section of a department store to grind fruits, vegetables, and soft-cooked meats. The mill strains as it grinds, so it's useful for separating the hulls from foods like corn or peas.

There are a few home-cooked foods to avoid in the early months. Certain vegetables—spinach, celery, lettuce, radishes, carrots, beets, turnips, and collard greens—shouldn't be fed to babies younger than three or four months old. (That's too young to feed babies solid food, anyway.) Those vegetables, bought fresh, may contain excessive nitrate, which can be converted to nitrite in the stomach of very young infants. Nitrite inhibits the blood's ability to carry oxygen.

Although honey is perfectly safe for adults and for children more than a year old, it should never be given to infants. Honey sometimes contains spores of the bacteria that causes botulism, a deadly form of food poisoning. Adults and children pass these spores on without harm, but infants haven't yet developed the proper defense mechanisms. The bacteria can multiply in a baby's intestines, with potentially fatal results.

Price

Heinz is the least expensive brand, costing up to about 10 cents less per package than comparably priced Gerber and Beech-Nut products. According to Heinz, the company's aim is to price their products 10 percent below Gerber's, which is achievable because of Heinz's minimal advertising expenses.

Earth's Best costs about 30 cents (or more) per package more than Gerber or Beech-Nut. Increased costs can be attributed to:

◆ the expense needed to farm organically (for instance, manpower costs)
◆ costly ingredients like chestnuts; they also do not add the cheaper sugars or starches to their products
◆ the cost of running a small business

It will be interesting to see if Earth's Best's prices will change now that it has been acquired by Heinz.

Growing Healthy products will cost the consumer about double what they will pay for Gerber or Beech-Nut products. Like Earth's Best, their products contain no added sugars and starches, and they too are a small business. Additionally, they have to deal with the costs associated with processing and distributing frozen foods.

There are several ways that the consumer can save money when feeding baby:

◆ **Make homemade baby food.** It is cheaper to mash a banana and to grind beef or chicken than to purchase commercially processed baby food. However, consumers must be reminded of the pesticide issue associated with raw produce and the proper sanitation techniques required in preparing homemade baby food. Depending on the homemade food, convenience also plays a role.
◆ **Substitute adult foods for some baby foods.** One can easily puree or grind most canned vegetables and fruits. If added sugars or salt are concerns, ingredient lines need to be read and compared. It is also easy to replace baby applesauce with adult applesauce and baby

juices with adult juices (watered down, if desired). If vitamin-C fortification is an issue (adult foods may not be fortified with as much vitamin C), label comparisons will have to be made.

◆ **Buy economy-size juices and dry cereals.** When buying these products, make sure they are used up before they expire. According to one manufacturer, opened juices will last about a week and dry cereals about a month. Single-serve, aseptically packed juices will always be the most expensive.

◆ **Use dry rather than jarred cereals.** Although they may be slightly less convenient, in that they require some preparation, they are much cheaper.

◆ **Switch to adult foods earlier.** Some manufacturers market line extensions, hoping that children up to age four or older will eat them. Since these products can be more expensive than adult food, switching at an earlier age (about one year is average) could help save on food bills.

◆ **Use coupons and take advantage of supermarket sales.**

Recommendations

The five commercial baby-food brands are nutritionally comparable so which brand to use is a decision that needs to be made based on other factors.

If cost is the driving factor, typically the Heinz brand is the obvious choice (assuming it's available in one's geographic area). Beech-Nut and Gerber will cost slightly more. But sales or coupons for individual models may alter this overall choice.

The Earth's Best brand is for people interested in supporting the development and viability of organic agriculture for future generations. While Earth's Best's foods cost substantially more, they also contain no added sugars, starches, or salt.

Growing Healthy may appeal to those looking for natural baby foods that are minimally processed and contain no added sugars, starches, and salt. Frozen baby food may be considered more convenient for some, but there will be a need for additional freezer storage space. The consumer should expect to pay much more for this brand.

Homemade baby food is yet another option. Although it can be less costly, it may also be less convenient.

Whatever the decision, it is important that the consumer use the nutritional and ingredient line information on the labels to compare brands and to select a wholesome and varied diet for baby.

Feeding accessories

Baby-food warmers can be useful for defrosting small portions of frozen homemade baby food. Most models come with a large suction cup on the base that helps to hold the dish in place while baby is eating. Some have pull-up tabs that make removal from the table or tray easier, or you can simply use your fingernail or the tip of a table knife to break the suction.

Our suggestion is to buy a dish that has a wide mouth for pouring in hot water and a permanently affixed cap on the water hole so that baby can't pull it off and possibly choke on it. Choose a model with steeply sloped sides, since it makes spooning up baby food easier.

Toddler eating time can be quite a mess. That's why bibs were invented. Bibs can be bought in disposable foam or paper versions and in more permanent washable, vinyl-backed terry or wipe-clean molded plastic. The disposable foam versions are lightweight, absorbent, and easy to store in a purse or diaper bag for use in restaurants or while traveling. Of the more permanent versions, the flexible, molded-plastic styles with a wide trough at the bottom are the most convenient. They don't have to be laundered, they can be easily wiped clean, they can be used over and over, and they catch liquids before they can reach the clothes.

Listings: Feeding accessories

Note: These products were not tested by Consumers Union. This alphabetical listing by category does not include all models available but rather is a selection of some widely distributed models. Descriptions are derived from authors' observations and manufacturers' claims.

MODEL	DESCRIPTION
BIBS	
Baby Bjorn Soft Bib *Regal & Lager* Model BB-710/Small; BB-720/Large, $5.90	Soft, flexible, molded plastic bib with a gutter pocket to collect liquid and food spills.
Parenting Concepts Turtle Tummy Bib Model GTTB, $12	A generous terry towel with a stretch turtleneck opening to cover baby from head to toe during mealtime. Available in a variety of colors.
Remond Le Neat Bib Model 2410, $5	Molded plastic bib with adjustable rear tab. Food-catcher trough at base of bib helps contain spills.

Listings: **Feeding accessories** *continued*

MODEL	DESCRIPTION
FEEDING DISHES, SPOONS, TRAINING CUPS, AND MISCELLANEOUS ITEMS	
Evenflo Food Warmer Dish Model 62250, $3.50	A brightly colored plastic feeding dish with three sections. The bottom half of the dish holds warm water to keep food warm. It is dishwasher-safe and has a child-resistant plug and suction cup on base that holds the dish securely to the table.
First Years No-Tip Bowl Model 1750, $5	A molded bowl in bright blue and red with an inward-curving lid that minimizes spills and tipping. Comes with plastic lid for storage.
First Years Tumble Mates Trainer Tumblers Model 1664, 4/$5	Four plastic cups with snap-on sipper spouts. Can be turned upside down but won't drip. Dishwasher-safe on top rack.
Gerber Hot Water Feeding Dish Model 76035, $8	A three-compartment dish. Hot water in the base of unit helps to keep food warm. Suction-cup base prevents spills. Molded of high-impact plastic; dishwasher-safe.
Kids II Baby Susan Revolving Baby Food Organizer Model 402-12, $10	Plastic lazy Susan with specially designed columns keeps baby food jars stationary to prevent sliding and breaking. Storage in center for feeding accessories.
Omron Happy Baby Food Grinder Model 700A, $10	Baby-food maker works manually; rotating handle connected to a blade under a strainer. An internal cylinder forces food upward into 4-ounce feeding dish on top. All parts are dishwasher-safe and can be sterilized. Comes with a long-handled, plastic feeding spoon.
Omron MagMag Advanced Training Cup System Model D785, $16	Two double-handled cups, two silicone nipples that fit on the cup lids, nipple covers, a plastic straw unit, a drinking spout, a slotted lid, and a no-leak travel lid. All parts except straws are washable in top rack of dishwater.
Playskool Microwave Warm 'n' Service Dish Model 3470, $4.30	Three compartments and removable spatter lid with easy-to-use handle. (Caution: Splatter and burn potential from overheating. Follow manufacturer's directions for microwave times. Not to be used for cooking or with small amounts of food, or heated for over three minutes.)
Prince Lionheart Stay Warm Bowl Model 2504, $6	Steep-sided, brightly colored bowl with a suction-grip base and release tab. Warm water can be poured into the base at the bottom and closed with a stopper to keep foods warm.
Remond Le Floating Fish Dish Model 2105, $17	See-through, nonelectric warming dish with plastic fish, turtles, and boats that float in the water in the dish. A suction-cup base holds the dish in place. Comes with a funnel for easy filling.
Sassy Feeding Bowl with Soft Bite Spoon Model 316, $4	Small, two-section baby-food bowl fits easily in the palm of an adult's hand for spoon-feeding. Thumb handle allows parent to hold bowl securely in one hand. Comes with a long-handled, "soft bite" spoon with cushioned bowl. Dishwasher- and microwave-safe.
Sassy Stay-Put Bowl Model 320, $9	Four suction cups prevent child from grabbing and overturning bowl. Bowl can be used alone, or with a removable sectioned-plate insert for smaller, separated servings of food. Plastic snap-on lid for storage. All pieces are microwave- and dishwasher-safe.

12

Gates

Adjustable gates that fit into doorways are often used as barricades to wandering toddlers. Manufacturers often call them security gates or safety gates, but they are not really very safe at all. If you buy a gate, purchase one that installs permanently with hardware into the door frame, and don't depend on any gate to guard your child at the top of a stairway. We found just one hardware-mounted gate that we can recommend for use at the top of a stairway, the *KidCo Safeway Gate G-20*, since it does not swing out over the stairs. All other hardware-mounted gates do swing out. So that you don't injure yourself, as many adults have already done, we also advise you not to attempt to step over these gates.

There are basically two types of gates on the market: those that mount with such hardware as screws and those that merely rely on the pressure applied to rubber bumpers to stay in place. We found that hardware-mounted gates, if properly installed, stayed in place better than pressure-mounted gates or "hardware" gates used as "pressure" gates. A more recent gate design is called a step-through, walk-through, or swing gate.

Pressure gates

Pressure gates rely on the pressure applied to bumpers to hold them in an opening. They usually have two panels that slide past each other to achieve the required dimensions of the door opening. A pressure bar or other locking mechanism then supplies the force that acts to wedge the gate in place.

Although pressure gates are convenient to install, it does not take much of a push to dislodge them. And those that hold a bit better will work out of the opening after awhile.

At best, you can use them where safety is not a major concern, such as in a doorway segregating two areas or at the bottom of a stairway to discourage a child from venturing up the stairs. But remain nearby to rush to the rescue of an adventurous child.

Manufacturing requirements

A voluntary standard for gates was developed by the American Society for Testing and Materials (ASTM) in cooperation with the Juvenile Products Manufacturers Association (JPMA). All the gates tested are certified to ASTM F1004.

The following represents the major requirements of that standard:

General requirements address
◆ Finish of parts and type of fasteners

Performance requirements address
◆ Size of openings
◆ Height of gate
◆ Strength of top rails and framing components (includes vertical dislodgement test)
◆ Bottom spacing
◆ Configuration of the uppermost edge

Labeling and warning statement requirements for
◆ A permanent and conspicuous label advising to install according to manufacturer's instructions
◆ Label stating intended for use with children from 6 to 24 months
◆ Warning that the product will not necessarily prevent all accidents
◆ Warning to install with the locking mechanism on the side away from the child (applies to pressure-mounted gates with locks anywhere except on the top of the gate, provided the lock is a dual-action lock or requires two distinct actions to unlock)
◆ Warning never to leave child unattended

Note: The current version of this standard does not require a minimum level of resistance to horizontal dislodgement nor a requirement that hardware-mounted gates must not swing out over a stairway. Also absent from the standard is a requirement that the top edge of the gate must be free of protrusions that can cause clothing or strings to entangle. Efforts are under way, however, to address these shortcomings.

Accordion gates: clear and present danger

Old-fashioned, accordion-style wooden gates that open to form diamond-shaped spaces with wide V's at the top have trapped children's heads and necks, causing death by strangulation. New accordion-style gates create smaller and much less dangerous openings, but some models have wooden tabs at the top that could ensnare a child's clothing or pacifier string.

Following an agreement with the Consumer Product Safety Commission (CPSC) in January 1985, the manufacturers of child safety gates permanently halted production of old-fashioned accordion gates like the one pictured below. Unfortunately, the agreement did not include a recall of the 10 to 15 million accordion gates still in use, or even of the smaller number that were still available in many retail outlets. A check in the New York area in 1993 found that these unsafe gates were available in some stores, including pet supply and hardware stores. They are also a staple item at yard sales.

The CPSC allowed those gates to remain in homes and stores in deference to their manufacturers' balance sheets, even though the CPSC's files show that accordion "safety" gates have been responsible for serious accidents, including fatalities, to children between 9 and 30 months of age. We strongly recommend against a gate of this type. If you already have one, replace it with one of the models free of entrapments or entanglements.

Accordion gates. An old unsafe accordion gate (left) and a more recent version (right). Note that tabs at the top of the newer gate can ensnare a child's clothing or pacifier string and result in accidental hanging.

Vertical slats

Even though federal regulations control the spacing between slats on cribs, there are no regulations or industry standards for the spacing in gates that have panels made of vertical slats or bars. Fortunately, no gates we tested seriously exceeded the recommended $2^3/_8$-inch spacing for cribs. Spacing in the 2 to $2^1/_2$-inch range, however, is the perfect dimension for entrapping a child.

Additional hazards

Active toddlers can climb over some gates, especially models that have widely spaced mesh or other means that allow a toehold. Fingers, toes, arms, or legs could get caught in the mesh or in between the sliding panels of some models. Several gates have hinged joints that can pinch fingers and sharp hardware that can result in cuts.

CAUTION
Pressure gates, or any gates for that matter, should never be trusted to protect a baby at any location, especially at the top of a stairway. There's no substitute for constant parental supervision.

Small parts, such as screws and mounting heads, can break off or loosen. Babies love to put small things into their mouths; if they ingest, inhale, or choke on these parts, they can suffocate—an all-too-common tragedy.

The gates we tested are relatively free of those hazards, but those we did not test or older gates can be hazardous.

Alternative to gates

As an alternative to a gate, you might consider installing an actual door, a screen door, or a half-door with a latch that is out of your child's reach. At the entrance to your toddler's bedroom, installing an additional screen door with a latch on the outside at your height, for example, would allow you and your child to be in continual visual contact while providing assurance that the child is not going to tumble down a stairway. This arrangement may also prevent your tot from roaming the house in the early morning hours while you're sleeping.

If you do install such a door, experts suggest adding a strong self-closing mechanism, particularly if there is a potential for injury in the area to be blocked off, such as a stairway leading to a basement. Unfortunately, a baby's fingers can be injured if a door with a self-closing mechanism slams too quickly. As a safeguard, install a pneumatic or hydraulic door-closer that comes with a pressure adjustment to slow the door down in the last few seconds prior to closing—and keep an eye on the child.

Rules for buying and using gates

Don't use a pressure-mounted gate where safety is a major concern. Tests have shown that pressure-mounted gates can dislodge under child-level forces. They are recommended for segregating same-level rooms.

Check finish and construction. Inspect hardware for sharp edges. Be sure wooden surfaces are smooth and splinter-free, as well as made with rounded rather than sharply squared edges. Vertical slats

Swing-out gate

Vertical wooden slats

Plastic mesh

Large-opening plastic mesh

or rods that are not flexible should be no more than 2 ⅜ inches apart.

Avoid gates that pose climbing hazards. Don't purchase a gate that could give your child a foothold, such as a wide-holed mesh gate.

Take measurements of the width of the opening with you when shopping. Measure the opening where you plan to install the gate, and don't buy a gate you'll have to extend beyond the width specified for the gate.

Follow the manufacturer's instructions. How and where you install the gate can make a difference. Follow installation instructions carefully and remember to check the hardware frequently.

Never use a pressure-mounted gate or hardware-mounted gate that swings out over the top of the stairs. No pressure-mounted gate tested was secure from dislodgement, and a hardware-mounted gate that swings out over the stairs is equally dangerous.

Place the pressure bar away from the child. Gates with a pressure bar should be positioned so that the child cannot tamper with it.

Never leave more than one to two inches clearance between the floor and the gate bottom. A large gap can let the child push or slip underneath the gate.

Keep large toys away. Such items can be used by the child to climb over the gate.

Discontinue use of the gate when the child reaches age two. Stop using the gate when the child reaches a height of about 36 inches or weighs 30 pounds (at about 24 months). A good rule of thumb is that the gate should be no less in height than three-quarters of your child's height.

Avoid buying or using gates with openings or protrusions at the top edge. Clothing, necklaces, strings around the neck, or sweatshirt drawstrings can get snared and cause strangulation.

Never leave the child unattended!

INSTALLATION TIPS

Hardware-mounted gates can be more reliable than pressure-mounted gates, but even hardware-mounted gates are not always safe. If an opening's sides are plasterboard without accessible wood backing, the gate's hardware may not hold securely. For the hardware to be effective, the plasterboard must have wood studs directly behind it. Use screws at least ⅝-inch longer than the screws supplied with most gates.

Recommendations

Hardware-mounted gates are relatively safe from dislodgement if properly installed and used, whereas pressure-mounted gates dislodge. That relegates pressure-mounted gates to segregating same-level rooms or areas where safety is not a major concern.

All of the gates tested can close off conventional door openings or openings 26 to 42 inches in width. Four hardware-mounted models are for openings from 60 to 108 inches.

Selecting the appropriate type and size of gate is the first decision you have to make. You may decide that you need more than one gate for the different applications as outlined below.

To opt for the top-rated but expensive *KidCo* models can burn a hole in your pocketbook, but if you need a gate for the top of the stairs you may have no other choice. The *KidCo Safeway Gate G-20*, at $60, is the only gate we tested that did not dislodge and at the same time does not swing out over the stairs, if installed correctly. (See upper left photo on p. 157.)

The other hardware-mounted gates are for installations where safety may be a concern, but they should not be used at the top of the stairs. Among those models are some we think are good values for your money. One such gate is the $19 *Gerry Baby Wood Slat Security Gate 1048*. It's simple to install and use, but those who continuously have to use the clasp may wish they had purchased the *Fisher-Price AutoLock Gate 9263* at $35.

To install any hardware-mounted gate requires making holes in a door frame or wall. Pressure-mounted gates may merely mar the door frame or walls. The *KidCo Gateway G-10* at $70 to $90 was the safest and most convenient pressure-mounted gate we tested. That gate swings open and closed with one hand, an important consideration with baby around. The other gates were less convenient, even the *Gerry Baby Soft Gate Nylon Mesh 524* at $22. The *Gerry* held reasonably well for a pressure gate, but you needed to use two hands as well as to bend down to near-floor level for opening and closing the opening. That gate is the only really compact gate for traveling (it rolls into a package 28 inches long and 3 inches in diameter).

Not recommended are all three *Seymour* hardware-mounted accordion gates because they have a top edge with openings and protrusions that can snare clothing, strings around a child's neck, or sweatshirt drawstrings, etc., with resultant risk of strangulation. (See cautions on accordion gates on p. 155.)

Ratings: Gates

Rated by type, hardware-mounted models were rated above pressure-mounted models because the latter was more prone to dislodging accidentally. Within type, we rated the models in order of decreasing overall score. That score is based on results of a panel test and laboratory tests. A panel of parents judged each model on ease of following the instructions, ease of installing, opening, and closing. Laboratory tests included tests for dislodgement and overall safety, as well as our judgments of structural integrity (or durability).

Scores for opening and scores for closing were at least Good (◖) or Very Good (◕) for all models. The *Fisher-Price AutoLock Gate 9263* and both *Kidco* models had Excellent (●) scores.

All hardware-mounted gates had Excellent (●) scores for dislodgement. Among the pressure-mounted models, the *Kidco Gateway G-10* scored Good (◖). All other pressure-mounted models scored only "fair" or "poor."

For safety, all models scored at least Good (◖), except the *Seymour 13-036-60, 13-084-33, 13-108-33* accordion gate models. The hazardous protusions at the top edge that could cause entanglement of a child's clothing brought its score down to Poor (●).

MODEL, DESCRIPTION	COMMENTS, RECOMMENDATIONS	

HARDWARE-MOUNTED GATES

Fisher-Price Auto-Lock Gate Model 9263, $34.99 **Product description:** Panels (2) slide past each other. Panels have plastic frame, semirigid plastic mesh filler. **To close:** Swing closed. **To open:** Press button while squeezing lock, swing open in either direction.	**Comments:** • Covers an opening 28 to 42 inches wide. • Gate height is 27½ inches. • You'll need a drill and screwdriver. • Single-handed operation. • Gate can be opened with one hand and closes automatically by gently swinging closed; panelists liked operating this gate. • Gate can easily be lifted out of the opening by an adult. • Swings in either direction; great for opening between same-level areas but not recommended for use at top of stairs or step between levels. • Smooth at top. **Recommendation:** Excellent and most convenient gate tested. Ease of opening ◕. Ease of closing ◕. Secure from dislodging ◕. Safety ◕.
KidCo Safeway Gate Model G-20, $59.99 **Product description:** Panels (2) overlap and bolt together. Panels have metal top and bottom edges and vertical tubular metal bar fillers. **To close:** Swing closed and lift to set into lock bracket. **To open:** Lift, slide out of bracket, and swing open.	**Comments:** • Covers an opening 24¾ to 43½ inches wide. • Gate height is 30½ inches. • You'll need a drill and a screwdriver. Plastic wrench supplied. • Can be fine-tuned to fit uneven openings. • Single-handed operation. • Panelists noted that instructions are unnecessarily complicated. • Unidirectional swinging of gate can be selected to prevent swinging out over stairs. • Smooth at top. • Vertical bars discourage climbing; no foothold. • Can be used as window guard (not tested as window guard). **Recommendation:** An excellent gate. The only gate tested that may be mounted at top of stairs because it does not swing out over stairs. Ease of opening ◕. Ease of closing ◕. Secure from dislodging ◕. Safety ◕.

MODEL, DESCRIPTION	COMMENTS, RECOMMENDATIONS	E ⊖	VG ⊖	G ○	F ◑	P ●

Gerry Baby Wood Slat Security Gate
Model 1048, $18.99
Product description: Panels (2) slide past each other. Panels have wood frame and vertical nonclimbable wood slats as filler. **To close:** Swing closed, squeeze and engage lock. **To open:** Squeeze lock to disengage and swing open.

Comments: • Covers an opening 27 to 48 inches wide. • Gate height is 24 inches. • May require predrilling only. • Can be fine-tuned to fit slightly uneven openings. • Single-handed operation. • Gate can be quickly removed from opening by unclasping hinge locks. • Although gate can be opened and closed with one hand, panelists disliked the lock; it hurt their fingers. • Swings in either direction; great for opening between same-level areas, but not recommended for use at top of stairs or step between levels. • Smooth at top. • Vertical bars discourage climbing; no foothold. **Recommendation:** At $19, this gate is the best value for your money, but check to see if you can squeeze the locking clasps without experiencing pain. Ease of opening ⊖. Ease of closing ○. Secure from dislodging ⊖. Safety ⊖.

Seymour Expansion Gate
Model 13-0360, $19.99
Product description: Accordion all-wood gate with metal hardware. **To close:** Swing and slide closed, engage lock. **To open:** Disengage lock, swing and slide open.

Comments: • Comes in three models that cover different width openings: one regular-size model (#13-0360), 11 to 37 inches wide; an extrawide model (#13-108-33), 26 to 116 measured inches wide (108 inches stated); and another extrawide model (#13-084-33), 21¼ to 89 measured inches wide (84 inches stated). • Gate height is 30 to 33 inches. • You'll need a screwdriver and maybe a level. • Can be fine-tuned to fit slightly uneven openings. • Single-handed operation. • Although gate can be opened and closed with one hand, panelists disliked fidgeting with the lock. • Swings in either direction; great for opening between same-level areas, but not recommended for use at top of stairs or step between levels. **Recommendation:** Choose another gate, since strings and loose clothing can entangle at the protrusions on the top edge of this model. Ease of opening ⊖. Ease of closing ○. Secure from dislodging ⊖. Safety ●.

North States Super Gate III
Model 8615, $19.95
(Can be hardware-mounted or pressure-mounted)
Product description: Panels (2) slide past each other. Panels have plastic frame and filler. **To close:** Swing and slide closed (hardware mount); slide closed (pressure mount), set lever in lock tap. **To open:** Release lock lever, swing open (hardware mount); lift out of opening (pressure mount).

Comments: • Covers opening 26 to 42 inches wide. • Gate height is 26 inches. • You'll need a screwdriver to hardware-mount (no tools required for pressure mount). • Single-handed operation. • Although gate can be opened and closed with one hand, panelists noted difficult use of lock lever; a lot of hand strength required. • Swings in either direction by selecting hinge plate position; great for opening between same-level areas, but not recommended for use at top of stairs or step between levels. Although limited in swing direction when selecting opposite hinge plate location, gate can still swing slightly over a stairway. • Smooth at top. **Recommendation:** There are better choices. Our panelists disliked installation and the amount of hand strength needed to lock and unlock the gate. Ease of opening ⊖. Ease of closing ○. Secure from dislodging ⊖. Safety ⊖.

HARDWARE-MOUNTED MODELS FOR EXTRA-WIDE OPENINGS

Gerry Baby Extra Wide Expansion Gate
Model 160, $29.99
Product description: Accordion all-wood gate with metal hardware and rigid plastic at top edge. **To close:** Swing and slide closed, squeeze and engage lock. **To open:** Squeeze lock to disengage, and slide and swing open.

Comments: • Covers an opening 25 to 60 inches wide. • Gate height is 29 to 32 inches. • May require predrilling only. • Can be fine-tuned to fit slightly uneven openings. • Single-handed operation. • Gate can be quickly removed from opening by unclasping hinge locks. • Although gate can be opened and closed with one hand, panelists disliked the lock; it hurt their fingers. • Swings in either direction; great for opening between same-level areas, but not recommended for use at top of stairs or step between levels. • Smooth at top. **Recommendation:** An excellent gate, but check in the store to see if you can squeeze the locking clasps without experiencing pain. Ease of opening ⊖. Ease of closing ⊖. Secure from dislodging ⊖. Safety ○.

Ratings: Gates *continued*

MODEL, DESCRIPTION	COMMENTS, RECOMMENDATIONS	E ⊖	VG ⊖	G ○	F ◑	P ●

MODELS FOR EXTRA-WIDE OPENINGS *continued*

Seymour Keepsafe Expansion Gate
Model 13-108-33, $34.99

See *Seymour Expansion Gate*, p. 161. Ease of opening ⊖. Ease of closing ○. Secure from dislodging ⊖. Safety ●.

Seymour Keepsafe Expansion Gate
Model 13-084-33, $29.99

See *Seymour Expansion Gate*, p. 161. Ease of opening ⊖. Ease of closing ○. Secure from dislodging ⊖. Safety ●.

North States Super Gate V
Model 8645, $34.95.
(Model 8645 no longer available; new model designation is 8648.)
Product description:
Panels (4) slide past each other. Panels have plastic frame, filler, hinge, and lock strips. **To close:** Swing and slide closed, lift slightly, fit locking pegs into lock strip and press down. **To open:** Push down locking clip, lift slightly, slide and swing open.

Comments: • Covers an opening 22 to 62 inches wide. • Gate height is 31 inches. • You'll need a drill and screwdriver. • Single-handed operation. • Gate can easily be lifted out of the opening by an adult. • Swings in either direction; great for opening between same-level areas, but not recommended for use at top of stairs or step between levels. • For somewhat easier opening and closing performance, hinge section and lock section should be offset in the opening (especially in a narrow opening); instructions fail to advise on this point. • Smooth at top. **Recommendation:** A good gate for wide openings. Gate slides and closes better in maximum-width opening than narrow opening and requires attention to proper alignment of hinge and lock rails during installation. Ease of opening ○. Ease of closing ○. Secure from dislodging ⊖. Safety ○.

PRESSURE-MOUNTED GATES

KidCo Gateway
Model G-10, $69.99
with G-6 Extension
+$19.99
Product description:
Fixed panel and swing-open/closed panel. Metal top and bottom edges with vertical tubular non-climbable metal bar fillers. **To close:** Swing closed, lift slightly, push down on lock lever at top edge of gate. **To open:** Depress secondary lock, move lock lever upward, lift slightly, swing open.

Comments: • Covers an opening 28 to 34 inches wide. • Gate height is 29½ inches. • Two wrenches supplied but no additional tools required. • Can be fine-tuned to fit slightly uneven openings. • Single-handed operation. • Panelists noted that instructions are unnecessarily complicated. • Smooth at top. • Vertical bars discourage climbing; no foothold. • Sticker noting Certification to ASTM F-1004 Safety Standard not encountered, but model listed in current JPMA directory for compliance with that standard. • For 36-inch opening you'll need to purchase Extension G-6,, $19.99. Wider extensions available. **Recommendation:** Excellent, highest rated pressure-mounted gate, but expensive. Very convenient gate, but instructions are unclear. Ease of opening ⊖. Ease of closing ⊖. Secure from dislodging ○. Safety ⊖.

MODEL, DESCRIPTION	COMMENTS, RECOMMENDATIONS	E ⊖	VG ⊖	G ○	F ◒	P ●

Gerry Baby Soft Gate Nylon Mesh
Model 524, $21.99
Product description: Fabric with metal poles that must be inserted in fabric sleeves. Nylon mesh filler. **To close:** Pull back telescoping poles, set and release poles. Must be performed at top edge and bottom edge of gate. **To open:** Pull back telescoping poles at top and bottom of gate and lift gate out of the opening.

Comments: • Covers an opening 27 to 42 inches wide. • Gate height is 27 inches. • No tools required. • Can be fine-tuned to fit slightly uneven openings. • Two-handed operation. • Smooth at top. • Sticker noting Certification to ASTM F-1004 Safety Standard not encountered, but model listed in current JPMA directory for compliance with that standard. **Recommendation:** Excellent gate. Great for travel, and fits well in very uneven openings. Ease of opening ⊖. Ease of closing ⊖. Secure from dislodging ◒. Safety ⊖.

Gerry Baby Quick-Release Gate
Model 222, $19.99
Product description: Panels (2) slide past each other. Panels have wood frame with plastic handle and plastic mesh filler. **To close:** After setting proper width, push down on top edge of gate. **To open:** Pull upward on handle and lift gate out of opening.

Comments: • Covers an opening 27 to 42 inches wide. • Gate height is 24 inches. • No tools required. • Can be fine-tuned to fit slightly uneven openings. • Single-handed operation. • Although possible to fully secure as well as remove gate with one hand, some strength is required. • Smooth at top. • After only a few uses, wood "sockets" at adjustment knobs broke and plastic locking cams broke off in some samples. • Warning/Instruction wording not visible when gate is in use, constituting a noncompliance with ASTM F-1004 Safety Standard. **Recommendation:** Good gate. Quick-release is the best part of this gate, although setting proper width (a one-time task) can be tedious. Ease of opening ⊖. Ease of closing ⊖. Secure from dislodging ◒. Safety ⊖.

Gerry Baby 4 Sure Pressure Gate
Model 525 (Sears), $17.99
Product description: Plastic filler with telescoping metal poles. **To close:** Pull back telescoping poles, set and release poles. Must be performed at top edge and bottom edge of gate. **To open:** Pull back telescoping poles and top and bottom of gate and lift gate out of the opening.

Comments: • Covers an opening 27 to 42 inches wide. • Gate height is 27 inches. • No tools required. • Two-handed operation. • Smooth at top. **Recommendation:** Good gate and fits well in very uneven openings. Ease of opening ⊖. Ease of closing ⊖. Secure from dislodging ●. Safety ⊖.

North States Super Gate III Model 8615, $19.95

See *North States Super Gate III*, p. 161. Ease of opening ⊖. Ease of closing ⊖. Secure from dislodging ●. Safety ⊖.

Ratings: Gates *continued*

MODEL, DESCRIPTION	COMMENTS, RECOMMENDATIONS	

PRESSURE-MOUNTED GATES *continued*

Gerry Baby Plastic Mesh Security Gate
Model 202, $10.99
Product description: Panels (2) slide past each other. Panels have wood frame, soft plastic mesh filler. **To close:** Slide to fit opening, press lever bar down. **To open:** Lift lever bar, lift gate out of opening.

Comments: • Covers an opening 26 to 42 inches wide. • Gate height is 24 inches. • No tools required. • Two-handed operation. • Although gate can be opened and closed with one hand, panelists noted difficult use of lock lever; a lot of hand strength required. • Smooth at top. **Recommendation:** There are better choices. Lacks fine-tuning capacity for uneven openings and openings that cannot be selected on its locking mechanism. Ease of opening ⊖. Ease of closing ⊖. Secure from dislodging ●. Safety ○.

Seymour Guardmaster Security Gate
Model 13-276-55, $13.99
Product description: Panels (2) slide past each other. Panels have wood frame, soft plastic mesh filler. **To close:** Slide to fit opening, press lever bar down. **To open:** Lift lever bar, lift gate out of opening.

Comments: • Covers an opening 27 to 41 inches wide. • Gate height is 24 inches. • No tools required. • Two-handed operation. • Although gate can be opened and closed with one hand, panelists noted difficult use of lock lever; a lot of hand strength required. • Smooth at top. • Notched bar broke in one of our samples. **Recommendation:** There are better choices. Lacks fine-tuning capacity for uneven openings and openings that cannot be selected on its locking mechanism. Ease of opening ⊖. Ease of closing ⊖. Secure from dislodging ●. Safety ○.

Fisher-Price Quick-Lock Gate
Model 9262, $29.99
Product description: Panels (2) slide past each other. Plastic frame and filler. **To close:** Slide to fit opening, press lever bar down. **To open:** Lift lever bar, lift gate out of opening.

Comments: • Covers an opening 26 to 42 inches wide. • Gate height is 26 inches. • No tools required. • Can be fine-tuned to fit slightly uneven openings. • Two-handed operation. • Although gate can be opened and closed with one hand, panelists noted difficult use of lock lever; a lot of hand strength required. • Smooth at top. **Recommendation:** There are better choices. Gate is quite flexible and can therefore be easily dislodged. Ease of opening ⊖. Ease of closing ○. Secure from dislodging ●. Safety ⊖.

13

Hazard reduction and childproofing products

What poses a safety hazard to your baby in your home is different for each stage of your baby's development. For example, crib mobiles may be great for tiny newborns, but they become a strangulation hazard when your baby can sit up—between five and six months of age—so you have to remove them. Your diaper-changing table becomes more dangerous as your baby begins to squirm and roll over—after the first two months—especially if you fail to fasten the restraining belt or keep your hand on your baby. Staircases, household chemicals under the sink, and medicine cabinets loom as hazards once your baby starts to crawl and climb up on things, after about five months of age. And outdoor swimming pools and passing cars are hazardous to all self-propelled babies and preschoolers who lack the restraint and judgment of more mature children.

It's never too early to begin mapping a household plan for protecting your baby. The best way to start is to register for a CPR and first-aid course from the Red Cross or local "Y" or rescue squad. Then make emergency plans for handling accidents and fires, and make sure everyone in the house knows what to do by rehearsing for emergencies.

It's important to survey your home with a critical eye. Get down on your knees and go through each room so you can see things from a toddler's point of view. It will help you discover sharp corners and other dangers you may otherwise have missed.

Kitchen

Sharp knives, glass bottles and dishes, household chemicals under the sink, burning-hot cooking surfaces, electric appliances that can be pulled to the floor—your kitchen is an arsenal of danger! For maximum safety, keep baby out of the kitchen when you cook. Use a gate at the door, or put baby in a play yard or in a high chair out of harm's way.

Dishwasher. Dishwasher detergent can cause severe, disfiguring chemical burns to a child's mouth. Keep dishwashing detergent away from your baby.

Cabinets. Remove all detergents and chemicals from under the sink and place them in a locking closet, or up high enough so they can't be reached by your curious tot. Keep plastic bags and kitchen wraps out of reach, especially those that have packaging with sharp, serrated edges.

Small appliances. Babies are injured when they tug on cords and pull coffeemakers, food processors, toaster ovens, and other appliances down on top of themselves. Wrap up and fasten cords so they can't be reached by using twist ties, rubber bands, or by taping cords to the wall with duct tape. Unplug appliances when they're not in use. Coffeemakers have caused fires even when turned off.

Refrigerators. Every year children die needlessly in refrigerator suffocation accidents. Typically, parents move an old, unused refrigerator outside for pickup. Children playing hide-and-seek decide to climb inside and close the door, and suffocate before they can be rescued. Remove the doors from old refrigerators and store them facedown. In addition, keep small refrigerator magnets out of your baby's reach.

Ranges. Does the front door of your oven become hot enough to cause burns? Remember, a baby's skin burns a lot easier than yours. If your baby can reach the oven, and the oven door has a front window that gets really hot, or if you have an older model with poor insulation, consider replacing it with a newer model or using a microwave oven placed high and out of baby's reach for family meals. However, microwaves should not be used for heating baby-food jars or milk bottles because they can create severe hot spots (food or milk can become hot enough to burn a baby's mouth and throat) or may cause jars or bottles to explode. If your range has front knobs, pull them off and store them out of reach until you need to cook. Turn all pot handles toward the back of the cooktop when you're cooking so that they can't get pulled on by baby. When possible, cook on the back burners.

Cabinets and drawers. Keep knives, scissors, and other sharp objects in drawers with child-resistant safety latches installed from the inside. Lock liquor away—it's dangerous for babies. Pad sharp corners of countertops, and keep stools and chairs out of reach so your baby won't use them for climbing.

Plastic bags. Plastic bags—garbage bags, laundry bags, grocery bags—can suffocate children who play with them. Lock them away.

Living room

Never leave your baby unattended. A baby will roam around the living room, for example, while you're temporarily busy in the kitchen or other area of the house. Babyproofing the living room should include measures to prevent shock hazards from electrical outlets and extension cords, burns from heat sources such as fireplaces and woodstoves, and cuts and bruises from sharp furniture edges.

Coffee tables. Coffee tables send over 70,000 babies and young children to emergency rooms every year. Children are hurt when they fall against sharp corners and edges. Use stick-on safety padding for table edges—or, better yet, completely remove the coffee table and store it away during the first three years of your baby's life.

Fireplaces and woodstoves. Babies are drawn to fire like moths to a flame. They don't realize that fires and heat sources are dangerous. Reinforce the words "HOT! DON'T TOUCH!" so your child comes to respect your warning. Keep matches and lighters safely out of children's reach. Consider installing a fireproof safety railing around the fireplace, keeping glass doors closed when fires are going, and putting fireproof padding around sharp brick edges on raised hearths.

Lamps. Babies may tug on lamp cords without realizing that lamps may topple. Wrap up cords using a cord shortener made for just that purpose, or use twist ties or rubber bands at the base of the lamp so there's no slack. Position lamp cords to the back, clearly out of baby's reach.

Electrical outlets. Typically, when accidents with electricity occur, a baby sticks a diaper pin or hairpin into an open socket, causing a sudden and severe shock. Use safety outlet covers to prevent contact with a live outlet. Check that all outlets have ground fault interrupters; if there are any missing, you should install them.

Extension cords. When a baby puts an extension cord in his or her mouth, saliva sets up a pathway for electricity, which can cause severe shock and mouth burns. Purchase new, safety-oriented cords equipped with locking plug holes. If you've got an old house that's overloaded with extension cords, for everybody's safety, consider getting the house rewired.

Area rugs. Secure all area rugs in place with a piece of foam carpet backing or double-sided self-stick tape.

Decks and porches. Falls from outdoor decks and porches can cause serious injuries. Check to be sure railings are no more than three inches apart. If they are, keep your baby away from them to prevent him or her from falling through. Furniture on small decks or custom-built benches can entice children to climb up and fall off. Keep doors to the deck closed and secured so baby can't go out when you're not watching. Put decals on glass patio doors so that you and your children won't crash into them on the mistaken perception that they're open.

Barbecue grills. Remove and store propane gas tanks where children can't reach them. Never leave a child near a hot grill while barbecuing.

Backyard

Sometimes tots slip out of the backyard when least expected by parents. Nearly all parents have tales of finding their naked two-year-old running down the street at dawn, or of discovering their baby poised on the edge of a neighbor's pool.

Outdoors, babies require constant adult vigilance. (Other children, such as siblings, should not be relied on to watch babies.) Installing a latch high on the backyard door and firmly locking and securing patio doors with a bar can help make certain that your youngster doesn't go AWOL. You may even want to purchase an alarm that sounds off if baby strays away from you. (See chapter 16 for information on baby monitors.)

Baby-size wading pools and swimming pools. Unprotected pools with as little as one inch of water can cause drowning accidents. That's because baby's heads are heavy and they can't easily right themselves. Make sure that all outdoor containers of water, including buckets and wading pools, are emptied and stored upside down or in the garage. If you have a back-yard pool or live near water, keep a life jacket on your tot outdoors. Surround your pool with a fence (required by most building codes) and a locking gate, and cover it during the off season. Swimming pool alarms for in-ground pools provide some measure of protection—they sound an alarm if a child falls in—but they tend to sound too many false alarms.

Ride-on toys. Tricycles and other ride-on toys can be hazardous for young children, who can fall easily. The lower the toy is to the ground, the less the falling distance. Don't purchase a wheeled toy until you're certain your child is mature enough to use it safely. A four-year-old can manage a tricycle fairly well, but a two-year-old can't. Don't try to rush your little one into balancing large-wheeled, imitation toy bicycles. They're dangerous. Be sure your home has a "safety zone" for riding toys away from traffic and steep hills or driveways; otherwise, don't buy ride-on toys. Equip your child with a bicycle helmet every time he or she uses a ride-on toy.

Swing sets. Often toddlers are hit while crossing or running between swings. Install swing sets so that they are securely anchored in concrete and won't tip over. Fill the entire play area with at least six inches of mulch or sand or other energy-absorbing material. Buy units with soft seats and rounded edges, and always supervise your child. Follow the safety instructions provided by the manufacturers of playground sets.

Bathroom

Restless toddlers will explore every nook and cranny in your home, including the bathroom. Typically, babies die in bathroom accidents in one of four ways: drowning, poisoning, scalding, or electrical shock. To protect your baby from bathroom accidents, keep him or her out of the bathroom by using a gate or by latching the outside of the door. You can also latch down everything inside the bathroom, including the toilet and diaper pail lids, so your baby can't get into anything. You may also want to cover the *inside* door lock with duct tape to keep baby from locking *you* out.

Medicine cabinet. Toddlers can be very inventive when it comes to climbing on sinks and getting into the medicine cabinet. Inspect your cabinet, and flush all outdated medications down the toilet. Install a locking medicine cabinet, or remove medicines and put them on a high shelf, or in a childproof locking box. Make sure that all medications from the pharmacy are in child-resistant packaging. Keep activated charcoal and syrup of ipecac available should your child be poisoned.

Bathtubs. A baby can drown in as little as one inch of water. Typically, a parent goes to answer the telephone or the door, and comes back to discover an unconscious baby facedown in water. *Always* stay close when giving your baby a bath. That means keeping one hand on the baby at all times and never leaving the baby to answer the phone or door. Suctioned and other types of bath seats have figured in the deaths of 18 babies since 1983—don't buy or use one. Install a rubber mat in the tub so that you and the baby won't slip. Infants can be bathed in a small tub that fits in the sink.

Toilet and diaper pail. Babies also drown in toilets and diaper pails. Buy a diaper pail that has a tamper-proof lid and is equipped with a locking device. Toilet locking devices are also available.

Hair dryers and radios. Handheld hair dryers and other appliances, such as radios, fans, and heaters, can cause fatal electrical shock when they fall into water. In addition, curling irons (and irons for clothes) cause deep burns. For maximum safety, don't store or use these appliances in your bathroom or near baby. Outlets in the bathroom must have ground fault interrupters.

Bedroom

Adult beds, waterbeds, and beanbag chairs. According to the U.S. Consumer Product Safety Commission, over 200 babies have suffocated or been strangled in adult beds since 1985. In most cases, babies became wedged between the mattress (or between the bed frame) and the wall. In some cases, adults have rolled onto a baby while the baby was in an adult bed. When a baby is positioned facedown on waterbeds and beanbag chairs, a suffocation pocket is created that can cause death. Use a crib for all napping and sleeping.

Unshielded windows. About 70 babies and children die in falls from windows every year. Don't depend on screens to keep your child from falling. Avoid placing furniture near windows that your child could use to climb up to the window. Open double-hung windows from the top instead of the bottom. Install locks that prevent sliding windows from opening more than five inches. If local fire codes permit, install window guards. Burglar bars should be easily removable in case of fire.

Basement and garage

Don't overlook your garage as a source of danger for your tot. A garage is simply not a safe place for children to be in. Install a lock on the door leading to the garage to keep tots from rambling out of the house, or consider installing a self-locking "Dutch door" that allows you to pass groceries into the kitchen without letting your toddler out. The number-one danger in your garage is your car. Automobile accidents are one of the leading causes of accidental child deaths. Babies can be run over when drivers don't see them. Be especially cautious when backing out of your garage—always take your time and make sure your kids aren't in the path of your car. Never leave your children unattended in a parked car. Lawn mowers, power tools, gasoline, and household chemicals are all dangerous, too, and should be kept completely out of a child's reach.

Basement stairs and other staircases. Over 25,000 babies are rushed to emergency rooms every year after wheeled baby walkers plummet down unprotected staircases, roll into fireplaces or against woodstoves, or tumble into swimming pools. Don't buy or use a walker. To prevent falls down basement stairs, install a lock as high as you can reach on the basement door, and keep it closed at all times. Make sure stairs are well lit, and keep all clutter and toys off steps. If railings to stairs and balconies are more than three inches apart, install Plexiglass to prevent your child from falling through.

Water heater. Turn the water heater thermostat down to 120°F to prevent painful scalding of a baby's sensitive skin.

Lawn mowers. Mowers throw rocks and can mangle small hands and feet. Keep your tot indoors until you've finished mowing, and never joyride your child on the mower. Pour gasoline into the mower while outdoors, not in the garage or basement, where spills can be ignited by the pilot lights of water heaters or furnaces.

Chemicals. Store gasoline, insecticides, antifreeze, and other dangerous chemicals behind locking cabinet doors. Keep all chemicals in their original containers, never transfer them to soda bottles or other beverage containers. Don't use bug spray in the house without cleaning up the pesticide residue.

Buckets. Over 200 toddlers and young children have drowned in five-gallon buckets since 1984. Typically, a baby finds a bucket with water, throws a toy in, and then leans over to retrieve it. Toppling in headfirst, and unable to get back out again, the baby drowns. Never leave a bucket of water, or other liquid, unattended when small children are around.

Power tools. Keep children away from your workbench when you are working there. Don't expose your child to risk by assigning tasks he or she doesn't have the hand skills to do safely. Store power tools and sharp objects out of reach. Install plug guards on outlets not being used.

Garage doors. Each year children die or suffer brain damage when they are crushed under automatic electric garage doors that are not sensitive enough to reverse when they encounter a small child's body. To test a garage door's sensitivity, place a two-inch-high block of wood on the floor in the path of the garage door to see if the door will stop and reverse. If the test fails, either operate the door manually or replace it with a door with optical sensors that can tell when something's in the way before closing. Caution your toddlers about garage and garage door dangers. Store tricycles and ride-ons toys in a safer place.

....

Ratings: Childproofing products

"Childproofing products" is a term used to describe products designed to reduce the risk of injury to children from such hazards in the home as electric shock, falls, burns, poisonings, drowning in toilets, and strangulation. We examined more than 30 products priced from $0.99 to $15.99 (manufacturer's suggested retail).

Overview of childproofing products

These products vary in design and purpose but have common features:

Age range. All childproofing products have an age range over which they are most effective. We hired consultants who were experts in child development, child safety, and environmental psychology to assess the age range over which common household items pose a risk of injury to children. They found that in most cases the lower end of the "at-risk" age range began at about seven months; the upper end varied depending on the hazard involved. They then assessed the age range over which each product effectively reduced the risk of injury from specific hazards. Individual product descriptions (to follow) specify the upper end of the "effective" age range determined by the consultants. For some products the upper end of that range may decrease by six months to one and one-half years if the child observes the safety device being operated regularly.

All age-range assessments assume proper installation and use of the childproofing product. Where applicable, Consumers Union personnel also conducted laboratory tests to determine a specific product's effectiveness, and the results were taken into account in the given effective age range.

Installation and removal. All childproofing products have to be installed, and most will eventually be removed. Improper installation can render a childproofing product ineffective and leave you with a false sense of security. Ease of installation was assessed by installing the products as directed by the instructions. We also considered what might happen if parents didn't follow the directions precisely. Ease of removal was assessed by following removal instructions when provided, or by removing the product in the most obvious manner when not. Where applicable, the surfaces on which these products were mounted were also checked for damage.

Ease of use. Most childproofing products have to be operated by an older child or adult to allow access to, or operation of, the item being protected against; afterward most have to be reset to reduce risk of injury from the protected item. Improper use can render a childproofing product ineffective while leaving the child's caregiver with a false sense of security. Where applicable, ease of use was assessed by using the products both with and without the instructions.

Durability. Childproofing products that can be easily damaged through normal use or reasonably foreseeable abuse can't be counted on to reduce a child's risk of injury. Engineering judgment was used to assess how vulnerable each product was to damage and how well these products would hold up to normal use, as well as various levels of abuse.

Each product was given an overall assessment called the **Bottom Line.** While the bottom line is an overall quality judgment strongly influenced by effective age range, ease of installation, ease of use, and durability, it is primarily based on the degree to which a product's protective capabilities do not rely on the conscientiousness of the last person who used it. This is because a major weak link in any protection scheme is the last person who used the protective device; a safety device can't effectively reduce the risk of injuries if it has not been reset properly or if someone forgets to reinstall it. Products that provide protection independent of the actions of the last user are eligible for a bottom-line score of Excellent. Products that require the last user to perform a single routine action, such as closing a drawer, to provide protection are eligible for a bottom-line score of Very Good. Products that require the last user to perform two actions, such as closing a door and then locking the protective device, to provide protection are eligible for a bottom-line score of Good. Deficiencies in the areas of effective age range, ease of installation or use, and durability will further reduce the bottom-line score.

The products on the following pages are grouped by category. Within each category the products are discussed in order of overall quality based primarily on the bottom-line assessment. When all else is equal, the products are listed in order of increasing price. When applicable, some low- or no-cost home remedy alternatives that will guard against specific hazards are provided.

Toilet lid locks

Toilet bowls are a drowning hazard for children ages ten months to two years who may fall in headfirst and not be able to lift their heads out of the water. Young children are also hazardous to toilets—children who are eight months to three and one-half years old may enjoy throwing whatever's at hand into the toilet, which could lead to a clogged waste line. Toilet lid locks are used to hold the toilet lid down to prevent a child from gaining access to the water in the bowl. Children under eighteen months old can't turn doorknobs, so keeping the bathroom door shut is an effective, no-cost means of keeping the youngest toddlers away from the toilet.

Product: *Gerber Model 76597 Toilet Lid Lock,* $3.93

Description: This product consists of a spring-loaded lever assembly mounted on the toilet lid with double-sided tape. The lever wedges against the toilet tank to keep the lid from being lifted.

Effective age range: This product can reduce the risks associated with unsupervised toilet access for children through age three and one-half.

Ease of installation: ⊜. The installation steps are straightforward, only minimal measuring was needed to ensure proper placement, and we had no trouble getting the backing off the double-sided tape. This product is not intended for use on padded toilet seat lids; the lack of a rigid mounting surface would reduce its effectiveness.

Ease of removal: ◖. The instructions don't mention removal, it is difficult to get the taped-on lever housing off the lid, and once it's pulled free the tape is likely to leave a gummy residue. We found that softening the tape up with the heat of a blow-dryer, pulling the lever housing loose, and then removing any tape residue with rubber cement solvent (found in any stationery store) makes the job easier. The tape adhesive or the removal steps outlined above may damage the finish of some lids, but toilet lid and seat assemblies are easy to replace.

Ease of use: ⊜. Locking the toilet lid was very easy—just close the lid and the spring-loaded lever automatically snaps into place. Disengaging the lever to open the lid was easy to do but required two hands (one to move and hold the lever and one to raise the lid). The lever is marked with an arrow to indicate which direction it should be moved, so its operation should be obvious to first-time users. If the space between the raised lid and the toilet tank is narrow, this model will keep the lid from staying up by itself.

Durability: ⊜. The materials used are not prone to breakage under normal use or even light abuse. The double-sided tape will provide a strong bond between the lever housing and the toilet lid. While a child three and one-half years old would not be able to dislodge the lid lock by trying to force the lid open, an older user will be able to. The tape should adhere adequately in the hot, humid conditions found in bathrooms.

The Bottom Line: ⊜. This product can serve as an effective deterrent to young children, but with some toilets it may prevent the lid from staying up by itself—a nuisance. The fact that it resets automatically when the lid is closed increases its deterrent value; however, users still have to remember to close the lid. (A sticker advising users to close the lid is included and is intended to be placed on the inside of the lid where it will be seen.)

E VG G F P
⊜ ⊖ ○ ◒ ●

Product: *The First Years Model 3350 All-purpose Safety Latch,* 2/$3.79

Description: Each device consists of a strap that is placed over the closed toilet lid to hold it down. The strap closes on one end with a Fastex-type buckle. Double-sided tape is used to attach one end of the strap to the toilet lid and the other end to the toilet bowl. (Two devices come in a package.)

Effective age range: This product can reduce the risks associated with unsupervised toilet access for children through age three.

Ease of installation: ⊖. The installation steps are straightforward: The straps require minimal adjustment, and we had no trouble getting the backing off the double-sided tape. This product is suitable for use with padded toilet seat lids.

Ease of removal: ◖. The instructions don't mention removal. It can be difficult to get the taped-on strap and buckle off the lid and bowl, and once it's pulled free the tape is likely to leave a gummy residue. Softening the tape up with a blow-dryer, pulling the strap and buckle loose, and then removing any tape residue with rubber cement solvent makes the job easier. The tape adhesive or the removal steps outlined above will not damage the porcelain bowl, but may damage the finish of some lids. However, toilet lid and seat assemblies are easy to replace.

Ease of use: ○. Closing the buckle to lock the lid was very easy. The two simultaneous motions needed to open the buckle require a bit of finger strength and dexterity but will be familiar to anyone who has used this type of buckle before. When the toilet is in use, this product will be unobtrusive provided the strap section is mounted on the lid and the buckle section is mounted on the bowl, as shown in the instructions. If mounted the other way around, the strap section may flop over the edge of the bowl, where it will be subject to being splashed by waste or may snag the clothing of someone using the toilet.

Durability: ⊖. The materials used are not prone to breakage under normal use or even light abuse. If the device is installed toward the front of the toilet per the instructions, it will be very difficult to detach the mounting tape from the side of the bowl by forcing the lid open. The farther toward the back of the toilet this product is installed, the easier it will be to force it open by raising the lid. The tape should adhere adequately even in the hot, humid conditions found in bathrooms.

The Bottom Line: ○. This product can serve as an effective deterrent to young children if older users always remember to close the toilet lid and relatch it. This product can also serve as a general-purpose safety latch to deter young children from opening appliance or cabinet doors.

E VG G F P
⊖ ⊖ ○ ◖ ●

In those applications it will be very effective when mounted out of the child's reach (better yet, when mounted out of the child's sight).

Product: *Safety 1st Model 125N Fold Away Toilet Lock,* $3.99

Description: This device consists of two straps that are placed over the closed toilet lid to hold it down. The straps close in the middle with a modified Fastex-type buckle, and are attached to both sides of the toilet with double-sided tape.

Effective age range: This product can reduce the risks associated with unsupervised toilet access for children through age three and a half.

Special considerations: If the toilet lid is left open, the dangling straps may attract young children and thereby increase the risk of toilet bowl drowning or plumbing being clogged. The straps are also long enough to get into the toilet bowl, which poses a hygiene problem.

Ease of installation: ○. The installation steps are straightforward; however, the straps may have to be cut to fit. It takes strong fingers to put the straps on their holders, and getting the backing off the double-sided tape can be difficult. This product is suitable for use with padded toilet seat lids.

Ease of removal: ◖. It can be difficult to get the taped-on toilet bowl mounts off the bowl, and once it's pulled free, the tape is likely to leave a gummy residue. Softening the tape up with a blow-dryer, pulling the strap mounts loose, and then removing any tape residue with rubber cement solvent makes the job easier. The tape adhesive or the removal steps outlined above will not damage the porcelain bowl.

Ease of use: ◖. Closing the buckle to lock the toilet lid was very easy. However, the buckle was a bit difficult to open because it's made of soft plastic that deforms under pressure, causing the buckle to bind. The three simultaneous motions needed to open the buckle may not be obvious to some older children or adults.

Durability: ⊖. The materials used are not prone to breakage under normal use or even light abuse. It is possible to detach the mounting tape from the side of the bowl by forcing the lid open, but the typical three-and-one-half-year-old would not be strong enough to do it. The tape adhered adequately even in the hot, humid conditions found in bathrooms.

The Bottom Line: ○. This product can serve as an effective deterrent to young children if older users always remember to close the toilet lid and relatch it.

Product: *Fisher-Price Model 0240 Toilet Lid Lock,* $5.25

Description: This device consists of a clamp that attaches to the toilet bowl and is placed over the edge of the closed toilet lid to hold it down.

E VG G F P
⊖ ⊖ ○ ◖ ●

Effective age range: This product can reduce the risks associated with unsupervised toilet access for children through age three.

Special considerations: The spacers used to mount the device can break and come loose. These spacers pose a choking hazard to children three years old and younger.

Ease of installation: ⊖. No tools were required, just finger dexterity and the ability to select the proper number of spacers to fit the clamp to the toilet bowl. The clamp must be positioned toward the front of the bowl in order to hold the lid down. However, this product will not work with some toilet bowl shapes, and it can't clamp onto toilet seat and lid combinations that are very high. This product is suitable for use with padded toilet seats and lids provided they are not too thick.

Ease of removal: ⊖. No tools are required, just a bit of dexterity to release the section of the clamp that secures it to the bowl. During removal, care must be taken to prevent a part of the clamp from falling into the toilet.

Ease of use: ◑. Locking the toilet lid was extremely easy—just pushing the clamp up over the edge of the closed lid while applying light pressure locks it in place. Opening the clamp was just as easy—disengaging the locking latches on either side of the clamp required no strength, little dexterity, and could be done with one hand. Although easy to use, operation may not be obvious to unfamiliar users. When the toilet is in use, this device is exposed to waste splash, and the clamp can annoyingly snag the user's clothes or bump the user's leg. This device gets in the way when cleaning the toilet.

Durability: ○. The materials used are not prone to breakage under normal use but may not withstand light abuse. On some toilets, older users can bypass this lid lock by forcibly lifting the lid. The clamp mounting assembly can be pried off the bowl, which can result in the device's mounting spacers breaking and coming loose.

The Bottom Line: ◑. This product can serve as a good deterrent to young children if older users always remember to close the toilet lid and relatch it. However, it's very obtrusive when using or cleaning the toilet, poses a hygiene problem due to waste splash, is more fragile than competing designs, and has pieces that can pose a choking hazard.

Bathtub safety products

During bath time, children seven months to four years old run the risk of hitting their heads on the tub spout due to unsteadiness in sitting or standing, or energetic play. Children ten months to four years old run the risk of hitting their heads on knobs for the same reasons, or from sustaining scalding injuries from turning on the hot water. Cushioned

E   VG   G   F   P
⊖   ⊖   ○   ◑   ●

bathtub knob covers and bathtub spout covers are intended to address these concerns. Scalding accidents can be prevented by setting the water heater temperature to no higher than 120°F.

Product: *Safety 1st Model 169 Tub Knob Cover,* 2/$4.99

Description: This product consists of two inflatable covers (one for each knob) that attach to the wall in back of the knobs with suction cups.

Effective age range: If they stay in place, these products can reduce the severity of impact injuries for children through age four. They can deter children from turning bathtub knobs through age one and one-half.

Ease of installation: ◖. It is difficult to blow up these products when installing them for the first time, and the suction cups must be applied to a smooth clean wall (although not noted in the instructions, applying water to the suction cups helps them stay in place). If the mounting surface is kept clean and the cover is left inflated, reinstallation is extremely easy.

Ease of removal: ◖. It's extremely easy to remove these products temporarily—just peel the suction cups off the wall. It's difficult to deflate the cover if these products are being removed for storage.

Ease of use: ◓. Just peel off two of the four suction cups to gain access to the tub knob, and press the suction cups back into place to cover the knob again.

Durability: ◓. The materials used are not prone to breakage under normal use or light abuse. We found that we could not separate the suction cups from the cover by pulling on the cover to try to free the cups rather than peeling the cups directly off the mounting surface.

The Bottom Line: ○. Provided they stay in place, these products should provide adequate impact protection for children in the risk age range. They are less effective at preventing older toddlers from turning the bathtub knobs. Although children can defeat this product at a young age, baths tend to be a well-supervised activity, and an attentive caregiver can stop a child from removing the covers.

Product: *Safety 1st Model 103 Bathtub Spout Cover,* $2.99

Description: This device consists of an inflatable cover that is force-fitted over the bathtub spout.

Effective age range: This product can reduce the severity of impact injuries for children through age four if it remains in place. Children over three years old can pull the cover off the tub spout.

Ease of installation: ◖. This product is difficult to blow up or deflate; when inflated, it fits snugly on most tub spouts.

Ease of removal: ◖. Once inflated, ease of reinstallation or tempo-

E VG G F P
◓ ◓ ○ ◖ ●

rary removal is excellent—just push it on to, or pull it off of, the spout.

Ease of use: ⊖. This product does not interfere with the operation of the tub spout.

Durability: ⊖. The materials used are not prone to breakage under normal use or light abuse.

The Bottom Line: ○. This product should provide adequate impact protection for children in the risk age range, provided it remains in place. Although children over three years old can defeat this product, baths tend to be a well-supervised activity, and an attentive caregiver can stop a child from removing the cover.

Medicine cabinet safety latches

Children twelve months to five years old may climb on a chair or sink to reach a medicine cabinet and gain access to hazardous materials. Medicine cabinet safety locks are intended to reduce the risks to young children associated with unsupervised opening of medicine cabinets.

Product: *Safety 1st Model 11611 Sliding Medicine Cabinet Latch,* 2/$1.19

Description: This product consists of a leaf-spring latch that is attached to the medicine cabinet door with double-sided tape. This device fits between the sliding doors and locks them closed. Two latches are supplied in each package.

Effective age range: This product can reduce the risks associated with unsupervised medicine cabinet access for children through age three and one-half.

Ease of installation: ⊖. Actually attaching the latch to the door is extremely easy. However, the doors have to be removed first, and that may be difficult to do with some cabinets.

Ease of removal: ◓. After removing the doors from the cabinet, it can be difficult to get the latch off the door. Although tape residue will remain, cleaning it off the glass surface of the typical sliding medicine cabinet door is not difficult (the instructions don't mention removal). The tape adhesive will not damage the glass mounting surface.

Ease of use: ⊖. To engage the latch, completely close both doors; to disengage it, depress its spring tabs and slide one door open. The latch is very visible, and its operation should be obvious to older users.

Durability: ⊖. The materials used are not prone to breakage, and in this application the double-sided tape will hold the device securely in place. The tape adhered adequately even in the hot, humid conditions found in bathrooms.

E VG G F P
⊖ ⊖ ○ ◓ ●

The Bottom Line: ⊖. This product automatically locks the doors whenever they are fully closed. However, there is no way to ensure that all users will always fully close the cabinet doors.

Product: *Safety 1st Model 11611 Cabinet Latch,* 2/$1.19
Description: This product consists of a spring-loaded latching mechanism that is attached to the medicine cabinet door and frame with double-sided tape. This device locks swinging-type medicine cabinet doors closed and is not normally visible or accessible to a young child when installed as intended (at the top of the cabinet, behind the door flange). Two latches are supplied in each package.
Effective age range: This product can reduce the risks associated with unsupervised medicine cabinet access for children through age four.
Ease of installation: ⊖. The installation steps are straightforward, and we had no trouble getting the backing off the double-sided tape.
Ease of removal: ◖. Once the latch parts are pulled off, it can be difficult to get the tape residue off the cabinet and door. Although the instructions don't mention removal, we found that rubber cement solvent makes it easier to remove any leftover tape residue. The tape adhesive or rubber cement solvent may damage some cabinet or door finishes.
Ease of use: ○. It's very easy to use if the cabinet door is pushed closed while the latch button is depressed, a bit difficult if the latch button is not depressed. Ease of disengagement was excellent—a light push on a button releases the latch. However, the latch is so inconspicuous that unfamiliar users may not realize that it's there and may try to force open the "stuck" medicine cabinet door. Shorter users will have a difficult time reaching the latch.
Durability: ◖. The materials used are not prone to breakage; however, the device can be dislodged from the mounting tape by forcing the door closed if the latch pieces are not aligned, and it took only a 15½-pound pull to force the door open.
The Bottom Line: ◖. This product is easy to use. However, its mounting does not hold it securely, and its inconspicuousness makes it prone to being dislodged by unfamiliar or forgetful users forcing the door open or closed.

General cabinet and drawer safety latches

Cabinet doors or drawers that can be pulled open while crawling or standing on the floor may allow children seven months to five years old access to hazardous materials. Children in this age range are also prone to slamming the cabinet door or drawer on their fingers, or pulling a drawer free of its housing and having it fall on them. Cabinet and drawer

E   VG   G   F   P
⊖   ⊖   ○   ◖   ●

safety locks and latches are intended to reduce the risks to young children associated with unsupervised opening of cabinets and drawers.

Product: *Safety 1st Model 115C Double Lock,* 3/$2.49

Description: This product consists of a plastic latch and catch that mount on the inside of a drawer face or cabinet door. When the drawer or cabinet door is opened slightly or pushed closed, the catch engages the latch, preventing the drawer or door from being opened farther or closed fully. Three latch assemblies are included in each package.

Effective age range: This product can reduce the risks associated with unsupervised drawer or cabinet access, and reduce the chance of catching fingers in a drawer or door for children through age four.

Ease of installation: ◖. Tools are needed, the catch and latch must be lined up precisely for proper operation, and working in tight spaces around the drawer opening or door makes installation difficult. Installation on metal drawers or cabinets is very difficult (but not impossible), and this latch will not work on some types of drawers.

Ease of removal: ○. Remove the four mounting screws. Installing this product will leave screw holes in the mounting surfaces; however, the screw holes are inside the cabinet or drawer so they won't normally be seen.

Ease of use: ◑. Engaging the latch was very easy—the latch automatically engages whenever the drawer or door is opened or closed past a certain point. Ease of disengaging the latch was very good—once the latch engages, just push down on the latch arm and open or close the drawer or door farther.

Durability: ◑. The materials used should be able to stand up to normal use and light abuse.

The Bottom Line: ◑. This product is not easy to install; however, it is an effective deterrent that automatically resets itself whenever the drawer or cabinet door is closed.

Product: *Safety 1st Model 116R Universal Drawer & Cabinet Latch,* 4/$1.59

Description: This device consists of a plastic latch and catch that mount on the inside of a drawer face or cabinet door. When the drawer or cabinet door is opened slightly, the catch engages the latch, preventing the drawer or door from being opened farther. Four latch assemblies are included in each package.

Effective age range: This product can reduce the risks associated with unsupervised drawer or cabinet access for children through age three and one-half.

E   VG   G   F   P
◑   ◑   ○   ◐   ●

Ease of installation: ◒. Tools are needed, the catch and latch must be lined up precisely for proper operation, and working in tight spaces around the drawer opening or door makes installation difficult. Installation on metal drawers or cabinets is very difficult (but not impossible), and this latch will not work on some types of drawers.

Ease of removal: ○. Just remove the four mounting screws. Installing this product will leave screw holes in the various mounting surfaces; however, the holes won't be readily noticeable.

Ease of use: ⊖. Engaging the latch was extremely easy—closing the drawer or door automatically resets the latch to engage the next time the drawer or door is opened. Ease of disengaging the latch was very good—open the drawer or door slightly, push down on the latch arm, and pull the drawer or door open farther.

Durability: ⊖. The materials used should be able to stand up to normal use and light abuse.

The Bottom Line: ⊖. This product is not easy to install; however, it is an effective deterrent that automatically resets itself whenever the drawer or cabinet door is closed.

Product: *Safety 1st Model 110 C Cabinet Slide Lock,* $1.39

Description: This product consists of a U-shaped rail with a slide-on catch. When fitted over the knobs or through the handles of a cabinet's doors, this device prevents access. It can also be used to prevent access to some types of drawers.

Effective age range: This product can reduce the risks associated with unsupervised drawer or cabinet access for children through age three and one-half.

Ease of installation: ⊖. The amount of finger strength and dexterity required to open or close the latch is well within the capacity of older children and adults, and unfamiliar users should be able to figure out how the device works. The device won't work on cabinet doors that lack handles or knobs, or that have very small or large knobs, or whose handles or knobs are more than 5½ inches apart. It can be used to lock drawers that are positioned one over the other, provided they have suitable knobs or handles that are within the spacing limit noted above. When used to latch drawers together, this device will not prevent access to the contents of the top drawer if both drawers are pulled out at the same time.

Ease of removal: ⊖.

Ease of use: ⊖. This product is used the same way it is installed and removed. For details, see Ease of installation.

Durability: ⊖. The materials used are not prone to breakage.

E ⊖ VG ⊖ G ○ F ◒ P ●

The Bottom Line: ○. This product is an adequate deterrent through-out most of the at-risk age range. Although it is easy to operate, it does require that the user close the drawer or cabinet door and then latch it shut. This extra step makes it less effective as a safety product than devices that engage automatically when the door or drawer is closed.

Product: *The First Years Model 3232 Cabinet Safety Lock,* $1.79

Description: Consists of a flexible plastic strap with a U-shaped catch. When fitted over the knobs or through the handles of a cabinet's doors, this device prevents access. It can also be used to prevent access to some types of drawers.

Effective age range: This product can reduce the risks associated with unsupervised drawer or cabinet access for children through age four.

Ease of installation: ○. Opening and closing the latch is a three-step process that, while not difficult, is tedious. The device is marked with a diagram that shows unfamiliar users how it works. The device won't work on cabinet doors that lack handles or knobs, that have very small or large knobs, or that have knobs more than 7¾ inches apart. It can be used to lock drawers that are positioned one over the other, provided they have suitable knobs or handles that are within the spacing limit noted above. When used to latch drawers together, this device will not prevent access to the contents of the top drawer if both drawers are pulled out at the same time.

Ease of removal: ○.

Ease of use: ○. This product is used the same way it is installed and removed. For details, see Ease of installation.

Durability: ◖. The materials used are not prone to breakage.

The Bottom Line: ○. This product is an adequate deterrent through-out most of the at-risk age range. Although it is easy to operate, it does require that the user close the drawer or cabinet door and then latch it shut. This extra step makes it less effective as a safety product than devices that engage automatically when the door or drawer is closed.

Product: *KinderGard Model 701 Cabinet Lock,* $2.49

Description: This device consists of a U-shaped rail with a U-shaped slide-on catch. When fitted over the knobs or through the handles of a cabinet's doors, this device prevents access. In the same manner, it also can be used to lock drawers that are arranged one over the other.

Effective age range: This product can reduce the risks associated with unsupervised drawer or cabinet access for children through age three.

Ease of installation: ◕. For door handles or knobs that are less than

4½ inches apart, the ease of sliding the catch on the rail was good, since the latch takes some dexterity to operate. If the door handles or knobs are between 4½ and 6¾ inches (5½ inches, according to the manufacturer) apart, ease of use was fair, since hard-to-attach extensions have to be fitted to the rail. The device won't work on cabinet doors or drawers that lack handles or knobs, or that have very small or large knobs, or whose handles or knobs are more than 6¾ inches apart. It can be used to lock drawers that are positioned one over the other provided they have suitable knobs or handles that are within the spacing limits noted above. When used to latch drawers, this device will not prevent access to the contents of the top drawer if both drawers are pulled out at the same time.

Ease of removal: ○.

Ease of use: ○. Easy to lock, very easy to unlock. The locking arm on the catch is a bit awkward to work with when locking the device but is less so when unlocking it. The amount of finger strength and dexterity required to operate the latch is well within the capacity of older children and adults, and unfamiliar users should be able to figure out how the device works.

Durability: ⊖. The materials used should be able to withstand normal use and light abuse.

The Bottom Line: ○. This product is an adequate deterrent throughout most of the at-risk age range. Although it is easy to operate, it does require that the user close the drawer or cabinet door and then latch it shut. This extra step makes it less effective as a safety product than devices that engage automatically when the door or drawer is closed.

Window blind safety products

Window blind cords pose a strangulation hazard to children ten months to three years old who may put their heads into cord loops or get their necks tangled in loose cords. The products that follow are generally used to shorten window blind cords to keep them out of the reach of toddlers. They do not address the more general risk of strangulation associated with older children playing with string or rope.

Tying a knot in the blind cord to keep it out of reach is a no-cost alternative that reduces the risk from this hazard. However, tying and untying a knot every time the window blind is adjusted is inconvenient; safety measures that are inconvenient tend not to be followed. A low-cost alternative would be to drive two 2½-to-3-inch round head wood screws into the window frame. The screws should be spaced about 2 inches apart and installed high enough to be out of a child's reach. The screws should be driven about 1 inch deep. Excess cord is wrapped around the protruding excess of both screws.

E   VG   G   F   P
⊜   ⊖   ○   ◖   ●

Product: *Mericon Model 0330 Window Blind Cord Wrap,* 4/$1.25

Description: This device is a clear plastic holder that is similar in size and shape to a large-size wing nut. It is attached to the window frame or wall with a screw. Excess window blind cord is wrapped around the holder(s) to keep it out of children's reach. One holder can be used for short cords, two for long cords. Four are supplied in each package.

Effective age range: This device can deter children through age two and one-half if properly positioned—the effectiveness of this product is based almost exclusively on how accessible it is to the child.

Ease of installation: ○. The installation steps are straightforward. However, a screwdriver is required, a pilot hole has to be drilled or made with a nail for each holder, and care must be taken to ensure that the holder(s) will be out of the child's reach even when the child is climbing.

Ease of removal: ⊖. Pop off the screw cover and unscrew the holder from the wall. Installing this product will necessitate damaging the mounting surface by putting a screw hole in it.

Ease of use: ⊖. The cord is just wound on, or unwound from, the holder(s).

Durability: ⊖. The holders themselves are not prone to breakage; however, pulling on the cord may dislodge them from a plasterboard wall if they are installed without anchors.

The Bottom Line: ○. This product can serve as a deterrent to young children if it is installed out of reach. Although this product is easy to use and window blinds are adjusted relatively infrequently, the user must still manually wrap the cord around the holder in order to keep the cord out of a child's reach.

Product: *Safety 1st Model 222 Window Blind Cord Wind-Up,* 2/$3.99

Description: This device consists of an enclosed spool that fits over the window blind cord. It is used to wind up excess cord to keep it out of a child's reach. Two units are supplied in each package.

Effective age range: This device can deter children through age three if properly positioned—the effectiveness of this product is based almost exclusively on how accessible it is to the child. By age three children may be attracted enough by it to climb after it, risking a fall.

Ease of installation: ⊖. The installation steps are straightforward, and no tools are required; however, the device may have to be repositioned a few times in order to achieve the desired cord height. Installing this product will not damage the window blind cord.

Ease of removal: ⊖. Just pop off the cover to release the cord.

Ease of use: ○. The cord is just wound on, or unwound from, the spool.

E ⊖ VG ⊖ G ○ F ◔ P ●

Although easy to do, every time you raise or lower the window blind you'll have to readjust the cord length, which can be tedious. The instructions indicate that when adjusting the blinds, the user should always pull on the portion of the cord above the device; pulling on the lower portion of the cord may cause the device to pop open and release the cord. The device itself is not marked to alert unfamiliar users to this problem.

Durability: ⊖. The spool is not prone to breakage and will not be subject to abuse in this application.

The Bottom Line: ○. This product can serve as a deterrent to young children if it is installed out of reach. Although this product is easy to use and window blinds are adjusted relatively infrequently, the user must still manually wind the cord into the holder in order to keep the cord out of a child's reach.

Product: *Gerber Model 76347 Break-Thru Window Blind Cord Tassels,* 4/$3.22

Description: Each set consists of two discs that fit together and come apart easily under pressure. The discs are intended to be tied on the bottom of the window blind cords to reduce the risk of strangulation from children putting their heads through cord loops. Four sets of discs are supplied in each package.

Effective age range: This product will reduce the risk of strangulation from having the head caught in a cord loop for children through age eighteen months. This product will not reduce the risk of strangulation from loose cords becoming wrapped around the neck, since it does not make the cord shorter or less accessible.

Special considerations: When not engaged, the individual discs are small enough to be a choking hazard for children three years old and younger.

Ease of installation: ⊖. The installation is straightforward, and the only tools required may be a pair of scissors. However, good dexterity is needed to thread the window blind cords through small holes in the discs, and cords thicker than $5/64$ inch won't fit. In some cases, installing this product will alter the window blind cord, since the cord will have to be cut. Note that many window blind cords are not looped, so adding this device to them serves no purpose.

Ease of removal: ⊖. It takes some dexterity to untie the knots in the cord.

Ease of use: ⊖. This product does not interfere with the operation of the window blind cord. If the discs become separated, it's easy to line up the two halves and press them back together.

Durability: ⊖. The materials used are not prone to breakage under normal use or light abuse, such as occasionally being stepped on.

E	VG	G	F	P
⊖	⊖	○	◓	●

The Bottom Line: Not Acceptable. This product reduces the risk of strangulation from very young children getting their heads caught in cord loops, and it does not rely on an older user to properly use it to be effective. However, it does not address the problem of loose cords becoming tangled around the neck, and because it may pose a choking hazard for young children, we consider it Not Acceptable.

Door safety products

Doors that can be pulled opened may allow children ten months to five years old access to hazardous appliances or materials. Children eighteen months to five years old may turn a doorknob to unlatch the door and wander from the home. Doors slamming shut could pinch the fingers of children one to four and one-half years old. Door-safety products are intended to reduce the risks to young children associated with unsupervised door operation. If you're worried only about toddlers getting their fingers pinched in the door, a low-cost alternative is to hold the door open with a hook and eyebolt—it's not difficult to install, and it's easy to use.

Product: *Safety 1st Model 221 Bi-fold Door Lock,* $1.49
Description: This product consists of a U-shaped channel with a knob-operated clamping mechanism. When this device is fitted over the top edge of a bi-fold door at the center joint, it prevents it from being opened.
Effective age range: If located out of reach, this product can reduce the chance of finger-pinching injuries as well as the risks associated with unsupervised access through bi-fold doors for children through age five.
Ease of installation: ⊖. Open the door and place the device over the upper edge. The device won't work on doors thinner than ¾-inch or thicker than 1⁵⁄₁₆ inches.
Ease of removal: ⊖. To remove the device, loosen the locking knob and lift it off the door edge.
Ease of use: ⊖. To lock the door, just slide the device into place over the center joint and turn the knob to tighten the clamp. To unlock, loosen the knob and slide it off the center joint. Small users with tall doors may need a step stool to reach the device. The finish of the door can be scraped if the clamp is not sufficiently released when sliding the device into, or out of, place.
Durability: ⊖. The materials used are not unduly prone to breakage, and in this application the device will not normally be subjected to abuse. Repeated drops on a concrete floor resulted in a cracked clamp knob; however, the device still worked.
The Bottom Line: ○. Although it is easy to operate, it does require

E	VG	G	F	P
⊖	⊖	○	◔	●

that the user close the door and then lock it shut. This extra step makes it less effective as a safety product than devices that engage automatically when the door is closed.

Product: *Safety 1st Model 518 Grip 'N Squeeze Door Knob Cover,* 3/$1.99

Description: This device consists of a soft plastic cup that fits over the doorknob. The cover makes it difficult for toddlers to grip the doorknob with enough force to rotate it. Three covers are supplied in each package.

Effective age range: If it remains in place, this model can deter children through age three and a half.

Special considerations: A two-piece rear retaining collar is used to hold the cover in place on the doorknob. Unless tape or some other means is used to hold the two halves of the retaining collar together, the collar will disengage when the sides of the cover are squeezed, even by a very young child. This not only allows access to the doorknob but also the retaining collar (one of the collar halves has small pointed tabs that could cut the mouth of a child who disengages it and places it in his or her mouth).

Ease of installation: ◒. Fit the cup over the doorknob and push the halves of the rear retainer collar together; it takes careful aligning to get the mating tabs on the collar to engage. Because of the problem noted in Special considerations, we suggest that you wrap duct tape around the circumference of the retaining collar to keep it from being disengaged.

Ease of removal: ○. The instructions don't mention how to disengage the rear retainer; however, once you discover how, it's easy—too easy, as noted below. This product will not damage the doorknob or the door.

Ease of use: ◕. According to the instructions, you should squeeze the cover from front to back to grip the knob and then turn it; we found this to be an awkward motion. It was easier to turn the knob by pushing the front of the rubber-backed cover against it. The cover automatically uncouples itself from the doorknob after every use. Unfamiliar users may squeeze the sides of the cover to turn the doorknob. This won't provide enough grip to rotate the knob but will cause the rear retaining collar to disengage, as noted above.

Durability: ◒. The materials used are not prone to breakage, and being mounted on the doorknob reduces the likelihood of the cover being subjected to abuse.

The Bottom Line: ●. As it is, we consider this product to be poor overall, since it's prone to being disengaged from the doorknob, and a child mouthing one of the parts of the retaining collar could sustain shallow lacerations to the mouth. Wrapping duct tape around the cir-

E VG G F P
◒ ◓ ○ ◕ ●

cumference of the retaining collar to hold it together alleviates these problems and makes this a much more effective product (we'd give it a Bottom Line score of O. Although this product is easy to use, those unfamiliar with its operation may have difficulty opening the door, which can cause problems in an emergency.

Product: *Safety 1st Model 240 Sure Catch Grip 'N Lock,* $1.99

Description: This device consists of a plastic latch arm that mounts on the baseboard and a spring-loaded receptacle that mounts on the door. When the door is opened so that the receptacle engages the arm, the door is kept from being pulled shut to prevent toddlers from getting their fingers caught in the door.

Effective age range: This device can deter children through age two and a half.

Ease of installation: ◔. The instructions omitted hints that would make installation easier (like drilling pilot holes for the screws), the screw head slots distorted easily, and working in tight spaces around the door made installation difficult.

Ease of removal: O. Just remove the four mounting screws. This device is not suitable for use with pressboard or hollow doors; the mounting screws will eventually pull out. Installing this product will leave screw holes in the door and baseboard.

Ease of use: ◔. The door has to be slammed against the latch arm for the receptacle to engage. (We suggest you avoid engaging the latch in sight of toddlers; it's almost guaranteed that they will follow your example and start slamming doors throughout the house.) Ease of disengaging the latch was good—although pulling the door loose takes more strength than a toddler can muster, it is not difficult for an older child or adult.

Durability: ◑. The materials used should be able to stand up to moderate-to-heavy abuse, but a moderate-to-heavy downward impact on the latch arm could break it loose from the baseboard.

The Bottom Line: ◔. This device can reduce the risk of finger-pinching injuries for young children if the door is latched consistently by other users. However, it is neither easy to install nor easy to use. The latch arm can also obstruct your vacuum cleaner.

Window safety locks

Open windows are hazardous to children ten months to six years old, who may play around and possibly fall out of an open window or close the window on their hands, heads, or necks. Window safety locks allow the window to be opened enough for ventilation but not enough for a

E   VG   G   F   P
◓   ◑   O   ◔   ●

child to get out, and keep the window from being opened farther or closed. Depending on the window, drilling a hole through the bottom window sash and into the top sash and inserting a nail may be an effective low-cost means of reducing the risk from this hazard for younger children. An effective (although inconvenient) no-cost alternative for all double-hung windows is to open only the top sash.

Product: *Safety 1st Model 140 Window Lock,* 2/$1.99

Description: This device consists of a hinged catch and two latch plates that attach to the window frame and sash with screws. This device allows the window to be opened to two different positions and keeps the window from being opened or closed farther. Two window lock sets are supplied in the package.

Effective age range: This device can deter children through age five.

Ease of installation: ◒. The installation steps are straightforward. However, a screwdriver is required, pilot holes have to be drilled or made with a nail, care must be taken to properly line up the catch and latch plates, and a tight working space may make it difficult to tighten the screws. This device is not suitable for mounting on windows with narrow frames (like those on most new vinyl and aluminum windows) unless the window frames are modified.

Ease of removal: ○. Opening the catch takes considerable finger strength and dexterity; however, once opened the catch and latch plates are just unscrewed from the window. Installing this product will necessitate damaging the mounting surfaces by putting screw holes in them. In addition, screwing into narrow sashes may crack the windowpane.

Ease of use: ◒. It takes little hand strength or dexterity to close the catch over the latch. Opening the catch takes considerable finger strength and dexterity.

Durability: ◕. The materials used are not prone to breakage, and being mounted on the window reduces the likelihood of the lock being subjected to abuse.

The Bottom Line: ◒. Although the installation is not easy and the device cannot readily be installed on newer windows, this product can serve as an excelent deterrent to young children if it is always used. However, the lock is not easy to open, so older users may not use it consistently.

Stove safety products

Stoves pose burn and scalding hazards (and in the case of gas stoves, gas leak and explosion hazards) to children one to eight years old who may contact hot items on or in the stove, or who may try to operate the stove itself. The following products are respectively intended to reduce access to the stove-top, deter access to the oven interior, and prevent the stove knobs from being turned.

An alternative to using a stove knob cover is to remove the knobs when the stove is not in use. This is an effective, no-cost way to prevent young children from operating the stove; just remember to keep track of the knobs. (Making it a habit to always put them in a designated, out-of-the-way location will reduce the chance of misplacing them.) An alternative to using a stove-top guard is to employ the common kitchen practice of turning the handles of pots toward the center of the stove top. Although this does not reduce the risk of young children burning their fingers on a hot pot, it does prevent them (or others in the kitchen) from pulling or knocking a hot pot off of the stove onto themselves.

Product: *Safety 1st Model 241 Oven Lock,* $1.59

Description: This device consists of a plastic latch and catch that are attached to the oven door and the side of the oven with double-sided tape. The lock is intended to prevent the stove door from being opened.

Effective age range: This model can deter children through age four.

Ease of installation: ◒. The installation steps are straightforward, but the latch and catch have to be aligned carefully to make sure they'll mate properly. This lock is not suitable for ovens that don't have enough clearance on the side (or top for microwave ovens) to mount the catch.

Ease of removal: ◑. The taped-on latch and catch must be pulled off the stove (heating the stove first makes this easier), and then any tape residue can be cleaned off with solvent (although the instructions don't mention this). The tape adhesive did not damage the finish of the stoves used to test this device.

Ease of use: ◒. Squeezing the latch prongs together while pulling off the catch at the same time is an easy operation for older children and adults with normal hand strength. Operation should be obvious to first-time users.

Durability: ◑. The lock itself is not prone to breakage or damage from the surface temperatures of a well-heated stove. The amount of force needed to pull the lock free of the mounting tape by pulling on the stove handle when the oven is cold (19 pounds for a full-size oven) should deter most toddlers. When the stove is well heated, it took only 12 pounds of force to separate the lock from the mounting tape—a three- or four-year-old may be able to pull it loose by pulling the oven door open.

The Bottom Line: ◑ (Conventional Ovens)/○ (Microwave Ovens). This product is easy to install and easy to use. However, it will only be effective if it is relatched after every use. Additionally, if the mounting

E   VG   G   F   P
◒   ◑   ○   ◐   ●

surface gets warm during oven operation, three- or four-year-olds may be able to defeat it by pulling hard on the door.

Product: *Safety 1st Model 243 Stove Guard, $9.99*

Description: This product consists of a plastic fence that is attached to the front of the stove with double-sided tape. The guard is intended to reduce access to items on top of the stove and to prevent pots of hot liquid from being knocked or pulled off the stove.

Effective age range: This product may deter children through age one and a half. Older children will be able to reach over the top of the fence or pull the fence off the stove.

Ease of installation: ⊖. The installation steps are straightforward.

Ease of temporary removal: ⊜. The fence posts snap off the taped-on mounts to allow the fence to be removed for cleaning.

Ease of complete removal: ◕. The mounts have to be pried off the stove (heating the stove first makes this easier), and then any tape residue can be cleaned off with rubber cement solvent. The tape adhesive did not damage the finish of the stoves used to test this device.

Ease of use: ○. Although it is intended that the guard remain in place while cooking, care must be taken not to bump into it, so some users may find the guard obtrusive, since they have to lift pots over it.

Durability: ●. The guard itself is not prone to breakage. However, the fence slats, which are force fit into place, can easily be pulled apart, allowing stove-top access. Children intent on getting to items on top of the stove will tend to push or pull on the guard. Depending on the direction, our measurements showed it takes $6\frac{1}{2}$ to less than $27\frac{1}{4}$ pounds of force to push or pull the guard free when the stove is cold, and only 2 to 4 pounds of force to dislodge the fence when the stove is well heated.

Special considerations: The guard will melt and catch fire if it is pushed onto the stove burners. In our tests, the open flame of a gas stove ignited the fence slats within five seconds. Once removed, the slats continued to burn for up to 30 seconds; in most cases the slats produced flaming drips, which could ignite other materials on or around the stove. The heating element of an electric stove took two minutes to ignite a slat that was in contact with it. Once ignited, the part of the slat that was on the heating element continued to burn strongly even after the stove was turned off.

The Bottom Line: Not Acceptable. This product is flammable and is easy for a child to dislodge, creating a serious fire hazard should it fall on a hot burner. This product will prevent only the youngest toddlers from accessing the top of the stove.

E   VG   G   F   P
⊖   ⊜   ○   ◑   ●

Product: *Safety 1st Model 242R Stove Knob Cover,* 4/$3.39

Description: This device consists of a cover and plastic retaining ring that fit over a stove knob. The covers are intended to prevent the stove knobs from being turned to operate the stove. Four cover assemblies are included in each package.

Effective age range: This model can deter children through age two. Older children may be able to access the stove knob by removing the cover through knocking or prying. Although the covers prevent the stove knobs from being turned, they themselves turn easily and may attract children as a source of play.

Ease of installation: ◓. Installation consists of pulling off the stove knob, sliding the retaining ring over the knob stub, replacing the knob, and snapping on the cover.

Ease of removal: ◓. Removal consists of reversing the installation steps. The cover assemblies will not fit over knobs that are wider than $2\frac{1}{4}$ inches. This product will not damage the finish of the stove or the knob.

Ease of use: ◓. Removing the cover to access a stove knob involves applying slight pressure on two tabs on the cover sides to release it from the retaining ring, then pulling the cover off. To replace the cover, the user aligns the tabs on the cover with the slots on the retaining ring and pushes the cover back into place. Since the cover is completely removed from the knob during stove operation, there is a tendency to eventually misplace the cover or leave it off.

Durability: ◑. The cover assemblies themselves are not prone to breakage and will not melt when placed on the top of a well-heated stove away from the burners. However, the cover can be knocked free of the knob when less than $4\frac{1}{4}$ pounds of force is applied on the side of the cover directly over one of the retaining tabs.

Special considerations: The cover will melt and catch fire if it inadvertently contacts a hot stove burner. In our tests, the open flame of a gas stove ignited the cover within 15 seconds when it was pushed up against a pot that was being heated. Once removed, the cover stopped burning. The heating element of an electric stove took two minutes to ignite a cover that was in contact with it (it did not ignite when pushed up against a pot that was being heated). Once ignited, the part of the cover that was on the heating element continued to burn strongly even after the stove was turned off.

The Bottom Line: Not Acceptable. This product is flammable and can be easily knocked onto a hot burner, creating a fire hazard. This product will prevent only the youngest toddlers from accessing the stove knobs.

E VG G F P
◓ ◓ ○ ◑ ●

Electrical outlet safety products

Electrical outlets and partially inserted electrical plugs pose shock, burn, and electrocution hazards for children seven months to six years. The following products are intended to reduce the risk of injury to children from electrical outlets.

Product: *Safety 1st Model 10401N Auto-Swivel Outlet Cover,* $1.99

Description: This device consists of a plastic electrical cover plate with spring-loaded swiveling outlet covers. This product is screwed over an electrical outlet in place of a regular outlet plate, and the swiveling covers automatically block access to the outlet's electrical contacts when plugs are removed from the outlet.

Effective age range: This product can deter children through age five.

Ease of installation: ⊖. The installation steps are straightforward; remove the original outlet cover plate with a screwdriver and replace it with this device using the included attachment hardware. Installation of this device will not damage the outlet or the wall surface around it. If this device is screwed tightly to an outlet that sticks too far out of the wall, the swiveling covers will bind on the outlet face and will not automatically swivel to cover the electrical contacts when a plug is removed. If the covers bind, slightly loosening the retaining screw(s) will allow them to move freely.

Ease of removal: ⊖. To restore the outlet to its original condition, reverse the installation steps.

Ease of use: ⊖. Insert an electrical plug as far as it will go into the slots in the swiveling cover, rotate the plug one-quarter turn, and push the plug into the outlet. When the plug is removed from the outlet, the swiveling cover will automatically snap back into place.

Durability: ⊖. The materials used are not prone to breakage. A heavy impact to the cover or a plug inserted in it may damage the cover housing.

The Bottom Line: ⊖. This easy-to-use product will reduce the risk of shock-related injuries to children throughout most of the at-risk age range. Once the plug is removed, it automatically resets its protective feature.

Product: *Safety 1st Model 10402 Outlet Cover,* 2/$1.99

Description: This product consists of a plastic electrical outlet enclosure with two slots at one end for the exit of electrical cords. This product is screwed onto an electrical outlet over the outlet plate and any plugs that have been inserted in the outlet. It blocks access to unused outlet contacts and prevents any plugs that have been inserted from being removed. Two covers are included in each package.

Effective age range: This product can deter children through age six.

Ease of installation: ○. Remove the original outlet cover plate screw, insert the plugs to be covered into the outlet, and screw the cover to the outlet over the plate and plugs. Installation of this device will not damage the outlet, outlet cover plate, or wall surface around it. This device will not fit over large plug-and-cord assemblies; forcing the cover over a plug-and-cord assembly that is too large could damage the cord. Plug cords may get in the way and make it difficult to screw the cover onto the outlet.

Ease of removal: ◒. To restore the outlet to its original condition, reverse the installation steps.

Special considerations: Placing the cover over the outlet may partially dislodge the plug from the outlet; the opaque material of the cover makes it impossible to see whether the plug has been dislodged. A cord that has a plug covered by this device can present a more serious tripping hazard than one whose plug can freely be dislodged from an outlet. Note that use of this device prevents the quick unplugging of an appliance as an alternate means of turning it off in case of an emergency.

Ease of use: ◕. Inserting or removing a plug from the outlet requires completely removing and reinstalling the cover. The best use for this product is with outlets that power fixed appliances whose plugs are seldom removed. However, many fixed appliances (like refrigerators and television sets) have plugs that are too large to fit under the cover.

Durability: ◒. The materials used are not prone to breakage; however, a heavy impact to the cover may damage it.

The Bottom Line: ◕. This product will reduce the risk of shock-related injuries to children throughout the full at-risk age range. However, it's not suitable for use with tall plugs or thick cords, and it introduces new problems such as an increased likelihood of an actual fall if someone trips over a cord, and the inability to "pull the plug" in case of an emergency.

Product: *Safety 1st Model 119 Shock Preventer,* 8/$.99

Description: This device consists of a plastic guard with three slots in the center portion for electrical plug blades. The guard is positioned against the plug face with the blades of the plug inserted through the slots in the guard. Eight guards are included in each package.

Effective age range: This product can reduce the risk of shocks, burns, or electrocutions to persons of all ages caused by a finger accidentally contacting the blades of plugs that are partially removed from

E VG G F P
◒ ◒ ○ ◕ ●

outlets but are still electrically live. This product will not deter anyone from intentionally touching the blades of a partially removed plug.

Special considerations: If the plug guards become separated from the plug, they are small enough to present a choking hazard to children three years old and younger.

Ease of installation: ⊖. Adults with average hand strength will have no trouble pushing the guards into place on plugs, or removing them from plugs. Although the guard will not damage the plug blades or the outlet, it does force the plug blades slightly farther apart.

Ease of removal: ⊖.

Ease of use: ⊖. Since the guard spreads the plug blades, this device makes it a bit harder to insert a plug into an outlet; however, it does not affect the ease of plug removal.

Durability: ⊖. The materials used are not prone to breakage, and can withstand heavy abuse.

The Bottom Line: ◔. This product will reduce the risk of shock-related injuries due to unintentional plug blade contact for all persons. However, it does not reduce the risk to anyone who intentionally tries to contact the blades. Although the guard may pose a choking hazard to toddlers once it is free of the plug, it is very unlikely that toddlers will be motivated enough by it to attempt to pull it loose.

Product: *Safety 1st Model 117N Outlet Cap,* 12/$.99
Description: This device consists of a plastic cap with two plastic prongs on one side. The prongs of the cap are pushed into the contact slots of unused outlets to block access to the contacts. Twelve caps are included in each package.

Effective age range: This product can deter children through age two and a half. Children older than this may have the hand strength, dexterity, and determination to defeat the caps if given enough time.

Special considerations: The samples of this model that we purchased for our tests were small enough to present a choking hazard to children three years old and younger. However, we also came across samples of this product that had the same model number and the same packaging, but were slightly larger, and so did not pose a choking hazard to toddlers.

Ease of installation: ⊖. The plugs are very easy to push into place. Installation of this device may loosen the outlet's contacts over time, but no more so than inserting an electrical plug would.

Ease of removal: ○. It ranged from very easy to very difficult. The cap has to be pried free of an outlet—this can be very difficult when

E VG G F P
⊖ ⊖ ○ ◔ ●

using a fingernail, but it is very easy when using a tool. The amount of force needed depends on how tightly the outlet's contacts clamp the cap's prongs.

Ease of use: ○. Using these devices involves the same steps as installing and removing them. Studies show that there is a strong tendency to forget to replace removed caps once an outlet is no longer being used.

Durability: ⊖. The materials used are not prone to breakage, and can withstand light abuse; however, since this device is likely to wind up on the floor, stepping on it may damage it.

The Bottom Line: Not Acceptable. This product will reduce the risk of shock-related injuries to children throughout the lower portion of the at-risk age range if used consistently. However, users are very likely to forget to reinstall them. As noted above, there appear to be at least two different sizes of this product that bear the same model number. One size is small enough to present a choking hazard to toddlers once it is removed from the outlet. Because the two different versions share the same model number and one version poses a choking hazard, we consider this model Not Acceptable.

Electrical cord safety products

Electrical cords may pose a tripping hazard to children seven months old and older. Toddlers may tug on a cord and be hit by the device it's connected to if it falls off a table or shelf, or they might sustain mouth burn injuries from chewing on cords. The following products are intended to reduce the risk of injury to children from electrical cords. An inexpensive alternative is to bind up excess cord with a zip tie (don't make it too tight or you will damage the cord insulation).

Product: *Safety 1st Model 218 Cord Holder,* 3/$1.49

Description: Each holder consists of a plastic case that is attached to the baseboard or wall with double-sided tape. The holders are used to attach loose electrical or telephone cords to walls and baseboards to prevent tripping and to make them less conspicuous to a child. Three holders are included in each package.

Effective age range: This device can make cords less attractive as play objects, and thus reduce the risk of cord-related injuries for all toddlers.

Ease of installation: ⊖. To install, separate the two halves of the holders (which takes a bit of finger strength and dexterity), then attach the back halves to the wall or baseboard using the supplied double-sided tape. A cord is positioned in the holders, and the front halves are

E VG G F P
⊖ ⊖ ○ ⊖ ●

snapped in place to retain it. The holders work best with 16 AWG type SPT-2 (the type of cord used on most extension cords and appliances) or smaller cords; the insulation of cords that are too thick may be damaged by the holders.

Ease of removal: ●. Separating the two halves of the holders to release the cord is not difficult, but it can be hard to get the taped-on portions of the holders off the baseboard or wall. Once the holders are removed, any tape residue that remains on the wall or baseboard must be removed, which may prove difficult (the instructions don't mention removal, but rubber cement solvent may make it easier to remove tape residue from some surfaces). The tape adhesive will damage the finish of most walls and some baseboards.

Ease of use: ○. Opening the holders to release the cord is not difficult. Closing the holders requires aligning the two halves and snapping them together. Since the holders will be positioned low on the wall or on the baseboard, operation may be awkward, since it's done by feel rather than by sight. This device is best used to hold the cords of appliances that will remain stationary most of the time.

Durability: ○. The materials used are not prone to breakage and can withstand light abuse. However, they can be damaged by a heavy impact, and if the cord is forcefully yanked out of the holder, the retaining slots on the covers may break. This is actually an advantage, since the holders are inexpensive and a cord can be pulled free of a holder in an emergency without damaging the cord.

The Bottom Line: ○. This product reduces the risk of young children sustaining electrical cord-related injuries by making the cord less attractive as a source of play. It also keeps electrical cords from being tripping hazards. Although not difficult to install or use, removing this device will probably damage the finish of your wall or baseboard.

Product: *Safety 1st Model 114 Retracting Cord Short'ner,* $1.99
Description: This device consists of an enclosed plastic spool that is used to wind up excess electrical cord to keep it out of a child's reach or to keep other persons from tripping.

Effective age range: This device can make electrical cords less attractive to all toddlers. However, the effectiveness of this product is based largely on how accessible or visible it is to the child. If the cord retractor is visible and accessible, it may exacerbate the problem of cord pulling, since children may be attracted by the device itself.

Ease of installation: ◒. To install this device, you line up a slot in the spool with an opening in its case, fold the cord in half, insert the cord through the case into the spool slot, and turn the spool knob. Installing this product will damage the cord insulation if it is wound too tightly. Cords much thicker than 16 AWG type SPT-2 will not fit in this device. We found that the device will shorten 16 AWG type SPT-2 cord up to 51 inches; thinner cords will be shortened more, thicker cords will be shortened less.

Ease of removal: ⊖. To remove the cord, reverse the installation steps.

Special considerations: This product is not suitable for use with high-current devices like heaters; tightly winding a cord carrying high current in an enclosed space will cause the cord to overheat.

Ease of use: ⊖. To shorten the cord, turn the knob to wind the spool; to lengthen the cord, hold the case and pull the cord out.

Durability: ⊖. The materials used are not prone to breakage and can withstand being stepped on; however, the retractor may be damaged if struck with a very heavy object.

The Bottom Line: ◑. The effectiveness of this product in reducing the risk of young children pulling on electrical cords depends solely on how inconspicuous or inaccessible it is once installed. If it is placed where it will be plainly visible from a toddler's vantage point, it may actually attract children to the cord. This product will cause power supply cords carrying high currents to overheat; accordingly, it is not suitable for use with devices that draw high currents.

Electrical switch safety lock

Wall switches are attractive to children one to six years old. If they control hazardous appliances like garbage disposals, operation of these switches by a child can have disastrous results. The following product is intended to reduce the risk of injury to children from hazardous wall switch-operated devices.

Product: *Safety 1st Model 128 Appliance Guard Switch Lock,* 2/$1.59

Description: This device consists of a plastic sliding latched switch cover. This product is screwed over a wall switch and cover plate. It locks the switch in either the Off or On position to prevent an appliance from being turned off or on. Two covers are included in each package.

Effective age range: This product can deter children through age five.

Ease of installation: ⊖. To install, remove the original switch cover plate screws, orient the switch lock over the switch handle, making sure that it will lock the switch in the desired position, and screw it into place using the longer retaining screws that are provided. It can be tricky to position the sliding switch cover over the switch without blocking access to the cover's mounting screw holes. Installation of this device will not damage the switch or switch cover plate.

Ease of removal: ⊖. To remove the lock, reverse the installation steps.

Ease of use: ⊖. To turn on (or off) a locked switch, press in the latching tab and slide the switch cover in one direction. To turn off (or on) the switch again, slide the switch cover in the other direction; the latching tab will automatically engage. Although the locks are not marked with use instructions, an unfamiliar user should be able to figure out how to use the switch without much difficulty.

Durability: ⊖. The materials used are not prone to breakage. Although a heavy impact to the cover may damage it, the locations where it will be installed make it unlikely to be subjected to this kind of abuse.

The Bottom Line: ⊖. This product is easy to install, remove, and use, and it is unlikely to be damaged. However, its application is very limited because it works only on wall switches and operating a wall switch is rarely hazardous.

Corner and edge bumpers

The corners of various household furnishings, including tables, low shelves, and fireplace hearths, pose impact hazards to children six months to two and one-half years old who are unsteady sitters or walkers. Corner and edge bumpers are intended to reduce the risk of injury to children in this age range from falling and hitting their heads on the corners of furniture. They also reduce the risk of injury to older children who may run into furniture corners during play. Since children who are learning to sit up or stand are at risk for hitting their heads on both the top and bottom corners of tables, cushioning both of these surfaces should be considered.

Product: *Safety 1st Model 111J Corner Cushion,* 4/$1.19

Description: This product is made of a soft plastic and attaches to the corner of furniture with double-sided tape. The cushions are supposed to soften the impact of a child falling against them, and prevent pointed corners from causing gouging injuries. Four cushions come in a package.

Effective age range: This product can reduce the severity of corner-impact injuries for people of all ages; it is especially useful with children through two and one-half years old who are practicing their standing, walking, and running skills.

Ease of installation: ○. The installation steps are straightforward; however, it takes dexterity and patience to properly position the tape on the cushions.

Ease of removal: ◖. It's not difficult to get the taped-on cushions off

E	VG	G	F	P
⊖	⊖	○	◖	●

the mounting surface. Any remaining tape residue must be removed with either soap and warm water or rubber cement solvent. The tape adhesive may damage some furniture finishes.

Ease of use: ⊖. This product does not interfere with the use of the table or countertop.

Durability: ⊖. The materials used are not prone to breakage, and the cushions should remain in place unless they are subjected to a very heavy impact or are removed intentionally.

The Bottom Line: ⊖. This product will reduce the severity of impacts and prevent gouging injuries from children falling against, or running into, furniture with pointed corners. The only reservation is that it may mar the finish of some furniture.

Product: *Safety 1st Model 246 Fireplace Edge and Corner Bumper,* $9.99

Description: This product consists of firm plastic bumpers that are attached to the corners and along the edges of a fireplace hearth with double-sided tape. The bumpers are intended to cushion the impact of a child falling against them, and will also prevent pointed hearth corners from causing gouging injuries. Enough material is provided to cover 90 inches of hearth edge and two corners; additional bumper sections can be mail-ordered from the manufacturer for $2.00 per section.

Effective age range: This product can somewhat reduce the severity of corner-impact injuries for children through two years old who are practicing their sitting and walking skills.

Ease of installation: ◑. Installing the bumpers requires fitting, measuring, and cutting the bumper sections. The instructions indicate that the supplied double-sided tape will adhere only to hearths made from relatively smooth brick or stone. For other surfaces, a masonry expert should be consulted to determine the best attachment means. This product is intended for raised fireplace hearths; it cannot be attached to flat hearths. The tape adhesive won't damage the hearth material.

Ease of removal: ○. It is not difficult to pull the taped-on bumpers off the mounting surface. Any remaining tape residue may be removed with either soap and warm water or rubber cement solvent (the instructions don't mention removal).

Ease of use: ⊖. This product does not interfere with the use of the hearth.

Durability: ◑. The materials used are not prone to breakage, but the cushions may not remain in place if they are subjected to more than a moderate impact. A motivated child could detach the bumpers. Hot embers that come in contact with the bumper will cause it to melt and smoke but not to ignite.

The Bottom Line: ◗. This product will somewhat reduce the severity of impacts and prevent gouging injuries from children falling against raised fireplace hearths. The reservations are that the bumpers are not easy to install, may not stay in place, and the firm plastic will not absorb as much shock as implied.

Railing guards

Stair, porch, or balcony railings with widely spaced slats may trap the heads of children seven months old and up, or allow them to fall through the railing. Safety products that guard against falling through railings are intended to reduce the risk of injury from these hazards. Effective, but costly, alternatives are to have vertical slats added to the railing to close the slat spacings to less than the child's head width, or to attach Plexiglas sheeting over the gaps between the slats or over the entire section of railing. Do not add horizontal slats—this will increase the risk of a toddler climbing up on, and falling over, the railing.

Product: *Safety 1st Model 179 Balcony Guard for Stair, Porch, and Balcony Railings,* $15.99

Description: This product consists of a 120-inch-by-33-inch plastic net and miscellaneous mounting hardware. The net is intended to prevent young children from falling through, or getting their heads wedged in, railings with widely spaced slats.

Effective age range: This product can reduce the risk of head entrapment and falls through the center of railings for children through three years old; however, this product may not prevent very small children from falling through the railing at the sides and bottom, and may introduce a strangulation hazard (see **Special considerations** below for further details).

Ease of installation ◗. Installation consists of attaching plastic clips to the netting at one-foot intervals and tying the clips to the top, side, and bottom railing with string so that the netting is pulled taut. For railings without bottom rails or slats that are spaced closely to an end wall, the string will have to be tied to eyebolts screwed into the walls at the sides and into the floor along the bottom of the railing.

Ease of removal: ◗. Removal consists of reversing the installation steps. If the installation requires the use of eyebolts, holes will be left in any surface that they were attached to.

Special considerations: After installing the net, we tested it with templates that represented the head sizes of children up to three years old, and with probes that are used to check openings in home playground equipment for head entrapment hazards. We found that if no railing slats blocked the gaps in the net at the sides and bottom, it was possible for children up to nine months old to squeeze completely through the gaps at the sides and bottom of the net. We also found that toddlers older than nine months could get their bodies through the gaps but not their heads. Toddlers who squeezed their bodies through a gap and then lost their footing could wind up hanging by their necks and could be strangled.

Ease of use: ⊖. This product does not interfere with the use of the railing.

Durability: ◑. While the net material itself is very strong, the mounting hardware is not up to the task. We found that pulling the net downward from the top or upward from the bottom will cause the knots in the string to slip. Once the knots slip and the securing string lengthens, the gaps at the top and bottom of the net get bigger. When the net was pulled upward or downward with a force of 10 to 18 pounds, the fastening clips opened and released sections of the net. The resulting opening could allow a young child to get through.

The Bottom Line: Not Acceptable. While this product can prevent toddlers from falling directly through or getting their heads stuck in the center portion of railings with widely spaced slats, it may not prevent very small children from falling through the sides or bottom. It also introduces the potential of strangulation for toddlers who work their bodies through a gap and then lose their footing. Additionally, a child pulling on the net can cause the retaining clips to disengage. Once the clip comes loose, the child may be able to get through the netting.

E   VG   G   F   P
⊖   ⊖   ○   ◑   ●

14

High chairs and booster seats

The traditional tall wooden high chair with wooden tray has largely given way to multijointed products of metal and plastic or all-plastic and hybrids that combine baby seats or carriers with a chair base or swing, etc. The spectrum of metal-framed chairs ranges from lower-price models with narrow stances, thin vinyl upholstery, and rattly trays to expensive units with large, wraparound trays that are easy to remove, reclining seats, and other special features. Since 1975, high chairs have been covered by a voluntary safety standard that calls for restraining belts, dependable locks for the chair and tray, good stability, and other features. Current standards address accidents like slipping out of the chair under the tray, a hazard known as "submarining." A few models already have passive restraints that are judged to reduce this hazard. Assembly can be difficult, so select a model that does not require you to assemble it. In purchasing a chair, the seatbelt latches and the tray operation are critical considerations, since you will be handling them every day. Look for a tray that allows single-handed operation. If space is at a premium, consider a model that folds compactly. And follow such rules as keeping an eye on your child while in the chair, always fastening the seatbelt, and never letting the child stand up in the chair.

You don't necessarily need to purchase a high chair before your baby is born, but at the age when he or she is sitting up and eating solid foods, it's helpful to have one for mealtimes. Some models let you place baby in a reclined "bottle-feeding" position even before the age of six months.

Most of the top-rated models covered by our October 1990 Ratings are still available as of this writing (most can still be found in stores even though they may not be listed in manufacturers' catalogs), but several manufacturers have introduced all-plastic high chairs of the folding type and some that don't fold. Although wooden chairs can have an old-fashioned charm, they have several practical disadvantages over metal-framed models. Without additional pads, they don't seem to be as comfortable for babies as more modern, padded metal versions. Often the seat may be too deep and the footrest positioned too low for the baby. Some have spindles at the back that are uncomfortable to lean against. Wood surfaces can be more difficult to clean than vinyl, and can get scratched when you try to pry up dried baby food with a knife or scrub it with a cleanser. Wooden chairs, as a rule, do not fold. This can be a major inconvenience. The trays on most wooden chairs do not operate as smoothly as the trays on metal and plastic chairs. With the help of lightly padded inserts, wooden high chairs can be made a bit more comfortable and form-fitting for smaller children.

Manufacturing requirements

Every year an estimated 9,000 accidents involving high chairs result in visits to hospital emergency rooms. Children under the age of one are most vulnerable to high-chair accidents. Falls from the chair constitute the major portion of serious injuries. A typical accident occurs when a parent puts a baby into the chair and closes the tray in front without fastening the restraint belt. The tray becomes unlatched, falling to the floor, with baby following it. Other accidents happen when babies push themselves and the chair over with their hands or feet, using a wall, kitchen counter, or table to push against, or when they stand up and teeter over, taking the chair with them. Sometimes babies "submarine" under the chair's tray because the crotch strap isn't being used to provide restraint. (This kind of accident kills, on average, four babies every year.)

As mentioned, high chairs may be measured against a voluntary safety standard and certification program that is administered by the Juvenile Products Manufacturers Association (JPMA). Certified chairs must meet the following requirements, although there is not always a guarantee that they do.

General requirements. These include the provisions that a chair must not have hazardous sharp edges or protrusions before and after testing, and must have a locking device to prevent accidental folding.

Performance requirements. These cover matters such as minimum withdrawal force for caps and plugs that a child can grasp between thumb and forefinger; drop tests of tray; disengagement tests of tray; load and stability tests of chair; protection from coil springs (rarely found in newer models) and scissoring; maximum size of holes; and restraining-system tests using a test child-dummy.

Labeling. This includes a requirement that a permanent conspicuous label should warn against leaving the child unattended and advise always securing the child in the restraining system. A label should also give the name and address of the manufacturer, distributor, or seller, and the model number and date code of manufacture.

Instructional literature. This should cover assembly, maintenance, cleaning, and operation.

Some chairs that meet the safety criteria have a seal of approval prominently posted on them, bearing the word "CERTIFIED" and the JPMA logo. We suggest that you remove the label when you get the chair home, since it might become a choking hazard.

We tested high chairs described in this chapter according to that standard and added a few durability tests of our own. Basically, the added tests were repetitive operations of the folding mechanisms and tray operations. We pushed the models to their limits (1,000 repetitions of each operation), so you can be sure that a chair rated high in durability won't collapse or become unsafe for quite a while.

Buying advice

Usually, what you are paying for in different metal or plastic models is the thickness of the vinyl and padding in the upholstery and the sophistication of the tray systems. Differences in padding thickness are relatively insignificant in relation to your baby's seating comfort, but vinyl quality is important. Inspect the seat upholstery to be sure that it is thick and won't puncture or tear easily. Inspect the heat-sealed seams along the front of the seat. They should not have sharp edges or be placed in such a position that they will scratch the back of your baby's legs.

Look for stability: A chair that has widely spread legs or a wide base is difficult to tip over. Check the restraining system; the seat's restraining belts should be designed to contact your baby firmly across the hips and between the legs so the child can't stand up or submarine under the tray. Restraints should be adjustable to accommodate a growing child.

Except for passive restraints, the safest restraint systems are those that are securely attached to the seat or low on the backrest frame. The child actually sits on the crotch strap, which should be looped into the waist belt. The buckles should be securely attached to the belt, and they must not slip when closed or when you pull on the belt.

Such a system may interfere with the diaper and may be a bit more inconvenient to use than those where the crotch strap attaches to the front edge of the seat. This latter type of belt fastening can permit easier entry and exit of the child, but in some variations the child can stand up or slip both legs on one side of the crotch strap. That could lead to a serious accident.

Regardless of what restraint system you encounter, be sure to use it, and keep an eye on the child. Remember that even the best system will not prevent accidents if you do not use it or use it incorrectly.

Check the tray. It should be operable with one hand while you're holding your baby. Operation includes adjusting the tray forward and backward, removing it, or swinging it to the side and back. Trays that wrap around are helpful in keeping food and toys on the tray. Other good tray features include a wide rim to contain spills, a tray angle designed so that spills go to the front rather than puddling near the baby, and stable hardware fittings so that the tray doesn't rattle against the chair's metal arms. Check the bottom of the tray to be sure that there are no exposed holes or sharp edges that can injure exploring fingers. Watch for peeling chrome, which is a potential hazard. Examine the seat; it will have to be able to withstand rough treatment. Look for smooth surfaces that can be cleaned easily and don't capture food particles. A lift-out seat comes in handy for daily cleaning. Some chairs offer lumbar support or reclining backrests as an accommodation to small babies who aren't yet able to sit up. The reclining feature is only for bottle-feeding, but for maximum safety of very young infants, bottle-feeding should only be done with baby in an adult's arms.

Check that the chair has a secure locking system to prevent inadvertent collapse. Usually, the chair folds by bringing the seat against the backrest. If you have limited space in your kitchen or dining area and plan to store the chair between meals, test the folding mechanism to see how easy it is to operate, and look for a chair that has a slender profile when it's folded. A chair should have a latch that engages automatically when the chair is fully opened, so it cannot fold accidentally. Finally, before you buy, check the high chair to see that there are no parts that can come off. Avoid a chair with parts small enough for a child to swallow or inhale, or that can choke the child. Easily removed caps or plugs at the ends of metal tubing frequently cause choking incidents. Of course, we did all the checking for you for the models in the Ratings on the next page.

Ratings: High chairs

As published in CONSUMER REPORTS, October 1990.

Listed in order of estimated quality, based primarily on safety and convenience. Closely ranked models differed little in quality. Models judged equal in quality are listed in order of increasing price.

Brand and model. If you can't find a model, contact the manufacturer; see list of addresses and phone numbers in Appendix B.

Price. The manufacturer's suggested or approximate retail price.

Safety. We followed procedures similar to those specified in government and industry safety standards to check the following: the strength of restraining systems and their ability to keep a child from falling or slipping out; small parts that could fit into a child's mouth, the strength of locking mechanisms; the chair's stability.

Convenience. A measure of how easy chairs were to assemble and use. Tests included folding and unfolding, buckling a child in, and moving trays.

Durability. How well chairs held up to repeated use and common accidents.

Comfort. Chairs we judged the most comfortable have padded seats and backrests with good head support.

Frame. Metal-framed chairs have largely supplanted wooden high chairs.

Open size. The large chairs range from 38 to 41 inches high, 22 to 25 inches wide, and 24 to 29 inches deep. The medium chairs range from 36 to 39 inches high, 19 to 23 inches wide, and 21 to 26 inches deep. The small chair is 35x20x23 inches.

Tray spill capacity. How much liquid each tray could hold. Even a small spill is likely to splash the floor or the baby.

Specifications and features. *All have:* • Tray, footrest, and restraint system. • Leg stance from 19½x19½ inches to 24x24inches. • Backrest from 14 to 20 inches high. • Seat width of 10 to 15 inches. *Except as noted, all have:* • Straight legs. • Effective seat height of 21 to 23 inches from floor. • Seat depth of 10 to 12 inches. • Tray that slopes down and away from child. • Wood trays on wood models. • 2 or 3 anchor points for restraint system. • Ability to fold for storage. • Locking mechanism that engages automatically.

Ratings: High chairs *continued*

Brand and model	Price	Safety	Conven-ience	Dura-bility	Comfort	Frame	Weight	Open size	Tray spill
Cosco 202	$75-80	⊖	⊜	⊜	⊖	Metal	16 lb.	Large	12 cup
Peg Perego 21-01-027	120	⊖	⊜	⊜	⊖	Metal	20	Large	16
Fisher-Price 9139	70	⊖	⊜	⊜	○	Metal	13	Large	12
Gerry 375	75	○	⊜	⊜	⊖	Metal	14	Large	12
Century 16-400	70	⊖	⊜	⊜	⊖	Metal	14	Large	15
Evenflo Sidewinder 260	47	○	⊜	⊜	○	Metal	13	Large	10
Aprica 244	120	○	⊜	⊜	○	Metal	13	Medium	9
Fisher-Price 9520	100	⊖	⊖	⊜	◒	Wood	16	Large	12
Little Tikes 7723 Playcraft	80	○	⊖	⊜	○	Plastic	17	Large	10
Graco 3320	44	⊖	○	⊜	○	Metal	13	Medium	12
Graco 3450	60	⊖	○	⊜	○	Metal	14	Medium	12
Chicco Spazie 64479	94	○	⊖	⊜	○	Metal	18	Large	12
Cosco Deluxe 329	39	⊖	○	⊜	○	Metal	12	Medium	7
Kolcraft 19070 AL	33	○	○	⊜	○	Metal	11	Medium	1/4
Child Craft 55000.03	220	○	○	○	◒	Wood	17	Medium	2
Welsh 3463 Love Bunny	59	○	○	○	○	Metal	13	Medium	1/4
Kolcraft 19300	50	○	◒	⊜	○	Metal	13	Large	17
Nu-Line 2712	105	○	○	○	◒	Wood	16	Medium	4
Simmons 512	189	○	◒	○	◒	Wood	20	Medium	1
Sears Cat. No. 37042	50	○	◒	◒	◒	Wood	15	Medium	1

Comments

Has U-shaped leg with plastic corner guards. Larger tray than most. Discontinued. **Plusses:** Folds more compactly than others. Backrest provides lateral support for very young child. Tray can be adjusted with one hand. Tray swings to side. Comes fully assembled.Can be folded and opened with one hand easier than others.

Six seat heights, 12 to 25 inches from floor. Detachable seat can be used as separate feeding seat. Has removable casters. **Plusses:** Backrest provides lateral support for very young child. **Minuses:** Does not fold for storage.

Has U-shaped leg with plastic corner guards. Larger tray than most. Discontinued. **Plusses:** Restraint system judged more effective than others at preventing child from putting both legs through one opening. Tray can be adjusted with one hand. **Minuses:** Plastic piece (too large to be a choking hazard) came off in tray drop test.

Has U-shaped leg with plastic corner guards. Larger tray than most. "First Meals" style tested now discontinued; available ony in "Forest Friends" style. **Plusses:** Has reclining backrest for bottle feeding. Backrest provides lateral support for very young child. Restraint system judged more effective than others at preventing child from putting both legs through one opening. Tray can be adjusted with one hand. **Minuses:** Pieces that broke off tray in drop tests judged to be a choking hazard.

Has U-shaped leg with plastic corner guards. Wider base than most. Larger tray than most. **Plusses:** Has reclining backrest for bottle feeding. Backrest provides lateral support for very young child. Restraint system judged more effective than others at preventing child from putting both legs through one opening. Tray can be adjusted with one hand. **Minuses:** Restraint system, although effective, was judged more difficult to use than others. Restraint system pulled out from single anchor point in our stress test. Single anchor point for restraint system.

Has U-shaped leg with plastic corner guards. Larger tray than most. **Plusses:** Tray swings to side. Can be folded and opened with one hand easier than others.

Replaced by **242,** approximately $133. **Plusses:** Folds more compactly than others. Comes fully assembled. Can be folded and opened with one hand easier than others. **Minuses:** More likely than others to fold accidentally.

Larger tray than most. Deeper seat than most. **Plusses:** Has removable plastic tray and armrest covers. Restraint system judged more effective than others at preventing child from putting both legs through one opening. Tray can be adjusted with one hand. **Minuses:** Does not fold for storage. Lacks floor glides. Plastic piece (too large to be a choking hazard) came off in tray drop test. Single anchor point for restraint system.

Plusses: Tray can be adjusted with one hand. **Minuses:** Does not fold for storage.

Plusses: Restraint system judged more effective than others at preventing child from putting both legs through one opening. Tray can be adjusted with one hand. **Minuses:** Restraint system, although effective, was judged more difficult to use than others. Single anchor point for restraint system.

Has U-shaped leg with plastic corner guards. **Plusses:** Restraint system judged more effective than others at preventing child from putting both legs through one opening. Tray can be adjusted with one hand. **Minuses:** Restraint system, although effective, was judged more difficult to use than others. Single anchor point for restraint system.

Larger tray than most. **Plusses:** Comes fully assembled.

Minuses: Automatic locking mechanism sometimes failed to engage.

Deeper seat than most. **Plusses:** Restraint system judged more effective than others at preventing child from putting both legs through one opening. **Minuses:** Tray slopes toward child; spills are more likely to overflow onto child. Lacks automatic locking system to prevent chair from folding accidentally; child's weight keeps chair open. Single anchor point for restraint system.

Minuses: Does not fold for storage. Lacks floor glides. Crotch strap attaches to tray; judged less safe than others. Wood tray broke in drop test.

Minuses: Tray slopes toward child; spills are more likely to overflow onto child. Lacks automatic locking system to prevent chair from folding accidentally; child's weight keeps chair open.

Has U-shaped leg with plastic corner guards. **Plusses:** Restraint system judged more effective than others at preventing child from putting both legs through one opening. **Minuses:** Single anchor point for restraint system. 2 of 4 samples couldn't be assembled because parts didn't line up.

Deeper seat than most. Larger tray than most. **Plusses:** Tray swings to side. **Minuses:** Does not fold for storage. Lacks floor glides. Crotch strap attaches to tray; judged less safe than others.

Plusses: Tray swings to side. **Minuses:** Does not fold for storage. Floor glides judged hard to attach.

Minuses: Does not fold for storage. Lacks floor glides. Tray scratches more readily than others; scratches more visible than on others. Wood tray broke in drop test.

....

Basic rules for safe use of high chairs

Use a seatbelt every time. Don't depend on the tray to hold in your baby. If the tray lock fails, the tray will fall with your baby and may result in more serious injuries than if the baby were to fall alone. If you're using an older model without a seatbelt, or for some reason the current restraint doesn't operate correctly, purchase a harness and attach it securely to the chair. Even the newest models with passive restraint systems must be used correctly.

Keep watch. Don't leave your baby unattended in a high chair or allow the baby to climb in unassisted or stand in the seat. Don't allow other children to play around the chair; they could knock or pull it over.

Use a high chair only after your baby can sit up. For safety's sake, babies shouldn't use a high chair until they can sit up unassisted, unless the chair is specifically designed for very young infants.

Check the tray's lock every time you use it. Be sure the tray is locked properly each time you use the chair.

Watch out for your baby's fingers and head. To prevent pinching or cuts, protect baby's hands when you're installing or removing the tray. When you swing the tray, don't hit the baby on the head.

Position the chair in a good place. The high chair should be used on a level surface. Place it well away from tables, counters, or walls that your child could push against, causing the chair to tip over. Forgo the use of area mats or rugs under the chair that can tip or destabilize the high chair.

Check the locking mechanism. When you unfold the chair for use, make sure the locking device is fully engaged.

RECENTLY INTRODUCED MODELS

We judged the following recently introduced high chairs worthy of consideration. Listed alphabetically they are:

Cosco Rise & Dine. $90. Adjusts to three heights and four reclined positions for feeding infants and toddlers.

Fisher-Price 9270 Adjustable High Chair. $125. Adjusts to six heights. Converts to youth chair for table height as well as low child's chair. (Similar models: 9271 and 9258.)

Gerry Baby 385 Adjust-A-Height Chair. $100. Adjusts to six heights. Converts to youth chair or play chair.

Gerry Baby 380 Easy Riser High Chair. $100. Adjusts to multiple heights.

Examine the high chair frequently for unsafe conditions. Stop using the chair if locks or latches no longer hold, if small parts come off, if vinyl is torn and exposes foam padding that a child can choke on, or if the tray is cracked.

Booster seats

A telephone book used to do the job of boosting a toddler who was too short to reach the table. Now special booster seats are available. The typical seat, made of molded plastic, is intended to rest on a full-size dining chair.

Booster seats are uncomplicated devices and have few parts that can break or wear out. With these products, however, safety is a much more important consideration than durability.

Safety straps are a necessity. Booster seats need two sets of straps: one to keep the child in place on the booster, one to keep the booster securely in place on the chair.

Basic rules for safe use of booster seats

A booster seat is not a substitute for a child safety seat or a restraint on an airplane. A booster seat is not designed to restrain a child in case of a collision.

Never use a booster seat as a tub seat. The booster seat is wholly plastic and can float. That could cause it to become dislodged, exposing the child to the risk of falling or drowning.

Never use a booster seat as a platform or step, unless specifically stated by the manufacturer. You may risk damaging the booster or hurting yourself.

Use a booster seat only if a child is able to sit up unassisted. Do not use any booster until a child is about one year old and can sit up securely without being propped.

Never use a booster seat that lacks the provision for fastening to an adult chair or that lacks a restraint strap. A booster without a proper restraining strap should be restricted to use on the floor. To avoid the child accidentally falling from a chair, always strap the booster to the chair before a child is seated, and release the strapping only after the child is no longer seated.

A booster seat should be used only on a sturdy chair with a seat larger than the booster. A booster can move slightly even when strapped to a chair. The chair seat area should be at least a few inches wider than the booster base. Avoid using a booster if the chair or the booster is cracked or broken. Don't use a booster on a pedestal-base chair, swivel chair, rocking chair, or bar stool, or on a bench that doesn't permit strapping the booster in place.

Never place a cushion between the booster seat and the chair or use a heavily padded chair. A pad or cushion could slip, upsetting the stability of the seat, or prevent you from properly strapping the booster seat to the chair.

A booster seat isn't a toy or for carrying. For safety's sake, don't let a child stand on a booster. If you carry a child in a booster, the seat's components may loosen or the child could slip out.

Keep child's hands out of the way while adjusting the seat, backrest, or tray (on those that have these features). Fingers or toes could get caught during adjustments, causing painful injuries.

Never leave the child unattended.

Recalls

PLAYSKOOL 1-2-3 High Chair
Plastic joints could crack and make chair collapse.
Products: 300,000 high chairs sold between 5/94 and 10/95 for $75.
What to do: Inspect chair, especially plastic pivot joints, and call 800-752-9755 if you spot any cracks. Company will send repair kit—or, if chair has cracks, company will replace chair.

THE FIRST YEARS INC. The First Years 3-in-1 Booster Seat
May not attach securely to full-size chair. Seat could fall off and injure child.
Products: 41,000 booster seats, model no. 4200, sold between 3/95 and 5/95. Plastic seats are 14 inches high and 12 inches deep. Seat and seatback are teal; arms and removable tray are white. White mesh belts can be attached to bottom of seat to restrain child and to secure seat to adult chair. Device folds for carrying; handle is molded into seatback. Belts may have improperly threaded buckles, or one of the two belts may be missing.
What to do: Call 800-533-6708 for information on how to repair belts. Not affected: newer 3-in-1 booster seats, which have 4-piece belt sets with properly threaded buckles; model no. 4200C appears on box.

15

Infant seats

Molded infant seats and wire-framed fabric seats are very handy in the months after a baby's birth. Even young babies who can't sit up on their own like to sit and watch parents moving about the room. Sometimes babies who experience discomfort after eating may be more at ease in a semiupright position in such a seat, even for napping, instead of being placed on their backs or sides.

Some models can be rocked, a motion that is usually soothing to a baby. These seats are more portable and lightweight—but they are also less stable—than the sturdy, heavyweight models designed to be used both as infant seats and child safety seats (see chapter 7 for information on child safety seats). Don't confuse the two versions of seats. The models reviewed here are not designed to transport a baby in a car; they provide no protection in the event of a crash.

Most of the approximately 3,700 infant seat-related accidents that occur every year involve seats and babies falling off tables, washing machines, or other elevated surfaces, either because of the babies' movements or because the seat's metal support wires were flimsy and gave way. Sometimes a baby is hurt when the parent trips and drops the seat to the ground.

When placing your child in an infant seat, observe the following safety rules: Never turn your back while the seat is on a table or other elevated surface. Be especially careful about smooth surfaces that may allow the seat to slide. Do not place the seat on a vibrating surface, such as a washing machine or dryer top, which could cause a seat to travel over the edge.

Buying advice

When you shop for a seat, look for a base or rear support that is wider than the seat itself. Press down on the unit from different positions to be sure it will stay in place and cannot be tipped over. If the seat is primarily held erect by a flip-back handle, try pressing down while the handle is in the rear support position to be sure that its locking mechanism holds securely and that slide movements will not cause the unit to flip over. Check the base for rubber tips or other nonskid surfacing to be sure that it will be safe on table-tops and won't "walk" from baby's motions. A sturdy, easy-to-operate safety belt is crucial and should be used every time a baby is put in the seat.

CAUTION
Infant seats are not substitutes for child safety seats, and should never be used to transport a baby in a car.

Parents have a choice of vinyl upholstery or washable fabric seat covers. Fabric seats are less sticky in summer and cozier in winter than vinyl, but they absorb stains and may become damp around a baby's diaper area. Vinyl, on the other hand, resists stains better and can be quickly mopped off and dried. However, the latest fabrics are just as easy to keep clean as vinyl.

Several companies produce versatile, multifunction seat pads that can be used with infant seats, strollers, high chairs, swings, and walkers. Two examples are *Basic Comfort's Universal Seat Insert* (Model 00002, $17) and *Noel-Joanna's NoJo Li'l Soft Seat* (Model 60, $26). Both offer removable head and neck support for small babies, and both are machine washable.

Listings: Infant seats

Note: These products were not tested by Consumers Union. This alphabetical listing does not include all models available but rather is a selection of some widely distributed models. Descriptions and Special Features or Precautions are derived from authors' observations and manufacturers' claims.

MODEL	DESCRIPTION, SPECIAL FEATURES OR PRECAUTIONS
Baby Bjorn Safety Seat Regal & Lager Model BB750, $50	A molded plastic, upright booster-style seat for babies who can sit up. It comes with a front restraining bar, two screw-on vises to fasten the front of the seat to a table, and a bottom strap to secure it to a supporting chair. **Special features or precautions:** Once the child reaches age three, the restraining bar can be removed and the seat used as a booster—but not as a booster seat in motor vehicles.
Century Kanga-Rocka-Roo Model 1545, $13	Four-position carrying handle for carrying, rocking, feeding, and play. Quick-lock buckle, three-point waist strap allows for easy entry and exit. Comes with thick, machine-washable pad and a removable, washable rear storage pouch. Also includes two suspended teething toys. **Special features or precautions:** Rocking base soothes and entertains baby.
Cosco Day Cradle Model 06-523, $29	Molded shell with contoured, rocking back and padded vinyl interior. Nonskid safety pads on base and built-in storage compartment in rear. Spring-action sprockets on handle allow it to rotate to any position, front or rear. Handle serves to support seat in upright position. Shoulder belt and crotch restraining system with press-tab release. **Special features or precautions:** Curved shape of handle allows it to hook over chair back for additional support.
Delta Luv Super Seat Model 9520, $30	A rocking baby seat with parallel hand grips on the handle that make it more comfortable to carry. Seat reclines to two positions. Base is rounded for rocking baby. Lining is machine washable. **Special features or precautions:** Useful as both carrier and rocker.
Fisher-Price Cradle Rocker Seat Model 9274, $35	Rocks side-to-side as a cradle or head-to-toe as a rocker seat. Base locks in an upright position for feeding. Dual handles lock together for carrying. Soft fabric crotch and waist restraint shield. Padded removable seat cover is machine washable and dryer safe. **Special features or precautions:** Rocking motion soothes and entertains baby.
Fisher-Price Soothing Bouncer Seat Models 9241/9242, $33	Bouncer seat has soothing vibrating motion that simulates a ride in a car. Gentle bouncing is generated by baby's own movement. Soft fabric restraint holds baby in place. Vibrator runs on one D battery and has On/Off switch. Pad is machine washable and dryer safe. Frame has slip-resistant pads. Model 9340 ($40) comes with an attachment that places toys within baby's arm reach. **Special features or precautions:** Baby's own motion can provide hours of stimulating entertainment.
Gerry Good Vibes Infant Carrier Model 037/033, $45	Plastic molded seat that sits on a flat stand. Three reclining positions. Poly-filled washable fabric upholstery. Crotch and lap belt with squeeze-release buckle. **Special features or precautions:** Base vibrates seat with a battery-operated spring-action motor with On/Off switch. Uses one D battery.
Gerry Snugli Bounce 'n' Play Model 307, $32	This flexible-framed infant seat lets baby create a smooth, soothing bounce. Includes a toy bar with five developmental toys. Features plush seat padding, including removable padded head support for newborns, and crotch and waist restraint. Folds flat for storage and transport. For age 0–20 months. **Special features or precautions:** Head support lets even young infants enjoy bouncing.

Listings: Infant seats *continued*

MODEL	DESCRIPTION, SPECIAL FEATURES OR PRECAUTIONS
Kolcraft Carri-Cradle Model 12000, $20	Molded, crescent-shaped shell has rounded back for rocking. U-shaped handle doubles as seat-support stand for multiple positions from upright to recline. Crotch and waist restraining belt with squeeze-release buckle. Padded vinyl seat pad. **Special features or precautions:** Tapered head area for upper body and head support.
Kolcraft Rock 'n' Play Infant Seat & Rocker Model 65001, $40	Metal-framed infant seat and rocker features a full-length rocking base. Reclining seat adjusts to multiple positions; converts to stationary infant seat. Three-point harness system keeps baby safely in the seat. Detachable toy bar provides entertainment; adjustable canopy provides shade from the sun. Folds flat for travel or storage. For newborn to 9 months or 18 pounds. **Special features or precautions:** Compact and versatile. Slip-resistance uncertain.
Summer Comfort Bouncer Seat Model 1145, $45	Wiggles with baby's every move, or can be gently rocked. Designed to conform to baby's shape. Fully quilted fabric cover, with storage pocket in rear, comes with matching head and body support cushion. Whole cover snaps off for washing. Two-position safety strap adjusts on both sides with buckles. Two-position toy bar includes toys, mirrors, and a rattle. Slip-resistant scratch protectors on base. Comes apart for travel and storage. For newborn to 9 months or 25 pounds. **Special features or precautions:** Includes educational toy bar.

16

Monitors

"What if my baby wakes up, and I don't hear the baby crying?" That's a familiar worry, especially if you've got a newborn in the house. Well, thanks to the wonderful world of technology, now you can turn on a baby monitor and listen in on or watch your baby—even if you're downstairs in the kitchen or out in the yard. And a baby monitor could alert you to abnormal sounds or sights like choking, which require quick action.

Audio monitors

These monitors are a lot like one-way walkie-talkies. They come with two components—one for the baby's room and the other for parents to tote around. The baby's unit is larger than the parent's unit and is designed to sit on a flat surface, acting like a transmitter. A tiny microphone picks up sounds that are then transmitted by a selected radio frequency to the receiver—located on the parent's unit.

Most monitors offer AC adapter cords for plugging both baby's transmitter and parent's receiver into electrical outlets, and most also offer a battery option. Unfortunately, baby monitors quickly use up batteries—a set can be depleted in only a matter of days of continual use. So plugging in a unit whenever you can will save you time and money. Even though most units have low-battery indicator lights, they can be easily overlooked. (*Shopping tip:* Stock up on batteries when they go on sale—for example, during the holidays—then store packets in the refrigerator. They keep longer that way.)

Some transmitters have built-in, soft night-lights that can be turned on or off, and may turn on automatically when baby makes noises. Other units play lullaby music for five to ten minutes, but don't expect the soothing sounds of a symphony. You're more likely to hear annoying sounds produced by a computer chip.

The parent's unit, called a receiver, is smaller and works like a specialized radio that's tuned to the frequency of the baby's transmitter. Designed for portability, this device usually resembles an overgrown beeper. Most come with a clip on the back so they can be fastened to your waistband or the outside of your pocket. While most require a battery, some have an adapter so you can plug the unit into a wall outlet to save battery power.

Antennas, usually flexible and covered with a cushioned sleeve, are fragile and shouldn't be gripped when carrying a monitor, even though some U-shaped antennas resemble carry handles.

Keep the baby monitor completely out of reach of your baby. Some babies have managed to wrap the monitor's electrical cord around their necks, nearly strangling themselves. Others have gotten the adapter loose from the monitor and chewed on the live end. Most transmitters operate best at distances less than 10 feet from a baby, so positioning the transmitter close enough to pick up sound, while keeping the cord out of baby's reach, is important.

Basic shopping tips

Audio-monitor features vary depending on the model you buy. Most models are generally priced between $30 and $40. Newer models have more features. For example, some are extrasensitive; others combine the baby's transmitter with a night-light.

The more compact a receiver, the more portable it is—but that increases the odds of misplacing one under a couch cushion. Occasionally, a unit will get lost, chewed on, or dropped into the toilet by an inquisitive tot.

Worthwhile monitor features include a light that indicates when your batteries are running low, and a light to alert you when your baby is making sounds, helpful in the event that you're not paying attention. One design even places multiple lights on the top of the unit so you can "see" how loudly or softly your baby is crying.

Most monitoring systems have a switch that enables you to choose one of two separate frequencies. If choice "A" is filled with static, you simply switch over to "B." Unfortunately, in densely populated areas such as in apartment buildings, where other people may be using monitors, you may have problems finding a clear channel. You may have to move the receiver in different directions just to fight the static.

All models have an On/Off switch, and some also offer a volume control knob so you can decide whether you want to hear baby's every breath, or only baby's cries. The volume control on some units causes a loud squealing sound if accidentally turned up too high.

Basic monitors have their drawbacks. Distance and barriers, like concrete walls, can alter your reception. Some models have special signal lights to tell you when you've moved out of range, a feature we think is a real plus.

Unfortunately, sometimes you may end up hearing more than you expect. If you live in an apartment building and your neighbors also own a monitor, you may find yourself responding to cries from someone else's baby. Or, you may find yourself listening to unwanted cellular telephone conversations picked up by your monitor. Conversely, baby-monitor broadcasts can also be picked up on cordless phones, including your own. The signals can even be read by police scanners a mile or more away. So watch your nursery conversations. And keep the box the unit came in (including the store receipt), in case your compatibility problems can't be resolved.

Monitor drawbacks

As with all electrical devices, monitors pose a shock hazard. They shouldn't be used near bathtubs, sinks, or swimming pools, or in wet basements. Propping the unit on a bed, sofa, or other soft surface may cause overheating when air vents are blocked. Monitors, like other delicate devices, can be damaged when they're dropped. They're also sensitive to sunlight, dust, moisture, and excessive heat.

One of the biggest drawbacks of monitors is the false sense of security they give a parent who may feel that the monitor is "watching baby," when, in fact, only a responsible human being can safely protect and monitor a baby. In the event your baby has a spiking fever or is being suffocated by soft bedding, your baby's silence is much more noteworthy than all those snorts, sighs, and whimpers. The truth is nothing can monitor your baby better than you can.

Catching the high-tech wave

Manufacturers are now introducing high-powered audio monitors that operate at 900 MHz—a frequency similar to that used by cellular telephones. These monitors allow for clearer transmissions at farther distances than weaker, more basic models. You can expect to pay for that advantage, though. Systems can cost $50 to $60. The new frequency may also seriously interfere with any cordless phones you have in your home.

Video monitors

In addition to audio monitors, state-of-the-art video systems for baby gazing are available. A scanner can be positioned in the nursery on a tall chest or mounted on the wall to peer into the crib. With a video monitor, you get to witness your baby's every move on a lightweight, small-screened black-and-white television monitor in another room. One model has a VCR plug to allow you to record your baby's movements. Units like these can cost over $200—a hefty sum for zeroing in on your sleeping baby. We looked at three similar systems, each consisting of a camera/transmitter for the nursery and a receiver that resembles a small black-and-white TV set—the *Fisher-Price Video Nursery Monitor,* $325; the *Smart Choice BabyCam,* $330; and the *Safety 1st Day 'n Night TV Monitor,* $300. The *Fisher-Price* and *Smart Choice* are available at retail; we bought the *Safety 1st* through a catalog (800-837-5437). We ran lab tests and had staffers try the *Fisher-Price* at home.

All three monitors have an array of infrared light-emitting diodes on either side of the camera's lens. Those LEDs provide enough illumination to monitor a baby even in a totally dark room. The *Fisher-Price* and *Safety 1st* have three times as many LEDs as the *Smart Choice,* and so work better in dark rooms.

Don't expect a crystal-clear image. In our tests, the best pictures weren't large enough or clear enough to reliably tell if a baby's eyes were open or if the child were breathing. But you could at least tell if the baby had turned over or covered its face. The *Smart Choice* produced too dim an image in total darkness; it could barely show a subject six feet away.

The real question is not how well these video monitors work, but whether you need one in the first place. Most of the staffers who tried one felt an audio monitor was enough; they didn't need to watch the baby on TV to feel reassured.

Listings: Monitors

Note: These products were not tested by Consumers Union. This alphabetical listing does not include all models available but rather is a selection of some widely distributed models. Descriptions are derived from authors' observations and manufacturers' claims.

MODEL	DESCRIPTION
DISTANCE ALARMS	
Casio Portable Child Locator Model IM-40, $25	Sounds when a child ventures more than 20 feet from parent; operates up to 50 feet. Pocket-size, with a key chain on parent's unit. Belt clip on child's unit. Transmits at 300 MHz.
MONITORS (AUDIO)	
Baby Trend Home & Roam Baby Monitor Model 2000, $40	Place transmitter close to baby and hook receiver on parent's belt to monitor baby while out of the room. Transmits sound remotely, through walls and doors to person wearing the receiver. Baby's transmitter operates on an A/C plug and has a night-light switch. Parent's receiver uses 9V battery or A/C adapter. FCC approved.
First Years Rechargeable Pocket Monitor Model 4100, $40	Small, beeper-size parent's unit is highly portable. Unit offers clear reception up to 360 feet, with a light to indicate when you are out of range. A choice of channels allows parent to find the clearest frequency. Built-in digital alarm clock lets parent keep up with feed and nap times. Uses rechargeable batteries. Comes with electrical cord for recharger.
Fisher-Price Cordless Nursery Monitor Model 1562, $53	This compact, rechargeable monitor system is highly portable—the receiver can be carried around during the day and recharged at night, remaining fully operational while charging. Charging indicator shows battery performance. Operates on two separate transmitter channels. Both receiver and transmitter have AC adapters and rubberized antennas.
Fisher-Price Sound 'n' Lights Monitor Model 1550, $52	Baby's unit has a carry handle on top. It has a power indicator, On/Off switch, a high/low range-selector button, two transmission channel options, and volume selector. Parent's monitor is small and compact. Both units can be battery-operated, have low-battery indicators, and come with AC adapters for use with electrical outlets. Light display on the parent's receiver indicates loudness of baby's sounds.
Fisher-Price Super-Sensitive Nursery Monitor Model 1555, $33	Battery- or line-powered operation for parent's receiver. Two channels to minimize interference. LED power lights on transmitter and receiver. Both transmitter and receiver have flexible antennas.
Gerry Clear Choice Rechargeable Monitor Model 618, $21	Parent's unit can be recharged, remaining fully operational while being recharged, allowing continuous service without concern for batteries running low. Other features include sound-light indicators, choice of low or high sensitivity, and automatic out-of-range indicator. Both units feature soft, flexible antennas. Baby's unit can be set on table or wall-mounted; parent's unit has belt clip.
Gerry Range Check Nursery Monitor Model 610, $40	This portable monitor has convenience "range check" button to alert parent when out of range of baby's unit. Has two-channel selection and a sound light for parents. Night-light on baby's unit. Plugs in.

Listings: **Monitors** *continued*

MODEL	DESCRIPTION

MONITORS (AUDIO) *continued*

Gerry Ultra-Sensitive Nursery Monitor Model 611, $30	Very sensitive—will pick up even the tiniest sounds. Parent's portable unit has LED sound lights that indicate nursery sounds. Also features pocket-size receiver unit with belt clip, volume control, and two-channel selection. Nursery unit has power light. Headphone jack. Both use 9-volt batteries (not included), or 110/120V AC adapter.
PlaySkool Deluxe Lullaby Monitor Model 30507, $40	An ultrasensitive monitor with clear reception. Sound-activity lights let parents "see" baby sounds. Plays five classic lullabies as you listen in on baby. Lullaby play time can be set for 5- or 15-minute intervals. Parent's receiver has belt clip. Includes two channels, power/battery indicator light, and out-of-range indicator light. Comes with two AC adapters. Portable mode requires four AA batteries and one 9-volt battery, not included.
Safety 1st Crystal Clear 900 MHz Monitor Model 49001, $60	A strong-powered transmitter for clear, wide transmission and reception. LED light display in addition to sound. Two-channel option and volume control. Comes with two AC adapters. Parent's receiver is compact and has a belt clip. Uses a 9-volt battery.
Safety 1st Musical Nursery Monitor with Auto Sensor Night-Light Model 205, $43	Voice-activated music soothes baby back to sleep when awakened. Manual override switch turns unit off. Automatically turns on at the sound of the baby. LED lights show sound levels. Night-light in base of baby's unit glows automatically when it is dark. Two-channel selection for greatest clarity.

MOTION DETECTORS

Casio Portable Infant Monitor with Motion Detector Model IM-100, $45	Baby's unit contains an adjustable motion detector with an infrared beam. An alarm sounds on the parent's unit when something passes through the beam. Motion is detected from a range of up to 15 feet. Parent's unit has an LED visual sound-level display and volume control. Clips easily to belt or stands independently. Two-channel selection. Sensitive microphone. Flexible antenna. Transmits at 49 MHz.

Recalls

GERRY BABY PRODUCTS Gerry Deluxe Baby Monitor
Wiring could overheat and catch fire.
Products: 990,000 audio monitors, model 602, manufactured between 6/88 and 5/90.
What to do: Inspect the back of the montor; affected units are embossed "GERRY DELUXE BABY MONITOR MODEL 602" and bear a manufacturer's date code that runs sequentially from "8806" to "9005." If your monitor is subject to recall, stop using it and call 800-672-6289 for instructions on how to return it for a free replacement. For more information, write to Gerry Baby Products, Att: Building R-602 Recall, 1500 E. 128th Ave., Thornton, CO 80241.

Nursery decor and accessories

When it comes to nursery furniture other than cribs, it's really not necessary to welcome your baby home with an entire coordinated suite in fine mahogany. Your baby cares only about basic things: being physically close to you, being fed, being rocked, and sleeping.

The price of baby furniture, including cribs, has escalated in the past few years. A simple, three-drawer chest costs hundreds of dollars. You may do better to shop in discount furniture stores for some usable nursery pieces (see chapter 9 for information on purchasing a safe used crib), or consider piecing together your child's nursery from quality used or unfinished furniture that you assemble yourself. You might even be able to use some of the furniture already in your home in the baby's room.

Conversion kits are available that allow you to turn the top of any waist-high chest into a changing table by screwing the support frame into the rear of the chest. (*Note:* These kits don't have guard rails. They're safe only if you put the safety belt around your baby.) You'll want to select a chest with a sealed, waterproof finish or laminated top. You may also consider using open shelving and easy-to-transport baskets to pile clean or dirty baby clothes. Once your tot begins to crawl and walk, you'll want to fasten shelving to the wall to prevent any dangerous accidents from shelving being tipped over.

Inexpensive chests are often cumbersome to use, may be poorly constructed, and may be unsafe. That's because their drawers are often difficult to pull out, or they may lack safety stops to keep them from falling out on your tot. Flip-top chests with diaper changing pads on top are also dangerous—they usually lack safety railings on all sides, they are unstable, they can flip over if a baby's weight is on the edge, and their drawers are difficult to access with the flip-top down.

Decorating nurseries

Crib sheets should be soft to the touch, without printed-on patterns. Smell sheets before you buy them. Avoid those with a chemical scent caused by the fabric-treatment processes. Since your baby isn't going to spend much time in the crib while awake, costly sheet designs simply aren't necessary. Fitted sheets are handy if the mattress is lightweight and bendable, but if it's stiff and heavy, fitted sheets may complicate sheet changing. And forget all the fancy items like window valances, pillowcases, and dust ruffles. Save your money for more practical items, like a good stroller.

Window dangers

When you're arranging your child's room, keep furniture and beds away from windows to reduce the potential for hazardous falls. The National Pediatric Trauma Registry recently found that among 8,722 falls by children, 28 percent fell out of windows. Twelve of those children died. Eighty percent of falls from windows occurred between April and September, when windows were more likely to be open. Seventy-four percent of the children falling from windows were between one and four years of age. Sixty-five percent of these children suffered serious head injuries, and the average length of hospitalization was five days. One out of three of these children stayed in intensive care units for one or more days. Most of the children fell from open windows with no screens on them. Screens that were not fastened securely were readily pushed out when children pressed or leaned against them. Falls were more likely in low-income homes that had no air conditioners, where families left windows open and there were no window guards.

Usually parents were in another room when accidents occurred. Toddlers often fell from window ledges they had seen grown-ups sitting on.

Nursery safety

Your baby's nursery may appear to be safe, but that's not always the case. Cribs, bedding, windows, toys, and decorations have all contributed to accidents. Since your baby will be spending a lot of time in the nursery without direct visual contact with you, you need to babyproof the room. The best way to keep your baby safe is by buying safe furniture and accessories.

WARNING!
There is a connection between some cases of Sudden Infant Death Syndrome (SIDS) and sleeping babies placed on their stomachs on fluffy quilted bedding, lambskins, or pillows. A pocket may form when babies are placed face-down, causing babies to slowly suffocate while rebreathing exhaled air. Babies should be placed on their backs or sides to sleep (unless otherwise instructed by a pediatrician), and never on pillows, thick quilts, or lambskins.

Cribs. Cribs have caused hundreds of baby deaths, especially older models with loose slats or broken hardware. All cribs manufactured since 1973 are required to meet stringent federal regulations for safety. Mattresses must fit closely on all sides. Slats must be no farther than $2\frac{3}{8}$ inches apart to prevent a tiny body from sliding through and entrapping the head, which causes suffocation. Dropsides should have safety locks to prevent accidental lowering; to prevent a baby from falling out, they should lower only partially. Don't use broken cribs, cribs with posts that could hang a baby by capturing clothing or strings, or heirloom cradles with slats that don't conform to current safety standards established by the U.S. Consumer Product Safety Commission (CPSC).

Pillows and quilts. Even though decorative nursery ensembles are appealing to the eye, your baby is much safer without them. A recent study conducted by the CPSC found a correlation between soft bedding—pillows, quilts, and sheepskins—and baby suffocation deaths. Never cover a mattress with garbage bags or bags from the dry cleaner —they've caused numerous deaths. Use plain, nonpuffy blankets for warmth, and inspect edges after each laundering for unraveling strings.

Baby proppers. The latest information on the relationship between baby positioning and SIDS has led to a multitude of new products designed to prop babies in a side or back position. Proppers are usually firm bolsters, and some are made in the shape of triangles. But these proppers can be just as dangerous as pillows (if not more so) if a baby's neck becomes captured over the edge of the propper and his or her airway gets blocked.

Bed warmers. A baby's skin is extremely sensitive to heat, and babies can be burned by temperatures that would seem comfortable to an adult. Don't be tempted to use an electric blanket, a heating pad, or a warm water bottle to heat your baby's crib.

Blinds and shades. Cords from blinds and shades, or from such wall hangings as balloon patterns, have caused strangulation deaths. Position the crib away from windows and away from walls with wall hangings. Roll dangling strings up and fasten them securely out of reach using twist ties or rubber bands.

The CPSC and the American Window Covering Manufacturers Association have the following recommendations for keeping a cord safely away from a baby: Clip the cord to itself or to the window covering with a clothespin or cord clip, or wrap it around a cleat mounted high up on the window frame.

Night-lights and humidifiers. Poorly constructed night-lights have caused fires and tempted tots to play with electrical outlets. If you use one, make sure it's Underwriters Laboratories (UL) approved. A safer alternative might be to use a lamp—with a flame-resistant shade and a 15-watt bulb—placed on a dresser, or just to leave the ceiling light on. Don't use steam humidifiers; the hot steam may cause burns. Buy a cold-water vaporizer instead.

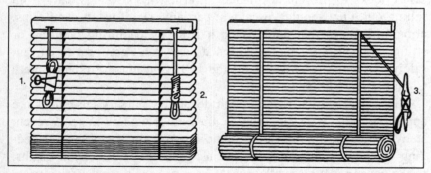

Cords can strangle tots. To keep cords out of reach of children, use these techniques: *1. Clamp or clothespin. 2. Tie the cord to itself. 3. Cleat. Or you can buy devices like the ones described in chapter 13 as a way to childproof your child's nursery.*

**WARNING!
FIRE HAZARD
WITH
NIGHT-LIGHTS**
To reduce the
chance of fire:
▲ Locate night-
lights away from
beds, where the
bulb might touch
flammable material.
▲ Look for night-
lights labeled by a recognized testing laboratory.
▲ Consider using night-lights that have cooler, mini-
neon bulbs instead of four- or seven-watt bulbs.

Toys. Over 150,000 babies and children are injured in toy-related accidents every year, according to CPSC estimates. Shop carefully for toys to ensure that they have no sharp edges, pinch points, or small parts that could hurt a baby. Heed package warnings such as: *"Not for use by children under three."* These warnings indicate that toys could harm or cause death to a younger child. Don't use mobiles or other hanging toys in your baby's crib after the baby is a few months old, and remove bumpers and toys once your tot is old enough to try climbing out of the crib.

Decorating tips

Babies spend a lot of time on their backs looking around. Bare ceilings can be made more interesting with suspended fabric kits or billowing fabric draped through rings on the ceiling. Even if you're not interested in wallpapering your baby's entire room, you may want to think about patterned borders, many of which are designed just for babies' and children's rooms. You can usually hang them yourself in only a few hours.

Many babies are fascinated by contrasts of light and dark, such as the pattern created by leaves fluttering outside the nursery window. Vinyl prism stickers, available in some science centers, break up light into colorful beams that are projected across the room onto the wall. An aquarium with a light and pump, stationed out of a baby's reach, can provide an interesting visual scene, although it can be an expensive and time-consuming investment. You may find that the pump is too noisy, but the monotonous sound may be soothing to some babies.

Salespeople may try to persuade you to invest in a fully coordinated suite of nursery furniture, or you may be tempted by a fancy brass crib or one with an arched canopy. But remember that the crib and diaper table will be outgrown in only two years. Plan ahead for the preschool years by purchasing open shelves that can store diapers and shirts now and toys later, and small chests with easy-to-open drawers with your self-dressing preschooler in mind.

Shopping for used baby equipment can be a way to save money. But be careful to select only those items that are totally safe and in good condition. Check the product recall information listed in selected chapters of this book to be sure you're not buying a dangerous lemon.

Cribs, playpens, high chairs, and other nursery items that are broken are likely to cause serious accidents. If furniture has been painted, you

NEW LIGHTING ALTERNATIVES

Night-lights offer several benefits (see warning about night-lights on p. 229). They can be handy for parents getting up for those midnight feedings and comforting when baby wakes up. They can also increase safety when toddlers need to get up in the night. For the infant, the *Fisher-Price Soothing Sounds Crib Light* (Model 1563, $19) cribside night-light also produces soothing sounds when activated by the infant's voice. The *Safety 1st Musical Nursery Monitor with Auto Sensor Night-Light* (Model 205, $43) begins to glow automatically when it is dark. Voice-activated music soothes baby back to sleep when awakened.

As baby becomes a toddler and starts potty training, access to the light switch will increase his or her confidence to get up in the night for trips to the bathroom. *Perfectly Safe's Kid Switch* (Model 86902, $8) brings a light switch down to a child's level. This wall plate extender, resembling an extra-long wall switch plate, creates a second switch 16 inches below the main switch, allowing parent and child to access the same switch. No wiring required; simply replace the current wall switch plate.

may want to consider removing or covering the paint, just in case it is lead based, and repainting it with a finish that you know is nontoxic.

You can paint a used chest, rocker, and table in coordinated colors as a part of your decorating scheme. A closet can be turned into a nursery nook by removing the door and installing a padded plywood changing platform. Shelves are also useful in the closet during the first few years, since only a few items of baby's clothing will need to be hung up, and those require only a few feet of hanging space. (*Note:* Older toy chests can be dangerous. New versions have slam-resistant hinges that make them safer, but Consumers Union believes open shelves are a better way to store toys.)

As an alternative to a night-light, consider installing a dimmer switch on the nursery's switch plate (and in your bedroom as well) that can lower the fixture's brightness at night so you can check in on your sleeping baby. (Remove the dimmer switch once your child is old enough to play with it.) Or use a lamp with a three-way brightness switch.

Think about your own comfort as well as your baby's when you plan a nursery. You can be fairly sure that you are going to be awakened by your child several times each night in the early months and periodically for several years thereafter. A comfortable rocking chair can be a special investment that will bring many nights of pleasure as you feed or comfort your baby. Look for one with flat armrests for support during breast-feeding or bottle-feeding.

A footstool or hassock will give you a place to put up your feet. A small table beside the chair can be used to hold late-night extras: a book, a reading lamp, a container for drinking water, and a radio or tape recorder for soft music.

Recalls

COSCO INC. Cosco Youth Options Toddler Bed Guardrails
Child could be trapped and asphyxiated by metal rods.
Products: 75,000 guardrails made between 8/1/91 and 6/10/92; sold with Cosco toddler beds, models 10T23 and 10T33, or separately (model 10T71). Guardrails are red, white, or blue, have ¾-inch tubular metal frame, and 2 thin horizontal metal rods with frame. Guardrails with 3 thin metal rods are not affected; nor are guardrails for full-size beds. Check label for 4-digit date-of-manufacture code. First two digits are week of year; last 2 digits are year.
What to do: Call 800-267-2614 for free modification kit.

EL RANCHO INDUSTRIES Wooden Bunk Beds

Space between mattress frame and guardrail could trap child's head and strangle child.

Products: 10,000 to 14,000 pine bunk beds, with twin-size upper and lower berths, sold between 5/90 and 10/12/94 for $200. Label on inside frame of bottom bunk identifies El Rancho or Seffi as manufacturer.

What to do: Call 800-622-7171 for replacement guardrail that should eliminate risk of head entrapment by closing up gap.

COSCO Children's Furniture

May tip over and injure anyone nearby if several drawers are opened at once or if heavy objects are placed in top drawers.

Products: 585,000 chifforobes (wardrobe/chest of drawers combinations) and 309,000 four-drawer dressers sold since 1991. White laminated furniture was sold unassembled. Affected chifforobes, models 80813 and 88813, consist of closet on left side and two shelves and three drawers on right side; they measure 51 inches high, 46 inches wide, and 16 inches deep, and sold for $89 to $109. Dressers, models 80413 and 88413, measure 38 inches high, 30 inches wide, and 16 inches deep; they sold for $79 to $89. Both items came with round, black plastic feet that can be attached to bottom of furniture. Cosco says feet make furniture tip easily.

What to do: Remove feet so furniture sits flat on floor.

18

Playpens

Playpens, sometimes called play yards, are relatively high-sided, enclosed play areas. Mesh playpens are the standard, whereas wooden pens have virtually disappeared from the market. Mesh sides that can be lowered while the baby is in the playpen can create a hazardous situation, trapping a baby in the folded mesh. (See illustration on p. 238.) For that reason, never leave the side down. You might consider purchasing a model with sides that lower only as a part of the folding-away process.

Choose a model that has well-protected hinges, supports that don't have a scissoring action, and a sturdy floor support underneath. No matter which model you choose, keep the child in constant view. If you purchase a portable crib with fabric and mesh sides, the type that we describe in the next chapter, you may not need a playpen. If you limit playtime and use it for only one child, the portable crib can suffice as a playpen.

Playpens are rapidly giving way to portable crib/playpens; both can be folded up for storage. The frame and legs of a playpen are usually made of steel or aluminum tubing. The top rail is vinyl covered and padded. Typically, the top rail is hinged so that one side or the other can be lowered to make it easier to lift the baby in or out of the pen. That's called a dropside. On many models the legs are padded and vinyl covered, too. Sides are made of nylon or polyester mesh that is taut when the playpen is properly set up.

Are playpens necessary?

Do parents really *need* a playpen? Some parents would answer a definite yes, since it temporarily frees them to do chores; also, many babies don't appear to mind being in a playpen. Other parents would give a qualified yes, perhaps because their babies don't tolerate being in a playpen for very long. Nevertheless, playpens can be useful when dinner is being cooked or a floor is being mopped, or during other

 Never leave your child unattended in a playpen. Always keep the child in view.

activities that require keeping baby in a confined space. Still other parents have found that their playpens have become cumbersome and rather costly toy containers that take up valuable floor space, or that their babies protest vigorously from the time they are placed in one until the time they are "freed" again. Under certain circumstances, a crib might serve your purpose (see chapter 9). Prices for playpens are about $100, or about the same as for portable cribs.

Manufacturing requirements

A voluntary safety standard for playpens was developed by the American Society for Testing and Materials (ASTM) in cooperation with the Juvenile Products Manufacturers Association (JPMA). Some of the requirements of the standard are the following: The mesh on playpens has to be tightly woven so that fingers do not get trapped and so that small buttons on a child's clothing cannot get caught, possibly causing strangulation. The vinyl material has to be thick enough so that children can't bite or pick it apart, getting foam caught in their throats and choking; there should be no sharp edges, protrusions, or points, and a minimal potential for scissoring, shearing, or pinching. The playpen sides should be at least 20 inches high, measured from its floor, to keep baby in. It should have strong railings and floors, with holes too small to catch fingers, toes, or buttons. There should be locking devices to prevent a child from lowering or folding the playpen side. A label is required to warn parents never to leave the dropside down. It is prudent to stop using a playpen when the child reaches a height of 34 inches or weighs 30 pounds.

There should be a permanent label with a warning on the product, stating, "Never leave your child unattended." But labels themselves can be a choking hazard if they peel off. All tags and labels within a child's reach, including those required by law on pads, should be removed by parents.

Playpen construction

At first glance, all mesh playpens look pretty much alike, but some notable differences emerge upon a professional inspection.

Legs. Typically, the legs on a playpen are either straight or have a hairpin curve at the bottom. Most straight-legged models have plastic glides capping the legs. Some tubular legs have plastic plugs instead of caps. Caution is required with both types because these pieces present a small-parts hazard: They can come off and a child could choke on them. The hairpin style lets bare metal touch the ground. The bare steel legs, usually chrome or nickel-chrome, plated or painted, will eventually scratch and can leave rust stains on damp carpeting. Some models have telescoping legs that may require depressing a spring-loaded button. In some instances such legs can be difficult to operate, so they may not be worthwhile unless you are concerned about storage space.

Casters. Straight-legged playpens sometimes have casters on two of the legs so that they can be moved about in wheelbarrow style. The most useful casters are three inches long or longer. Two-inch casters do not travel as well over carpeting as the larger ones do. But in most instances even the models that lack casters were fairly easy to move a short distance when set up.

Hinges. The mechanism that operates a dropside should be easy for an adult to use but impossible for a child inside or sibling outside of the playpen to operate. The same applies to the locking hinges on playpens without a dropside. A multistep mechanism usually does the trick. Many models have a sliding plastic cover that has to be moved in order to operate the hinge. Some models have a spring-loaded lock that has to be pressed to operate the hinge. Both designs work relatively easily for adults, although there are differences in the degree of ease.

Floors. The floors of most playpens are made of hardboard, such as Masonite, that is split in the center for folding. Most have a center leg underneath for support. Most floorboards and center legs are adequate to support the equivalent of a jumping baby's weight. But not all floors are equally sturdy, and some can break as they age. Examine the floor when you inspect the playpen for wear and tear. Stop using the playpen at the first indication of floor failure. Floors can also present a finger- or toe-pinching hazard, since baby can reach the floor easily around the edges of the pad.

Floor pads. Most playpens offer a removable vinyl-covered pad that fits over the floor. That kind of pad is judged better than one that is permanently attached, since it can be removed for cleaning and can be reversed to increase the pad's life. Just keep an eye on the child, who might explore the floor beneath the pad and get caught in "cutouts" or where the sections of the playpen's floor meet. Inspect the pad frequently; it can get damaged, permitting the child to pick at the foam inside and choke on it. Use only the pad that comes with the playpen. Never add extra pads. Children have suffocated when parents added additional pads to the playpen.

Padding on rails. Padding on the top rail of most models prevents bumped heads and other injuries. Some less expensive playpen models may come with no padding at all on the top or side rails. A playpen's frame should be padded wherever a baby might bump it. Padded legs are also an advantage, unless a pen's tight mesh is designed in such a way that it protects baby from falling into the legs. The plastics used in playpens are not flameproof. Although a lit cigarette might only burn or melt a hole in the plastic, a burning wooden match could ignite the material.

PLAYPEN SAFETY HAZARDS

The U.S. Consumer Product Safety Commission estimates that every year about 3,000 babies and children are treated in emergency rooms for injuries related to wooden or mesh playpens; some even die. The most dangerous hazards exist in mesh models with dropsides. When a side is left down, very young babies can creep or roll into the pocket of loose mesh and vinyl between the bottom of the sides and the playpen's rigid floor, where they can become trapped and suffocate. Between 1985 and 1991, approximately 20 babies died in this kind of accident across the nation. So far, no mandatory federal corrective actions have been taken, other than requiring manufacturers who wish their products to be certified (on a voluntary basis) to place a warning on the playpens telling caregivers never to leave the sides down.

Some manufacturers have responded to the safety hazard by producing new models that have sides that lower only during the folding-away process. With these models, both sides lower at the same time the floorboards come upward.

Keep the playpen away from heat sources such as fireplaces, radiators, etc.

Draft guard. A strip of vinyl, usually the same material as that used on the floor pad and top rail, connects the mesh sides of the playpen to the floor on most models as a way of minimizing drafts. On most models the so-called draft strip is tightly attached to the floor, so that there are no gaps. But on some models the draft guard is merely stapled to the floor, leaving gaps that could trap a baby's fingers. Staples could come loose, too, and could possibly be ingested by a baby. We suggest that you inspect the underside of the playpen periodically to see how well the draft guard is attached to the floor, and by what means. If staples come out or if gaps appear, repair the unit or stop using it.

Upholstery. Upholstery on the top rail of mesh-sided playpens is usually constructed of reinforced or embossed vinyl. Upholstery elsewhere on the unit is generally not reinforced. Since babies tend to chew on things, it's important that the covering of the top rail be adequately tooth-proof. Playpens that are certified to the ASTM standard are required to have a surface covering that can withstand a baby's chewing. However, inspect the vinyl periodically anyway.

Sides. To prevent fingers, toes, buttons, etc, from getting caught, the openings in the mesh on the sides of the pen should be fine enough to stop a one-quarter-inch-diameter probe from entering. The finer the mesh, the more resistant it is to bursting or becoming damaged.

Some models have pull-up handles built into the sides. The handles for pulling up are for a relatively narrow age range when babies cannot quite stand up alone but have sufficient motor skills to try. Some models may have other types of built-in activity toys. We suggest that you inspect all parts of the playpen frequently and stop using it if anything becomes unsafe. In addition to the advice that follows, check chapter 19 for advice on the safe use of portable cribs; similar advice applies to playpens.

PLAYPEN STANDARDS FOR PORTABLE CRIBS

Portable cribs bearing a certification sticker are certified (as of this writing) to the voluntary industry standard for playpens. So, if you already own a portable crib or are thinking of buying one, you may not need a playpen. A separate standard for portable cribs has been developed and is expected to go into effect soon. It will have most of the requirements now standard for full-size cribs.

Basic rules for safe use of playpens

Keep dropsides up. If you use a playpen with lowering sides, always keep the sides in the upright position to protect your baby from rolling or creeping into a suffocation pocket (see drawing below), and to prevent tots from pinching their fingers on the unlocked hinge mechanism.

Take out large toys or boxes. Babies may fall out of the playpen when they use toys or boxes, etc., in an attempt to climb out.

 WARNING!
Never leave an infant in a playpen with the sides down. A baby may roll into the space between the mattress and the loose mesh side, causing suffocation.

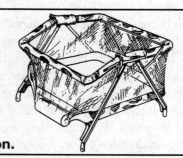

Don't tie anything across the top. If you hang a toy from the side of the pen, the suspended strap should be short enough so that it won't entangle a baby's neck. It should never be more than seven inches long.

Frequently check vinyl and padding for holes. Your baby may try to teethe on the sides of padded railings, chew off pieces of vinyl or foam, and choke. Inspect the floor pad for the same reasons. Do not replace the pad that comes with the playpen with a thicker pad. Thicker pads may be more comfortable, in your opinion, but they can be a fatal suffocation hazard to your baby.

Watch out for staples. Inspect staples under the floorboard frequently to make sure they are secure and that there's no danger your baby could pull them out and ingest them.

Clip loose threads. Babies can get fingers entangled in unraveled stitching and can choke on loose threads. A thread more than seven inches long can also cause strangulation.

Don't use a broken playpen. Safely discard a mesh pen that has holes in the side. It may trap your baby's fingers or toes or, worse, your baby's head, causing strangulation. Don't use a playpen with a broken floor, missing or loose bars, or malfunctioning hardware. Your baby may gain access to the holes in the floorboard and trap fingers, toes, or legs.

Stop using the playpen when the child can climb out. When toddlers show signs of being able to climb over the side of the playpen, it is time to allow them to roam free of it. Definitely stop using the playpen when your child reaches a height of 34 inches or a weight of 30 pounds.

Don't leave the playpen outside. Sun and rain can damage the playpen and make it unsafe. If you have to clean it, most manufacturers recommend a mild soap solution.

Never leave a child in the playpen unattended. You should always have baby in sight and be on the alert for unsafe situations. It may be hard to follow that rule to the letter, but you should be vigilant.

Playpens are available from the following companies: Baby Trend, Century Products, Cosco, Evenflo Juvenile Furniture, Fisher-Price, Graco Children's Products, and Kolcraft Enterprises.

19

Portable cribs

Portable cribs are not yet certified to a newly developed safety standard for non-full-size cribs, a standard that is nearly identical to that for full-size cribs. Until they are, a portable crib should never be used as a substitute for a full-size crib. Its design poses risks that aren't present in a full-size crib. One such design component, the soft sides of a portable crib, may result in entrapment and subsequent suffocation of a small child. Such an entrapment is less likely in wooden or metal slat-sided, full-size cribs. But for convenience, traveling, play, and occasional naps, a portable crib is a good investment. Expect to pay about $80 to $150. The *Graco Pack N Play, Century Fold 'N Go, Evenflo 341 Happy Camper,* and *Fisher-Price 3-In-1 Travel Tender 9157* have few safety problems and the most to offer in convenience. If you decide to buy a portable crib, we suggest that you assess a potential purchase carefully and follow the safety precautions we've outlined on page 243.

A portable crib manufactured before 1997 should never be used in place of a full-size crib, but it comes in very handy for occasional overnight visits, and it can be set up practically anywhere for play or a nap. Sometimes referred to as a travel crib, or as a combination crib and play yard, portable cribs resemble conventional playpens but differ in that they are rectangular instead of square, fold up compactly, and come with a carrying case. Most have a plastic or metal frame, woven fabric and mesh sides, and a hard, segmented bottom with an inch or so of padding. But there are throwbacks, too—bulky, slat-sided wooden models that are time-consuming to assemble and disassemble and difficult to stow in a car.

Basic considerations

As of this writing, most portable cribs meet the voluntary safety standard for playpens. But, safety considerations aside, some "portables" are easier to live with than others.

First and foremost, you want a model that's quick and easy to set up. The most convenient have no loose parts or locks that require twisting or turning to engage or free up. The *Century Fold 'N Go, Graco Pack N Play, Evenflo 341 Happy Camper,* and *Fisher-Price 3-In-1 Travel Tender 9157* are all one-piece units that will take you less than a minute to set up (after a few tries). You merely stretch them out, pop the locks, and insert the floor.

A portable crib should be portable. More than the differences in weight, it's the way a crib folds up into a package that makes one crib easier to carry than another. The *Century, Graco, Evenflo,* and *Fisher-Price* models fold into tidy rectangular packages, about one foot high, one foot wide, and 29 to 34 inches long—small enough to fit inside the trunk of a subcompact car. Each comes with a nicely designed carrying case with short, centrally located handles that make for good balance.

All the models measure at least 22 inches from the crib floor to the top rail—high enough to keep children from climbing out until they are 34 inches tall. Inspect a crib for problems such as sharp edges, finger entrapments, and small parts. None of the holes in the mesh of the *Century, Graco, Evenflo,* and *Fisher-Price* are large enough (more than one-quarter inch in diameter) to catch fingers, toes, or small buttons. In addition, the side rails of those models can withstand 50 pounds of downward force—another safeguard that helps to make sure a child won't get out.

Recommendations

Portable cribs are a good investment for parents who travel or want to keep a watchful eye on their napping child in a room outside the nursery. A portable crib can also be used for playing, so you may not want to spend additional money for a playpen (although a playpen offers more play area).

The *Century,* $90, *Graco,* $142, *Evenflo,* $80, and *Fisher-Price 9157,*

Graco Pack N Play

$100, are worth considering. They set up and come apart swiftly, are relatively lightweight, and are easy to carry. Four mesh sides let you view the child from any angle (most have two mesh sides and two fabric sides, though).

Basic rules for safe use of portable cribs

Erecting the crib. Use the portable crib only after it has been fully erected, which includes securely locking the top rails. Check the assembly and the locks before each use. Never use the portable crib if any parts are missing or broken, or if the mesh or the vinyl is torn. If a hole appears in the vinyl or fabric, making foam accessible to your child, the child can choke on pieces of the foam.

Using the right pads. Never add a mattress or pad thicker than one inch to a mesh-sided unit, since that can cause your child to suffocate between the side and the edge of a thick pad or mattress. Never add padding or other objects that could permit your child to climb out. Use the portable crib only with the pad provided.

Strangulation hazards. Be cautious about corner posts and other protrusions that stick up or out. Don't place strings, cords, or necklaces around your child's neck, or dress the child in loose-fitting clothing. These things can become entangled on the protrusions and cause strangulation. Don't suspend strings, cords, or toys with strings in or over the portable crib. Strings longer than nine inches can also cause strangulation.

Cords. Never place the portable crib near a window where your child has access to blind cords. Never place the crib near a wall hanging with cords. These cords can cause strangulation as well.

Fire hazards. Keep the portable crib away from stoves, heaters, campfires, and other heat or fire hazards.

Sides up. Beware of a potential suffocation pocket in mesh-sided models. Such a pocket can be created between the floor and a side if the side is left in the down or unlocked position. If your child rolls into such a pocket, he or she can suffocate. Therefore, never leave the side down, and make sure it does not accidentally fold down during use.

Transporting. Never carry or move the portable crib with your child in it. Never use a portable crib to hold a child in a moving vehicle. A crib is neither an approved car bed nor an approved child safety seat.

Occupancy. Never allow a second child or large pet in the portable crib with your baby.

For temporary use only. Never use a portable crib as a substitute for a full-size crib for full-time use. Follow this rule until portable cribs are in compliance with a safety standard for non-full-size cribs.

Watch for climbing. Use the portable crib only if your child is unable to climb out. This is typically when the child is less than about 30 inches in height and weighs less than 30 pounds.

Never leave your child unattended.

20

Portable
hook-on chairs

Hook-on chairs were introduced in 1969 by the Kantwet Company, with its *Feed-N-Play* unit. Commonly, the chairs are called "Sassy seats" for a popular brand manufactured by the Sassy Company. There are now a half-dozen manufacturers of this product.

At first glance, a hook-on chair appears to be a handy alternative to a high chair. Its design is relatively simple: a seat and backrest attached to a metal frame. Rather than sitting on the floor, the chair's frame slides onto a tabletop and it is held in position, cantilever-style, by friction and the weight of the child. Most chairs also come with locking mechanisms, suction cups, or spring latches that are supposed to enhance a chair's holding ability.

The advantages of hook-on chairs are that they are very lightweight and fold compactly so that they can be put in the car trunk for trips and carried along for outings. They also allow your child to join the rest of the family at the table for meals, which, according to one manufacturer, "encourages mealtime social development." Some families prefer to forgo such social training, since some babies grab at plates, spill liquids, complain vociferously, and manage to trash their eating areas thoroughly.

A typical portable hook-on chair has straps similar to those on a full-size high chair. The straps should be used to keep a child securely in the hook-on chair, because such a seat can easily be dislodged if a child's feet are planted in the right place and the child pushes back and loosens the chair from its moorings.

Some chairs have pulled away from the tabletop when tested to the current voluntary industry standards. The chairs that stay put have a lock or clamp that holds them firmly in place. Those that simply hook onto the table and cantilever off the edge are less secure.

A hook-on chair can't be safely hooked onto every table. The tabletop should be at least a half-inch thick; anything much thinner could be too flimsy to support the chair and its occupant. (Glass-topped tables aren't suitable either; the glass could break.) The table should also be stable, with construction that doesn't allow it to tip over easily; that rules out all but the heaviest pedestal tables, which can tip from the weight the baby adds to one side.

Countertops make a poor place for a hook-on chair; the child could easily push against the base of the counter and work the chair free.

Hook-on chairs don't do well in tests for durability. End caps and other small parts fall off. Pieces bend. Plastic parts come loose.

Recommendations

For baby feeding full-time, we recommend a high chair. For occasional feedings or eating out, use a portable hook-on chair, but use it carefully. Special attention needs to be paid to where you hook the chair, since this product cannot be used without a table. The portable hook-on chair might be safe, but the table may not be.

The three models listed below were top-rated by CONSUMER REPORTS in October 1990 and are currently being marketed. They come fully assembled and fold for storage or transport. They are relatively easy to attach to the table while resisting dislodging from the table in simulated normal use. They have a webbing-belt restraint system. They were rated equal in safety and convenience.

Graco Tot-Loc 3000 ($22). Weighs eight pounds. Durability judged poor; more easily damaged if dropped on tips of grips (after dropping onto the ground, the locks failed to hold on tables two inches thick). Comfort for child judged good.

Graco Deluxe Tot-Loc 3045 ($35). Identical to Graco 3000 above, except that it comes with a tray. The tray has a spill capacity of four cups of liquid.

Sassy Executive 050 ($42). Weighs five pounds. Durability judged fair. Comfort for the child judged average. Table locks have dual latches; provide effective backup to keep chair attached to the table.

Lacks tray; not a disadvantage. Lacks padding; a slight disadvantage.

Note: The above models are certified to meet the requirements of the American Society for Testing Materials (ASTM) F1235. The only other portable hook-on chair currently certified is the *Baby Trend 82.*

Basic rules for safe use of hook-on chairs

Setting up the chair. Use extreme caution when folding or erecting a chair, to avoid pinching the child's fingers or your own. The child should be secured in the chair at all times by a restraining system. (Use the chair only with a child capable of sitting upright unassisted.)

Proper use. Check the stability of the table before using. Do not hook the chair onto the leaf of a table. Do not use with a card table. Do not use on glass, marble, a loose-top table, or a single-pedestal table. Use only on tabletops that are sturdy. Do not use without all tips (or suction cups) attached securely. Always use the restraint system.

Table surface. Keep the seat and table surface clean and dry. Do not use with tablecloths or place mats.

Discontinue. Discontinue use before the child reaches the maximum weight stated by the manufacturer. Discontinue use if the child, when seated in a hook-on chair, is able to move the chair "arms" on the tabletop. Discontinue use if the chair is broken or damaged. (Examine the chair frequently for loose screws, worn parts, torn material, exposed foam, and sharp edges and points.) Contact the manufacturer immediately for replacement parts or service.

Transporting. Do not drop the chair on a hard surface while transporting it; it could become damaged. Do not release, fold, or carry the unit with the child in it.

Placement. Do not place an ordinary chair under the hook-on chair or position the hook-on chair on a counter or near other structures that could be used by the child to push up or off from the table. Do not allow other children or pets to play near or walk under the hook-on chair while it is in use.

Never leave the child unattended or out of view.

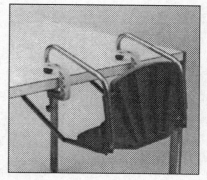

Portable hook-on chair and tray

21

Strollers

Light- and medium-weight strollers and combination carriage/strollers dominate the market. Large carriages and oversize strollers are rarely bought. Your main decision will be whether to buy a carriage/stroller, a lightweight stroller, or both. Specialty strollers that double as car safety seats or can be used by runners are also available. Try out different models in the store—including some of each style—before you buy. Look for important safety features, such as reliable restraint belts, brakes, overall stability, and a mechanism to prevent the stroller from folding or collapsing accidentally if the primary locking system fails or is not fully engaged. Check to see that the model you're considering is free from small parts a child could swallow, inhale, or choke on. Check to make sure all openings at the bottom and around the perimeter of the child area can be closed. (Your infant's legs and torso can slip through openings without closures, and the opening's edges can then trap the child's head, causing strangulation.) Shop around, since actual prices are often substantially below manufacturers' suggested prices.

The lightweight "umbrella" strollers that have replaced the bulky, heavy baby carriages or huge, nonfolding strollers of decades ago represent a revolution in convenience. They fold compactly for easy stowing in the trunk of a car and are light enough to be hung over your arm. The combination carriage/strollers made their debut in 1986 and quickly became a favorite mode of transport for babies. In addition to their utility and convenience, most have adequate safety features.

Although strollers have been improved significantly in recent years, 15,000 children are injured seriously enough in stroller-related accidents to require hospital emergency room medical treatment each year. Especially disturbing are design-related deaths. Since 1986, more than a dozen infants under seven months of age (some as young as seven weeks) died in carriage/strollers when they slipped through leg openings between the front edge of the seat and the handrest bar. Some new carriage/strollers provide protection against this hazard with closeable or restricted openings. To avoid such dangers, parents should buy the safest product possible and try to use it in accordance with basic rules for stroller safety.

**WARNING!
STRANGULATION**
**Never leave a
child unattended
in a stroller because
the child may slip
into a leg opening,
become entrapped
by the head, and die.**

For parents with two stroller-age children, there are "multiple-occupancy" strollers. We prefer tandem models (one child behind the other) to the side-by-side type. Sales figures show that most consumers choose the tandem design. The tandems are easier to maneuver, fold more compactly, and are easier to use with only one passenger. They are as wide as single-occupancy strollers but a bit longer; negotiating store aisles with tandem strollers can be as easy as with single-child strollers. Their rival, the side-by-side stroller, takes a bit more clearance to maneuver. But the latter may reduce squabbles between siblings about who sits in which seat. (If their weight is different, the side-by-side can veer to one side.)

Runners can take their babies along in all-terrain strollers built for runners. There are several good models (see photo on p. 260).

New products, such as combination child safety seat/strollers, appear periodically. Some car seat manufacturers that carry a line of strollers also market combination child safety seat/strollers.

Buying advice

If you try out strollers in the store before you buy one, you can see for yourself how the restraining belts operate, how the folding and locking mechanisms work, and how the stroller can be maneuvered. Operating these features gets easier after a while. In most instances, accessories to make the stroller more comfortable and protective in sun or rain will cost extra (except for the canopy or hood).

Should you buy a combination carriage/stroller, a lightweight stroller, or both? If your baby is very young, you will probably want to purchase a unit that reclines almost completely. All the carriage/stroller combinations recline to about 5 to 10 degrees from the flat position. Look for adequate side and rear protection from the stroller's frame, or for upholstery sides

Carriage/stroller combination

Lightweight stroller

Child safety seat/stroller

Tandem carriage/stroller

that will prevent the child from accidentally rolling out, being hit from the side, or being injured should the stroller tip over backward.

The following additional points are important to look for when purchasing a stroller:

A sturdy, reliable restraint belt. Look for a seatbelt that fits securely around the sides and front of your child's waist, and provides direct crotch restraint to prevent the child from climbing out, standing up, or slipping out of the stroller. Crotch straps that loop into the waist belt are better than those that merely attach to the handrest bar of the carriage/stroller. Most of today's strollers come with nylon webbing waist and crotch belts that connect and have plastic, squeeze-type buckles. A buckle design we like is in the form of a T; the T is attached to the crotch strap, and the right and left waist belt parts buckle into that T separately. Some restraint belt buckles may be difficult to release, and others may require double-threading, which is time-consuming and may not hold unless belt buckles are threaded and fastened securely.

Some strollers have belts that fasten across the stroller rather than around the baby, leaving a gap on the sides that might enable a toddler to get out. Choose a model with belt buckles and restraint systems that are factory-attached and threaded securely. Even with instructions, some parents may not thread the buckles or attach the belts properly.

Stability. Look for a stroller with a wide, long wheelbase and a seat that is mounted low and deep within the frame. The stroller should resist tipping backward when you press downward lightly on the handles.

Brakes. Look for brakes that lock both rear wheels positively by engaging sprocket arrangements at the wheels, rather than those that rely solely upon pressing against the tire. "Tire-pressure" brakes are

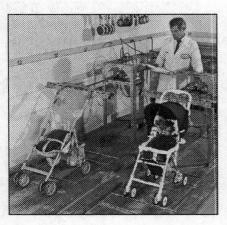

Durability test. To check how well strollers hold up structurally on rough road or sidewalk surfaces, we place a 40-pound test weight in each and move them back and forth over sets of simulated road or sidewalk bumps. To speed up the test, we use two tracks. Stroller speed is held at normal walking speed, and the test is stopped after structural damage occurs. Many strollers go the distance, a total of about 50 miles of bumps.

generally unreliable because they can permit unwanted rolling of the stroller forward or backward. This can occur even though the brake pads contact the tire. Strollers have one-, two-, and four-wheel brakes. Two-wheel brakes can either be set independently for each back wheel or engaged simultaneously with a foot-operated mechanism.

Steering ease. Try steering the stroller to see if it can be pushed in a straight line without veering when you use one hand. Wheels should be aligned; in the case of double wheels, all eight tires should contact a level floor and rotate when the stroller is in motion. Generally, the larger the wheel diameter, the easier it is to negotiate curbs and sidewalk irregularities (and sand during a beach outing). Some strollers have front wheels that can be locked into a forward-facing position or unlocked to swivel freely. Swiveling front wheels make a stroller more maneuverable for turns, whereas stationary wheels or locked swivel wheels may function better on rough surfaces.

Secondary safety latch. After you set up the stroller, a locking mechanism should keep the stroller open. Many strollers have only a single locking mechanism. Some models offer a single lock and an automatic or manual safety catch, which means it will take two release actions to fold the unit. In that way, if the main lock fails, the secondary latch or lock prevents further collapse after the stroller has started to fold.

Children who are caught in strollers that accidentally collapse could be injured, possibly seriously. Some strollers, especially older designs, have unsatisfactory metal slip-rings that slide down over the overlapping edges of the frame's tubing to hold the handle erect; these can easily become mispositioned or slide out of place, causing collapse. If you come across a stroller with that design, reject it.

Look for secondary safety locks that automatically or manually

Stability test. *This test addresses stability problems that result from a sloping sidewalk, for example. We test each stroller by gradually increasing the slope until we reach an angle of 12 degrees, the benchmark required by the ASTM voluntary standard; then we increase the steepness of the slope until the stroller tips over.*

engage, or pick models with folding mechanisms that eliminate accidental folding. Models requiring two distinct releases for folding or those with a mechanism that prevents accidental release are also more secure than models with locks that can be kicked inadvertently, resulting in accidental folding.

Sturdiness. It's difficult for a parent to judge the sturdiness of a stroller by simply looking it over. Some common failure points in strollers include snaps that rip from the upholstery and sewn-on crotch straps that stretch and tear. Many strollers are shipped only partially assembled, so it's important to put the components together correctly to keep the canopy from flapping in the wind, the seat and crotch straps from failing, and so on. A hazard that is reported from time to time is an improperly sewn or attached backrest. When reclined, the top edge of the backrest could slip off the backrest frame, allowing the child to fall out of the stroller from the back. Check that the fabric backrest is securely fastened to the backrest frame.

Frame safety. Look for a stroller frame that has no hazardous sharp edges or protrusions. A child's fingers and hands can be hurt by the folding and opening of the frame, so keep the child and older siblings well away when you fold or set up the unit. Small fingers and toes can be injured in the gaps between metal parts, and in coils of uncovered springs, so examine the stroller you are considering very carefully. X-joints, where two frame tubes fasten together, are especially hazardous because they can act like a large pair of scissors. Handles on carriage/stroller combinations reverse, presenting a potential pinching or shearing hazard. Plastic caps on the ends of tubes should be securely fastened so that a child cannot remove and choke on them.

Handlebar height and folding length. A stroller's handlebars should

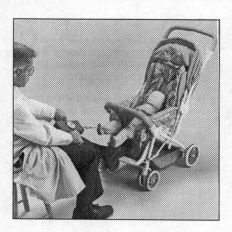

Testing the entire restraint system. Fully buckled into the restraint system, the test dummy is pulled repeatedly with a 45-pound force. Buckles and straps must not release, and the dummy must remain secured in the system.

be at a comfortable height for the parent. An ideal height is at waist level or a little below. The plastic or rubberlike covering of the gripping part of the handles should be securely attached so that it does not slip or shift. If you have a small car, you should consider the bulk and length of the folded stroller and whether it will fit into your car trunk.

Manufacturing requirements

On the whole, strollers are safer now than they were in the past. Federal regulations cover such things as sharp edges and parts small enough to be swallowed, inhaled, or cause choking.

An additional voluntary standard that most manufacturers follow is one sponsored by the Juvenile Products Manufacturers Association and issued by the American Society for Testing and Materials (ASTM). Models meeting that standard bear a sticker or tag stating that the stroller has been tested "for compliance to ASTM F-833 safety standards for carriages/strollers." These are the standard's chief requirements:

General requirements. No hazardous sharp edges or protrusions before and after testing, and a locking device to prevent accidental folding.

Performance requirements. Load tests of seat and footrest; stability tests with a child dummy in carriage or stroller; stability tests to simulate a child climbing in; brake requirements limiting the rotation of braking wheel(s); and restraining-system tests using a child dummy; as well as a test that addresses the strangulation hazard to infants guaranteeing that their legs can't slip through openings, which could lead to the child's neck being caught.

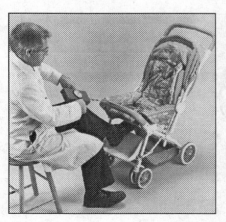

Testing the attachment of restraint straps. *To check that the restraint system is securely anchored to the stroller, we test each strap separately by pulling on it repeatedly with a force of 45 pounds.*

Labeling requirements. These requirements specify a permanent, conspicuous label advising that the child should never be left unattended and should always be secured in the restraining system. Instructions show the recommended sequence for placing and removing occupants from units designed to carry more than one child. The label must also identify the name and address of manufacturer, distributor, or seller and the model number and date (code) of manufacture.

Instruction literature. This covers assembly, maintenance, cleaning, and operation.

Multiple-occupancy strollers

Nowadays there are strollers with four seats, three seats, and two seats. You won't come upon many four- and three-seaters on an actual stroll, but two-seaters are seen with increasing frequency. As noted previously, tandem two-seaters outsell side-by-side models. A side-by-side unit is appropriate mainly for twins or children of about the same weight; it is normally intended for stroller-age children rather than carriage-age children, since a side-by-side is typically a coupling of two lightweight strollers. The children face in the same direction. A tandem stroller, on the other hand, seats two children, who could be siblings of different ages, one behind the other. A tandem unit is easier to maneuver, particularly with one hand, than a side-by-side stroller. A tandem model works better with only one baby on board than the side-by-side design does, since uneven weighting doesn't cause a tandem to veer to one side (at least not as much as the side-by-side type). And a folded tandem model

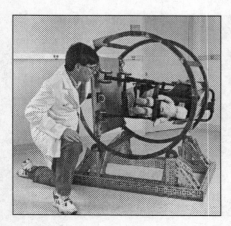

Occupant retention tests. All strollers should have a restraint system to keep a child in the stroller. In this test, the stroller is rotated 360 degrees around its side-to-side axis. At the end of the test, the test dummy in the stroller must still be restrained.

does not take up much more space than a single-occupancy model, while a folded side-by-side unit normally requires twice as much storage space.

In general, multiple-occupancy strollers have the same features as single-occupancy carriage/strollers, such as a reclining backrest, sunshade canopy, and swiveling front wheels.

Stroller and child safety seat combinations

Century had an award-winning first a few years ago with their *4 in 1 System*. Their *590* model infant child safety seat mates with a stroller, and the stroller converts from an infant stroller to a toddler stroller, while the child safety seat also doubles as an infant seat and carrier. In stroller use, this combination was a hit with parents. The price of the system ($130) was less than the price of most strollers sold separately. That attraction sparked competitive designs from other companies with dual manufacturing lines in child safety seats and strollers. *Century Deluxe Smart Fit 4-in-1 System* (regularly $180, but often sold at about $140) meets all motor vehicle safety requirements for infant child safety seats and the applicable standard requirements for strollers.

Among the competitors are the very similar *Kolcraft Plus Infant Car Seat and Stroller 4* ($160). Another competitor in this "combination" market is the *Safeline Sit'n'Stroll* ($140). As a convertible child safety seat, it can be used as an infant seat as well as a toddler child safety seat, whereas the retracting wheels and handle—once extended—make it into a stroller. It's not your best choice as an infant carriage/stroller, however, since it does not let you recline the backrest as in other carriage/stroller combinations or the Century and Kolcraft systems. It's also a bit hefty, and there is a design flaw in the brake levers; if you step on the brake too hard a few times, you will find that the brake will engage when you don't intend it to engage. However, as a child safety seat it's a very safe performer.

Stroller maintenance

Your stroller will suffer more outdoor wear than most of your other baby equipment, but there are some simple things you can do to prolong its life and usability. Park the stroller inside, protected from dust, dirt, and dampness. Check the stroller for loose screws, worn parts, and torn material or stitching from time to time. Replace or repair the parts as needed. The telephone numbers and addresses of the stroller manufacturers mentioned in this book are listed in Appendix B so you can order spare parts and accessories.

Clean metal surfaces by wiping them with a damp cloth. Periodically lubricate moving metal parts, such as brake hinges, axles, and joints, with small amounts of light household oil. To clean vinyl upholstery, use mild soap and water. Then rinse thoroughly with clean water and allow to dry naturally. Strong detergents, bleaches, solvents, and abrasive cleansers may damage vinyl and fabric. Avoid soaking the seats completely, since this may soften pressboard seat pans, etc.

Vomit and urine on fabric can be cleaned with a mild solution of bicarbonate of soda in water (one teaspoon per pint).

Follow the manufacturer's instructions for cleaning, if they are provided.

Basic rules for safe use of strollers

Don't open or fold the stroller near your child. Scissoring actions can trap small fingers and cause injuries. Be sure the stroller is securely locked in the open position before loading your child.

Always use the restraint belt. Use it to protect against sudden starts and to prevent your child from standing up, climbing out, or slipping out of the stroller. Consider purchasing an additional restraining harness if you have a very active toddler. With very young infants, however, you will probably forgo using a restraint.

Don't let an infant under seven months sleep in the carriage/stroller unattended. Very few carriage/strollers let you close openings, such as the foot-end opening between seat and handrest bar, to prevent infants from partially slipping through, causing entrapment and possible strangulation. (*Note:* 1997 models—if certified—should be safe in this respect.)

To prevent backward tipping, do not suspend a package or purse from the handles. Hooking things on the handles makes the stroller more apt to tip backward. Never put a second child in the stroller unless it is designed for two. Don't set packages or other objects on top of the canopy—it might collapse and injure your child.

Don't rely on the brakes. Don't expect the brakes to hold the stroller or carriage on an incline.

Don't try to carry the stroller with your child in it. If you're not careful, you could easily trip, hurting yourself and your child. Use elevators rather than trying to balance the stroller on escalators when shopping in department stores. (Many stores actually prohibit strollers on escalators.)

Don't use or carry a stroller with your child in it on stairs or steps. Your child could fall out and get hurt. Or, you and the stroller (with child in it) could fall down the stairs.

Look before you cross the street. Be particularly cautious when pushing the stroller out in front of you into traffic, especially when you are emerging from between parked cars. Parents often misjudge the length of the stroller when they are preparing to cross a street, and drivers can easily miss seeing a low-profile stroller. Cross at the corner, and look carefully before you cross.

Don't let children play with the stroller. Strollers aren't toys. It's especially dangerous to allow children to give each other rides in the stroller.

Stop using the stroller when your child weighs more than about 36 pounds. Most children who weigh that much are about three years old and may be too active or too tall for safe use of the stroller.

Don't reverse the handle while your child is in the stroller. Most carriage/stroller combinations have reversible handles. A child's fingers, arms, or hands may get caught when you move the handle from front to back or back to front if the child is in the unit. Always check to see that the locking mechanism of the handle is securely engaged.

Keep your child's hands away from the backrest when making adjustments. Be careful when adjusting the reclining backrest on models where the recline bracket (shaped like a rooster comb) is exposed to children.

Watch those adhesive stickers and small parts. Parts that were secure when the stroller was new can work loose over time. Check plastic caps, belt buckles, and adhesive stickers. Keep small parts such as nuts and bolts out of your child's reach. (Parts can fall off the stroller after some use and can choke a baby or toddler.)

Follow proper entry and exit sequence for multiple-occupancy strollers. With multiple-occupancy strollers (tandem strollers, for example) follow the manufacturer's instructions with respect to entry and exit sequence for the children. An improper loading or unloading sequence can upset a stroller's stability; it could tip over and hurt your children. And again, never leave a child unattended.

Strollers for runners

The trouble with taking care of a baby is that sometimes it can cut into a parent's time for activities like jogging. In addition, parents who live in rural areas often have to negotiate less-than-ideal terrain when they take baby out in the stroller. These problems have given rise to strange-looking crafts. Called all-terrain strollers, they're often depicted in ads that show mom running while pushing an all-terrain unit in front of her with baby in it.

Racing Strollers, Inc., is perhaps the best-known manufacturer of this type. They have several models in the $250 range.

Racing Strollers Baby Jogger

22

Swings

A swing can be a pleasant diversion for a baby. The types of swings available include mechanical windup and battery-powered models. Within either type are cradle/swing combinations and models that use a removable infant seat or infant car seat. The latest models don't have the problem of insufficient battery power to sustain the swing's motion—as long as you heed manufacturers' advice to stop using the swings once your baby reaches the swing's weight limit: 25 pounds for a few models, 16 or 17 pounds for others.

A safety standard for swings does not yet exist. Therefore, it's important to heed some commonsense rules. Three safety practices are important:

◆ Stay with the baby during playtime in a swing.
◆ Always use the restraining belt supplied.
◆ Discontinue use when your baby reaches the unit's weight limit.

An automatic swing takes advantage of a baby's love of rhythmic motion. The swing consists of a baby seat suspended by tubular support arms, typically in an A-frame structure with a swinging device built into the top crossbar. Others have a base that receives the infant seat or infant car seat. Some units offer attachments for both a cradle and a seat. The seats of some models can be used as a feeding stand or carrying device. The swing's tubular legs have a wide stance for stability. Some parents find that the device takes up too much room to be practical. To save space, one model has a base stand, a plastic base occupying an area about 15 to 25 inches. Although the idea may be tempting, this model should not be used on a table or other high place. Other swings have a U-shaped base with no overhead beams.

The two basic types of swings are those that run from 15 to 30 minutes per manual winding and battery-powered models that run for many hours on a set of batteries. Some parents found older versions of the swing too noisy with their clacking, ticktock sounds; the new models run more quietly. Earlier versions also had mechanical problems, and there were reports of the winding mechanism shattering and sending metal pieces flying through the air. Now mechanical swings are more durable and have encased winding mechanisms to prevent such accidents.

The cradle attachments that come with some models tend to rock the baby, causing continuous rolling from side to side if the restraining belts are not used to keep the baby in a single position. A more natural motion, according to some experts, would be to swing the baby from head to toe, as do the models we think are worthy of your consideration.

There are anecdotal reports of near suffocation of babies who fell forward into the padded front bar of a swing's seat and were unable to right themselves. A second type of accident may occur when a baby who is too large for the swing manages to pull on a frame leg and topple out. Another accident scenario with potentially fatal results might involve an older sibling playing with the swing and getting his or her head or neck caught between the suspension tubing and the swing seat.

Babies thrive on human contact, and although a swing may in some ways simulate for your baby what it feels like to be carried, a swing should never be considered a substitute for holding or spending time with your baby.

Recommendations

When purchasing a swing, ask a salesperson how long the swing will run on a single winding, or on a set of batteries if it's battery operated. Select the one with the longest run. Noise shouldn't be an issue; current models run almost silently. Battery-powered models emit a low "churn" with each pass of the swing and shouldn't present a problem.

Check the unit for sturdiness by giving it a good shake. Examine the seat carefully to be sure that it will be comfortable for your baby and that the plastic edges of the seat's legs are not sharp. If you decide to buy a model with a cradle attachment, inspect the underside of the cradle. It should have sturdy flooring that cannot break or detach from the frame.

A battery-powered swing, although normally more expensive than its mechanical counterpart, might seem more convenient, but some models can have problems with the power. The swing may get out of sync and at times slow down almost to a standstill from the weight of the baby. We think you'll find the mechanical windup swing with long running time more trouble-free than battery-powered models.

Before you purchase a swing, remember that your baby will outgrow it after only a short time. Once your baby can sit up unassisted, he or she could get out or catch hold of the side legs, throwing the swing off balance. As babies become heavier, they may overwhelm the unit's swinging mechanism.

CAUTION
Three safety precautions are important when using a swing:
▲ **Stay with the baby constantly during playtime in the swing.**
▲ **Protect your baby by always using the restraining belt provided with the swing.**
▲ **Stop using the swing as soon as your baby reaches the weight limit for the unit.**

You should also determine whether you have enough room for it. The legs of most swings are about three feet in width and depth, so you will need a floor area of about nine square feet.

Be careful when you place your baby in the seat of the swing. In some units you have to hold the seat absolutely still while you're doing that. The baby can fall out if the seat moves backward while loading baby. Limit the amount of time your baby swings, especially at a high or fast setting; in fact, the high setting may be too "violent."

Here are some recommended models:

Century Freedom 2in1 Swing, $120. Natural-arc, head-to-toe swing motion. Base accepts infant car seat (no need to buy an extra infant car seat). Has an upright and a reclined position. Battery operated. Variable speed control. Base footprint area is about 2 by 2 feet. Swing is open at the top for access from above and all sides. **Similar model:** *Century Freedom Swing* (no infant car seat).

Fisher-Price Cradle Rocker Seat 9273 (as well as **9274** and **9253**), $75. Rocks side-to side as a cradle, or head-to-toe as a rocker seat. Base locks upright as a feeding seat. Has handles for carrying. *Caution:* Don't place this unit on a table or a countertop.

Gerry 802 Easy-Sit Swing, $90. Glide-swing motion. Battery operated. Base footprint about 2½ by 2½ feet. Swing is open at the top, with access to baby from all sides.

Graco 2-position Swing, $80. Battery operated. Head-to-toe swing motion with two speeds. Base footprint area is about 2½ by 3 feet. Swing is open at the top, but extends above the swing seat.

Basic rules for safe use of swings

Inspection. Check for sharp edges, points, protrusions, or pieces small enough to choke a baby, such as peeling chrome, paint, stick-on labels, etc. Check to make sure there are no openings or small parts in which your baby's fingers or toes could become entrapped or sheared off. Don't use a damaged, broken, or incompletely assembled swing.

Temporary use. Stop using the swing once the baby is able to lean forward in it, becomes very active, or reaches the weight limit stated on the unit.

The seat. Check that the seat is securely attached to the swing frame. Lock the seat or hold it securely while seating or removing your baby. Remove the baby before removing the seat from the frame.

The restraint device. Use the restraint device (not the tray) to secure baby prior to starting and during use of the swing.

Duration. Don't use a swing for an extended length of time (no more than half an hour), and never use the swing for your baby's naps.

Proper handling. Don't push a swing as hard as you would a playground swing. Don't lift a seat by the tray when baby is in the swing.

Entrapment hazard. Don't allow a sibling to play with the swing. In some models, a head-entrapment hazard exists between the tubular suspension frame and the seat.

Transporting. Never use a swing seat as a child safety seat in a motor vehicle.

Battery-powered units. Set at low speed prior to starting (or start and set at low speed in some units). Use high-speed setting only when the batteries start to run down. Remove batteries when the unit will not be used for a long time.

Don't leave your baby unattended in the swing.

23

Toilet-learning aids

Potties come in lots of sizes, shapes, and colors (including clear plastic). They're great confidence builders for the transition time when tots still can't balance themselves well on full-size toilet seats. Plus, they can help soothe a child's secret fears about being flushed away forever.

There are basically three kinds of potties available: molded plastic chamber pots, floor models that resemble miniature adult toilets with adapters for the regular toilet seat, and adapter rings designed only for use on the adult seat. A relatively recent innovation is an adapter that comes with an attached stepladder—clever, but awkward to fold and unfold when adults are sharing the use of the toilet.

The three most important factors to consider when potty shopping are comfort, convenience, and safety. The seat should be small enough to fit a toddler, with no sharp joints that could pinch or edges that could scratch. All parts should lock securely together and be easy to clean. Toilet-seat adapters should be easy to install and remove, with no danger of accidentally coming loose.

Although potty shopping with a tot can be daunting, it can also produce positive results. Letting your child help you select a "big boy" or "big girl" seat is a good way to reinforce an "I can do this" attitude.

Once a stable, easy-to-use model has been selected, it pays to compare prices. Larger discount chains, such as Wal-Mart and Toys 'R' Us, usually offer better bargains than smaller baby goods stores. And yard and garage sales are good places to find bargains.

....

One-piece chamber pot

Molded, one-piece potties are the simplest and most inexpensive units for first-time learners. They occupy minimal floor space, and their low-slung design helps smooth those awkward moments when a child is still mastering how to back into the right position.

Their compact design means they can be used virtually anywhere—even in the backseat of a parked car for emergency situations. Many come in bright primary colors, such as green, red, and blue, and are shaped like colorful animals for a touch of playfulness. Clear plastic pots allow trainees to see what they are doing—a step some people believe will help tots graduate to adult toilets sooner. (Prices: $7–$10.)

Disadvantages: Pots have to be emptied into regular toilets, which can cause spills. If a pot lacks a slip-resistant base, it may slide out from under a child. (*Hint:* For easier cleaning and better traction, place a rubberized kitchen mat underneath.)

....

Adapter rings

Doughnut-shaped adapters that fit directly into a full-size toilet seat give small users extra comfort and security. Instead of having to be emptied like pots, they take full advantage of the toilet's flushing system. Some adapters are made of hard plastic with hooks on the underside to lock them firmly onto the adult seat, whereas others, like those constructed of vinyl-covered soft foam, simply fit into place, but are not as safe. A "boy" shield in the front can help reduce cleanups. Small, flat-folding adapters slip easily into a purse or diaper bag for shopping jaunts or travel. (Price: $5–$15.)

Disadvantages: Climbing onto and off of a full-size toilet is a daunting task for most tots. There's another major hassle: The adapter has to be repeatedly removed when anyone else needs to use the toilet. Rings and toilet seats don't always match, and a loose-fitting adapter could cause a child to fall. Some models have "safety belts," but strapping a child down can be counterproductive, especially with rebellious two-year-olds.

....

Convertibles

Stable convertible seats often resemble miniature toilets. They have small pots positioned on the inside that slide out for emptying. There's usually a seat ring that can be removed and used as a toilet-seat adapter. Some models convert into sturdy, kid-size step stools when their tops are locked into position. (*Shopping Hint:* Look for handles on either side of the seat that will help tots with positioning.) (Price: $10–$20.)

Disadvantages: These multipiece units have more parts to clean than simple, one-piece chamber pots, and spills are likely. Here's a typical scene: A child attempts to remove the pot from the unit, but the pot hits the side of the seat and spills everywhere, resulting in a crying child and an annoyed parent with a cleanup job. So test the pot to see how easily it slides in and out of the seat. *Warning:* Some convertibles have flimsy parts that don't snap firmly together, which could cause painful pinches or falls.

Listings: Potties

Note: These products were not tested by Consumers Union. This alphabetical listing does not include all models available but rather is a selection of some widely distributed models. Descriptions and Special Features or Precautions are derived from authors' observations and manufacturers' claims.

MODEL	DESCRIPTION, SPECIAL FEATURES OR PRECAUTIONS
Baby Bjorn Little Potty Model BB-765, $9	Lightweight molded portable "chamber pot." **Special features or precautions:** Excellent backup potty for travel.
Baby Bjorn Potty Chair Model BB-760, $20	Low, one-piece unit with a wide, tip-resistant base. Flexible splash guard for boys. Lightweight, molded, portable "chamber pot." **Special features or precautions:** Smooth, rounded armrest and back support.
Baby Bjorn Splash Proof Potty Model BB-763, $9.90	A plastic molded chamber potty with a high splash guard that is angled to deflect the stream downward into the bowl. A rim around the base secures the potty to prevent sliding. Rear carry handle. Seat is contoured for comfort. Available in five colors. **Special features or precautions:** Design makes it easier to keep bathroom clean and hygienic.
Children on the Go Folding Potty Seat Model 800, $10	A folding plastic potty seat that is wide enough to cover the entire standard toilet rim. Hinges are engineered not to pinch. Four large rubberized seating pads and position guides keep seat securely in place. **Special features or precautions:** Folds to fit into its own self-sealing carry case that can fit in a glove compartment or purse.
Children on the Go Soft Seat Potty Seat Model 810, $10	Thickly cushioned vinyl soft seat adapter for standard toilet ring. Soft ring can be removed from the base for cleaning. Fits all standard toilet seats. **Special features or precautions:** Side handles to help tots position themselves on the seat and provide added balance.
Children on the Go Soft Seat Potty Trainer Model 812, $20	Stable canister base holds pot for use as potty chair in early stages of training. Later, the soft-cushioned vinyl seat with side handles can be used as a standard ring adapter. The lid can be closed to make a step stool. Also includes soft rubber deflector and oversize pot. **Special features or precautions:** Easily used as step stool.

Listings: **Potties** *continued*

MODEL	DESCRIPTION, SPECIAL FEATURES OR PRECAUTIONS
Cosco Toilette Plus Model C7-320, $15	Floor potty with a lidded top. Potty can be removed by lifting the upper seat. **Special features or precautions:** Potty base turns over to create a two-level step stool.
Cosco Toilette Trainer Model 07-116-PRX, $10	Resembles a standard adult commode but in bright blue, yellow, or red. The top removes to become a toilet-seat adapter. **Special features or precautions:** Potty must be removed from the rear, a disadvantage.
First Years 2-Way Trainer Toilet Model 4000, $10	Wide-based, molded plastic two-way potty seat. Can be used as a floor unit, or the snap-out ring adapts a standard toilet seat. **Special features or precautions:** Removing the potty from the rear of the seat is difficult at best. Deflector for boys has a rough interior, which could cause injury.
First Years Step-by-Step Toilet Trainer Model 4025, $17	Three-piece unit includes a potty section lifted from the top for easy emptying, a seat section with a supportive back that can be used as an adapter on a standard toilet, and a slip-resistant base that can be turned over to make a step stool. Low deflector built into the potty is designed to be used by both boys and girls. Carrying handles on both sides. **Special features or precautions:** Built-in deflector means there is one less small piece to lose. Potty must be taken off in order to use base as step stool.
Fisher-Price 1-2-3 Potty Model 9329, $16	For use in all stages of potty training. Use as freestanding floor potty, then detach seat for use on standard toilet; base becomes a step stool when turned over. Contoured seat and back for comfort. Handles on each side for lifting seat off potty and helping tot to balance. **Special features or precautions:** Potty must be taken off in order to use base as step stool.
Fisher-Price Step Stool Potty Model 9328, $13	A floor potty with a contoured seat and seat back. Pot can be lifted out from the front. With lid down, can be used as a step stool. Comes with deflector. Made of sturdy plastic, with skid-resistant feet and built-in carrying handles on each side. **Special features or precautions:** Attractive and usable as step stool long after need for potty is over.
Gerry First Potty Model 486, $10	A stand-alone potty with detachable contoured seat that fits standard toilet. Molded side handles and contoured seat back. Front-loading chamber pot has safety lock. **Special features or precautions:** Absence of lid eliminates possibility of use as a step stool.
Gerry Potty Pro System Model 487, $18	A stand-alone potty with a closing lid. Molded handles and contoured lid front. Front-loading chamber pot with safety lock. **Special features or precautions:** Lid allows easy use as step stool.
Mommy's Helper Cushie Tushie Toilet Adapter Model 11157, $10	A cushioned vinyl potty adapter that sits on top of standard toilet seat ring. Sized to fit a child's bottom, seat eliminates the fear of falling in. Fits standard and most elongated toilet seats. For ages 2–5 years. **Special features or precautions:** Vinyl seat cover is easy to clean.
Sanitoy Nursery Needs Potty Plus Model 1527, $16	Lidded potty seat, a folding travel seat ring, a booster seat, and a step stool all in one. Pot awkwardly pulls out from the back of the unit. **Special features or precautions:** Belt is supplied when the seat is being used for a booster on a regular chair.
Summer All In One Potty Training System Model 8000, $25	Features include a toilet-paper holder on the side, and an "I'm Done" squeaker button. Lid folds down to become a step stool. The one-piece potty cup with built-in splash deflector is easy to remove. Comes in bright aqua or yellow. **Special features or precautions:** Built-in splash deflector means that there is one less small piece to lose.

24

Toys

With the seemingly endless rows of boxes stacked on store shelves these days, buying toys for your baby can be a time-consuming process. From the huge array of mobiles, activity boxes, teethers, rattles, and squeeze and push toys, it's hard to know what's going to be right for your baby. This chapter will give you the practical guidance you need for buying safe, age-appropriate toys while saving money at the same time.

Toys and affluence

In our affluent society, supplying babies and young children with toys has become a national obsession, particularly among parents and grandparents. Alongside food, clothes, and shoes, we assume that every child must have an abundant supply of playthings. Backing that obsession is a huge monetary investment by the toy industry. Toys are a whopping $20 billion industry in the United States. In 1995, parents and gift-givers spent over $638 million for baby toys alone.[1]

Deep-pocketed toy advertisers reinforce the concept that toys are not just an add-on to a child's life but a child's right. Millions of dollars are spent to bombard parents and children through the media with toy advertising. Small children appear in commercials hugging stiff plastic

[1] Source: Toy Manufacturers of America, communiqué, May 1996.

HOW TO PLAY WITH YOUR NEW BABY

Choose the right time to play. The best time for play is when your baby is wide awake, calm, and alert. If your baby is fussy, try putting him or her to your shoulder to look out behind you. Often that's all that's needed to help your baby calm down. Don't try to engage your baby in play if he or she is restless and unhappy. It probably means your baby is hungry, sleepy, or feeling some other discomfort.

Move in close. A young baby's eyes can best focus on objects about 12 to 18 inches from his or her face. Arrange a position so that your baby's face is aligned with yours and the two of you are looking eye to eye. You can sit in an armchair or in bed supporting your baby's head with your cupped hands. Or, you can put your baby on your own chest as you lie flat with a pillow under your head.

Make it short and sweet. Don't be disappointed if your baby looks at you only for a minute or two. Small babies have very limited abilities to pay attention. You can play with them for only a short while before they get tired.

Slow down and talk. Your baby will respond best if you slow down your movements and speech so that they are calm and deliberate. A baby is more apt to listen to a soft, high-pitched voice than one that's too loud or too fast to follow. Try slowly moving a bright object horizontally about 12 inches from your baby's face while saying: "Here's a ball. It's nice and red, s-e-e-e?"

Read baby's signals. Imitating your baby's sounds and gestures is a good way to sensitize yourself to his or her unique play style. If your baby gurgles, babbles, or squeals, try duplicating those sounds. Gaze aversion—the turning of eyes or head to the side—is a baby's way of signaling that he or she is overwhelmed. Surprisingly, the best way to respond is imitation. Soon your baby will glance your way again. That's his or her way of signaling interest in playing again.

Each baby is unique. It won't take long to discover what your baby likes. Babies differ in the sense modalities that most appeal to them. Some are visually oriented and like to feast on objects and patterns with their eyes. Others are more attuned to sounds and are entranced with music and talking. Still others are "touchy-feely" types who would prefer to be rocked, moved, caressed, or massaged—anything but left to sit in a baby seat.

When it's time to stop. Young babies sometimes find adults' entreaties overwhelming. Sneezing, hiccupping, fist sucking, yawning, fretting, or outright crying are potent messages from your baby that playtime is probably nearing an end and it's time for nursing or a nap.

dolls while exclaiming "I love you!" to them, or screaming with delight at the performance of huge toy trucks or grotesque play monsters.

Toys are never quite as pleasing and entertaining to babies and young children as parents and grandparents envision they're going to be. We buy them in childlike anticipation that our tots will be overjoyed with them and play contentedly for hours. But it doesn't take long to discover that babies are often more attracted to the brightly colored wrapping paper and the flashy ribbons on the box than to the toys inside.

Relationships come first

Let's set the record straight: Babies need people a lot more than they need objects. Parents, siblings, grandparents, and other caregivers teach babies about the world. It's through warm human interaction that babies and young children learn that the world is a trustworthy place. Or, the lesson may be that the world is a lonely place, in spite of all the objects.

It's these important people, too, who teach babies to enjoy sights, smells, and textures within the context of loving faces, hugs, and aromas. Babies thrive on the attention of caring parents who carry them, talk to them, caress them, and give them the sophisticated verbal and physical stimulation that nurtures the young.

Deceptive advertising warnings

The American Academy of Pediatrics has issued a warning about deceptive toy advertising that touts toys as valuable educational tools. The academy holds that there is no scientific evidence to back claims that any toy, toy system, or toy environment is necessary or even desirable for enhancing a child's learning.

Advertising claims by manufacturers that toys teach skills, such as "cause and effect," "object permanence," or "manual dexterity," or ads that imply there are critical periods when a baby or child's development must be exploited, are deceptive, according to the academy.

The result of these unfounded claims is that parents end up spending a great deal of money unnecessarily, feeling unfounded guilt when they can't afford these products and worrying needlessly when their children don't show the benefits the advertising promises to deliver.

Rather than fall for manufacturers' ploys, the academy reminds parents that no manufactured mechanical or electronic device can serve as an adequate substitute for direct parent-child interaction. It recommends that parents play with their children more, offer a variety of playthings, and recognize that common household objects may be just as adequate as so-called developmental toys.[2]

Injuries and toy regulations

Recent estimates show that children ages one to five spend up to 85 percent of their waking hours in play of some sort. The connection between children and toys can be both good and bad. It's good when play is pleasurable; it's bad when children get hurt.

An estimated 133,100 children and adults were treated in U.S. hospital emergency rooms for toy-related injuries in 1994. Half the injuries involved children under five years of age, and 60 percent of toy-related fatalities involved children under six.

Since 1980, nearly 200 babies and children have died from choking on toy latex balloons, marbles, and small balls. There were 18 toy-related deaths in 1994, according to the U.S. Consumer Product Safety Commission (CPSC). Thirteen of these deaths were associated with choking. The CPSC estimates that an additional 3,200 children were treated in hospital emergency rooms for choking on or swallowing small toy parts.

The U.S. Child Safety Protection Act was enacted in 1994 in response to the toll of toy-related choking accidents. The law, in response to previously inadequate toy regulations, enables the CPSC to require manufacturers to put warning labels on toys intended only for children three years of age or older so that parents will know when toys are dangerous for small children. Products with these warnings include balls, balloons, marbles, and certain toys and games having small parts.

Voluntary toy standards

Toy safety standards are voluntary, not mandatory. Manufacturers are not required to follow these standards. That makes it difficult for par-

---

[2] American Academy of Pediatrics, "Advertising of 'Toys That Teach,'" *American Academy of Pediatrics Committee on Infant and Preschool Child,* Publication RE0014, reaffirmed February 1990.

ents to know whether a toy is safe or not. Most reputable U.S. manufacturers not only adhere to these safety standards but exceed them. Often
they will put a notice on toy packages that states that it conforms to
ASTM-F963, the code for the voluntary standard. There are additional
numbers following the standard designation. Typically, you will see the
following designation: ASTM-F963-95. The "95" indicates the standard was revised in 1995 and that the toy is safer than a toy that com-
plies with the 1992 revision or an earlier revision.

Here are some of the important requirements of that standard:

◆ **Squeeze toys and teethers.** These products must be made large enough
so that they cannot enter and become lodged in an infant's throat.

◆ **Crib toys.** Toys intended to be attached to a crib must have strings
short enough to prevent them from becoming wrapped around a
child's neck. Crib gyms must be labeled so that parents know to
remove the product from the crib when the child can pull up on
hands and knees. (Some children have been strangled when they fell
across crib gyms stretched across a crib.)

◆ **Toy chests with hinged lids.** These products must have a lid support device to hold the lid open in any raised position to prevent it
from falling unexpectedly on a child's head or neck. Free-falling
hinged lids have been responsible for strangulation deaths, mostly of
children under the age of two. Toy chests must also have ventilation
holes to prevent suffocation.

◆ **Projectile toys.** Projectiles fired from toys must not be small, and those
exceeding a specified energy level must have a resilient tip that is not
detachable. The discharge mechanism of these toys must be designed to
prevent discharge of improvised projectiles, such as pencils or pebbles.

◆ **Riding toys.** Toys intended for children to ride on must not collapse
or tip over when subjected to overload and stability tests.

◆ **Battery requirements.** Toys intended for children under three years of
age must have battery compartments that cannot be opened without the
aid of a coin, screwdriver, or other common household tool. Similarly,
toys for children of *all* ages that contain small batteries must have battery compartments that cannot be opened without the aid of a tool.

Balloon dangers

Balloons are extremely dangerous and shouldn't be used as a child's
toy. Latex toy balloons are one of the leading causes of choking deaths

from children's products—responsible for one out of three deaths. Two recent deaths resulted when physicians carelessly inflated latex examining gloves and handed them over to children to play with.

In a typical balloon-related accident, babies chew on and swallow a piece of an uninflated balloon that may have been inflated only moments earlier. At least one death occurred when a helium-filled balloon was tied on the railing of a baby's crib at naptime. The baby proba-

THE HAZARDOUS SUBSTANCES ACT

Under the Federal Hazardous Substances Act, all toys sold in the United States must meet the following requirements:

❖ **Small parts.** No small parts that could pose a choking hazard are allowed on toys and other articles intended for use by small children under three years old. That includes small balls and marbles, which account for about one out of five choking deaths.

Small parts. Beware of wheels that can be removed to expose a sharp metal rod, parts that can pinch, or parts small enough to cause choking.

❖ **Rattles.** Must be large enough so that they can't become lodged in a baby's throat or separate into small pieces.

❖ **Sharp points and edges.** Must follow manufacturers' technical guidelines (via testing) to eliminate hazardous sharp points and edges on toys made for children under eight years of age.

❖ **Lead in paint.** The amount of lead and other heavy metals that can be used on toys and other children's articles is limited to a low level. (Lead in paint is limited to .06 percent.)

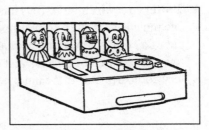

Sharp points. Toys with sharp points and edges are dangerous because babies frequently fall on them. Inspect all toys for hazards before you let youngsters play with them.

❖ **Electrically operated toys.** Must have precautions to prevent electric shock and burn injuries from poorly constructed electric toys and other children's products.

❖ **Toys for older children.** Lawn darts have been banned because

bly pulled the balloon down and caused it to deflate before suffocating on a piece captured in the throat.

All latex balloon packages sold in the United States now carry the following statement: *"Warning:* Choking hazard. Children under eight years can choke or suffocate on uninflated or broken balloons. Adult supervision required. Keep uninflated balloons from children. Discard broken balloons at once."

---

of the number of injuries and deaths associated with their use. "Clacker" balls on a cord designed to knock into each other must be made of a material that won't shatter or fly off the ends of the cords. The sound level on toy caps must either be limited or carry a warning label regarding potential hearing loss.

Sharp edges. When left in the crib, these sharp edges have caused abrasions of the eye in babies. Remove hard objects, such as building blocks, from the crib.

Rattles. A cheap rattle breaks easily, exposing sharp edges that can cut and pellets that can become lodged in the windpipe, causing suffocation.

Multiple dangers. This stuffed toy is highly flammable and could easily be set afire by a careless cigarette. Ears have sharp, piercing wire. Eyes can be pulled off to expose sharp metal sprockets. Babies have suffocated by choking on button eyes. Hair comes off by the handful and is eaten by babies.

Crib toy dangers

Numerous babies and young children have died in incidents involving baby rattles. The largest rattle involved in an accident measured five-eighths of an inch in diameter at the bulb end. Either the rattles were partially swallowed while the babies were sucking on them, or tots fell with the rattles in their mouths, causing them to be jammed to the back of the mouth. Squeeze toys and teethers with handles small enough to lodge in a baby's throat also have been involved in choking incidents.

What can you do if you already have such products or intend to buy them? You can check all rattles, squeeze toys, and teethers for small ends that could extend into the back of a baby's mouth. If one is too small for safety, throw it away. Check to see that rattles are not broken or have not come apart at the seams, exposing small pellets that might be swallowed or inhaled, or cause choking. Never leave a rattle or toy in a child's crib. If the toy becomes lodged in his or her mouth, the child would not be able to remove it unaided or cry for help. Be sure that squeeze toys, teethers, or pacifiers cannot be compressed so that the entire object can enter a child's mouth and block the airway.

Crib gyms and other brightly colored toys that stretch across the crib or are suspended from its sides can provide stimulation and exercise for very young infants. But these toys can be a hazard to older, more active babies. The CPSC has reports of infants who were strangled or became entangled in crib gyms or other toys stretched across or suspended from their cribs or playpens. If you decide to install a gym, make sure it is installed correctly so that it can't be pulled down into the crib. Remove it when your baby is able to push up on hands and knees. Toys that hang by a string over a crib or playpen should be well out of your baby's reach.

If a toy's packaging specifies that it is for a particular age group, the toy is unsafe for younger groups. For safety's sake, abide by the recommended age range on the package.

No-choke testing tube

We examined the Toys to Grow On *No-Choke Testing Tube*, designed to weed out toys and other articles too small to be used safely by young children. Small toys can cause suffocation by lodging in the child's mouth and blocking the air passages, or they can be ingested or inhaled, or cause choking. We judged this device better than no device at all for preventing such hazards, but it is important to know that it isn't foolproof. The tube can help identify most of the hazardous items that can cause choking, but when you conduct the safety survey of your home, we recommend that you be on the lookout for objects that are less than 1¾ inches in diameter (the *No-Choke Testing Tube* has a cavity diameter of 1¼ inches).

Batteries and babies don't mix

Increasingly, battery-operated toys are being sold as suitable for baby play. The list includes battery-operated cars, activity boards that make sounds or talk, and imitation telephones and computers that activate when buttons are pushed to create lights, noise, or voices.

One drawback of these toys is that they *do* everything, with little action demanded from the baby. These electronic devices usually carry a big price tag, and keeping them stocked with batteries can be costly.

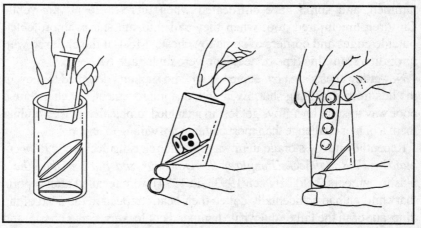

The No-Choke Testing Tube (left) is similar to the device used by the government and toy manufacturers to test toys for children under three years of age. The test cavity has a diameter of 1¼ inches, a depth on one side of 1 inch, and a depth on the opposite side of 2¼ inches. The samples of the Toys to Grow On tube we examined were very close to these dimensions, but two of the three samples would not have been in compliance with the dimensions required in the federal standard for toys to be used by children under three years of age. According to the manufacturer, the tube is designed to err on the small side—that is, it will reject some possibly safe objects but will uniformly screen those that are too small for safety. If an object fits entirely within the cylinder (middle), it would fail the government test. You should not let this object get into the hands of a child under age three. Although this toy (right) does not fit entirely within the cylinder and would therefore pass the government test, it is important to know that it could still injure your child.

Their biggest disadvantage is the batteries themselves. Batteries weigh toys down, and battery covers and screws can work loose. When that happens, there is a danger that a baby will mouth the battery, choke on it, or receive chemical burns.

Each year, babies are rushed to emergency rooms because they have ingested small, button-size batteries that in some instances must be surgically removed.

Our suggestion: Stick to nonbattery-operated toys until your child gets older.

Toy storage

Toy chests with heavy hinged lids are dangerous. Children have died when their heads became entrapped after lids fell on their necks and heads. Children have also gotten trapped inside chests when latches jammed, and some have suffocated when there were no air vents. Children are injured, too, when they fall into the sharp, unprotected outside edges and corners of some toy chests. Most of the children who have died from this type of accident were under age two.

Newer toy chests are now equipped with lid supports designed to prevent the lids from slamming shut. Even with this improvement, toy chests are a poor way to store toys. Toys get lost in a tangled jumble that makes finding them a bigger challenge than most children are willing to undertake.

Recently, one toy storage item was cited for causing accidents. *Rubbermaid's Li'l Roughneck Humphrey the Dinosaur and Bubbles the Whale* plastic hampers (sold between 1993 and 1994) were recalled after reports that children had accidentally gotten their heads trapped in the head of the dinosaur or in the tail of the whale hamper. Foot lockers, cedar chests, and small decorator storage cubes (with features similar to steamer trunks) have also resulted in deaths when used as toy storage devices.

Rather than using a toy chest, we recommend storing toys on low, open shelves that have been safely secured to the wall with brackets or screws to prevent them from toppling over if a tot tries to climb on them.

Tips for buying safe toys

Simply because a toy appears to have been designed with babies in mind is no guarantee it's going to be safe. Of the 117 different toys that have been recalled by the CPSC, 85 had small parts that were choking or aspiration hazards, 16 had excess lead in painted surfaces, 10 were rattles that presented choking or aspiration hazards, 4 had sharp points, and 2 contained hazardous chemicals inside.

WARNING!
Remove any crib gyms, mobiles, or toys strung across the crib, portable crib, or playpen before your child is five months old.

Even with federal monitoring, baby toys can still cause harm. Activity boxes with protruding knobs and sharp edges can hurt a baby who falls against them. Large pillowlike teddy bears left in the crib can suffocate a baby. Arms and legs of stuffed toys can be chewed on and can get lodged in a baby's throat while still attached to the toy. Other choking hazards include neck ribbons and pom-poms that can be bitten off and swallowed, or fabric toys with weak seams that can be gnawed open to expose small rattles and stuffing. Push toys with canisterlike containers can rupture at the seams, releasing small throat-size balls.

Some toy packaging carries specific age recommendations with statements such as, *"Not Recommended for Children Under Three Years of Age."* These age guidelines are not "ability" standards. Yet parents see these labels and assume *their* babies are smarter than most babies under three and proceed to buy the toy anyway. Not all toys are labeled by age or provide explanations as to why they may be inappropriate for specific age groups, so beware.

What babies want

Babies love textures, colors, and novelty. When you shop for baby toys, look for bright, primary colors with interesting patterns. Toys should be lightweight and the right size for small hands to grasp. A variety of textures make toys more intriguing—for example, soft, furry, smooth, or shiny surfaces. The toy should *do* something in response to baby's actions, not simply demand the baby to be a passive observer.

The best toys adapt to more than one stage of a child's interests and abilities. At best, there should be a fit between a baby's specific unfolding skills and inner drives to explore. But deluging a baby with dozens of toys is counterproductive—they only cause confusion and litter the baby's room and the rest of the house.

SAFETY BASICS

Every toy you buy for your baby should be:
◆ The right age for your baby, according to the manufacturer's rec-
  ommendation on the toy's packaging (but keep in mind that recom-
  mended age ranges are not 100 percent foolproof)
◆ Large enough so that it can't be swallowed or get stuck in the throat
◆ Without sharp edges
◆ Unbreakable
◆ Free of small parts that could be pulled off, such as eyes, buttons,
  or wheels
◆ Without hinges or pinching parts
◆ Without hidden wires
◆ Filled with pure (if stuffed), soft stuffing with no sharp pieces
◆ Colored with dyes that will not bleed
◆ Made without hair that can be pulled off
◆ Strong enough to withstand chewing
◆ Without strings longer than seven inches

Here are additional suggestions for preventing accidents with toys:
◆ Discard colorful wrapping paper (the ink may contain lead) and
  plastic wrappers, which may pose a suffocation hazard.
◆ Instruct older siblings to keep their toys away from baby.
◆ Think twice before buying a ride-on toy for your baby or tot. If you
  do buy one, make sure there are no stairs to fall down, or hard surfaces that could hurt the baby in case of a fall. Outdoors, beware of
  curbs, sloping driveways, open pools, ponds, or other dangers that
  could cause harm in a fall.
◆ Supervise your baby closely when he or she is playing with toys,
  and remove any toys that show the potential for harm. Get rid of broken toys—they're usually the most dangerous.
◆ Never allow a toddler to run with a toy in his or her mouth.
  Tragedies have occurred when a fall forced a rattle into the throat of
  a child with such force that parents were unable to remove the rattle
  in time to prevent suffocation.

Keep yourself informed about toy and other baby-product hazards.
The CPSC has an automated toll-free Product Safety Hotline, which lists
the most recent toy and product recalls (800-638-2772). You can also
inform the CPSC if any product injures your baby.

When babies begin to creep, crawl, and cruise from one piece of furniture to another, their play lives become dominated by the continual urge to find some new feat to master, some tiny intricacy to finger, or new object to mouth. At that point, toys compete with VCR buttons, the dirt in the potted plants, the hole in the couch upholstery, and the pots and pans stored in the kitchen drawer.

Energetic toddlers need toys that are sturdy enough to withstand being shaken, banged, thrown, or dropped. They want toys they can push, squeeze, roll, shake, or pull. Since they have limited strength and coordination, avoid overly large, heavy, or cumbersome items. But toys for quiet play are also helpful, such as cardboard or fabric "first" books.

Enjoyable toys don't have to cost a mint. With a little imagination, you can turn everyday objects and situations into opportunities for play. Batting an inflated paper bag may keep your two-month-old's attention, jangling a set of measuring spoons or keys might appeal to a six-month-old, or pushing an upside-down plastic laundry basket around the living room may be engaging to a newly walking tot. Bath toys from household items are likely to appeal to one- to two-year-olds—plastic containers (some with holes in the bottom), a washcloth, cups of different sizes, or a ladle.

Thrift and consignment stores or yard and garage sales are often good sources for well-made toys that are still in perfect condition but have been outgrown. Examine these toys carefully to ensure that they're age-appropriate for *your* child and that there aren't any broken, loose, or small parts or long strings that could lead to choking or strangulation.

You can save money on new toy purchases by shopping at large-scale discount operations, such as Burlington Coat Factory's Baby Depot, Toys 'R' Us, Baby Superstore, LiL' Things, Target, Wal-Mart, Kmart, and warehouse outlets like Sam's Club. The best toy bargains can be found during seasonal sales, such as those during the holidays, when the competition for consumer dollars heats up.

A word of warning: Don't be so bent on saving money that you settle for poorly constructed items often sold inexpensively in grocery stores, drugstores, service stations, or dollar-buys-all import stores. Flimsy plastic toys often have small parts that can break off easily or sharp edges that can be dangerous to babies and young children. It makes more sense to save up and buy one quality toy than to squander money on five cheap toys that won't last and that are potentially unsafe.

The right toys for the right age

Note: These toys have not been tested by Consumers Union. Toy descriptions and recommended ages are based, in part, on information provided by manufacturers. The inclusion of these toys in this book does not imply an assurance of their safety. (Toys are described in detail following the table.)

AGE SKILLS	TYPE OF TOY TOY SUGGESTIONS
1 month Alert for only brief periods of time. Wants to be held and rocked. Lifts head briefly to gaze at faces, lights, and contrasting patterns, but can't reach for them. Brings fists into range of eyes and mouth. Thrusts arms and legs. Hearing is fully mature.	Toys with high-contrast patterns, such as black-and-white pictures, bull's-eyes, checkered patterns, and simple faces. Musical crib mobiles with bright patterns that face downward toward the baby. Unbreakable mirror that fastens to crib bars. **Learning Curve Toys Lamaze Infant Development System Cribside Graphic Panels** (Model 97102, $11.99). **Fisher-Price Reversible Crib Mirror** (Model 3702, $10).
2–3 months Briefly raises head and chest by pushing with arms when placed facedown. Brief smiles to family members and toys. Cycles arms and legs. Opens and closes hands. Watches faces and can follow moving objects. Swipes at objects and is learning to grasp them.	Same toys as above. Rattles or other toys with small sections that can be grasped with a fist. Toys should be smooth-edged, with no sharp points for safe mouthing. **International Playthings Early Start Child Development Toys Tracking Tube** (Model CT507, $9.95). **Kids II Infant Development Foot Rattles** (Model 3541, $6).
4–8 months Rolls from front to back and back to front. Sits briefly, first with support, then alone. Can reach with one hand and grasp objects. Moves things from one hand to another. Pats and strokes textures. Plays with feet. Searches for sources of sounds.	Textured soft toys that can be safely mouthed. Soft balls with sounds inside. Musical toys and rattles. Chewable vinyl or cloth baby books. Toys with flaps or lids that can be opened and closed. **International Playthings Prime-time Playthings Figure 8 Rattle** (Model CT507, $8.95). **Tomy Multi Gym Walker** (Model 1598, $59.99).
8–23 months Sits alone, then propels forward on belly, learning to balance on hands and knees, and finally crawls on all fours. Pulls up to stand and cruises holding on to furniture. Stands and then walks taking two or three steps without support. Pincer grasp. Shakes, bangs, throws, and drops toys. Searches for hidden objects and takes objects out of containers. Pokes into holes with index finger. Enjoys baby games such as "Peek-A- Boo," "Where's Baby?" and waving "bye-bye."	Stacking and building toys with rounded edges, bath toys, squeeze toys, soft dolls, puppets, cars, lightweight balls, baby books, musical toys, push-pull toys, and toy telephones. **Discovery Toys Hide Inside** (Model 1350, $18.98) *Note: ages 12 months and up.* **Fisher-Price Baby's First Blocks** (Model 1024, $6.50). **Fisher-Price Little Red Ride-On** (Model 1067, $21.50) *Note: ages 9–36 months.* **Learning Curve Toys Lamaze Infant Development System Stacking Rings** (Model 97302, $19.99). **Lego Dublo Baby X-Large Stack 'N' Learn Set** (Model 2086, $19.99). **PlaySkool Steady Steps Busy Band Walker** (Model 50004, $29.99). **Today's Kids Play 'N Fold Clubhouse** (Model 370, $75) *Note: ages 9 months to 3½ years.* **Gerber Busy Camera** (Model 76756, $10) *Note: ages 12–18 months*

AGE SKILLS	TYPE OF TOY TOY SUGGESTIONS
2–3 years *Two years:* Walks unaided. Pulls toys behind while walking. Stands on tiptoe. Can run. Kicks a ball. Climbs stairs and onto and off furniture. Can build block towers, likes playing with large balls, turns pages on books, can use sorting toys. Piles blocks and then knocks them down. Likes toys that can be taken apart and put back together again. Likes to imitate. Plays simple make-believe with toy animals and dolls. *Three years:* Climbs, kicks balls, pedals tricycle, can draw with crayon, builds with blocks, turns handles. Plays make-believe with dolls, animals, and people. Sorts objects by shape and color. Simple puzzles.	*Two Years:* Cardboard books, blocks, nesting toys, simple sorting toys, buckets and shovels, dolls and balls, child-size trucks, cars, and trains, bath toys, swings, toy telephone, child keyboard. *Three years:* Building blocks, puzzles with knobs, clay, crayons and paper, outdoor play equipment, props for make-believe play, dolls, and stuffed animals. **Discovery Toys Measure Up! Cups** (Model 1640, $10). **Little Tikes Soft Rocking Cow** (Model 1554, $50). **Little Tikes Junior Activity Garden** (Model 1536, $72). **Oddzon Products Koosh Preschool Boingo Ball** (Model 8115, $17). **PlaySkool First Ride Trike** (Model 50005, $29.99). **Step 2 Wagon for Two** (Model 7303, $55). **Tomy Push 'N Go Vehicles** (Model 1012, $7.50 each).

Toy suggestions

Note: The following photos and descriptions correspond to the toys mentioned in the table above. Toys are listed alphabetically. For further information on these products, contact the manufacturer (see Appendix B).

Discovery Toys Measure Up!
Cups (Model 1640, $10). Twelve
cups from 1³/₄ to 3⁵/₈ inches in
bright, primary colors. They can fit
one inside the other or be stacked,
knocked down, filled up, and
emptied out. (Manufacturer's age
recommendation: from 12 months.)

Discovery Toys Hide Inside (Model
1350, $18.98). A softly padded,
square box with six stuffed shapes,
each with a unique sound and texture.
For dump-and-fill fun. Cube is 6¹/₂
inches. Figures are between 3¹/₂
and 4¹/₂ inches. (Manufacturer's age
recommendation: from 12 months.)

Fisher-Price Baby's First Blocks *(Model 1024, $6.50). A yellow canister shaped like an oatmeal box comes with 23 colorful blocks in three different shapes for sorting, stacking, and dropping. The lid for the canister has holes to match the block shapes. (Manufacturer's age recommendation: 6–24 months.)*

Fisher-Price Little Red Ride-On *(Model 1067, $21.50). A toddler ride-on toy with wide wheelbase. It has a large handle to make it easier to get on and off. Seat lid covers a storage compartment underneath. (Manufacturer's age recommendation: 9–36 months.)*

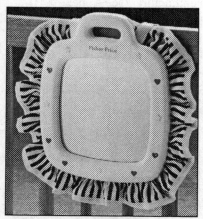

Fisher-Price Reversible Crib Mirror *(Model 3702, $10). A mirror that attaches to the crib by straps. Has a fabric frame—one side has black-and-white stripes, the other a colorful floral pattern. Carry handle at top. Fabric can be removed for washing. (Manufacturer's age recommendation: 0–24 months.)*

Gerber Busy Camera *(Model 76756, $10). A red plastic camera-like toy with five toddler features: spinning balls, ratchet sound, squeaker button, peek-through camera lens, and easy-to-hold carrying handle. (Manufacturer's age recommendation: 12–18 months.)*

International Playthings Primetime Playthings Figure 8 Rattle (Model CT507, $8.95). A rattle just the right size for baby's grasp. Two rings rotate around a center core making a ratcheting sound. (Manufacturer's age recommendation: 3–12 months.)

International Playthings Early Start Child Development Toys Tracking Tube (Model CT507, $9.95). The clear center in this barbell rattle has a slow-moving red bead. The two soft ends invite teething, squeezing, shaking, and drumming play. (Manufacturer's age recommendation: 0–18 months.)

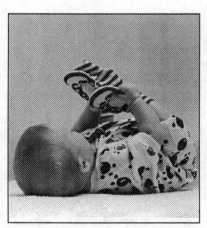

Kids II Infant Development Foot Rattles (Model 3541, $6). Soft knit socks fit comfortably on baby's feet. High-contrast characters rattle with every kick of baby's foot. Available in dalmatian, pony, and teddy bear characters. (Manufacturer's age recommendation: 0–6 months.)

Learning Curve Toys Lamaze Infant Development System Stacking Rings (Model 97302, $19.99). This five-piece set of cushioned rings can be slipped onto and taken off of a soft post. Each ring has its own hidden sound. (Manufacturer's age recommendation: 6 months and up.)

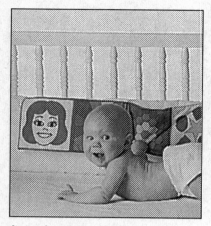

Learning Curve Toys Lamaze Infant Development System Cribside Graphic Panels (Model 97102, $11.99). These soft fabric panels attach to the crib with ties. Can be folded to make baby's first book. (Manufacturer's age recommendation: birth and up.)

Lego Dublo Baby X-Large Stack 'N' Learn Set (Model 2086, $19.99). This colorful set contains a rounded-edge elephant, a rattling penguin, a walrus, a car, a mirror block, a special rock-and-spin piece, and building blocks with a base. (Manufacturer's age recommendation: 6–24 months.)

Little Tikes Soft Rocking Cow (Model 1554, $50). A high-backed, molded plastic ride-on rocker with a wide stable base. Easy-grip handles and smooth rocking action. The cow's soft black-and-white spotted body is easily removed for machine washing. (Manufacturer's age recommendation: 12–36 months.)

Little Tikes Junior Activity Garden (Model 1536, $72). A molded plastic, circular play area with a swinging door, a squeaking doorbell, and a crawl-through tunnel. Garden contains three soft, squeezable vegetables for shape sorting and a chirping birdhouse. (Manufacturer's age recommendation: 9–36 months.)

Oddzon Products Koosh Preschool Boingo Ball *(Model 8115, $17). A supersoft, super bouncy ball in a large size that makes it easy to bounce, kick, or throw. Panels on the ball depict zoo animals. (Manufacturer's age recommendation: 1 year and up.)*

PlaySkool Steady Steps Busy Band Walker *(Model 50004, $29.99). A push toy with all the sounds and activities of a one-kid band. Wide base for stability. (Manufacturer's age recommendation: 9 months and up.)*

PlaySkool First Ride Trike *(Model 50005, $29.99). A push-along toy, a ride-on, and a first trike for toddlers. Has footrests for baby's feet and a restraint belt to help keep tot securely in place. Wide base and chunky wheels with easy mount and dismount. (Manufacturer's age recommendation: 12–36 months.)*

Step 2 Wagon for Two *(Model 7303, $55) and* **Tag-Along Trailer** *(Model 7304, $30). A roomy molded green wagon with high sides and a latching side door. The Tag-Along Trailer is for carrying an extra passenger, toys, or picnic supplies. (Manufacturer's age recommendation: 1½ years and up.)*

Tomy Multi Gym Walker *(Model 1598, $59.99). As an activity gym, it suspends toys over baby to entertain with sounds, colors, and shapes. It then can be transformed into a tyke-size stroller. (Manufacturer's age recommendation: 3 months and up.)*

Tomy Push 'N Go Vehicles *(Model 1012, $7.50 ea.). Child-size colorful vehicles—a train, a plane, or a truck—that speed along once the head of the small driver has been punched down. No batteries required. (Manufacturer's age recommendation: 12 months and up.)*

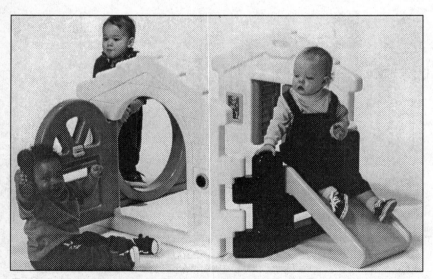

Today's Kids Play 'N Fold Clubhouse *(Model 370, $75). A molded plastic indoor-outdoor activity center with a crawl-through window with working shutters, a small slide, a photo picture frame, and a portable echo phone. The front door has a turning key, drop-through slot, ringing doorbell, clicking light switch, and note holder. Hinges allow the center to fold flat for storage. (Manufacturer's age recommendation: 9 months to 3½ years.)*

Toys for outdoor play

Outdoor swings for babies and tots

Most babies love being rocked in a swing. The motion soothes and pacifies them. Babies should not be put into a swing, however, until they are capable of sitting up unassisted. Some babies have had their heads fall forward into swing fronts and were not able to sit themselves back up again, causing strangulation. Toddlers are often hurt in playground accidents because they fail to understand the pendulum action of swings and get knocked over in the process.

Baby and toddler swings can be fun, but it's important that they have a secure safety-belt system to keep babies from falling out. In May 1995, PlaySkool recalled its *1-2-3 Swing* after 50 consumers called to report that children had fallen out of the swing. The problem was a restraint shield in the front of the swing that appeared to be in the locking position when, in fact, it wasn't. As a result, children were falling from the swing.

The edges and surfaces of a swing should be smooth, with no ragged seams or corners. Avoid swings with sharp hinges or other moving parts that could entrap small fingers, and never leave a child unattended in the swing.

Ride-on toys and trikes

Almost as soon as tots are able to balance on one leg and are able to straddle a toy, they're eager to roll around on wheels. But just as with baby walkers, which injure over 20,000 babies a year, ride-on toys present hazards. Most ride-on accidents occur when children fall over with the toy or fall off of it. They also inadvertently roll down stairs, over curbs, or into swimming pools, sustaining head injuries or drowning.

Sometimes ride-on accidents result from parents trying to push children into bicycling skills before they have adequate physical coordination to ride safely. The safest ride-on toys are those that have wheels wide apart, which prevents them from tipping over, and are low to the ground, so that an unstable tot won't have far to fall if he or she loses balance.

Tricycles are appropriate only for children who are secure walkers—from about two to five years of age. Take a safety survey before you purchase a tricycle. The major causes of injuries to young children on trikes include falls when they try to get on, being hit by vehicles in driveways and streets, and falling over with the trike when it goes over rough surfaces, such as curbs or sidewalks, or when sharp turns are made.

Check out the area around your home where your tot will be riding to be sure that it is a safe distance from traffic dangers. Since trikes have no brakes, there should be no rough surfaces or steep inclines that could cause your child to lose control.

It's easier to shop for a tricycle without your youngster along. That way, you can calmly choose the safest options within your price range without getting into a battle with your young titan. Again, as with ride-on toys, stable, low-slung models are much safer than those with high-riding seats. Look for widely spaced wheels, too. Avoid tyke-size bicycles with training wheels. They fall over too easily and are difficult to control. Most tricycles come in either 10- or 12-inch wheel sizes. Don't buy a model that's larger than your child in the hopes that he or she will grow into it. It's much safer to get one that fits.

While you're shopping, don't forget to pick up a toddler safety helmet in the size of your child's head circumference. It will protect your child from head injuries—the most serious result of tricycle mishaps.

Outdoor play equipment

Nearly 200,000 children each year are injured in accidents with outdoor play equipment. Typically, children are injured when they fall down on such hard surfaces as concrete or asphalt, or when they tumble from gym sets, monkey bars, merry-go-rounds, etc. Sometimes children's legs get burned on hot metal surfaces from sliding boards during the summer, and sometimes children accidentally strangle themselves when clothes, strings on clothes, or neck scarves catch on sliding boards or other high devices. Head injuries are the most serious consequence of play equipment falls, and studies show that the higher the equipment from the ground (children will climb to the highest point possible), the greater the chance of severe injury.

Currently there is an effort from the Playground Equipment Manufacturers Association (PEMA) to certify backyard play equipment to the ASTM safety standard, but certification was not in effect as of this writing. (The ASTM safety standard is voluntary.) Manufacturers may state in their advertising or catalogs that their products meet the ASTM safety standard or the CPSC's recommendations for some playground equipment; however, even with a stringent certification program, there remain questions about safety.

Follow a few basic safety rules when choosing outdoor play equipment. The play equipment chosen should be the right size and sophistication for the children using it. It should also fit into the backyard properly. Tall slides and high climbing devices can be dangerous for small children, who are more awkward and apt to fall. Avoid any devices that have protrusions, such as screw heads or sharp edges, that could hurt a child in a fall. Inspect moving parts on swings and gliders prior to purchasing them to ensure that there are no locations that could conceivably crush fingers or small hands. Allow for at least 6 feet of free room surrounding the set, as well as room above the set to ensure a safe fit.

Children should always be supervised when they're playing outdoors. Toddlers, in particular, don't seem to understand how swings work, and they may walk directly into or between swings.

Equipment should be installed carefully to prevent as many accidents as possible. The legs of swings, sliding boards, or climbers should be set in concrete below the ground to ensure maximum stability. The ground underneath the equipment should be covered with soft bark or sand, or protected with energy-absorbing matting to prevent injuries from falls. If the yard backs onto a street, a protective fence should be installed. Swings should be placed facing away from walls or tree trunks, yet in the shady area of the yard for use on glaring, hot days. Sandboxes should have a cover to prevent them from being used by cats and other animals, and to keep out rain and mildew.

If you're interested in outdoor play equipment, libraries often carry books on how to construct the wooden play centers that are available in stores. Large children's toy stores, such as Toys 'R' Us, also carry standard swing sets, wading pools, sandboxes, and other play equipment. Companies with mail-order children's outdoor play equipment often advertise in the classified sections of parenting publications, and equipment suppliers for day-care and early childhood education centers often have toll-free telephone numbers offering free outdoor equipment catalogs.

Recalls

DAKIN INC. Big Top Playmates
Pom-poms could come off of soft-fabric toys and choke child.
Products: 66,500 animal toys, sold between 2/94 and 4/95, including bear, bunny, and elephant soft-fabric dolls (item no. 40319); finger puppets (item no. 40320); bottle-hugging dolls (item no. 40321); dolls attached to musical mobile (item no. 40324); ring-shaped rattles with soft plush animal head and feet (item no. 40325); and crib attachments (item no. 40335). These toys have pink, yellow, and blue trim and $1/2$-inch pom-poms. Tag includes item number, product name, and "THE FRASER COLLECTION, DAKIN, INC. San Francisco, CA, Product of China." Mobile sold for $50; other toys, $5 to $15.
What to do: Cut off and discard pom-poms.

DAN-DEE INTERNATIONAL Teddy Precious Indian Girl Stuffed Bear
Small beads that decorate Native American-style sash could come off and choke child.
Products: 11,600 light brown stuffed bears sold between 3/95 and 3/96 for $13 at Kay-Bee toy stores. Bear is 18 inches long and comes with brown vinyl dress and headband trimmed with Native American embroidery. Pink label on bear's foot says, in part: "Teddy Precious." Blue-and-white tag on bear's lower back reads, in part: "DAN-DEE INTERNATIONAL LIMITED, JERSEY CITY, NJ 07305... MADE IN CHINA." Some tags also include: "SKU #089318."
What to do: Return bear to Kay-Bee toy store for refund.

DAVIS BROS. WHOLESALERS Baby's Bucket-Sorting Toys
Small parts could come off and choke child.
Products: 5,000 toys sold between 3/93 and 2/94 for $2 to $3. Toy consists of 17¼-inch round bucket with handle and 9 shaped pieces that fit through corresponding cutouts in bucket's yellow lid. Square, hexagonal, triangular, and circular pieces have attached small animal figure, which could come off. Label on box says "MADISON LTD., HACKENSACK, NJ, . . . MADE IN CHINA."
What to do: Return toy to store for refund.

KID DIMENSION Littlest Pet Shop Tea Set
Small, removable plastic animals on teapot and sugar bowl could choke child.
Products: 42,000 sets sold between 7/94 and 11/94 for $10. Set, made of pink, blue, purple, and red plastic, is about ⅔ normal size and includes teapot with lid, serving tray, sugar bowl with lid, creamer, 4 cups, 4 saucers, and 4 spoons. Plastic animals on cups and creamer are permanently attached. Toy package is labeled, in part: "Littlest Pet Shop Tea Set featuring adorable Hangimal characters, No. 27310, 1994 Kid Dimension Inc., a subsidiary of Hasbro, Inc., Pawtucket, RI." Newer set without hazardous small parts has starburst label on package that reads: "Contains No Small Parts."
What to do: If child is younger than 3 years old, return set to store for refund.

PLAYSKOOL Durasport Moon Bouncer Inflatable Vinyl Toy
If toy is improperly inflated or placed on hard surface, child could fall or bounce out and suffer serious injury.
Products: 142,000 toys sold since 11/94 for $60. Toy is designed for children ages 3 to 6 to bounce and jump in. It has red circular base that inflates to 5½ feet in diameter. Side walls, resembling three stacked yellow rings, inflate to 16 inches from jumping surface.
What to do: Phone 800-683-5847 for free set of gauges and instructions to help ensure proper inflation. Outdoors, place toy on energy-absorbing surface like sand or mulch. Indoors, use padded surface; carpeting may not be sufficient to prevent injury.

25

Walkers

A walker is a wheeled frame and seat that allows babies who can already sit up to propel themselves around by using toes and feet. As many as 3.6 million walkers are sold annually in the United States. Sadly, the government estimates that 28,500 injuries related to walker accidents are treated annually in emergency rooms. Babies in walkers can plummet down stairways or steps between levels; turn over in walkers that are snagged by cords, door thresholds, and carpet edges; roll themselves against hot stoves and heaters; fall over concrete curbs; or tumble into swimming pools. A child in a walker can go faster than a parent can run to rescue him or her. Despite its name, the device won't speed up your baby's inborn walking schedule and may, in fact, interfere with needed pulling-up, crawling, and creeping experiences.

Given the high accident potential of walkers and their brief period of usefulness, we question whether a walker is a worthwhile purchase. In fact, a coalition of consumer groups including Consumers Union would like to see walkers banned. Despite our support for a ban on their sale, we continue to report on them because of their continued popularity, not because we endorse them. If you do decide to buy one, we suggest a model such as Evenflo's *The Walker Alternative* (also known as *The Exersaucer*) or any of about a half dozen models of walker alternatives on the market today. The Evenflo model has a curved or dished base instead of wheels, and is designed to let a baby rock and bounce or jiggle and spin, but not scoot around. It also has fold-down stabilizing legs. If you already have a walker, we recommend that you hook your walker to a walker anchor, a device that you fill with sand or water. As a result, the child in the walker can move in a circle around the anchor but can't move or dislodge the anchor easily. *Safe Baby Steps* is one such device, and is available from Delta Enterprises Corporation for about $20.

Limit the time you allow your baby to stay in a walker to no more than 30 minutes (during which time you should continuously keep your eye on the child), and don't allow the walker to be used near stairways, steps between levels or ledges, or on uneven surfaces.

Types

It has been estimated that half of all babies in the United States use walkers. There are several types currently available. Most have circular, rectangular, or square bases and four to eight casters. A locking mechanism is located under the front tray of some units for positioning the height of the seat. Some models offer only a single height. In others, the interior seat or crotch strap is adjustable for height. Seat height should be adjustable, since it is essential to keep both of the child's feet on the ground at all times. Interior seats vary in back height and the amount of padding on the upholstery. Some models enable babies to bounce in them. Most have rimmed trays, some offer small turning knobs or other toylike devices attached to the tray, and some have removable U-shaped frames that dangle toys in front of the baby.

The high accident toll from walkers

Even though babies respond positively to being in a walker, the injury toll to them in walker-related accidents is so high that walkers could be considered one of the most dangerous of all baby products. Sale of walkers in Canada is, for all practical purposes, nonexistent. The Canadian government, recognizing that children in walkers frequently fall down stairways, ruled that walkers have to be made so that they can't go through a normal door 89 centimeters (35 inches) wide. Currently, there is only one such walker on the market.

Parents should also be wary of old-style X-frame walkers that are no longer being made but are still available in garage sales. These designs have been responsible for many injuries, including finger amputations when a baby's hand gets caught in the closing X-joint of the frame. Such models should be discarded.

Walkers:
Conclusions of selected medical research

Walkers cause serious head injuries. Head injuries result when walkers fall down stairs. One study found that walker-related head injuries represent the third most common cause of head injuries to children under two years of age.[1] In some cases, falls down stairs occurred even when parents had installed gates, according to another study, which found that one-third of falls down stairs happened with gates in place. Either the gates were closed incorrectly or they didn't hold up to the impact of a walker.[2] (For more information on gates, see chapter 12.)

 Children walk when ready to walk. If by the age of 18 months your child has not yet learned to walk, don't buy a walker; instead, check with your pediatrician.

Walkers are being misused. The main reason for purchasing a walker, according to 75 percent of the parents questioned in one survey, was to pacify their babies and keep them quiet and happy. Sometimes parental misuse of the walker can contribute to accidents. One study found, for instance, that even though their babies were hurt seriously enough in walker-related accidents to be taken to the hospital, two-thirds of the parents put the babies back in walkers again within two months. Babies most likely to be seriously hurt in accidents were those who spent as much as an hour or more a day in them.

They don't help babies walk sooner. Do walkers encourage a baby to walk? The answer is no, even though parents often believe differently. One survey found that 59 percent of walker buyers were under the impression that the walker would help their babies walk sooner, but research indicates otherwise. This misconception is encouraged by such manufacturers' statements as "This unit is designed to assist

---

[1] Partington, M., et al., "Head Injury and the Use of Baby Walkers: A Continuing Problem," *Annals of Emergency Medicine* 20 (1991): 52–54.

[2] Reider, M. J., Schwartz, C., and Newman, J. "Patterns of Walker Use and Walker Injury," *Pediatrics* 78 (1986): 488–493.

infants in learning to walk" or "This walker is only to be used by toddlers . . . ready to learn to walk."

Walkers call for an entirely different set of leg and back actions than those required for crawling or balancing on two feet. One study compared babies who spent time in a walker with their twin brothers or sisters who were not put in a walker. The babies who used walkers walked with stiff legs and shortened steps, and they leaned forward more than their siblings who were given floor freedom. Some studies appear to indicate that walkers, rather than speeding up a baby's ability to walk, may actually impede it.[3] The American Academy of Pediatrics recently had this to say about walkers: "Beyond parental impressions that infants 'seem happier' in walkers, it does not appear that any real benefits of using a walker can be found to balance the considerable risk of injury."[4]

Safety standards for walkers

Consumer protection for walkers currently for sale in stores is a combination of mandatory regulations and a standard set by the major manufacturers. All walkers have to pass certain federal requirements. For example, walkers should be designed so that they don't create a "small parts" problem, which can lead to choking if a child puts these parts into the mouth. A few years ago, walker manufacturers, in cooperation with the U.S. Consumer Product Safety Commission (CPSC) and the American Society for Testing and Materials (ASTM), issued a voluntary safety standard that allowed them to certify walkers that pass their tests. The standard sets forth the kinds of tests that walkers have to pass to show that they won't accidentally fold when being used, that they are stable against tipping, that children cannot slip through a leg opening with both legs and the body, and that the seams and materials will hold up under normal wear. The standard also includes labeling requirements and requirements for instructional literature. Walkers that are certified are labeled: "Juvenile Products Manufacturers Association Certified. This model tested by an Independent Laboratory for Compliance to ASTM F-977 Safety Standard for Walkers."

Neither the voluntary standard nor the mandatory requirements contain safeguards against the most frequently occurring and most danger-

---

[3] Ridenour M., "Infant Walkers: Developmental Tool or Inherent Danger," *Perceptual Motor Skills* 55 (1982): 1201–1202.

[4] Committee on Injury and Poison Prevention, the American Academy of Pediatrics, "Injuries Associated with Infant Walkers," *Pediatrics* 95(5) (May 1995): 778–780.

ous accidents—falling down steps or stairways while the child is in the walker. At best, you will find a label that warns you never to use the walker near stairs, steps, or thresholds.

 Given the high accident toll from walkers and the limited time of their usefulness, it is questionable whether you should have a walker at all.

But labels warning parents about the hazard of walkers falling down stairways and steps has not reduced the number of tragic accidents. As a result, a coalition of consumer groups including Consumers Union petitioned the CPSC in 1992 to ban walkers. In March 1993 the CPSC denied that petition, but it is now working with industry officials, under the auspices of the ASTM, to include a requirement in the ASTM standard that will address the hazard of walkers falling down stairways. This process, while well underway, will not be completed before 1997.

Safety tips

Our central recommendation regarding the use of walkers is not to use them. They don't help babies learn to walk, and they cause thousands of injuries every year. But if you still intend to use a walker, we urge you to heed these warnings:

- Never leave a child unattended.
- Never use a walker near stairs, steps, or thresholds. Check that surfaces are flat and free of objects that may cause the walker to tip over, either indoors or outdoors.
- Using a walker anchor (see p. 294) can keep a walker confined to an area of about 8 feet by 8 feet.
- To reduce the chance of a child slipping out of the seat, check that both feet touch the floor, and never carry the walker with a child in it.
- Read the manufacturer's instructional literature, and heed the warnings contained in it.

Since we recommend against buying any wheeled walker currently manufactured, we advise parents instead to use other products that keep a child of that age group busy and in safe surroundings. Mounting criticism of walkers because of the high number of injuries has caused some manufacturers to look for alternatives. The makers of these new products have designed them without wheels and the mobility so dangerous to children. The seats and decks are similar to seats and decks of wheeled walkers. Some seats can turn within their base when the child turns. One model, which resembles a treadmill, is combined with a seat.

We believe that the risk of falling down stairs, the main hazard in using walkers with wheels, is much lower when you use one of these alternative walkers because these products are relatively stationary. Therefore, opt for one of these nonmobile walkers rather than a conventional walker with wheels. One model we can recommend is Evenflo's *The Walker Alternative,* also called the *Exersaucer* ($55).

The Walker Alternative (Exersaucer)

If you use one of these alternative walkers, follow the same recommendations as for conventional walkers. Also, heed any warnings listed in the instructional material included with the products.

Appendix A

Babies and accidents:
A national overview

In the past, childhood accidents were considered unavoidable—*"they just happened"*—or parents were blamed for not watching children closely enough and allowing them to get hurt. But accidents happen even when babies and children are being monitored because parents aren't always able to foresee the potential dangers in their homes, yards, and cars.

Until recently, it wasn't clear exactly how our nation's babies were being injured in accidents. Now massive injury data are making things clearer. The sheer numbers of accidental deaths and injuries to babies and young children across the nation make a strong statement about the vulnerability of our youngest citizens. Parental negligence is to blame in some instances, but in many cases accidents could have been prevented if parents knew more about what is dangerous for babies, and how homes and cars can be made safer for these dynamic, small beings who quickly get into trouble.

When it comes to protecting babies and young children, stiffer regulations and better enforcement of existing regulations are needed. Federal regulations covering child safety seats, cribs, small parts, and protective caps for medications, for example, have already saved the lives of hundreds of babies and young children.

The best thing you can do to keep your baby safe is to continually monitor him or her. Expect the unexpected. No amount of precaution measures and "baby-proofing" can protect your baby as well as your own constant vigilance.

The national toll of baby injuries

Accidents, not diseases, are the leading causes of death and disability in children ages one to four.[1] In babies younger than one year, physical ailments cause more deaths, while accidents are the second largest killer. Suffocation causes the most baby deaths.

In 1994, accidents were responsible for the deaths of 3,200 one- to four-year-olds. It has been estimated that for every child who dies in a specific accident, 45 other children are hospitalized for similar occurrences, and 1,300 are rushed to emergency rooms.[2]

In 1994, some 827 toddlers up to three years old were killed in automobile accidents, making it the leading cause of death for children in that age range. The next biggest killers were fires (571 deaths) and drowning (550).

Unintentional deaths to babies

The following table is based on injury statistics from 1992. The National Safety Council and other injury-prevention experts now use the terms "unintentional injuries" and "unintentional deaths" instead of "accidents" when talking about safety because most accidents are clearly preventable.

AGE	MOTOR VEHICLES	FIRES	DROWNING	SUFFO-CATION	FALLS	POISONING	FIRE-ARMS
0–12 months	160	98	86	229	26	10	1
1 year	225	132	199	43	24	21	3
2 years	232	187	154	21	24	4	10
3 years	210	154	111	12	6	5	12
TOTAL	827	571	550	305	80	40	26

Source: The National Safety Council, *Accident Facts, 1995 Edition,* Customer Relations, National Safety Council, 1121 Spring Lake Dr., Itasca, IL 60143. To order, call toll-free: 800-621-7619; fax: 708-285-0797.

[1] National Safety Council, *Accident Facts, 1995 Edition,* Itasca, IL 1995.
[2] Gallagher, S.S., et al., "The Incidence of Injuries Among 87,000 Massachusetts Children and Adolescents: Results of the 1980–81 Statewide Childhood Injury Prevention Program Surveillance System," *American Journal of Public Health* 74 (1984): 1340–1347.

When babies and children are in serious accidents their heads often bear the brunt of lasting damage. Approximately 10,000 U.S. children under five will suffer permanent disabilities from brain injury this year. One reason head injuries are so common is that children have large heads in relation to their weak, vulnerable necks and spines. In 1994, 673 children under five years of age died while riding in motor vehicles; 362 of these children were unrestrained, and many more were restrained improperly. (To learn more about how to protect your child from automobile injuries, see chapter 7.)

Fire safety

House fires are the second leading cause of injury deaths for young children after motor vehicle accidents. The 1990 statistics show that of the 522 deaths to children under five, the leading causes of fire were young children playing with matches, lighters and other ignition sources, and faulty or misused heaters or extension cords.

Severe burns are only one way fires kill. In fact, only one in three home-fire victims dies from burns. More than half of fatal fires happen at night when people are asleep, and most people don't die in the room where the fire begins. Smoke and toxic fumes are the leading cause of fire deaths. Fires use up oxygen. Since young children's metabolisms, heart rates, and respiration systems work faster than those of older children and adults, they suffocate sooner in toxic smoke-filled rooms. So deaths may occur in only a matter of minutes after a fire starts.

Most home fires occur between December and March—the periods of coldest weather and longest darkness—and are often sparked by fireplaces, portable electric or kerosene heaters, and Christmas tree lights. Cooking equipment is another major cause of home fires. Stove burners, microwave ovens, and countertop appliances (such as toasters, coffeemakers, and toaster ovens) are the most frequent starting points of fires. Our suggestion is to unplug countertop appliances when you're not using them, and don't leave the room while they're in operation.

Plastic baby bottles left to boil can also cause fires and release toxic fumes. Typically, fires start when parents put the bottles in a pan of water to sterilize them and then leave the room, falling asleep on a couch or bed. The water boils away; the bottles melt and catch on fire, emitting toxic fumes that damage babies' lungs.

Smoking is another cause of fire. It is responsible for one out of three home fires that result in death. If there's a smoker in your home (a regrettable situation with a baby around), use sturdy, nontip ashtrays that put cigarette butts out of children's reach. Buy only child-resistant lighters.

Don't have easy-to-ignite, wooden matches in your home, and keep all matches out of children's reach. In addition, never smoke in bed.

Fire-protection devices. To survive a fire in your home, you've got to be prepared to take immediate action. Smoke detectors and other fire-protection equipment—such as sprinkler systems and fire extinguishers—are critical safety devices. Installing and maintaining a smoke alarm can cut your family's risk of dying in a home fire by almost half.

Some smoke alarms are battery powered, while others plug into electrical outlets or are wired directly into the home's electrical system. Some detectors use an "ionization" sensor, and others use photoelectric-type sensors. The important issue is whether the smoke detector has been tested by an independent testing laboratory, such as Underwriters Laboratories (UL). Look for a notification of this on the detector's packaging.

Smoke detectors should be installed on every level of your home. The National Fire Protection Association recommends that families sleep with all bedroom doors closed to slow the spread of smoke and flames in the event of a fire. If you sleep with bedroom doors closed, then smoke detectors should be installed inside bedrooms, too. Smoke detectors are not recommended for kitchens, bathrooms, attics, or garages because cooking fumes, steam, or automobile exhaust may cause nuisance alarms.

The National Institute of Standards and Technology estimates that 60 to 80 percent of fire deaths could be prevented if homes had sprinkler systems. Automatic sprinkler systems have now become affordable and practical for use in private homes. They act instantly to snuff out fires and reduce toxic gases.

Create an escape plan. Escaping a fire isn't always as simple as walking out of the door. That's why advance planning is important. The National Fire Protection Association (NFPA) recommends that you create your family's escape plan using a drawing of your home that includes all windows, doors, outdoor features, and possible obstacles to escaping.

Use this plan to create primary and alternate escape routes for you and your baby out of every room. Plan for at least two ways out of each room in the event that fire blocks one escape. Draw these routes on your floor plan, remembering that the two danger signs at any escape route are smoke and heat. Opening windows may only serve to draw smoke into a room. If you must open a window, open a crack at the top and one at the bottom. Smoke will be drawn out from the top.

If you have a two-story home, determine if you can climb out onto a roof or balcony. If you can't, then you should purchase noncombustible, independent-laboratory-tested escape ladders for second-story bedrooms. Store them permanently near the windows but in such a way that an exploring tot cannot gain access to them. Draw the ladder positions on your family plan. Note where you will meet other family members once you've exited the home.

Post your plan near your telephone along with the fire department's emergency number, your address, directions to your home, and telephone number. Revise your plan whenever living arrangements change. Remember: If you're in the home and the fire is spreading rapidly, get everyone out first and call for help from another home.

Keep a fire extinguisher in the kitchen, at least 10 feet from the range, so you can easily get to it if a fire breaks out. It pays to carefully read operating instructions before an emergency. If your garage is attached to your home, keep a second extinguisher there. Also, install carbon monoxide detectors in your home according to the manufacturer's recommendations.

Here are additional fire protection suggestions:

◆ Install glass doors or protective screens in front of the fireplace to keep fireplace sparks from igniting carpeting or wood. Install a fire-resistant rug in front of the mantel. Have your chimney cleaned every year, and don't try to burn the Christmas tree, green wood, wrapping paper, or trash in the fireplace. If you use a woodstove, install a thermometer in front and continually monitor the stove for overheating.

◆ Refuel kerosene heaters outside the home and use only K-1 kerosene. To prevent the buildup of carbon monoxide, keep a window partially open to allow for fresh air when using unvented fuel-operated heating devices.

◆ Consider using a nonflammable Christmas tree. If you use a live tree, don't place it near heating sources or fireplaces, and keep it watered—dry trees ignite easily. Use only safe, nonfrayed extension cords for lights, and don't overload electrical outlets.

◆ Locate your baby's nursery next to your bedroom, preferably with a connecting door, and install large, reflective numbers at your curbside or mailbox so firefighters can quickly find your home in the event of a fire.

◆ Mark your child's window with a decal to alert firefighters. *Tot Finder Fire Rescue Decals* (Model 600G, 2/$2.95) are available from the Perfectly Safe Catalog. The mail-order company also carries a *Compact Fire Extinguisher* (Model 83801, $19.95) and a *Portable Escape Ladder* (2-story, Model 89602, $89.95, and 3-story, Model 89603, $129.95).

❖ Write for "Fire in Your Home, Prevention and Survival," a free 47-page brochure with hundreds of fire-safety tips for families: National Fire Protection Association, One Batterymarch Park, Quincy, MA 02269-9101.

Scalds and burns

Over 30 percent of all burns to children come from hot liquids, foods, and water from faucets and tub spouts. One hospital study found that hot water scalds represented over 36 percent of all hospital burn injuries and 20 percent of burn deaths. Babies between six months and two years of age are seven times more likely to be rushed to emergency rooms for burns than older children.

These types of accidents occur when children fall into tubs filling up with hot water, or when hot water faucets are turned on by children. Some children burn their hands simply by putting them under hot running water.

The single best way to protect your baby from being accidentally scalded by hot water is to turn down the thermostat on the hot water heater. According to the American Academy of Pediatrics, thermostats on hot water heaters should be set no higher than 120°F. Studies show that a temperature only five degrees hotter can result in a full-thickness skin burn in only thirty seconds. If you can't control the temperature of the water in your apartment, then consider installing an antiscald device that will slow water to a trickle in a tub spout if it reaches a critical temperature.

One survey conducted by researchers at the William Beaumont Medical Center in El Paso, Texas, found that over 88 percent of water heaters tested were putting out water temperatures that dangerously exceeded 120°F. The researchers found that most parents were unaware that temperatures that high posed a burn danger to their children.

Here are additional safety practices to protect your child from scalding:
❖ Remember that children can get contact burns from car restraints, vinyl stroller seats, and children's playground equipment exposed to the hot sun. Cover your baby's child safety seat and stroller with a blanket or towel when not in use. Bury the metal latch in the car seat so that the sun doesn't hit it directly. Use playground equipment with caution, and only in the early morning on hot days, when it has had time to cool down overnight.
❖ Don't allow your baby or young child to sit in your lap while you're holding a mug of hot coffee or other hot liquid. Use a sealed-top mug and keep it away from your child's reach.
❖ Don't hold your baby while cooking.

Drowning

Approximately 550 babies age three and under died in drowning accidents in the United States in 1992. In 18 U.S. states, drowning is the number-one cause of death for children ages one to four. For every child who drowns, four children are hospitalized for near-drowning. One third of those who are unconscious when they're admitted to the hospital will survive but suffer significant brain damage. Babies and toddlers can drown in as little as one inch of water. Children under one year of age most frequently drown in bathtubs, buckets, or toilets. Children age one to four most often drown in home or apartment swimming pools.[3]

Researchers at the UCLA Medical Center in California studied the effects of near-drowning on 166 children, ages six months to twelve years of age. Eighty-seven percent of the accident victims were under five years of age. The most important factors in determining how long recovery takes after a near-drowning is how long the child stayed under water and how quickly the child got CPR.

The researchers concluded that all parents, siblings, and caretakers of children should learn how to apply rapid, effective artificial respiration —especially mouth-to-mouth breathing.[4] Learning how to give CPR and to intervene when your baby chokes is important. Call your local American Red Cross chapter, or your local rescue squad, to find out how to enroll in a CPR or first-aid course.

Here are ways to protect your baby from drowning:

❖ Take a first-aid and CPR course even before your baby is born. ("Infant and Toddler Emergency First Aid" [Vol. 1] is a 36-minute video with CPR instructions. It can be ordered for $29.95 plus $4.95 for shipping and handling from Apogee Communications Group, 159 Alpine Way, Boulder, CO 80304, or by calling toll-free: 800-210-5700.)

❖ Pool alarms and pool covers don't keep children from drowning. If you have a backyard pool, separate the pool from your home and yard by installing four-sided climb-proof fencing at least four feet high around the pool. Doing that can decrease the chance of your baby's drowning by 50 percent. Install a self-closing gate, with the latch too high to be reached by a young child, and arm it with a door alarm.

❖ Remove the ladder from aboveground pools.

❖ Wading pools are not harmless, and many children have drowned in pools that contained less than three inches of water. Never leave your

---

3 Committee on Injury and Poison Prevention, The American Academy of Pediatrics, "Drowning in Infants, Children, and Adolescents," *Pediatrics* 92(2): August 1993, 292–294.

4 Kyriacou, Demetrios, et al., "Effect of Immediate Resuscitation on Children with Submersion Injury," *Pediatrics* 94(2): August 2, 1994, 137–142.

child alone in one, and always empty it and store it where water can't gather in it after use. Dump water from buckets and baby wading pools.

◆ Inexpensive water wings and flotation devices give children (and their parents) a false sense of safety. Always watch your children when they're around water, even when they are wearing flotation devices. If you decide to purchase an infant life vest, it should fit snugly, have leg loops to prevent it from coming off over your child's head, and be more buoyant at the top and behind the head so your child will bob upright with his face out of the water, rather than face downward.

◆ Be cautious with large buckets. Approximately 228 children, most about 8 to 14 months old, have drowned in five-gallon utility buckets from January 1984 to March 1994. In a typical bucket-drowning incident, a parent has brought home a bucket that originally held paint or other substances. The bucket is then used to mop floors, or to wash a pet. A toddler, left unattended, crawls to the bucket and begins to play with the water. The tot then falls into the bucket, can't get upright again, and drowns. It's important to empty all buckets completely when not in use, and always supervise the baby when you are using a bucket containing liquid.

◆ Never allow your toddler to go into the bathroom unless you intend to keep close watch. Install a toilet-lid locking device to prevent the lid from being raised and the child from falling in.

◆ Don't buy or use suction-based bathtub seats. They aren't safe, and may fall over, vaulting baby face-downward into water.

Choking and suffocation dangers

Babies and young children have a natural tendency to put objects in their mouths. They die when these small objects become trapped in their throats, plugging up their airways. Of the 449 children who died in choking accidents between 1972 and 1992, over half were babies and toddlers under three years of age. In 1994, statistics showed 1,539 children were treated for ingestion or aspiration injuries from balloons, small balls, or marbles, and six children died from balloon-related accidents.

Toy latex balloons are one of the leading causes of pediatric choking deaths from children's products—they are responsible for one out of three choking deaths, and two recent deaths happened when physicians unadvisedly handed their latex examining gloves blown up like balloons to children during visits.

The U.S. Consumer Product Safety Commission (CPSC) now requires that all latex balloons be labeled as follows: "Warning: Choking hazard—children under eight years can choke or suffocate on uninflated or broken balloons. Adult supervision required. Keep uninflated balloons away from children. Discard broken balloons at once."

Balls and marbles account for about one out of five deaths to babies and children, as do toys and toy parts, such as miniature baby rattles attached to baby-shower gifts. One out of three deaths are from small objects not intended for use by babies and young children—bolts, bottle caps, buttons, keys, lipstick tubes, safety pins, screws, and thumbtacks. The small objects most likely to kill are those that are circular and shaped to form a perfect plug in a baby's small throat.

A recent survey of 165 cases of choking in children found that over half of the children requiring surgery had choked on coins. Seventy percent of the objects were rounded. They included pieces of vegetables, grapes, nuts, seeds, popcorn, cookies, candy, hot dogs, and chicken bones. Nonfood items that lodged in children's throats included toys, pen caps, metal, batteries, wire, wood, dirt, beads, pins, crayons, staples, glass, feathers, or string.[5]

Learn and practice choking rescue techniques designed especially for babies. The Heimlich maneuver—hugging a child from behind and thrusting a fist under the rib cage to cause an object from the throat to be ejected—is dangerous for infants and may cause internal injuries. Choking babies should be turned face down with their heads lower than their bodies, and thumped between the shoulder blades.

Here are steps you can take to protect your child from suffocation dangers:

◆ Beware of small, detachable parts on toys. Even though the CPSC regulates small toy parts for babies and young children, older brothers' and sisters' toys, such as vending machine balls and marbles, are not regulated by the same standard.

◆ Cut foods into bite-size pieces, and discourage play during eating.

◆ Keep coins, peanuts, balloons, beads, and watch batteries away from small children.

◆ If your child chokes, don't put your finger down your child's throat blindly hoping to pull the object out. This may only force it deeper and cause suffocation.

◆ You should also protect your child from crib and mattress (see chapter 9) and nursey decor (see chapter 17) suffocation hazards.

Falls

Fall injuries can occur when babies crash into coffee tables, topple out of cribs, tumble down stairs, or fall off counters, tables, couches, and other raised surfaces. Coffee tables are the number-one home injurer of

5 Rimell, F. L., Thome, A., Jr. et al., "Characteristics of Objects That Cause Choking in Children," *Journal of the American Medical Association,* December 13, 1995, 274(22): 1763–1766.

babies and young children, sending over 70,000 of them to emergency rooms each year.

Falls from cribs occur when parents inadvertently leave the dropsides down, or when tots try to climb out, often using toys as stepping stones. Falls from baby products such as high chairs, changing tables, and strollers happen when parents forget to fasten restraining belts.

Once toddlers can crawl or walk, their falls are caused by their lack of balance and their limited walking, climbing, and running skills. Children this age can't make sound judgments about heights or dangers.

The National Pediatric Trauma Registry found that of 8,722 falls by children, approximately one out of four were out of windows, usually in their own homes. Children ages one to four made up 74 percent of the falling victims; 65 percent of these children suffered serious head injuries. The average length of hospitalization was five days, and one out of three children stayed in the intensive care unit one or more days.

Most of the children fell from open windows that had no screens, or screens that weren't fastened securely and came loose when children pressed or leaned against them. Usually, their parents were in another room when the accident happened. Toddlers often fell while sitting on window ledges, just as they had seen their parents do.

Here's how to protect your child from dangerous falls:

◆ Don't depend on window screens to keep your child from falling out. They're not childproof. In fact, newly manufactured screens bear a warning label to that effect. Leave that label in place so that other family members are aware of the potential screen danger.

◆ Install grids or safety bars on upstairs windows to protect kids. They should be childproof but easy to open by an adult if there's a fire or other emergency.

◆ If you have no safety bars, close and lock windows when your child is around. For ventilation, open the top window and leave the bottom shut.

◆ Keep furniture away from windows to prevent children from climbing to window ledges or sills and falling out.

◆ Remove the coffee table for the first three years of your baby's life, or install protective padding on it and other sharp-edged furniture and countertops.

◆ Install hardware-mounted safety gates at the top and bottom of staircases that don't have doors.

◆ Secure basement and outside doors with locks that are too high to be reached by a young child.

◆ Always use the safety belts on baby products such as changing tables, strollers, and high chairs.

❖ Protect your child from outdoor playground equipment such as tall sliding boards, hard swings, and monkey bars. Be especially cautious if playgrounds are covered with uncushioned surfaces, such as concrete, asphalt, dirt, or grass.

Lead poisoning and water contamination

Lead is an invisible, tasteless, and odorless heavy metal. It is toxic to humans and accumulates in the body causing brain, nerve, and kidney damage, anemia, and even death. It's dangerous even in small amounts, especially to babies, children, and pregnant women. Babies and young children can be exposed to lead when it's dissolved in tap water used to prepare formula. It enters drinking water when plumbing systems, which carry water inside homes, have lead pipes and lead soldering.

Older homes pose the most danger, both from contaminated water and from lead dust. Lead may be contained in walls in homes painted prior to 1978. The lead dust and old paint chips accumulate on windowsills, deteriorating porches, and in the dirt around the home. It is then tracked onto carpeting, where it can stick to the hands and clothing of crawling babies. The biggest threat of lead contamination occurs when older homes are being renovated while families are still living in them. If surfaces containing lead are sanded and scraped, children may be exposed to dangerous lead dust from the floor and air.

Lead can also be found in lead crystal or pottery containers. Acidic fruits and fruit juices, and baby foods containing tomatoes should not be stored in these containers because they may leak lead into the juices and foods. According to the Food and Nutrition Service of the U.S. Department of Agriculture, some imported canned juices, such as those found in ethnic stores, may have seams soldered with lead.

Lead can leach into food from ceramic ware that has been improperly fired or has a formulated glaze that lets lead leach into food or drink. Incidents of lead poisoning have occurred with decorative pottery ware not intended for food use. Acidic foods, such as orange juice, tomato juice, and other fruit juices; tomato sauces; vinegar; and wine stored in improperly glazed lead containers are potentially the most dangerous. Lead can also be leached from ornate leaded glass decanters used to store wine or other beverages containing alcohol. While most ceramic ware purchased in the United States meets federal standards for lead safety, old bowls, pitchers, decanters, and those wares purchased from other countries may not be safe.

However, lead poisoning is more likely to occur when hot water dissolves lead from plumbing materials. Babies have suffered lead poisoning from drinking infant formula made with hot tap water, which, when boiled, concentrated the lead even more.[6]

In addition to lead, if your home has copper pipes, you may have too much copper in your water. Even though copper can be beneficial at lower levels, when it exceeds 1.3 milligrams per liter (mg/L) in water, it can pose a health risk to babies and young children. Acute copper exposure can cause nausea and diarrhea.

If you use well water, you should also have your water tested for high levels of nitrates, especially if you live in an agricultural area, have home gardening activity near your water supply, or if animal or human waste has the potential of entering the well. If the nitrate level in the well water is above 10mg/L, feed your baby water from a safer source. Just as with lead, boiling water for more than one minute after it reaches a boil concentrates nitrates.

Bottled water may be the only alternative for formula preparation if your water is contaminated. If you decide to use bottled water, distilled water may be your best choice, since it contains fewer contaminants than bottled spring or mineral water. In spite of Food and Drug Administration (FDA) requirements that bottled water products be clean and safe for human consumption, bottled water may contain potentially high levels of harmful contaminants that are not allowed in public drinking water. One study of 37 brands of bottled mineral water found that 24 of them contained one or more substances that did not comply with federal drinking water standards.[7] Fluoride levels also vary among different brands. Contact the water bottler for specific testing results that would indicate the quality of products.

If you decide to invest in a water-filtration system for your home, be aware that carbon, sand, and cartridge filters will not remove lead. Those units that use reverse osmosis and distillation are more effective. Where the device is located in relation to pipes with lead is important. You may decide only to have a device installed under the kitchen sink or, if levels are high, you may want a more costly system that filters water for the entire home.

Here are some measures you can take to protect your baby from lead in water:

❖ Have water tested for lead and other metals by a reputable testing facility.

❖ If you discover lead in your water, ask your physician about using

---

[6] Shannon, M.W., and Graef, J.W., "Lead Intoxication in Infancy," *Pediatrics,* 1992 (89): 87–90.

[7] Allen, H.E., et al., "Chemical Composition of Bottled Mineral Water," *Archives of Environmental Health* (44): 1989, 192–216.

distilled bottled water for powdered or concentrated formula, or use ready-to-feed formulas that do not require mixing with water.

❖ Always draw water for formula and juice preparation, drinking, and cooking from the cold water tap. Water from water heaters is at risk for a higher level of metal accumulation.

❖ To clear lead from water, allow the cold tap water to run for about two minutes until it is as cold as it will get before collecting it for formula or food preparation. This tactic doesn't work in high-rise buildings, or where city or county pipes have lead in them. Water for formula can be prepared by collecting it in the evening after the water has been running for cooking and dishwashing. It should then be stored in a clean container for use the next day.

❖ If water is going to be boiled to prepare formula, don't overboil (to prevent excessive water evaporation).

❖ Pour canned juices into clean glass or plastic containers to store them. Fruit juices should never be stored in lead crystal containers or pottery containers. Avoid canned juices from ethnic stores or imported from other countries.

❖ Buy and use toothpaste from nonmetal containers.

❖ Consult with your local environmental protection agency for advice on protective measures to take prior to renovating an older home so that you are certain you and your children will be protected from lead exposure.

Poisonings

According to the American Association of Poison Control Centers, 26 children under five died when they swallowed medicines and household chemicals in 1994. Fortunately, child-resistant packaging for medicines has lowered the toll from this kind of poisoning from the early 1970s, when over 200 children were poisoned by medicines every year.

Although most baby poisonings occur at home, some accidents occur when babies visit baby-sitters' and grandparents' homes. In fact, one out of five child poisonings involve medications belonging to grandparents who elect not to use child-resistant safety caps on their medicine bottles, fail to lock up medications, or keep toxic chemicals under sinks where babies can easily reach them.

In 1992, iron poisonings resulted in 20,004 calls to poison control centers for children under six. Iron supplements have been responsible for 305 poisoning deaths to children, making them the leading cause of poisoning deaths to children under six in the United States. Between 1986 and 1994, approximately 38 children ages nine months to three years of age died after they had ingested iron-containing products. Between June 1992 and January 1993 alone, five toddlers died after eating their mothers' prenatal iron tablets. The children had consumed as few as 5 pills and as many as 98.

Soon after swallowing iron tablets, a child will become nauseated, vomit, have diarrhea, and may suffer gastrointestinal bleeding. These problems may then progress to shock, coma, seizures, and death. Even if a child doesn't have these symptoms or appears to be recovering, medical evaluation should still be sought. Treatment becomes difficult once iron has been absorbed from a child's intestine into the blood-stream. Children who survive iron poisoning can experience problems such as gastrointestinal obstruction and liver damage up to four weeks after ingesting the poison.

Child-resistant packaging does not mean it is *childproof.* To be legally defined as child-resistant, packaging must take longer than five minutes for 80 percent of five-year-olds to open. A persistent, skilled child under five may break into child-resistant packaging in less time than that.

Poisons usually act on children's stomachs and central nervous systems quickly. Children who seem fine may suddenly develop unusual symptoms. They may not be able to follow objects with their eyes, or may show symptoms of sluggishness. Suspect a problem if you find an open or spilled bottle of pills or an open container of a dangerous product nearby. Your child may have burns, stains of the substance around the lips or mouth, or an odd smell on his or her breath.

For household chemical ingestion, immediately follow the first-aid instructions on the bottle, then call the poison control center or your doctor. For poisoning from pills, contact your poison control center or physician. If you have to go to the hospital, take along the pill bottle.

Here are some tips to prevent your child from being poisoned:

◈ Install a locking cabinet for all potentially poisonous substances, including prenatal vitamins, if you have a child six months or older in your home.

◈ Keep medications off countertops and bedside tables. Don't put them in easy-to-reach medicine cabinets or leave them in your pocketbook.

◈ Always close medicine containers as soon as you've finished using them, secure child-resistant tops, and keep them out of your child's sight and reach.

◈ Keep pills in their original containers.

◈ Carefully follow the label directions for administering medicine to your children to avoid accidental overdoses or misdoses that could result in poisoning.

Appendix B

List of manufacturers

Ameda/Egnell Corp.
755 Industrial Dr.
Cary, IL 60013
Tel: 800-323-8750; 847-639-2900;
Fax: 847-639-7895

Apogee Communications Group
159 AlpineWay
Boulder, CO 80304
Tel: 303-443-8473; 800-210-5700;
Fax: 303-443-0500

Aprica USA, Inc.
411 Hackensack Ave./10th Floor
Hackensack, NJ 07609
Tel: 201-883-9800

Babies' Alley/La Rue International
20 West 33rd St.
New York, NY 10001
Allan Silvers, VP/Sales, Laura Murphy,
Account Executive
Tel: 212-563-1414; Fax: 212-563-3396

Baby Bjorn/Regal & Lager, Inc.
1990 Delk Industrial Blvd., Suite 105
Marietta, GA 30067
Tel: 800-593-5522; 770-955-5060;
Fax: 770-955-1997

Baby Boom/Carter's
1 East 33rd St./10th Flr.
New York, NY 10016
Tel: 212-686-4666; 212-686-2656;
Fax: 212-686-5976

Baby Bundler, Inc.
17310 S.W. Bryant
Lake Oswego, OR 97035
Tel: 800-253-3502; Fax: 503-699-1132

Baby Trend, Inc.
13407 Yorba Ave.
Chino, CA 91710
Tel: 800-328-7363; 909-902-5568;
Fax: 909-902-5578

Babyville Distribution Co.
4576 East Second St., Suite C
Benicia, CA 94510
Tel: 800-967-2830; Fax: 707-746-5915

Babyworks
11725 N.W. West Rd.
Portland, OR 97229
Tel: 503-645-4349; Fax: 503-645-4913

Baby Wrap Products, Inc.
P.O. Box 100584
Denver, CO 80250-0584
Tel: 303-757-5564; Fax: 303-692-8297

Badger Basket Co.
111 Lions Dr., Suite 220
Barrington, IL 60010
Tel: 847-381-6200; Fax: 847-381-6218

Banix Corp.
11835 Carmel Mountain Rd., Suite 1304
San Diego, CA 92128
Tel: 800-443-1863; 619-673-1863;
Fax: 619-673-1863

Basic Comfort, Inc.
45 Lincoln St.
Denver, CO 80203
Tel: 800-456-8687; 303-778-7535;
Fax: 303-778-0143

Bassett Juvenile Products Division
Main St.
P.O. Box 626
Bassett, VA 24055
Tel: 540-629-6000; Fax: 540-629-6220

BB Marketing, Inc.
8825 S. 184th St.
Kent, WA 98031
Tel: 800-251-9150; Fax: 206-656-2921

Burlington Basket Co.
P.O. Box 808
Burlington, IA 52601
Ken Tomkins
Tel: 800-553-2300; 319-754-6508;
Fax: 319-754-5991

Carta Kid (*see* Prince Lionheart)

Casio, Inc.
570 Mt. Pleasant Ave.
Dover, NJ 07801
Tel: 800-962-2746; 201-361-5400;
Fax: 201-361-3819

Century Products, Inc.
9600 Valley View Rd.
Macedonia, OH 44056-2096
Tel: 216-468-2000; Fax: 216-468-4337

Child Craft Industries, Inc.
501 E. Market St.
P.O. Box 444
Salem, IN 47167-0444
Tel: 812-883-3111; Fax: 812-883-1819

Children on the Go
860 Chaddick Dr., Unit E
Wheeling, IL 60090
Tel: 847-537-3797; Fax: 874-537-3961

Cosco, Inc.
2525 State St.
Columbus, IN 47201
Tel: 812-372-0141; Fax: 812-372-0911

**Cultural Exchange
Entertainment Corp.**
80 S. Eighth St.
IDS Center, Suite 1760
Minneapolis, MN 55402
Tel: 612-339-1254; Fax: 612-339-2052

Delta Enterprise Corp.
175 Liberty Avenue
Brooklyn, NY 11212-8012
Tel: 718-385-1000; Fax: 718-385-8455

Desta Products (*see* Prince Lionheart)

DEX Products, Inc.
601 Stone Rd.
Benicia, CA 94510
Tel: 800-546-1996; 707-748-4199;
Fax: 800-546-1057 or 707-748-4190

Discovery Toys
6400 Brisa St.
Livermore, CA 94550
Tel: 510-370-3532; Fax: 510-370-0289

Evenflo Co., Inc.
1801 Commerce Dr.
Piqua, OH 45356
Tel: Consumer Line: 800-233-5921

First Alert/BRK Brands
3901 Liberty St.
Aurora, IL 60504-8122
Tel: 800-323-9005 (Consumer Hotline);
708-851-7330; Fax: 708-851-7330

The First Years, Inc.
1 Kiddie Dr.
Avon, MA 02322-1171
Tel: 800-225-0382 (ext. 581);
508-588-1220; Fax: 508-583-9067

Fisher-Price, Inc.
636 Girard Ave.
East Aurora, NY 14052-1879
Tel: 800-432-5437; 716-687-3000;
Fax: 716-687-3476

Gerber Childrenswear, Inc.
531 S. Main St./P.O. Box 3010
Greenville, SC 29602
Tel: 864-235-1615; Customer Service:
800-4-GERBER; Fax: 864-240-2972

Gerber Products Co.
445 State St.
Freemont, MI 49413-0001
Tel: 616-928-2000; Consumer Line: 800-
4-GERBER; Fax: 616-928-2723

Gerry Baby Products Co.
1500 E. 128th Ave.
Thornton, CO 80241
Tel: 303-457-0926; Consumer Relations:
800-525-2472; Fax: 303-450-3486

Graco Children's Products, Inc.
Main St.
P.O. Box 100
Elverson, PA 19520
Tel: 215-286-5961

Great Kid Company (*See* Prince
Lionheart)

Hoohobbers of Chicago, Inc.
4748 S. St. Louis
Chicago, IL 60632
Tel: 312-890-1466; Fax: 312-890-1467

Indisposables Cotton Diaper Co. Ltd.
4159 McConnell Dr.
Burnaby, B.C. Canada V5A 3J7
Tel: 604-415-0200
Tel: 800-766-7037; 410-877-0692

Infantino, Inc.
650 Arizona St.
Chula Vista, CA 91911
Tel: 800-365-8182; 619-420-1221;
Fax: 619-420-0836

International Playthings
120 Riverdale Rd.
Riverdale, NJ 07457
Tel: 201-831-1400; Consumer Line: 800-
445-8347; Fax: 201-616-7775

Jolly Jumper, Inc.
P.O. Box M
Woonsocket, RI 02895
Tel: 800-628-5168; 401-765-5950;
Fax: 401-766-7103

Kel-Gar, Inc.
P.O. Box 796934
Dallas, TX 75379-6934
Tel: 800-388-1848; 214-250-3838;
Fax: 214-250-3805

KidCo Inc.
901 E. Orchard Ave., Blvd. E
Mundelain, IL 60060-3016
Tel: 708-970-9100

Kids II
(formerly Pansy Ellen Products, Inc.)
1015 Windward Ridge Pkwy.
Alpharetta, GA 30202
Tel: 770-751-0442; Fax: 770-751-0543

KinderGard Products (subsidiary of
Mace Security International)
160 Benmont Ave.
P.O. Box 679
Bennington, VT 05201
Tel: 800-255-2634; 802-447-1503
(ext. 222); Fax: 800-545-6223 or 802-
442-3823

Kinderkraft
8220 W. 30th Court
Hialeah, FL 33016
Tel: 800-822-6748; 305-557-1481;
Fax: 305-362-7884

Kolcraft Enterprises, Inc.
3455 W. 31st Pl.
Chicago, IL 60623
Tel: 312-247-4494; Consumer Line: 800-
453-7673; Fax: 312-376-7972

Lands' End, Inc.
1 Lands' End Lane
Dodgeville, WI 53595
Tel: 608-935-4633; Customer Service:
800-356-4444; Fax: 608-935-4135

Learning Curve Toys
311 W. Superior, Suite 416
Chicago, IL 60610
Tel: 312-654-5960; 800-704-TOYS(8697);
Fax: 312-654-8227

LEGO Systems, Inc.
555 Taylor Rd.
Enfield, CT 06082
David Lafrennie, Sr. Public Relations
Mgr.; or Katherine Lee, Asst. Public
Relations Mgr.
Tel: 860-749-2291;
Consumer Affairs: 800-453-4652;
Shop-at-Home: 800-453-4652

Little Tikes Co.
2180 Barlow Rd.
P.O. Box 2277
Hudson, OH 44236-0877
Tel: 800-321-0183; 216-650-3175;
Fax: 216-650-3318

Longwood Forest Products, Inc.
201 Lakeland Rd.
Blackwood, NJ 08021
Tel: 609-227-5505; Fax: 609-227-5897

McKenzie Kids
P.O. Box 82095
Portland, OR 97282-0095
Tel: 503/238-7675; Fax: 503-238-7974

Medela, Inc.
4610 Prime Pkwy.
McHenry, IL 60050-7005
Tel: 800-435-8316; 815-363-1166;
Fax: 815-363-1246

Million Dollar Baby
Distribution Office
1520 Beach St.
Montebello, CA 90640
Tel: 800-282-3886; 213-728-9988;
Fax: 213-722-2805

Mommy's Helper
P.O. Box 780838
Wichita, KS 67278-0838
Tel: 800-371-3509; 316-636-9512;
Fax: 316-634-2783

Mondail Industries Ltd.
600 Mondail Pkwy.
Streetsboro, OH 44241
Tel: 216-626-4490; Cust. Service: 800-843-6430; Fax: 216-626-4491

Motherwear, Inc.
P.O. Box 927
Northampton, MA 01061
Tel: 800-950-2500

Murphy Diaper System
24 Sullivan Ave.
Newton, MA 02164
Tel: 800-762-9890

Mustang Survival, Inc.
3870 Mustang Way
Bellingham, WA 98226
Victor Baca
Tel: 800-526-0532; 360-676-1782;
Fax: 360-676-5014

NoJo (formerly Noel Joanna, Inc.)
22942 Arroyo Vista
Rancho Margarita, CA 92688
Tel: 800-854-8760; 714-858-9717;
Fax: 714-858-9686

North States Industries, Inc.
1200 Mendelssohn Ave./Suite 210
Minneapolis, MN 55427
Tel: 612-541-9101

Nursery Needs/Sanitoy, Inc.
1 Nursery Lane
P.O. Box 2167
Fitchburg, MA 01420
Tel: 508-345-7571; Fax: 508-342-5887

OddzOn
240 Hacienda Ave.
Campbell, CA 95009
Tel: 800-75KOOSH; 408-866-2966;
Fax 408-866-2972

**Okla Homer Smith Furniture
Manufacturing Co.**
416 S. 5th St.
P.O. Box 1148
Fort Smith, AR 72902-1148
Tel: 800-647-3876; 501-783-6191;
Fax: 501-783-5767

Omron Healthcare, Inc.
Juvenile Division
300 Lakeview Pkwy.
Vernon Hills, IL 60061
Tel: 800-634-4350; 847-680-6200;
Fax: 847-680-6269

Pansy Ellen Products, Inc. (*see* Kids II)

Parenting Concepts
P.O. Box 1437
526 Grizzly Rd.
Lake Arrowhead, CA 92352
Tel: 800-727-3683; 909-337-1499;
Fax: 909-337-0969

Pearcy Co.
03621 County Rd. 12-C
Bryan, OH 43506
Keith Pearcy
Tel: 419-636-4193; Fax: 419-636-9220

Peg-Perego U.S.A., Inc.
3625 Independence Dr.
Ft. Wayne, IN 46808
Tel: 219-484-3093

Perfectly Safe
7245 Whipple Ave., NW
North Canton, OH 44720-7198
Tel: 330-494-2323; 800-837-KIDS;
Fax: 216-494-0265

PlaySkool, Inc./Hasbro, Inc.
1027 Newport Ave.
P.O. Box 1059
Pawtucket, RI 02862-1059
Tel: 800-242-7276; Fax: 401-727-5901;
Consumer Line, 800-PLAYSKL (800-
752-9755)

Prince Lionheart
2421 S. Westgate Rd.
Santa Maria, CA 93455
Tel: 800-544-1132; Customer Service:
800-ROCKABYE; 805-922-2250;
Fax: 805-922-9442

Racing Strollers, Inc.
2609 River Rd.
P.O. Box 2189
Yakima, WA 98907
Tel: 509-457-0925

Remond for Babies
Div. of Handy Chair Corp.
6105 Portal Way
Ferndale, WA 98248
Tel: 800-426-9244; 360-384-0446;
Fax: 360-384-0544

Rev-A-Shelf
2409 Plantside Dr.
P.O. Box 99585
Jeffersontown, KY 40299
Tel: 800-626-1126; 502-499-5835;
Fax: 502-491-2215

Rock-A-Bye Baby, Inc. (*see* Prince
Lionheart)

Rosie's Babies/Diplomat Corp
25 Kay Fries Dr.
Stony Point, NY 10980
Tel: 914-786-5552; 800-247-9063;
Fax: 914-786-8727

Safeline Corp.
1777 S. Belaire St./Suite 300
Denver, CO 80222
Tel: 800-829-1625; 303-455-8335

Safety 1st, Inc.
210 Boylston St.
Chestnut Hill, MA 02167
Tel: 800-962-7233; 617-964-7744;
Fax: 617-332-0125

Sanitoy, Inc.
Nursery LAne
P.O. Box 2167
Fitchburg, MA 04120
Tel: 508-345-7571

Sara's Ride, Inc.
2737 Laramar St.
Denver, CO 80205
Ru Ciel, VP/Mktg.; Robert Griego, Pres.
Tel: 303-292-2224; Fax: 303-292-3543

Sassy, Inc.
1534 College S.E.
Grand Rapids, MI 49507
Tel: 616-243-0767; Fax: 616-243-1042

Sears
3333 Beverly
Hoffman Estates, IL 60179
Tel: 847-286-2500

Seymour Housewares Corp.
855 N. Chestnut St.
Seymour, IN 47274
Tel: 800-457-9881

Simmons Juvenile Products Co., Inc.
613 E. Beacon Ave.
P.O. Box 287
New London, WI 54961
Tel: 414-982-2140; Fax: 414-982-5052

Smart Choice/Exxis Security
1220 Champion Circle, Suite 100
Carollton, TX 75067
Tel: 800-683-9947; 214-280-9675; Fax:
214-280-9680

Soft Steps
177 NW 129th Pl.
Portland, OR 97229
Tel: 800-816-6715 (access code 77);
503-641-3407

Step2 Corporation
10010 Aurora-Hudson Rd.
P.O. Box 2412
Streetsboro, OH 44241
Tel: 216-656-0440; 800-347-8372; Fax:
216-655-9685

Summer Infant Products, Inc.
33 Meeting St.
Cumberland, RI 02864-8322
Tel: 401-725-8286; Customer Service:
800-9-BOUNCER; Fax 401-725-7019

Tabor Industries/Desta, Inc. (*see*
KinderKraft)

TL Care, Inc.
P.O. Box 77087
San Francisco, CA 94107
Tel: 415-626-3127; Fax: 415-626-2983

Today's Kids
13630 Neutron Rd.
Dallas, TX 75244
Tel: 214-404-9335; Fax: 214-404-9227

Tomy America, Inc.
450 Delta Ave.
Brea, CA 92621
Tel: 714-256-4990; Fax: 714-256-4835

Tough Traveler, Ltd.
1012 State St.
Schenectady, NY 12307
Tel: 800-GO-TOUGH (800-468-6844);
518-377-8526; Fax: 518-377-5434

Toys to Grow On
P.O. Box 17
Long Beach, CA 90801
Tel: 800-428-4414

Tracers Furniture
30 Warren Pl.
Mt. Vernon, NY 10550
Tel: 914-668-9372; Fax: 914-668-9368

Two Little Girls, Inc.
617 Huntington Ave.
San Bruno, CA 94066
Tel: 800-437-2229; 415-873-2229; Fax:
415-873-0498

Unisar, Inc.
151 W. 19th St.
New York, NY 10011
Tel: 212-989-5219; Fax: 212-691-1318

Welsh Co.
1535 S. 8th St.
St. Louis, MO 63104
Tel: 314-231-8822

White River Concepts
924-C Calle Negocio
San Clemente, CA 92673
Tel: 800-824-6351; 714-366-8960;
Fax: 714-366-1664

Index

Abbott/Ross Laboratories, 41, 42, 43

Accidents. *See individual types of baby products;* Safety

Air bags and child safety seats, 83–85

Airplanes, child safety seats for use in, 90–91

Allergies, food, 145–46

American Academy of Pediatrics, 32, 35, 42, 72, 80, 271–72

American Dietetic Association, 42

American Home Products, 41

American Medical Association, 42

American Society for Testing and Materials (ASTM), 2, 3, 110, 154, 234–35, 290, 296, 297

American Window Covering Manufacturers Association, 228

Apnea, 80

Association of Women's Health, Obstetrics and Neonatal Nurses, 42

Audio monitors, 219–21, 223–24

Baby food. See Foods for babies

Baby-food warmers, 151, 152–53

Baby formula. *See* Formula, baby

Baby powder, talcum-based, 127–28

Baby showers, 8

Backpacks
  advantages over soft carriers, 21
  buying advice, 15–16
  disadvantages of, 14–15
  distinguished from soft carriers by use, 14
  features, 20–21
  listings, 21–22
  safety, 15
  See also Soft carriers

Backyard, baby-proofing the, 168–69

"Bait and switch," 8

Balloon dangers, 273–75

Basement safety, 170–71

Bassinets, 23, 24
  listings, 26–27
  safety, 23, 24

Bathing accessories. *See* Bathtubs and bathing accessories

Bathroom safety, 31–33, 169–70
  childproofing products, 172–80
Bath seats, 5, 6, 32
Bathtubs and bathing accessories,
    29–30, 33–34
  baby bathing basics, 30–31
  listings of baby bathtubs, 34
  safety, 29, 30, 31–33
  safety products, 177–79
Batteries for toys, 273, 277–78
Beds, 114, 170
Bed warmers, 228
Beech-Nut Nutrition Corporation,
    133, 134, 135, 136, 137, 140,
    144, 145
Bibs, 5, 151
Booster seats, 71, 75–78, 88–89,
    91, 93, 213–14
Booties and socks, 103
Bottled water, 45–46
Bottle-feeding, 35–52
  bottled water, 45–46, 310
  bottle heater, 39, 51
  disposable bottle systems,
    37–38
  formula. See Formula, baby
  injuries from bottles, 40
  juices and sweetened beverages,
    44–45, 141–42
  listings of bottles and acces-
    sories, 50–51
  nipples, 46–48
  quick tips, 38
  standard bottles, 37, 38–39
  sterilization, 37, 39, 51
Botulism, 45, 149
Breast-feeding, 40, 42–43, 53–63
  books on, 55
  breast pumps. See Breast pumps
  freezing breast milk, 58
  health benefits of, 53–55
  nursing accessories, listings
    of, 63
  nursing bras, 56
  preparing to succeed, 55
  storing breast milk, 58–59

  thawing frozen breast milk, 59
  See also Bottle-feeding
Breast pumps, 8, 57–58
  battery-operated and electric,
    listings of, 61–62
  choosing, 59–60
  hand-operated, listings of, 61
  listings, 61–62
Bristol-Myers Squibb, 41, 43
Bumpers
  corner and edge, 200–202
  crib pads, 118
Burns, protecting against, 11, 32,
    228, 304
Buying plan, creating your, 5–6

Cabinet and drawer safety
    latches, 180–84
Carriers
  framed. See Backpacks
  soft. See Soft carriers
Carrycots, 23, 24–25
  listing, 27
  safety, 23, 25
Center for Science in the Public
    Interest (CPSI), 139
Centers for Disease Control, 45
Cereals, 140–41, 150
Certification stickers, 2–4, 110,
    206–207, 296
Chairs, portable hook-on, 245–47
Changing tables, 5, 6, 65–68
"Cheating Babies," 139
Chests, 9, 225–26
  cribs combined with, 9
Childproofing products, 172–203
  for the bathtub, 177–79
  bumpers, corner/edge, 200–202
  cabinet and drawer safety
    latches, 180–84
  door safety products, 187–89
  electrical cord safety products,
    197–199
  electrical outlet safety products,
    194–197

electrical switch safety lock, 199–200

medicine cabinet safety latches, 179–80

overview of, 172–73

railing guards, 202–203

standards for evaluating, 172–73

for stove safety, 190–93

toilet lid locks, 173–77

window blind safety products, 184–87

window safety locks, 189–90

Child Safety Protection Act, 272

Child safety seats, 69–94

additional do's and don'ts, 89–90

air bag dangers, 83–85

airplanes, use in, 90–91

booster seats, 71, 75–78, 88–89, 91, 93

buckle problem with Century safety seats/strollers, 86

built-ins, 88

comfort, 78–80

convertible seats, 70–71, 72–73, 74–78, 92–93

crash test results, 73–78

importance of, 69

infant-only seats, 70, 71–72, 73–78, 92–93

installation of, 80–81, 82–85

loaner programs, 87

maintenance of, 85

Ratings, 92–93

recalls, 8, 85–86, 94

recommendations, 86–88

rentals, 86

saving money on, 5

used, 4, 81, 87

warning against leaving child alone in a car, 79

Choking, 10, 102, 145, 158, 276–77, 279, 280, 306–307

no-choke testing tube, 276–77

Clothing, 95–104

basics for when baby arrives, 95–96

booties and socks, 103

dressing tips, 98–99

hazards, 102

nightgowns and pajamas, 5, 99, 102

overdressing, warning against, 98

recalls, 103–104

selecting, 96–98

shoes, 103

sleepwear, 5, 99, 102

for summer, 101–102

for toddlers, 99–100

underwear, 100

for winter, 101

Clothing storage, 5

Consumer Product Safety Commission (CPSC), 1, 2, 40, 102, 114, 119, 128, 155, 227, 229, 236, 276, 283, 296, 297

hotline number, 3–4, 8, 119, 280

Conversion kits, 225

Corner and edge bumpers, 200–202

Cradles, 23, 25–26

listings, 27

safety, 23, 25–26

Crib gyms, 276, 279

Crib mattresses, 8–9, 105–106, 114, 116–18

choosing, 116–17

recommendations, 117–18

Cribs, 105–18

assembly, 107

bumper pads, 118

casters, 106, 107, 108

certification label, 110

chests combined with, 9

dropsides, lowering, 107–108

infant cushions, ban on, 119

injuries and deaths, 105, 106

inspections, periodic, 107, 110

mattress adjustment, 108–109

overloading, 113

portable, 233, 234, 241–44

recommendations, 109–10

safety standards, 105–106, 227

sales tactics, 8–9
Sudden Infant Death Syndrome (SIDS), 114–16, 227
time for moving to a bed, 113
types of, 107
used, 4, 105, 110–11
Crib sheets, 226

Department of Agriculture, Food and Nutrition Service, 44–45
Department of Transportation, 85
  Auto Safety Hotline, 85–86
Desserts, 144
Detroit Testing Laboratory, Inc., 2
Diaper bags, 129–30
Diaper pails, 32, 128, 130, 169
Diaper pins, 128
Diapers, 121–28
  diaper rash, 126–27
  diaper service, 121, 123, 124–25
  disposable, 121, 123–24, 125, 126
  environmental issues, 125
  recommendations, 125–26
  reusable cloth, 121, 122, 124, 126
  saving money on, 5
  using a combination of alternatives, 121–22, 126
Dinners for babies, 144
Discount stores, shopping at, 4–5, 225, 281
Door safety products, 187–89
Drawer and cabinet safety latches, 180–84
Drowning, protecting against, 31, 32–33, 305–306

Earth's Best, Inc., 133–34, 135, 137, 138, 139, 143, 144, 149, 150
Electrical cord safety products, 197–99

Electrical outlet safety products, 194–97
Electrical switch safety lock, 199–200
Environmental Working Group, 146

Falls, protecting against, 9–10, 202–203, 226, 307–09
Federal Aviation Administration (FAA), 90–91
Federal Trade Commission (FTC), 41, 139
Feeding accessories, 151–52
Finger entrapment, protecting against, 11
Fire safety, 243, 301–304
Food and Drug Administration (FDA), 2, 4, 8, 43, 46, 137, 147
Food intolerances, 132
Foods for babies, 8, 131–52
  allergies, 145–46
  categories of, 134–35
  cereals, 140–41, 150
  choking on, 145
  desserts, 144
  dinners, 144
  expiration dates, 143
  first six months, 131
  fruits, 142, 148
  ingredients, 138–40
  jars, checking for safe, 147
  making your own, 147–49, 150
  manufacturers of, 132–35
  meat, 143–44, 148
  money-saving ideas, 149–50
  nutritional labeling, 137
  organic, 133
  other foods, 144–45
  pesticides, 146–47
  preparing your own, 5
  price, 149–50
  recommendations, 150–51
  with salt added, 140–41
  with starches added, 138–40
  starting solids, 131–32

with sugar added, 138
trends in the market, 135–36
vegetables, 142–43, 147–48
with vitamin C added, 140
Food warmers, 151, 152
Formula, baby, 8
leftover, 36
mislabeled, 43
politics of, 40–44
precautions, 44
preparing, 36–37, 44
saving money on, 5
soy-based, 35–36
sterilized, 37
temperature, 37
types of, 36
Framed carriers. *See* Backpacks
Front carrier. *See* Soft carrier
Fruits, 142, 148
Furniture. *See* Nursery decor and
accessories; *individual pieces
of furniture*

Garage safety, 170–71
Garage sales, 4
Gates, 153–64
accordion, 155
alternatives to, 156–57
hardware-mounted, 153, 159–62
hazards, 156–58, 159
manufacturing requirements,
154–55
pressure-mounted, 153–54, 156,
157–58, 159, 162–64
Ratings, 160–64
rules for buying and using,
157–58
vertical slats as hazard, 156
Gerber Products Company, 133,
134, 135, 136, 137, 138, 139,
140, 142, 143, 144, 149, 150
Gift registries, 8
Growing Healthy, Inc., 134, 135,
137, 138, 139, 140, 143, 149,
150

Handed-down clothing, 96
Hazardous Substances Act, 274–75
Hazard reduction around the
house, 165–71
See also Childproofing
products
Heatstroke, 98
Heinz, 133, 134, 135, 136, 137,
139, 140, 144, 149
High chairs, 6, 205–14
accidents, 205, 206
buying advice, 207–209
manufacturing requirements,
206–207
plastic, 205, 206
Ratings, 210–11
recently introduced models, 212
rules for safe use, 212–13
safety standards, 205, 206
saving money on, 5
wooden, 205, 206
Honey, 45, 148–49
Hook-on chairs, portable, 245–47
Humidifiers, 228

Infant cushions, 119
Infant formula. *See* Formula, baby
Infant Formula Act of 1980, 44
Infant seats, 5, 215–18
Information, gathering, 7–8
Injuries to babies. *See* Safety;
individual products
International Standards Organ-
ization, 83
ISOFIX, 83

Journal of the American Medical
Association, 145
Juices, bottle-feeding of, 44–45,
141–42
Juvenile Products Manufacturers
Association (JPMA), 2, 3, 8,
156, 206–207, 234, 255,
296–97

Kitchen safety, 166–67

La Leche League, International, 8, 55
Lead poisoning, 309–11
Lighting, 228–29, 230, 231
Living room safety, 167–68

Manufacturers, contacting, 8
Mead Johnson & Company, 41
Meat, 143–44, 148
Medicine cabinet safety latches, 179–80
Midas Muffler Brake Shops, Project Safe Baby, 87
Milk
  breast milk. *See* Breast-feeding
  cow's, 35
  formula. *See* Formula, baby
Monitors, 6, 219–24
  audio, 219–20, 223–24
  drawbacks of, 222
  high-tech, 222
  how they operate, 219–20
  Ratings, 223–24
  safety, 220
  shopping tips, 220–21
  video, 222
Motherwear, Inc., 56

National Campaign for Pesticide Policy Reform, 146
National Highway Traffic Safety Administration (NHTSA), 2, 4, 8, 73, 84, 85, 90
National Institute of Child Health and Human Development, 115
National Pediatric Trauma Registry, 88, 226
National Transportation Safety Board, 90
Nightgowns, 5, 99, 102

Night-lights, 228–29, 230
Nipples, 46–48
Northwestern University, Memorial Hospital, 43
Nursery decor and accessories, 225–33
  crib sheets, 226
  decorating tips, 229–30
  lighting alternatives, 230, 231
  money-saving ideas, 225–26, 230
  safety, 226–29
  window dangers, 226
Nursing bras, 56
Nursing Your Baby (Pryor), 55
Nutrition Labeling and Education Act (NLEA), 137

One-product-does-everything designs, 9
Orthodontic nipples, 47

Pacifiers, 48–50
  dangers, 49–50
  recalls, 52
Pajamas, 99, 102
Pesticides, 146–47
Pillows, 227
Plastic bags, 112, 113
Playground Equipment Manufacturers Association (PEMA), 290
Playpens, 6, 233–39
  construction of, 235–37
  cost of, 234
  manufacturing requirements, 234–36
  necessity of, determining, 234
  portable crib alternative, 233, 234
  rules for safe use, 238–39
  safety, 233, 235–37, 238
Poisonings, 311–12
Portable cribs, 233, 235, 241–44

Portable hook-on chairs, 245–47
Potties, 266–68
Premature babies, clothing for, 96
Proppers, baby, 227–28
Pryor, Karen, 55

Quilts, 227

Railing guards, 202–203
Rattles, 276, 278
Recalls, 8
    See also individual products
Registries, gift, 8
Response Surface Methodology
    (RSM), 132
Rockers, 9
Ross/Abbott Laboratories, 41, 42,
    43
Runners, strollers for, 250, 260

Safety
    certification stickers, 2–4, 110,
        208, 296
    childproofing products. *See*
        Childproofing products
    hazard reduction around the
        house, 165–72
    overview of dangers to babies,
        9–12, 299–312
    standards, 1–2, 9
    See also specific baby products
Safety seats. *See* Child safety
    seats
Sales tactics, 8–9
Seatbelts, 86, 87
Shampoo, 29
Sheets for cribs, 226
Shoes, 103
Skin care products, 8
Sleepwear, 5, 99, 102
Soaps, 29, 30
Socks and booties, 103
Soft carriers, 6, 13–20
    buying advice, 15–16
    disadvantages of, 14–15
    distinguished from backpacks
        by use, 14
    listings, 17–20
    safety, 15
    strap-ons, 17
    types of, 16
    See also Backpacks
Specialty stores, shopping at, 4
Sponges, foam, 33
Squeeze toys, 273, 275, 276
Stove safety products, 190–93
Strangulation, protecting against,
    10–11, 102, 155, 165, 228,
    243, 249, 250
Strollers, 249–60
    accidents, 250
    all-terrain, 250, 260
    buying advice, 251–55
    combination carriage and, 249,
        250, 251–52
    combination child safety seat
        and, 72, 249, 250, 251, 257
    lightweight "umbrella," 249,
        251
    maintenance, 257–58
    manufacturing requirements,
        255–56
    multiple-occupancy, 250, 256–57
    rules for safe use, 259–60
    for runners, 250, 260
    safety features, 249, 253–55
    saving money on, 5, 6
    side-by-side, 250, 256–57
    tandem, 250, 251, 256
Sudden Infant Death Syndrome
    (SIDS), 114–16, 227
Suffocation, protecting against,
    11, 112, 113, 114, 115, 119,
    236, 273–75, 277, 280,
    306–07
Summer clothing, 101–102
Sweetened beverages, bottle-
    feeding of, 44–45
Swings, 261–64
    outdoor, 289

Teethers, 273, 276
Testing of products by Consumers Union, 12
Toilet-learning aids, 265–68
Toilet lid locks, 173–77
Towels, 29
Toys, 6, 10, 231, 269–92
    affluence and, 269–71
    age appropriate, 282–88
    age guidelines, 282–83
    balloon dangers, 273–75
    batteries for, 273, 277–78
    buying safe, tips for, 278–79
    crib toy dangers, 276
    deceptive advertising, 271–72
    desirable, 279–81
    Hazardous Substances Act, 274–75
    injuries and deaths from, 229, 272, 273–78
    money-saving ideas, 281
    no-choke testing tube, 276–77
    for outdoor play, 290–91
    playing with your new baby, 270
    recalls, 291–92
    relationships coming ahead of, 271
    riding, 273, 280, 289–90
    safety basics, 280
    safety standards, 272–73
    storage of, 273, 278
    toy chests, 273, 278
T-shirts, 5

Underwear, 100
Underwriters Laboratories, 228
UNICEF, 44

Vegetables, 142–43, 148
Video monitors, 222

Walkers, 293–98
    accident potential of, 293–95, 297
    medical research, 295–296
    safety, 296–98
    types of, 294
Wall Street Journal, 42
Washcloths, 29
Water, bottled, 45–46, 310–11
Water beds, 114, 170
Water contamination, 309–11
Water heater, setting of, 11, 32
Window blinds and shades, 228
    safety products, 184–87
Window dangers, 226
Window safety locks, 189–90
Winter clothing, 101
Womanly Art of Breast-feeding (La Leche League, International), 55
World Health Organization, 44

Yard sales, 4, 96
Yellow Pages, 8
Youth beds, 114